SOCIO-ECONOMIC REVIEW 2015

Towards a Just Society

Securing Economic Development, Social Equity and Sustainability

Seán Healy, Austin Delaney, Ann Leahy, Michelle Murphy, Brigid Reynolds and Jason Robinson

Social Justice Ireland

SOCIO-ECONOMIC REVIEW 2015

ISBN No. 978-1-907501-14-2

First Published April 2015

Published by
Social Justice Ireland
Arena House
Arena Road
Sandyford
Dublin 18

www.socialjustice.ie

Tel: 01- 2130724

e-mail: secretary@socialjustice.ie

TABLE OF CONTENTS

1.	Introduction and Main Recommendations	7
2.	A Guiding Vision and a Policy Framework	17
3.	Income Distribution	37
4.	Taxation	73
5.	Work, Unemployment and Job-Creation	102
6.	Public Services	117
7.	Housing and Accommodation	130
8.	Healthcare	172
9.	Education and Educational Disadvantage	203
10.	People and Participation	220
11.	Sustainability	235
12.	Rural Development	255
13.	The Global South	269
14.	Values	284

Annexes (annex numbers are linked to corresponding chapter numbers above)

Annex 3: Income Distribution	289
Annex 4: Taxation	303
Annex 5: Work, Unemployment and Job Creation	311
Annex 11: Sustainability and Environment	314
Annex 13: UN Millennium Development Goals	318

References	321

1
INTRODUCTION AND MAIN RECOMMENDATIONS

After years of coping with the crisis and its consequences Ireland currently faces major choices. What kind of future do we want for Ireland? What level of services should we aspire to, in areas such as education and health? What level of infrastructure is required in areas such as public transport and social housing? How much of Ireland's services and infrastructure should be provided by the state? What would be the appropriate level of taxation for Ireland in the years ahead? Do we have any views on the distribution of wealth and power in our society?

It is time to have a real debate about our economic and social priorities in the years ahead; whether, for example, it is time to reduce taxes for higher-rate taxpayers, or whether it is time to invest in our social services and infrastructure and strengthen our social security system; whether we want to return to a privately-financed system of housing provision that leads to vacant homes, broken banks and record numbers on the social housing list, or whether we wish to create a society that guarantees quality accommodation for all; whether we wish the standard of healthcare to depend on the contents of our wallets, or the common demands of our humanity. Whether, in a word, we wish to collectively pursue the public purpose, or return to the petty politics of private greed.

There are key questions to be addressed. These include:
- Where does Ireland want to be in 2025?
- What should be its guiding vision?
- What infrastructure is required?
- What services are required?
- How are such infrastructure and service requirements to be delivered?
- How are they to be financed?
- How are decisions on these issues to be made?
- How and on what basis is progress on these issues to be measured?

These are the questions addressed in *Social Justice Ireland*'s Socio-Economic Review for 2015.

A Guiding Vision

Social Justice Ireland believes that Ireland should be guided by a vision of becoming a just society in which human rights are respected, human dignity is protected, human development is facilitated and the environment is respected and protected. The core values of such a society would be human dignity, equality, human rights, solidarity, sustainability and the pursuit of the common good.

Having these as guiding values would ensure that Ireland became a nation in which all women, men and children have what they require to live life with dignity and to fulfil their potential: including sufficient income; access to the services they need; and active inclusion in a genuinely participatory society.

These are not minority views as is sometimes stated, but reflect the aspirations of the majority of Irish citizens. Indeed, in February 2014, 85% of the members of the Convention on the Constitution convened by the Government voted to afford greater constitutional protection to Economic, Social and Cultural (ESC) rights. This included a recommendation to include explicit mention of rights to housing, social security, essential healthcare, the rights of people with disabilities, and linguistic and cultural rights, in the Irish Constitution.

What infrastructure is required?

By the mid-1990s there were major deficits in economic and social infrastructure across Ireland. In the years that followed there was a dramatic increase in investment in infrastructure which lasted until the economic crash of 2008. This investment led to real improvements in areas such as motorways, airports and public transport.

At the same time major infrastructure gaps remained in areas such as water, broadband, energy, social housing, healthcare facilities and schools. The low level of investment in the 2008-2014 period resulted in the deterioration of both physical and social infrastructure. This is very obvious in areas such as healthcare. The critical areas requiring investment now are: water, social housing, public transport, especially rural transport, roads, education, healthcare, energy, broadband and environment.

Current provision in each of these areas falls well short of what is required for maximum effectiveness and efficiency at the present time. Further pressure will come with the increasing population, changing age structure and growing demands driven by changes in technology and pressures in areas such as climate change. Addressing these infrastructure deficits will require much greater investment than is currently available or planned.

In this context it is important to ensure that investment is supported to provide fair outcomes for all and not just to make the rich richer. The creation of wealth does not necessarily lead to a reduction in poverty. It is important to ensure that investment is focused on areas that prevent regressive, unequal income distribution impacts.

What services are required?

There have been significant cuts to social services and welfare payments in the 2008-14 period. *Social Justice Ireland* believes many of these cuts were socially destructive and counter-productive. We also believe that Government could have taken different decisions that took greater care of those who were vulnerable and did not have such a negative, detrimental impact on jobs. In effect, the social impact of austerity policies was not factored into the original calculations. Irish society will be coping with the fallout of this failure for quite some time to come.

Substantial additional investment in social services is required

a) To ensure that current provision is not eroded further as this would have significant future costs.
b) To address the additional requirements flowing from demographic changes as the population grows and, for example, the numbers of older people and those with disabilities within this larger population also grow.

The critical areas of service provision that need to be addressed are:

- Income – to ensure everyone has sufficient income to live with dignity which would lead to a dramatic reduction in poverty.
- Work – to ensure everyone seeking work has access to meaningful work, particularly in a situation of high long-term unemployment.
- Accommodation – to ensure everyone has access to appropriate accommodation.
- Health – to ensure everyone has access to essential healthcare.
- Education – to ensure everyone has access to basic education.

Finally, the goal of universal provision for all must remain, particularly in the area of health, where inequalities persist between the insured and uninsured population, as well as within the uninsured population. These inequalities will grow as user charges are introduced, and access to medical cards is restricted.

How are the necessary infrastructure and service requirements to be delivered?

In recent years there has been a growing emphasis on cutting back the State as a means of promoting a post-crisis recovery. The basic assumption underpinning this approach is that the entrepreneurship and innovation delivered by the private sector is the key to recovery. A dynamic and competitive private sector is contrasted with a bureaucratic and sluggish public sector. This view is promoted in the media, argued by most business people and accepted by many politicians to a point where it is taken to be 'common sense'.

But this is not in keeping with the facts. What needs to be learned is that 'private good, public bad' is a slogan not supported by evidence. There are meaningful and substantial roles for the private sector, the public sector and the community and voluntary sector in providing infrastructure and services. Each of these sectors has strengths in particular areas and weaknesses in others.

What is required is recognition that the delivery of the infrastructure and services already identified needs different combinations of public, private and community and voluntary sectors. Whatever the issues being addressed, ranging from climate to demography and far beyond, they require comprehensive engagement by all three sectors. The level of engagement will vary depending on the issue and the required response. Decisions should be based on evidence. Their implementation should be subject to appropriate regulation. None should be demonised and false narratives should not be propagated.

How are infrastructure and services to be financed?

Infrastructure and services are financed by taxation and private financial sources investing in these areas. There can be endless debate about the balance between these. Here we wish to make three points. If Ireland's current deficits in infrastructure and services are to be addressed then:

a) Ireland's total tax-take must be increased, which can be done while maintaining Ireland's position as a low-tax country.

b) There must be a substantial increase in the benefits accruing to the State where public investment has led to major gains for private sector entities.

c) There is a need for off-balance sheet investment if current deficits are to be addressed.

The evidence for each of these, as well as for the other points being made in this introduction, is clearly set out in the following chapters.

How are decisions on these issues to be made?

The changing nature of democracy has raised many questions for policy-makers and others concerned about the issue of participation. Decisions often appear to be made without any real involvement of the many affected by the decisions' outcomes. In the context of the issues being addressed here there are challenges facing society if it is to genuinely engage people in shaping the decisions that affect them. *Social Justice Ireland* believes such engagement to be one of the seven basic rights referred to already. It also raises issues concerning the seventh of those rights i.e. the right to cultural respect. *Social Justice Ireland* believes there are three key issues to be addressed in this context:

a) Development of a deliberative democracy process

b) Engagement of all sectors in a deliberative process of social dialogue

c) Evaluation as a tool for ongoing learning

How and on what basis is progress on these issues to be measured?

Sustainable development is of critical concern. The future of the planet, including Ireland, depends on decisions taken now. Sustainable development is our only means of creating a long term future for Ireland. Environment, economic growth and social needs should be balanced with consideration for the needs of future generations. This has to be a central concern when progress is being measured. Sustainability and the adoption of a sustainable development model presents a significant policy challenge: how environmental policy decisions with varying distributional consequences are to be made in a timely manner while ensuring that a disproportionate burden is not imposed on certain groups e.g. low income families or rural dwellers.

This policy challenge highlights the need for an evidence-based policy process involving all stakeholders. The costs and benefits of all policies must be assessed and considered on the basis of evidence only. This is essential in order to avoid the policy debate being influenced by hearsay or vested interests or the un-reflected exercise of power.

Creating a sustainable Ireland also requires the adoption of new indicators to measure progress. GDP alone as a measure of progress is unsatisfactory, as it only describes the monetary value of gross output, income and expenditure in an economy.

A Policy Framework for a Just Society

How then might we summarise the proposals we are making in policy terms, proposals we believe are the key requirements if Ireland is to be guided by the vision we set out above? In chapter two we set out a Policy Framework for a Just Society. In it we identify five key areas for policy development if this vision is to be achieved:

a) The first is macroeconomic stability, which requires a stabilisation of Ireland's debt levels, fiscal and financial stability and sustainable economic growth, and a substantial increase in investment. How that investment might be sourced is also addressed.

b) The second is the need for a just taxation system, which would require an increase in the overall tax-take towards the European average; such an increase should be implemented equitably and in a way that reduces income inequality while ensuring that the corporate sector pays a fair share.

c) The third area is decent services, the securing of social services and social infrastructure, the prioritisation of employment, and a commitment to to securing seven basic social, economic and cultural rights.

d) The fourth area is that of good governance, which requires the promotion of deliberative democracy, new processes in policy evaluation and a deliberative process of social dialogue in a society that promotes the common good.

e) Fifth, policies must be adopted that create a sustainable future, through the introduction of measures to protect the environment, promote balanced regional development, and develop new economic and social indicators to measure performance, alongside traditional national accounting measures such as GNP, GDP and GNI.

This table summarises our proposed policy development framework.

A Policy Framework for a Just Ireland

Macro-economy	Taxation	Social Services	Governance	Sustainability
Debt sustainability	Bring total tax-take towards EU average	Secure services and social infrastructure	Deliberative democracy & PPNs	Promote climate justice and protect the environment
Fiscal and financial stability and sustainable economic growth	Increase taxes equitably and reduce income inequality	Combat unemployment and underemployment	Reform policy evaluation	Balanced regional development
Investment programme	Secure fair share of corporate profits for the State	Ensure seven Social, Economic and Cultural rights are achieved	Social dialogue - all sectors in deliberative process	New indicators of progress and new Satellite National Accounts

Chapter 2 of this Socio-Economic Review addresses these and related issues in detail.

The main policy proposals for moving towards a just society contained in chapters 3 to 13 are summarised below.

Chapter 3 – Income Distribution

- Adopt targets aimed at reducing poverty among particular vulnerable groups such as children, lone parents, jobless households and those in social rented housing.
- Examine and support viable, alternative policy options aimed at giving priority to protecting vulnerable sectors of society.
- Carry out in-depth social impact assessments prior to implementing proposed policy initiatives that impact on the income and public services that many low income households depend on. This should include the poverty-proofing of all public policy initiatives.

Chapter 4 – Taxation

- Increase the overall tax take towards 34.9 per cent of GDP (i.e. a level below the high tax threshold identified by Eurostat).
- Broaden the tax base and make the tax system fairer.
- Secure a fair share of corporate profits for the State.

Chapter 5 – Work, Unemployment and Job Creation

- Launch a major investment programme focused on creating employment and prioritise initiatives that strengthen social infrastructure, including a comprehensive school building programme and a much larger social housing programme.
- Expand funded programmes supporting the community to meet the growing pressures arising as a result of the recent economic downturn.
- Put in place a new programme targeting those who are very long-term unemployed (i.e. 5+ years).
- Seek at all times to ensure that new jobs have reasonable pay rates and adequately resource the labour inspectorate.

Chapter 6 – Public Services

- Develop an integrated public transport network ensuring that commuters can access local, regional and national transport services.
- Ensure adequate support and funding of public library services including the provision of open-access information technology.
- Ensure the roll out of rural broadband to all households and premises across the State.

Chapter 7 – Housing and Accommodation

- Fully resource the Social Housing Strategy and expand its scale to effectively eliminate the 90,000+ households currently on the waiting list.
- Ensure adequate resources are allocated within the various stakeholders involved in Construction 2020 providing the datasets to ensure that construction policy is made on the basis of accurate and up to date data.
- Implement specific policies aimed at protecting the rights of tenants to a secure home while addressing the issue of accidental landlords.

Chapter 8 – Healthcare

- Roll out the nine Community Healthcare Organisations and 90 Primary Care Networks intended, inter alia, to support Primary Care Teams as envisaged in the 2015 HSE Service Plan.
- Recognise the considerable health inequalities present within the Irish healthcare system, develop strategies and provide sufficient resources to tackle these.
- Give far greater priority to community care and restructure the healthcare budget accordingly to deliver on the commitment to enable groups like older people to live in their own homes for as long as possible. Care should be taken to ensure that the increased allocation does not go to the GMS or the drug subsidy scheme.

Chapter 9 - Education

- Invest in universal, quality early childhood education.
- Set an ambitious adult literacy target and ensure adequate funding is provided for adult literacy programmes.
- Increase resources available to lifelong learning and alternative pathways to education.

Chapter 10 – People and Participation

- Immediately increase the weekly allowance allocated to asylum-seekers on 'direct provision' to at least €65 per week for an adult and €38 for a child and give priority to recognising the right of all refugees and asylum-seekers to work.
- Adequately resource the PPN structures for citizen engagement at local level and ensure capacity building is an integral part of the process.
- Ensure that there is real and effective monitoring and impact assessment of policy implementation using an evidence-based approach. Involve a wide range of perspectives in this process, thus ensuring inclusion of all sectors in a new deliberative process of social dialogue.

Chapter 11 – Sustainability

- Communicate a common understanding of sustainable development across all Government departments, policy makers, stakeholders and civil society. This should underpin all public policy decisions.
- Account for the economic value of biodiversity in all environmental policy decisions.
- Develop Shadow/Satellite national accounts to move towards a more sustainable, resource efficient model of development.

Chapter 12 – Rural Development

- Prioritise rolling out high speed broadband to rural areas.
- Develop a new national rural strategy. This strategy should be part of a new national spatial strategy.
- Publish a rural and regional economic development policy statement and incorporate it into national economic and employment strategies.

Chapter 13 – Global South

- Renew Government's commitment to meet the United Nations target of contributing 0.7 per cent of GNP to Overseas Development Assistance. Recognising that the deadline of 2015 will be missed, *Social Justice Ireland* proposes that the new date should be 2020 and a clear pathway should be set out to achieve this.
- Take a far more proactive stance at government level on ensuring that Irish and EU policies towards countries in the South are just. Ensure that Irish businesses

operating in developing countries - in particular Irish Aid country partners - are subject to proper scrutiny and engage in sustainable development practices.

- Continue to support the international campaign for the liberation of the poorest nations from the burden of the backlog of unpayable debt and take steps to ensure that further progress is made on this issue.

2

A GUIDING VISION AND A POLICY FRAMEWORK

On one reading of Ireland's current situation all is well and the future looks bright. Economic growth has been dramatic and challenging fiscal targets have been exceeded. Employment is growing and unemployment is falling. Exports are growing, strongly supported by the weakening of the Euro. Interest rates are at an historic low.

A different reading of Ireland's current situation can be seen when issues such as the rise in poverty and social exclusion, the continuing very high levels of public and private debt and the failure to reverse the multiple hits taken by the vulnerable since the crash of 2008 are taken into account. The high levels of emigration and youth unemployment add to this down-side of Ireland today.

It is clear that the social impact of austerity policies was not considered from the beginning and, as a result, a great many people were damaged unnecessarily. Living standards fell by 14 per cent between 2007 and 2011 before recovering slightly up to 2013 (CSO, 2015) By then, however, it was still below the standard of living in 2004. *Social Justice Ireland* has constantly argued that Government could have achieved its fiscal targets in a manner that cared more for those who were vulnerable and had a less negative impact in areas such as employment.

Government was not helped by the failure to restructure the Eurozone's design and by the decision of the European Commission and the European Central Bank to persist with policy frameworks that have resulted in the monetary union's spectacularly poor performance. The continuing refusal to recognise that creditors as well as debtors are responsible for their actions has also made the situation even more difficult for Ireland.

As Ireland reflects on the legacy of the crisis there is a widespread desire not to repeat the mistakes that created the crash in the first place. There is also a widespread concern that decision-making may revert to the failed patterns of the past. In this chapter *Social Justice Ireland* sets out its views on how Ireland can ensure the future does not repeat the mistakes of the past. It sets out a guiding vision for a just society and a policy framework that would deliver a just future for all.

2.1 A Guiding Vision for a Just Society[1]

Ireland needs a combination of vision and pragmatic policies that can truly move the country towards a desirable and sustainable future. *Social Justice Ireland* advocates a new guiding vision to shape the future direction of Irish society. We believe that Ireland should be guided by a vision of becoming a just society in which human rights are respected, human dignity is protected, human development is facilitated and the environment is respected and protected. The core values of such a society would be human dignity, equality, human rights, solidarity, sustainability and the pursuit of the common good.

Human dignity is central to our vision. It demands that all people be recognised as having an inherent value, worth and distinction regardless of their nationality, gender, ethnicity, culture, sexual orientation or economic and social position. *Social Justice Ireland* believes that the State must uphold and promote human dignity, treating all citizens and non-citizens alike with dignity and respect.

The need for greater equality is closely linked to the recognition of human dignity and the desire for social justice. Great disparities in wealth and power divide society into the rich and the poor, which weakens the bond between people and divides society between the lucky and the left-out, between the many and the few. A commitment to equality requires society to give priority to this value so that all people can achieve their potential.

The development and recognition of human rights has been one of the great achievements of the 20th century. In the 21st century human rights are moving beyond civil and political rights to embrace social, economic and cultural rights. In this context *Social Justice Ireland* believes that every person has seven core rights that should be part of our vision of the future i.e. the right to sufficient income to live life with dignity; the right to meaningful work; the right to appropriate accommodation; the right to relevant education; the right to essential healthcare; the right to real participation and the right to cultural respect. Policy decisions should be moving towards the achievement of each of these rights. Care should be taken that decisions are not moving society or the economy in the opposite direction.

Solidarity is the recognition that we are all bound, as human beings, one to another,

---

[1] The authors have addressed this issue in details in a range of other publications, most recently in Reynolds et al 2014 pp. 29-31.

within nations, between nations and across generations. Many policy decisions taken in recent years are unjust to future generations. Solidarity requires all people and all nations to recognise their duties to one another and to vindicate the rights of their fellow members of society. Solidarity enables people and communities to become the shapers of their own destiny.

Sustainability is a central motif for economic, social and environmental policy development. Central to this is the recognition that economic development, social development and environmental protection are complementary and interdependent. None of these objectives can be achieved by ignoring any of the others. Respect for the natural environment is not a luxury to be indulged in but an imperative that cannot be ignored.

A commitment to the common good is also critical. The right of the individual to freedom and personal development is limited by the rights of other people. The concept of the 'common good' originated over 2,000 years ago in the writings of Plato, Aristotle and Cicero. More recently, the philosopher John Rawls defined the common good as 'certain general conditions that are...equally to everyone's advantage' (Rawls, 1971 p.246).

Social Justice Ireland understands the term 'common good' as being 'the sum of those conditions of social life by which individuals, families and groups can achieve their own fulfilment in a relatively thorough and ready way' (Gaudium et Spes, 1965 no.74). This understanding recognises the fact that the person develops his or her potential in the context of society where the needs and rights of all members and groups are respected (Healy and Reynolds, 2011). The common good, then, consists primarily of having the social systems, institutions and environments on which we all depend work in a manner that benefits all people simultaneously and in solidarity. A study by NESC states that 'at a societal level, a belief in a "common good" has been shown to contribute to the overall wellbeing of society. This requires a level of recognition of rights and responsibilities, empathy with others and values of citizenship' (NESC, 2009, p.32).

This raises the issue of resources. The goods of the planet are for the use of all people - not just the present generation but for generations still to come. The present generation must recognise it has a responsibility to ensure that it does not damage but rather enhances the goods of the planet that it passes on - be they economic, cultural, social or environmental. The structural arrangements regarding the ownership, use, accumulation and distribution of goods are disputed areas. However it must be recognised that these arrangements have a major impact on how society is shaped and how it supports the wellbeing of each of its members in solidarity with others.

Social Justice Ireland believes that the values outlined above must be at the core of the vision for a nation in which all women, men and children have what they require to live life with dignity and to fulfil their potential, including sufficient income, access to the services they need and active inclusion in a genuinely participatory society. We believe the vision for Ireland set out here should guide policy development and decision-making in the period ahead. Guided by this vision Ireland would move towards becoming a just society.

2.2 A Policy Framework for a Just Society

To achieve our vision and to build a just society we propose a policy framework that identifies five key policy areas for reform.[2]

- The first is macroeconomic stability, which requires a stabilisation of Ireland's debt levels, fiscal and financial stability and sustainable economic growth, and an immediate boost to investment, which has collapsed during the crisis. (Dealt with here and in chapter 4)

- The second is the need for a just taxation system, which would require an increase in the overall tax-take towards 34.9% and eventually towards the European average; such an increase must be implemented equitably and in a way that reduces income inequality. (These issues are dealt with in detail in chapter 4).

- The third area is social protection, the strengthening of social services and social infrastructure, the prioritisation of employment, and a commitment to quantitative targets to reduce poverty. (Chapters 3, 4, 5, 6, 7, 8 and 9).

- The fourth area is that of the governance of our country, which requires new criteria in policy evaluation, the development of a rights-based approach, and the promotion of deliberative democracy. (Chapter 10).

- Fifth, policies must be adopted that create a sustainable future, through the introduction of measures to promote climate justice and protect the environment, the promotion of balanced regional development, and promotion of new economic and social indicators to measure performance, alongside traditional national accounting measures such as GNP, GDP and GNI. (Chapters 11, 12 and 13).

---

[2] The authors have presented an earlier version of this framework in Healy et al. (2013).

Table 2.1 - A policy framework for a Just Ireland

Macro-economic stability	Just taxation	Decent services	Good governance	Real sustainability
Debt sustainability average	Bring Taxes towards EU infrastructure	Secure services and social PPNs	Deliberative democracy & and protect the environment	Promote climate Climate justice
Fiscal and financial stability and sustainable economic growth	Increase taxes equitably and reduce income inequality	Combat unemployment & underemployment	Reform Policy Evaluation	Balanced regional development
Investment programme	Secure fair share of corporate profits for the State	Ensure seven Social, Economic and Cultural rights are achieved	Social dialogue – all sectors in deliberative process	New indicators of progress and new Satellite National Accounts

i) Ensuring macroeconomic stability

Ensuring macroeconomic stability requires a reduction in Ireland's debt burden, the launching of an investment programme and a restoration of fiscal and financial stability. All of these measures are connected. An investment programme will contribute to growth which would in turn lower Ireland's deficit and real debt burden. A reduction of, or commitment to reduce, Ireland's debt burden will increase confidence in the capacity of Ireland's economy to expand and for the country to fully exit the EU/IMF programme without the requirement of additional credit facilities or the activation of the Outright Monetary Transactions (OMT) programme, thus reducing yields on Irish Government debt.

Ireland's macroeconomic policy will be severely constrained if current parameters are maintained. Since Economic and Monetary Union (EMU), monetary policy has rested with the European Central Bank, and the single currency has prevented the kind of currency devaluation engaged in by Ireland during the late 1980s (Kinsella, 2013). Following the introduction of the fiscal rules, Ireland's fiscal policy will also be constrained as noted in Box 2.1.

Box 2.1 Fiscal Compact

The Stability and Growth Pact (SGP) is seen as the cornerstone of budgetary discipline in the EU. One of the results of the diagnosis of the economic crash as a public finance crisis was the strengthening of this framework which governs Member States fiscal rules; there has been an increase in surveillance and the disciplining role of the European Commission has been strengthened. Additionally, the Commission was tasked with identifying and preventing macroeconomic imbalances, such as the persistent current account imbalances which built up during the early and mid-2000s.

The legal framework is contained in the 'six pack' of five regulations and a directive, applying to the EU28, the 'two pack' which applies to the Euro area Member States and increases monitoring by the European Commission – including submission of national budgets no later than 15 October – and the 'Fiscal Compact', an intergovernmental treaty (Britain and the Czech Republic did not sign it) which requires the direct transposition of the SGP measures into national law.

The SGP rules state that:

- Government deficits must be 3% or less;

- Government debt to GDP ratio must be 60% or less; and

  - Government structural deficits must be 0.5% or less.

- The structural deficit may be up to 1% if debt to GDP is significantly below 60%. However, the SGP requires a $1/20^{th}$ reduction in debt per year if a country has a debt to GDP ratio above 60%. The requirements of the Fiscal Compact have been given effect in law in most European countries.

The 3% and 60% limits are enshrined in Art. 126 of the Treaty and in Protocol 12 accompanying the Treaty

Ireland is currently in the Excessive Deficit Procedure (EDP) which requires the reduction of the General Government Deficit to under 3% of GDP.

The $1/20^{th}$ rule applying to the path of debt reduction will fully apply to all these countries once they exit the EDP. Until 2019 Ecofin and the European Commission will determine whether the pace of debt reduction is adequate. After that it is expected that the rule will apply to all.

One of the reasons this whole process is important to countries emerging from very difficult circumstances is that under the Six-Part/Two-Pack arrangements public spending is governed by an 'expenditure benchmark', which limits growth in government expenditure. When a member-state has not achieved its Medium-Term Budgetary Objective (MTO), a reference rate for growth in government expenditure is calculated based on potential growth estimates and a convergence rate of expenditure is provided which must be followed to achieve the MTO.

There is some concern that the Compact and wider EU fiscal rules contain a number of very difficult challenges for countries who have been struggling for some time. However, it is likely that these rules will remain in place and will have to be adhered to. Given the operation of the 'Expenditure benchmark', any increase in expenditure above the benchmark by Ireland would require revenue increases.

Consequently, if Ireland does not continue to experience high economic growth rates it may well be unable to invest the necessary resources to improve economic and social infrastructure and services for a very long time. In practice this could result in persistent high unemployment, high levels of poverty and ongoing social exclusion.

Serious care is required to ensure that the investment required to produce a well-functioning economy, to develop inclusive labour markets, to secure adequate income support and to ensure that access to high-quality services for all is not impeded by the requirements of the SGP, which were developed for a different purpose. The EU has had a major focus on its economic concerns in recent years but paid far too little attention to the social impacts of the decisions it made and the initiatives it took. Ireland did not address the social impacts of the Bailout measures from the beginning with very unfair consequences. Now there is an urgent need to rebalance the economic and social aspects of Irish society.

a) Debt Sustainability
The debt-to-GDP ratio peaked in 2013 at 123.3%, and declined in 2014 and is set to continue doing so. By 2016, the Department of Finance indicated, in a 2014 publication, that 14.3% of general government revenues would be devoted to servicing Ireland's debt (Department of Finance, 2014: C20). The unexpected rise in economic growth means this number is likely to have fallen. Ireland returned a primary surplus in 2014 – the budget deficit less interest payments. However Ireland still faces substantial debt challenges given the scale of the debt and its vulnerability to international developments. It is recognised by Irish policymakers that the Irish banking sector is still unprepared for widespread losses on distressed mortgages (e.g Honohan, 2013).

There has yet to be a full recognition by European partners that a large proportion of Ireland's debt was accumulated in the course of rescuing the Irish banking sector, and ensuring that there was relatively lower burden-sharing than would have been expected in any other enterprise. This part of Ireland's debt represents a direct subsidy by the Irish public of international bondholders and the European banking system. The total cost of the banking rescue has been €64bn, of which €12.6bn has come directly from the Exchequer, €30.7bn through promissory notes and €20.7bn from the National Pension Reserve Fund (NPRF).[3] Of the €192bn in gross government debt in 2012, over 20% was accounted for directly by the bank recapitalisation alone.

If there are no additional liabilities arising from the banking sector and no further economic shocks, Ireland's debt may be sustainable, assuming continuing low government debt yields and economic growth. However, deflation in the Eurozone could have implications for Ireland's real debt burden if it continues. To increase debt sustainability, European authorities should also consider further changes to the status of the government bonds which were issued to replace the promissory notes including further extending the maturity and considering a lower interest rate. Such measures could also be further applied to the loans received under the EU/IMF Programme, in a similar manner to the EFSF loans.

b) Fiscal and financial stability and sustainable economic growth
The connection between fiscal policy, output and employment has been at the heart of the austerity debate in Ireland and Europe. Reducing government expenditure and/or increasing tax revenues are not the same thing as reducing the deficit, and meeting deficit reduction targets requires rapid underlying growth. Ireland should make the case for a European-wide approach to growth, one that takes account of the spill-over effects of combined fiscal consolidation. Unfortunately the fiscal rules introduced militate against a European-wide fiscal expansion, though breaching the rules is allowed in 'extraordinary circumstances'.

Sustainable employment growth can be underpinned by an investment programme that invests in both economic and social infrastructure. Kelly and McQuinn (2013) have noted that, given the relationship between government's fiscal accounts and the balance sheets of the banking sector, austerity could have a deeper impact than thought by policymakers given the concomitant increase in mortgage arrears and business loan defaults on banking balance sheets, which necessitate greater levels of recapitalisation. This was not appreciated by policymakers during the crisis as austerity led to bank bailouts which led to further austerity.

The government urgently needs to tackle the infrastructure deficit and low levels of investment in Ireland. *Social Justice Ireland* welcomes the establishment of the Strategic Banking Corporation of Ireland (SBCI) as a first step towards a fully functioning Strategic Investment Bank, modelled on the German state owned KfW Bankengruppe, European Investment Bank.

---

[3] Parliamentary Question 18719/12.

c) An Investment Programme

Investment as % of GDP in Ireland in 2013 was 10%, the lowest in the European Union (Eurostat 2013) despite three other EU countries participating in troika (EC-ECB-IMF) bailout programmes and the poor investment base in Ireland. Since then there has been significant improvement (see Table 2.2), though it is from a low base.

Table 2.2 – Projected Growth in Investment, 2014-2015

	Department of Finance	ESRI	IMF	European Commission	Central Bank of Ireland	OECD
2014	14.6	14.2	4.4	12	11.9	10.6
2015	12.7	12.8	6.2	6.5	9.2	11

Source: Department of Finance (2014), Duffy et. al. (2014), IMF (2014), European Commission (2014)., Central Bank of Ireland (2014), OECD (2014)

In 2014, the European Commission (EC) proposed a European Investment Plan for Growth and Jobs 2015-2017 to spur economic development and investment in Europe. The Plan is based on three pillars: structural reforms to modernise and preserve the economy, fiscal responsibility to restore confidence and the sustainability of public finances, the need to boost investment, with the launch of a European Funds for Strategic Investments (EFSI). The new EC plans to commit €21 billion worth of funds (€8 billion from the EU budget, €8 billion guarantees from the EU and €5 billion from the European Investment Bank) to generate €63 billion worth in loans, and increasing investment to the value of €315 billion.

The government has created a new investment fund – the Ireland Strategic Investment Fund (ISIF) - using the NPRF's €6.8bn discretionary investment portfolio. The fund is orientated towards commercial investment opportunities such as energy, broadband and water. Domestic economic investment is sorely needed to provide employment and provide much-needed infrastructure; this would reduce short-term unemployment and increase the long-run productivity of the Irish economy.

The Strategic Banking Corporation of Ireland (SBCI) is a new company launched in 2014 and is based in the National Treasury Management Agency. The SBCI will provide over €800m credit for SMEs and will include long lending terms for capital investment, and interest holidays, typically around 18 months. The SBCI will be initially financed by €150 million from the Kreditanstalt für Wiederaufbau (Germany state development bank, the second largest commercial German bank) and €650 million from the European Investment Bank (EIB) and the Ireland Strategic Investment Fund (ISIF).

Social Justice Ireland believes that there must be an off-balance sheet investment programme particularly in the housing market, as we proposed in our briefing document, *Investing for Growth, Jobs & Recovery* (*Social Justice Ireland*, 2013). This would directly create employment and also enhance growth, which would contribute to reducing the deficit by reducing unemployment and increasing tax returns. We propose that the investment programme target both economic *and* social infrastructure, including the construction of social housing units, investment in water infrastructure, and investment in primary care facilities.

ii) Towards a Just Taxation System
Policy will be heavily constrained in the years immediately ahead, not least by the requirement under the 'six-pack' that additional discretionary expenditure must be funded by additional discretionary revenue. The current trajectory of government policy is for a reduction in total expenditure (including interest rates) and a reduction in total revenue (of which tax revenue is by far the largest component) to 2018. The Department of Finance's *Fiscal and Economic Outlook 2015* shows total revenue falling to 32.1% of GDP and total expenditure falling to 31.8% of GDP in 2018. By comparison, the most recent data show that the EU was estimated to have a total revenue of 45.3% of GDP and total expenditure of 47.9% of GDP in 2013 (Eurostat, 2015). What is the basis for the Government's proposed trajectory in these areas? As discussed in chapter 1, it is time Ireland had a real debate about the levels of services and infrastructure it seeks to have in the coming decade or two and how these are to be financed.

Graph 2.1 – Total Revenue and Total Expenditure as a % of GDP, 2004-2018[4]

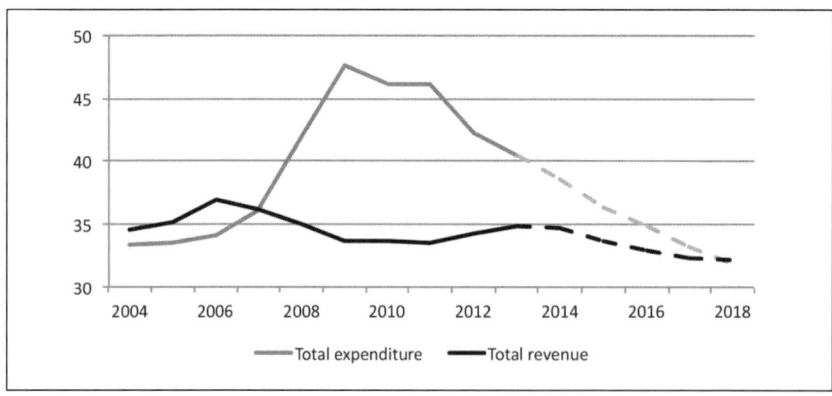

Source: Eurostat (2015), Department of Finance (2015).
Notes: *Figures to 2013 are taken from the AMECO database.
** The cost of recapitalisation of banking institutions has been removed.
*** Figures from 2013 to 2018 are taken from *Budget 2015, Table A.2.1*

---
[4] Total expenditure takes account of all government expenditure, including interest payments, which in the April 2014 Stability Programme Update account for some 4.9% of GDP per annum between 2016 and 2018 and 4.8% of GDP annum in 2019.

As a society, can Ireland provide high-quality public services to all while allowing total expenditure to fall as a percentage of GDP? And if there is an improvement in various indicators should additional revenue be used to reduce taxes or increase expenditure? *Social Justice Ireland* believes a new policy framework is required; one that recognises the need to increase taxes towards 34.9% of GDP in order to fund the public services that we need, while implementing new criteria for policy evaluation. This would have the additional value of maintaining Ireland as a low-tax country.

The American jurist Oliver Wendell Holmes once said that 'taxes are the price we pay for a civilised society'. *Social Justice Ireland* has long argued that Ireland's total tax-take is simply too low to pay for the services and infrastructure required to ensure human dignity for all. We also believe that the incidence of taxation falls too heavily on the shoulders of those on middle and low incomes. Therefore, the overall tax take must rise and this must be done in such a way that the burden falls of those most able to bear it.

a) Bring Taxes towards the European average
Ireland's tax-take in 2014 was 31.7% of GDP, some 4% below the European average. The Department of Finance believes that the total tax-take as a % of GDP will be 31.5% of GDP by 2016. Table 2.3 indicates the difference in the projected additional tax yield if Ireland's tax burden moved closer to the European average than that indicated by the Department of Finance in the April 2013 Stability Programme Update. There has been some debate on the appropriate measures of Ireland's fiscal capacity in recent years, given the difference between Ireland's GNP and GDP. The Irish Fiscal Advisory Council (IFAC) has suggested a hybrid measure in the form: [H = GNP+0.4 (GDP-GNP)] (IFAC, 2012: 53). *Social Justice Ireland* has argued that the tax-take should be increased to 34.9% of GDP, below the Eurostat threshold defining a low-tax country. An equivalent figure under the IFAC would be to increase taxes to a level that fluctuates around 39.5% of H.

Table 2.3 – Potential Irish Total Tax Revenues, 2014-2018 (€bn)

Year	Tax as % GDP	Tax as % of H	Total Tax Receipts	The Tax Gap (GDP)
2014	31.7%	36.0%	55,245	5,577
2015	31.9%	36.3%	57,914	5,446
2016	31.5%	36.0%	59,574	6,430
2017	31.3%		61,442	7,067
2018	31.2%		63,882	7,576

Source: Department of Finance (2014: 49-50).
Notes: *The Tax Gap is calculated as the difference between the projected tax take and that which would be collected if total tax receipts were equal to 34.9% of GDP.

As we noted before, the reliance on a relatively low level of taxation to fund vital public services certainly contributed to the scale of the crisis in the public finances. Ireland can never hope to address its longer-term deficits in infrastructure and social provision if we continue to collect substantially less tax income than that required by other European countries (cf. chapter 4 for a more detailed discussion of this issue). There should also be a public debate on the appropriate level of taxation required over the next twenty years to fund our public services and social security system. Future policy development will likely involve increasing public spending and tax levels as well as changes in how services are delivered. These questions should be openly debated instead of avoided by policymakers.

b) Increase taxes equitably
If Ireland is to increase its total tax-take, it must do so in a fair and equitable manner. *Social Justice Ireland* believes that the necessary tax reforms should be partly attained by increasing income taxes for those on highest incomes, and by reforming the tax code and broadening the tax base. This will involve shifting taxation towards wealth, ensuring those who benefit the most from Ireland's economic system contribute the most, in the most efficient manner.

Social Justice Ireland advocates a minimum effective tax rate of 6 per cent for corporation tax, reform of reliefs accruing to those paying the marginal tax rate, and the introduction of a Financial Transactions Tax (FTT) in line with proposals outlined by the European Commission and accepted by leading member-states.

c) Reduce income inequality
Income inequality, gender inequality and inequality of opportunity are problems in Irish society. They produce a range of negative outcomes for those who are poor and/or excluded. Growing inequality exacerbates the negative effects on people who are poor and/or excluded. Pickett and Wilkinson (2011) have pointed to the negative consequences of inequality for all sections of society, pointing to better outcomes in everything from subjective well-being to lower crime in more equal societies. Stigliz (2013) has warned of the wider effects of inequality on the political economy of a nation, as wealthier citizens gain an outsize influence in policy formulation, reducing opportunities for the majority through their choices of policy. In Ireland, increases in social protection payments, particularly between 2004 and 2007, played an important role in reducing inequality. This has been reversed since 2010, as successive governments prioritised cuts in expenditure over increases in taxation, raising serious questions for Irish society.

While budgets in 2008 and the years immediately following were progressive, changes in taxation and expenditure since 2010 have been regressive, with the increase in VAT impacting particularly significantly on those with the lowest incomes (Callan et. al.,

2012, 2013m 2014). This does not take into account cuts to public services, which have a greater impact on those who rely on services; the sick, poor and vulnerable. The Gini coefficient, a measure of income inequality, has risen from a low in 2009 of 29.3 to 31.3 in 2013 (CSO, 2015). Reducing inequality must be a core objective of Government policy. Though the promotion of pre-distribution income equality is important, redistribution through tax and spending decisions should be used to achieve greater equality in Ireland.

- *Secure fair share of corporate profits for the State*
A key part of Ireland's industrial strategy has been to attract foreign domestic investment through the use of a low headline corporation tax rate. However, this has recently caused reputational damage due to the utilisation of the Irish tax regime by multinational corporations to avoid taxes on their corporate profits. In practice, this policy has delivered some short-term gains in terms of foreign direct investment. In the medium-term, the main beneficiaries of Ireland's tax regime may well be multinational corporations and Irish professional services companies providing tax and legal services.

A key medium-term priority must be the reconceptualization of the role of the Irish corporation tax regime. Under international pressure from the G20 and OECD, controversial loopholes have been closed but a serious discussion must take place about the role of corporation tax in Ireland's industrial strategy, and the role of 'brass-plate' companies headquartered in Dublin for tax purposes.[5] We advocate Ireland change its stance towards the corporation tax debate in Europe and negotiate a Europe-wide minimum headline corporation tax of 17.5%.

iii) Securing Decent Services
There have been significant cuts to social services and payments since 2008. *Social Justice Ireland* believes many of these cuts have been socially destructive and counter-productive. Many cuts have been capricious and were implemented without an adequate examination of their impact. Moreover, in reducing the deficit the balance between expenditure reductions and taxes was weighted disproportionately towards cuts. Investment in social infrastructure is required now to ensure that it is not eroded further which could potentially have significant future costs. Gross capital expenditure has fallen from €9bn in 2008 to €3.5bn in 2015, and a social infrastructure deficit will inevitably emerge in a climate of underinvestment as the population continues to grow. The CSO estimates that the population will rise from its current level of 4.5 million to somewhere between 4.8 and 5.3 million by 2026. Finally, the goal of universal provision for all must remain, particularly in the area of health, where inequalities persist between the insured and uninsured population, as well as within

---

[5] See Department of Finance (2013) for recent adjustments to Ireland's corporation tax policy.

the uninsured population. These inequalities will grow as user charges are introduced, and medical cards removed. As we have noted before, given the widespread aspiration in Irish society for these services, the issue of taxation must be addressed.

a) Secure services and social infrastructure
Between 2008 and 2014 Government cut spending by €20,159m while increasing taxes by €10,180m: a ratio of €2 in spending cuts for €1 in tax rates. Measures were, and are, required to reduce the deficit, but they should not fall disproportionately upon the most vulnerable in society. Cuts to services and social protection payments ensure that they do.

Social Justice Ireland believes that the ratio of spending cuts to tax increases should have been the reverse of what was implemented. Future tax and spending policy should prioritise the building of Ireland's social infrastructure, including as a priority social housing, primary and mental health facilities, and early education facilities. Adequate social infrastructure and services are necessary to achieve sufficient dignity and equality for all citizens, from children to older people, particularly in the context of an increased total fertility rate and gradually ageing population.

b) Combat Unemployment & underemployment
Unemployment has begun to fall, and by 2014, 213,600 people were unemployed and the unemployment rate was 9.9% (CSO, 2015). Out of this, 123,400 people were long-term unemployed, accounting for 57% of those who are unemployed. The Government aims to deliver full employment [2.1 million jobs] by 2018 (Department of Social Protection. 2015).

Government currently operates a number of schemes such as the Community Employment Programme, Tús, and Rural Social Scheme which support part-time jobs. However, government has also introduced schemes such as JobBridge, an unpaid internship programme which provides an additional €50 a week for working between 30 and 40 hours, and the Local Government Social Employment Scheme, which provides an additional €20 a week for working 19.5 hours a week for a local authority, with the potential for sanctions if the person refuses. There are dangers in the latter schemes, such as labour market displacement, exploitation, demoralisation, and the erosion of the principle of a 'fair day's wage for a fair day's work'. They can also ignore the underlying lack of employment opportunities in the economy.

The Nevin Economic Research Institute (2014:1) has pointed to the fact that there is currently 1 vacancy for every 24 jobseekers. Combining the rate of underemployment – those involuntarily working part-time and seeking full-time work – with the rate of unemployment shows that some 329,100 people, or 15.2% of the labour force, are seeking more work. Without significant public and social investment, it is simply not conceivable that employment will grow in the non-traded sector. Policy discussions on 'labour market activation' often do not take this reality into account, and political rhetoric can verge on the demonization of the unemployed.

c) Ensure seven Social, Economic and Cultural Rights are achieved
There is a real danger that Irish society will permit those on the lowest incomes, and in particular those dependent on social welfare, to fall behind once again, as it did in the late 1990s. From 2006, Ireland's poverty levels had been slowly falling, driven by increases in social welfare payments delivered in the Budgets of 2005-2007. These increases compensated only partly for the extent to which social welfare rates had fallen behind other incomes in society over the preceding two decades. However, these advances have been reversed since 2009 with the at risk-of-poverty-rate rising from a low of 14.1% in 2009 to 15.2% in 2013, consistent poverty has risen from a low of 4.2% in 2008 to 8.2% in 2013 while the deprivation rate has risen from a low of 11.8% in 2007 to 30.5% in 2013 (CSO, 2015:1). In 2013, the single largest demographic group at-risk-of-poverty was children; nearly one in five was at risk of poverty (CSO, 2015).

It would be a great mistake for Ireland, and Irish policy makers, to repeat the experience of the late 1990s. At that time, economic growth benefited only those who were employed while others, such as those dependent on pensions and other social welfare payments slipped further and further behind. We believe that policy should now provide equity in social welfare rates across genders, adequate payments for children, and higher payments for those with disabilities.

Social Justice Ireland believes strongly in the importance of developing a rights-based approach to social, economic and cultural policy. The need to develop these rights is becoming ever more urgent for Ireland in the context of achieving recovery. Such an approach would go a long way towards addressing the growing inequality Ireland has been experiencing. Social, economic and cultural rights should be acknowledged and recognised, just as civil and political rights have been. *Social Justice Ireland* believes seven basic rights should be acknowledged and recognised. These are the rights to sufficient income to live life with dignity: meaningful work; appropriate accommodation; relevant education; essential healthcare; cultural respect; and real participation in society. To be vindicated, these rights will require greater public expenditure and provision of services.

iv) Reforming Governance
It has been widely recognised that Ireland's governance was poor in certain areas prior to the economic crisis, particularly in relation to financial regulation. Moreover, the economic crisis has led to government making rash and hasty decisions without consultation, whether in relation to financial or budgetary policy, which have been recognised as damaging or – in the case of the bank guarantee – catastrophic.

Reforming governance and widening participation are a necessity; below are three immediate priorities required to achieve this.

a) Democratic Deliberation
Decisions taken by government must be openly debated both inside and outside the Oireachtas. Since 2008, austerity measures have been implemented in a haphazard manner, with little public debate and often a lack of explanation and justification for the measures taken. Instead of reasoned debate with citizen and civil society participation, decisions have been taken at an elite level. For example, Government has provided a high-level forum called the IFSC Clearing House Group for the financial industry, and 23 changes in the Finance Act 2012 were made to accommodate this group (McGee, 2012). A number of actions taken during the crisis lacked democratic accountability and legitimacy.

Social Justice Ireland believes that a new social model for Ireland must be founded on the idea of deliberative democracy, in which decisions about what kind of society and economy Ireland needs are founded upon reasoned, evidence-based and enlightened debate, and in which decisions taken by government are justified and accessible to the general public.[6] A deliberative decision making process is one where all stakeholders are involved, but the power differentials are removed (Healy and Reynolds, 2011). In such a process stakeholders are involved in the framing, implementing and evaluating of policies and measures that impact on them. Each citizen should have a role and voice in how our society is governed. The Public Participation Networks in Local Authorities are providing an opportunity for real engagement between local people and the local authorities across the country (for further information on this cf. chapter 10).

b) Reform Policy Evaluation
Policy evaluation has been extremely poor in some cases throughout the crisis. *Social Justice Ireland* welcomes the steps taken by Government to increase their research and evaluative capacity. However, we believe that Government should also take steps to increase the transparency of budgetary and other important decisions, which are often opaque. Government should publish their analysis of the distributional impact of budgetary measures, and engage in public debate in light of that analysis. Previously, the Government published Poverty Impact Assessment Guidelines provided by the Office of Social Inclusion (2008) in the budgetary documentation using the ESRI's SWITCH tax-benefit model which captures the distributional impact of changes in most taxes and benefits, but this practice was discontinued from Budget 2010. Government should reintroduce this practice and also adopt a gender equality

---

[6] See Gutmann & Thompson (2004) and Healy and Reynolds (2011) for more on the concept of deliberative democracy.

analysis and apply it to each budgetary measure. This should be a statutory responsibility for Government.

c) Social Dialogue

Now that the economy is beginning to improve and some additional resources are likely to be available, Government is proposing to begin a process of social dialogue as it prepares a multi-annual plan for Ireland's development. Such a process is very welcome as long as it is fair in both its approach and its outcomes. Social dialogue in various forms is common across Europe's most successful economies and can play a key role in building a sustainable recovery here in Ireland.

Some reports suggest this social dialogue will deal with pay and taxation issues and map out the road ahead for some years. These are critically important issues as they determine the disposable income that people with jobs will have. There are four key issues that need to be recognised however before Government decides on the shape of such a process:

- People with jobs will be very aware of the importance, not just of pay and tax, but also of what is known as 'the social wage' i.e. the services and infrastructure to which they have a right.

- Many people do not have jobs; these include older people, many of those who are ill or have a disability as well as those who are unemployed. These are among the most vulnerable in Irish society today.

- There are many issues beyond wages and taxes that must be addressed. Increasing investment, ensuring access to credit for SMEs and enhancement of capabilities in the economy and society are just a few of these issues.

- If a social dialogue process deals with the issues of pay and taxation before social services and infrastructure are addressed then the concerns of only a part of the population will be given priority. Ensuring this is avoided requires explicitly factoring in the needs of all at the beginning of the process.

These issues should be approached in an integrated manner. Government will make the final decisions on all policy issues. That has always been the case. But it is important that any new approach adopted by Government is integrated and inclusive.

A social dialogue process would be a very positive development for Ireland at this point in our recovery. Government needs to engage all sectors of society. Otherwise lop-sided outcomes that will benefit those who are engaged in the social dialogue process while excluding others, most notably the vulnerable, are likely to emerge. If Government wishes the whole society to take responsibility for producing a more viable future then it must involve all of us. Responsibility for shaping the future should be shared among all stakeholders.

There are many reasons for involving all sectors in this process: to ensure priority is given to well-being and the common good; to address the challenges of markets and their failures; to link rights and responsibilities. When groups have been involved in shaping decisions they are far more likely to take responsibility for implementing these decisions, difficult and demanding as they may be. A process of social dialogue involving all and not just some of the sectors in Irish society would be a key mechanism in maximising the resources for moving forward and in ensuring the best possible outcomes for Ireland.

Ireland urgently needs to set a course for the future that will secure macroeconomic stability, a just tax system, strengthened social services and infrastructure, good governance and a real commitment to sustainability. A social dialogue process that includes all the stakeholders in Irish society would go a long way towards achieving such a future. There are lessons to be learned from the old social partnership process. It is important that this learning is based on evidence and not on the caricature of social partnership that is often presented by commentators.

One way to begin the process would be for the National Economic and Social Council – NESC - (an existing instrument of social dialogue involving broad sectors of Irish society, independent experts and Government Departments which has continued to produce clear analysis and sensible recommendations), to produce a balanced assessment of the strategic priorities to be pursued under the leadership of the Government in the period ahead.

v) Creating a Sustainable Future
Sustainable development is development which meets the needs of the present while not compromising the needs of the future. In this regard financial, environmental, economic and social sustainability are all key objectives. In light of this, new indicators must be compiled measuring both well-being and sustainability in society, and used as an objective beside the traditional measures of GDP and GNP. These indicators should help in ensuring that issues such as climate justice and balanced regional development are prioritised.

a) Support climate justice and protect the environment
Climate change remains the largest long-term challenge facing Ireland today. The challenge of reducing Ireland's fossil fuel emissions should not be postponed in the face of the current recession. We believe that Ireland should adopt ambitious statutory targets regarding the limitation of fossil fuel emissions, and introduce taxation measures necessary to compensate for the full costs of resource extraction and pollution. While the publication of the Climate Action and Low Carbon Development Bill 2015 was welcome there are not adequate sectoral targets or quantitative measures against which individual stakeholders can measure their progress.

The economic crisis has, for obvious reasons, focused attention on economic growth and financial stability. This should not come at the expense of the physical environment, as the failure to tackle climate change now will have significant impacts into the future, including on food production, regional and global ecosystems, and on flood-prone countries and regions.

b) *Balanced Regional Development*
A sustained recovery requires balanced regional development. The boom years saw an attempt to redress growing regional imbalances in socio-economic development through National Spatial Strategy (2002-2020), though it failed to do so, partly because of Government's own initiatives such as the decentralisation programme for public servants (Meredith and van Egeraat, 2013).

During the recession, particular regions of Ireland have suffered more than others The unemployment rate in Mid-East is the lowest in the country at 8.5% while the South East is the hardest hit with an unemployment rate of 11.9% (CSO, 2015). Rural areas have been severely impacted by cuts in services. The authors believe that policy must ensure balanced regional development through the provision of public services – including cultural, economic and social services - and through capital spending projects, and the adoption of a new National Spatial Strategy, which could be formulated through a deliberative national debate.

c) *New indicators of progress and Satellite National Accounts*
Creating a sustainable Ireland requires the adoption of new indicators to measure progress. GDP alone as a measure of progress is unsatisfactory, as it only describes the monetary value of gross output, income and expenditure in an economy. The *Report by the Commission on the Measurement of Economic Performance and Social Progress*, led by Nobel prize winning economists Amartya Sen and Joseph Stiglitz and established by President Sarkozy, argued that new indicators measuring environmental, financial sustainability, well-being, and happiness are required.

The National Economic and Social Council (2009) has published the *Well-Being Matters* report, which suggested that measures of well-being could be constructed that capture data on six domains of people's lives that contribute to well-being including: economic resources; work and participation; relationships and care; community and environment; health; and democracy and values. We believe that a new social model should deploy such indicators alongside national accounting measures. The OECD Global Project on Measuring the Progress of Society has recommended a use of such indicators to inform evidence-based policies (Marrone, 2009: 23). They would serve as an alternative benchmark for success.

2.4 Conclusion

So, having set out our vision for Ireland and presented a policy framework for a just society and provided some details of the policy initiatives required under each of its five pillars we now move on to look in much greater detail at key aspects of these five pillars.

We provide a fuller analysis of both the first pillar, **macroeconomic stability**, and the second pillar, a **just taxation** system, in chapter 4 where we also set out a more detailed set of policy proposals.

We address the third pillar, **decent social services**, in chapters 3 – on income distribution; 4 – taxation; 5 - work, unemployment and job creation; 6 - public services; 7 - housing and accommodation; 8 – healthcare; and 9 – education and educational disadvantage). On each of these we provide an analysis and critique of the present situation, set out a vision for a fairer future and make a detailed set of policy proposals aimed at moving in that direction.

The fourth pillar, **good governance** is addressed in chapter 10, where we again provide analysis and critique together with concrete policy proposals.

The fifth pillar, **real sustainability**, is addressed in chapters 11 – sustainability; 12 - rural development; and 13 - the global south following the same approach.

Chapter 14 provides further details on the values that underpin our approach, our focus and our proposals.

3.
INCOME DISTRIBUTION

The persistence of high rates of poverty and income inequality in Ireland requires greater attention than they currently receive. Tackling these problems effectively is a multifaceted task. It requires action on many fronts, ranging from healthcare and education to accommodation and employment. However, the most important requirement in tackling poverty is the provision of sufficient income to enable people to live life with dignity. No anti-poverty strategy can possibly be successful without an effective approach to addressing low incomes.

This chapter addresses the issue of income in five parts. The first (section 3.1) examines the extent and nature of poverty in Ireland today while the second (section 3.2) profiles our income distribution. The final three sections address potential remedies to these problems by outlining the issues and arguments surrounding the introduction of a living wage (section 3.3) achieving and maintaining an adequate social welfare income (section 3.4) and the introduction of a basic income (section 3.5). All address issues related to the achievement of one pillar of Social Justice Ireland's Core Policy Framework (see Chapter 2), 'Securing Decent Services'.

3.1 Poverty

While there is still considerable poverty in Ireland, there has been much progress on this issue over recent years. Driven by increases in social welfare payments, particularly payments to the unemployed, the elderly and people with disabilities, the rate of poverty significantly declined between 2001 and 2009. However, since reaching a record low level in 2009 it has increased, climbing to a higher level in each of the years 2010-2012. This change was driven by budgetary policy which reversed earlier social welfare increases.[1]

---

[1] Irish household income data has been collected since 1973 and all surveys up to the period 2008-2010 recorded poverty levels above 15 per cent.

Data on Ireland's income and poverty levels are now provided by the annual *SILC* survey *(Survey on Income and Living Conditions)*. This survey replaced the *European Household Panel Survey* and the *Living in Ireland Survey* which had run throughout the 1990s. Since 2003 the *SILC / EU-SILC* survey has collected detailed information on income and living conditions from up to 120 households in Ireland each week; giving a total sample of between 4,000 and 6,000 households each year.

Social Justice Ireland welcomes this survey and in particular the accessibility of the data produced.[2] Because this survey is conducted simultaneously across all of the EU states, the results are an important contribution to the ongoing discussion on relative income and poverty levels across the EU. It also provides the basis for informed analysis of the relative position of the citizens of member states. In particular, this analysis is informed by a set of agreed indicators of social exclusion which the EU Heads of Government adopted at Laeken in 2001. These indicators (known as the updated-Laeken indicators) are calculated from the survey results and cover four dimensions of social exclusion: financial poverty, employment, health and education. They form the basis of the EU Open Method of Co-ordination for social protection and social inclusion and the Europe 2020 poverty and social exclusion targets.[3]

What is poverty?

The National Anti-Poverty Strategy (NAPS) published by government in 1997 adopted the following definition of poverty:

> People are living in poverty if their income and resources (material, cultural and social) are so inadequate as to preclude them from having a standard of living that is regarded as acceptable by Irish society generally. As a result of inadequate income and resources people may be excluded and marginalised from participating in activities that are considered the norm for other people in society.

This definition was reiterated in the 2007 *National Action Plan for Social Inclusion 2007-2016 (NAPinclusion).*

---

[2] However, we note the delay in publishing the 2013 results, the third such delay in recent years. At a time when income and living standards data are central to much public policy analysis and formation, it is crucial that the SILC data, from the 2014 survey onwards, returns to being published in a timely way.

[3] For more information on these indicators see Nolan (2006:171-190).

Where is the poverty line?

How many people are poor? On what basis are they classified as poor? These and related questions are constantly asked when poverty is discussed or analysed.

In trying to measure the extent of poverty, the most common approach has been to identify a poverty line (or lines) based on people's disposable income (earned income after taxes and including all benefits). The European Commission and the UN, among others, use a poverty line located at 60 per cent of median income. The median disposable income is the income of the middle person in society's income distribution. This poverty line is the one adopted in the *SILC* survey. While the 60 per cent median income line has been adopted as the primary poverty line, alternatives set at 50 per cent and 70 per cent of median income are also used to clarify and lend robustness to assessments of poverty.

The most up-to-date data available on poverty in Ireland comes from the 2013 *SILC* survey, conducted by the CSO (published January 2015). In that year the CSO gathered data from a statistically representative sample of 4,922 households containing 12,663 individuals. The data gathered by the CSO is very detailed. It incorporates income from work, welfare, pensions, rental income, dividends, capital gains and other regular transfers. This data was subsequently verified anonymously using PPS numbers.

According to the CSO, the median disposable income per adult in Ireland during 2013 was €17,551 per annum or €336.63 per week. Consequently, the income poverty lines for a single adult derived from this are:

50 per cent line	€168.31 a week
60 per cent line	€201.98 a week
70 per cent line	€235.64 a week

Updating the 60 per cent median income poverty line to 2015 levels, using published CSO data on the growth in average hourly earnings in 2014 (+1.7 per cent) and ESRI projections for 2015 (+1.3 per cent) produces a relative income poverty line of €208.08 for a single person. In 2015, any adult below this weekly income level will be counted as being at risk of poverty (CSO, 2014; Duffy, FitzGerald, McQuinn, Byrne and Morley 2014: 3).

Table 3.1 shows what income corresponds to the poverty line for a number of household types. The figure of €208.08 is an income per adult equivalent figure. It is the minimum weekly disposable income (after taxes and including all benefits) that one adult needs to be above the poverty line. For each additional adult in the household this minimum income figure is increased by €137.33 (66 per cent of the poverty line figure) and for each child in the household the minimum income figure is increased by €68.67 (33 per cent of the poverty line).[4] These adjustments reflect the fact that as households increase in size they require more income to meet the basic standard of living implied by the poverty line. In all cases a household below the corresponding weekly disposable income figure is classified as living at risk of poverty. For clarity, corresponding annual figures are also included.

Table 3.1: The Minimum Weekly Disposable Income Required to Avoid Poverty in 2015, by Household Types

Household containing:	Weekly poverty line	Annual poverty line
1 adult	€208.08	€10,850
1 adult + 1 child	€276.75	€14,430
1 adult + 2 children	€345.41	€18,011
1 adult + 3 children	€414.08	€21,591
2 adults	€345.41	€18,011
2 adults + 1 child	€414.08	€21,591
2 adults + 2 children	€482.74	€25,172
2 adults + 3 children	€551.41	€28,752
3 adults	€482.74	€25,172

One immediate implication of this analysis is that most weekly social assistance rates paid to single people are almost €20 below the poverty line.

How many have incomes below the poverty line?

Table 3.2 outlines the findings of various poverty studies since detailed poverty studies commenced in 1994. Using the EU poverty line set at 60 per cent of median income, the findings reveal that 15 out of every 100 people in Ireland were living in poverty in 2013. The table shows that the rates of poverty decreased significantly after 2001, reaching a record low in 2009. These decreases in poverty levels were welcome. They were directly related to the increases in social welfare payments delivered over the Budgets spanning these years.[5] However poverty increased again in the period 2010-2012 as the effect of budgetary changes to welfare and taxes, as well as wage reductions and unemployment, drove more low income households into poverty.

---

[4] For example the poverty line for a household with 2 adults and 1 child would be calculated as €208.08 + €137.33 + €68.67 = €414.08.
[5] See table 3.8 below for further analysis of this point.

Table 3.2: Percentage of population below various relative income poverty lines, 1994-2013

	1994	1998	2001	2005	2007	2009	2012	2013
50% line	6.0	9.9	12.9	10.8	8.6	6.9	9.2	7.8
60% line	15.6	19.8	21.9	18.5	16.5	14.1	16.5	15.2
70% line	26.7	26.9	29.3	28.2	26.8	24.5	24.2	22.9

Source: CSO (2015) and Whelan et al (2003:12), using national equivalence scale.
Note: All poverty lines calculated as a percentage of median income.

Because it is sometimes easy to overlook the scale of Ireland's poverty problem, it is useful to translate the poverty percentages into numbers of people. Using the percentages for the 60 per cent median income poverty line and population statistics from CSO population estimates, we can calculate the numbers of people in Ireland who have been in poverty for a number of years between 1994 and 2013. These calculations are presented in table 3.3. The results give a better picture of just how significant this problem really is in Ireland today.

Table 3.3: The numbers of people below relative income poverty lines in Ireland, 1994-2013

	% of persons in poverty	Population of Ireland	Numbers in poverty
1994	15.6	3,585,900	559,400
1998	19.8	3,703,100	733,214
2001	21.9	3,847,200	842,537
2003	19.7	3,978,900	783,843
2004	19.4	4,045,200	784,769
2005	18.5	4,133,800	764,753
2006	17.0	4,232,900	719,593
2007	16.5	4,375,800	722,007
2008	14.4	4,485,100	645,854
2009	14.1	4,533,400	639,209
2010	14.7	4,554,800	669,556
2011	16.0	4,574,900	731,984
2012	16.5	4,585,400	756,591
2013	15.2	4,593,100	698,151

Source: Calculated using CSO on-line database population estimates, Whelan et al (2003:12) and CSO SILC reports (various years).
Note: Population estimates are for April of each year.

The table's figures are telling. Compared to 10 years ago, 2005, there are over 66,000 less people in poverty; even accounting for the recent increases. Notably, over the period from 2004-2008, the period corresponding with consistent Budget increases in social welfare payments, almost 140,000 people left poverty. Despite this, since the onset of the recession and its associated implications for incomes (earnings and welfare), the number in poverty has increased once again, rising by almost 60,000 since 2009.

The fact that there are almost 700,000 people in Ireland living life on a level of income that is this low remains a major concern. As shown above (see table 3.1) these levels of income are low and those below them clearly face difficulties in achieving what the NAPS described as *"a standard of living that is regarded as acceptable by Irish society generally"*.

A further context to these poverty rates and numbers is the changing value of the poverty line. As outlined above, the line is calculated as a percentage of median income and over the course of recent years this has declined. In 2007 the CSO reported the median income in Ireland (the income of the middle person in the income distribution) to be €19,794 and found that this decreased by more than 11 per cent, to €17,551, by 2013. As the poverty line is calculated as a proportion of this income it also declined, dropping by almost €26 per week (€1,345 per annum). Recent changes in the rate of poverty should be seen in the context of these changes. Even with a lower poverty line, poverty has notably increased.

Annex 3 provides a more detailed profile of those groups in Ireland than are living in poverty.

The incidence of poverty

Figures detailing the incidence of poverty reveal the proportion of all those in poverty that belong to particular groups in Irish society. Tables 3.4 and 3.5 report all those below the 60 per cent of median income poverty line, classifying them by their principal economic status. The first table examines the population as a whole, including children, while the second table focuses exclusively on adults (using the ILO definition of an adult as a person aged 16 years and above).

Table 3.4 shows that in 2013, the largest group of the population who are poor, accounting for 25.7 per cent of the total, were children. The second largest group were the unemployed (20.4 per cent). Of all those who are poor, 32.1 per cent were in the labour force and the remainder (63.5 per cent) were outside the labour market.[6]

---

[6] This does not include the ill and people with a disability, some of whom will be active in the labour force. The SILC data does not distinguish between those temporally unable to work due to illness and those permanently outside the labour market due to illness or disability.

Table 3.4: Incidence of persons below 60% of median income by principal economic status, 2003-2013

	2003	2005	2006	2010	2012	2013
At work	16.0	15.7	16.1	13.5	12.6	11.7
Unemployed	7.6	7.5	8.3	15.1	19.0	20.4
Students/school	8.6	13.4	15.0	12.3	14.2	15.2
On home duties	22.5	19.7	18.4	17.3	15.4	15.0
Retired	9.0	7.5	5.8	4.4	6.0	5.8
Ill/disabled	9.1	7.9	8.0	5.4	6.9	4.4
Children (under 16 years)	25.4	26.8	26.6	29.2	24.1	25.7
Other	1.9	1.6	1.8	2.8	1.8	1.8
Total	100.0	100.0	100.0	100.0	100.0	100.0

Source: Collins (2006:141), CSO SILC Reports (various years).

Table 3.5 looks at adults only and provides a more informed assessment of the nature of poverty. This is an important perspective as children depend on adults for their upbringing and support. Irrespective of how policy interventions are structured, it is through adults that any attempts to reduce the number of children in poverty must be directed. The table shows that in 2013 almost one-sixth of Ireland's adults with an income below the poverty line were employed. Overall, 43.2 per cent of adults at risk of poverty in Ireland were associated with the labour market.

Table 3.5: Incidence of adults (16yrs+) below 60% of median income by principal economic status, 2003-2013

	2003	2005	2006	2010	2012	2013
At work	21.4	21.4	21.9	19.1	16.6	15.7
Unemployed	10.2	10.2	11.3	21.3	25.0	27.5
Students/school	11.5	18.3	20.4	17.4	18.7	20.5
On home duties	30.1	26.9	25.1	24.4	20.3	20.2
Retired	12.0	10.2	7.9	6.2	7.9	7.8
Ill/disability	12.2	10.8	10.9	7.6	9.1	5.9
Other	2.5	2.2	2.5	4.0	2.4	2.4
Total	100.0	100.0	100.0	100.0	100.0	100.0

Source: Collins (2006:141), CSO SILC Reports (various years).

The incidence of being at risk of poverty amongst those in employment is particularly alarming. Many people in this group do not benefit from Budget changes in welfare or tax. They would be the main beneficiaries of any move to make tax credits refundable, a topic addressed in Chapter 4.

The Scale of Poverty - Numbers of People

As the two tables in the last section deal only in percentages it is useful to transform these proportions into numbers of people. Table 3.3 revealed that 698,151 people were living below the 60 per cent of median income poverty line in 2013. Using this figure, table 3.6 presents the number of people in poverty in that year within various categories. Comparable figures are also presented for 2005, 2009 and 2011.

Table 3.6: Poverty Levels Expressed in Numbers of People, 2005-2013

	2005	2009	2011	2013
Overall	764,753	639,209	731,984	698,151
Adults				
At work	120,066	91,407	103,942	81,684
Unemployed	57,356	82,458	121,509	142,423
Students/school	102,477	93,325	107,602	106,119
On home duties	150,656	115,058	128,097	104,723
Retired	57,356	30,043	31,475	40,493
Ill/disability	60,415	40,909	35,135	30,719
Other	12,236	9,588	15,372	12,567
Children				
Children (under 16 yrs)	204,954	176,422	188,852	179,425
Children (under 18 yrs)	n/a	223,084	232,039	218,521

Source: Calculated using CSO SILC Reports (various years) and data from table 3.3.

The data in table 3.6 is particularly useful in the context of framing anti-poverty policy. Groups such as the retired and the ill/disabled, although carrying a high risk of poverty, involve much smaller numbers of people than groups such as adults who are employed (the working poor), people on home duties (i.e. working in the home, carers) and children/students. The primary drivers of the 2005-09 poverty reductions were increasing incomes among those who were on home duties, those who are classified as ill/disabled, the retired and children. Between 2005 and 2009 the numbers of workers in poverty declined while the numbers of unemployed people in poverty notably increased. This reflected the rise in unemployment in the labour market as a whole during those years. As the table shows, the increase in poverty between 2009 and 2013 can be principally explained by the increase in poverty among people who are unemployed and the retired.

Poverty and social welfare recipients

Social Justice Ireland believes in the very important role that social welfare plays in addressing poverty. As part of the *SILC* results the CSO has provided an interesting insight into the role that social welfare payments play in tackling Ireland's poverty levels. It has calculated the levels of poverty before and after the payment of social welfare benefits.

Table 3.7 shows that without the social welfare system almost 50 per cent of the Irish population would have been living in poverty in 2013. Such an underlying poverty rate suggests a deeply unequal distribution of direct income – an issue we address further in the income distribution section of this chapter. In 2013, the actual poverty figure of 15.2 per cent reflects the fact that social welfare payments reduced poverty by almost 35 percentage points.

Looking at the impact of these payments on poverty over time, it is clear that the increases in social welfare over the period 2005-2007 yielded noticeable reductions in poverty levels. The small increases in social welfare payments in 2001 are reflected in the smaller effects achieved in that year. Conversely, the larger increases, and therefore higher levels of social welfare payments, in subsequent years delivered greater reductions. This has occurred even as poverty levels before social welfare increased. A recent report by Watson and Maitre (2013) examined these effects in greater detail and noted the effectiveness of social welfare payments, with child benefit and the growth in the value of social welfare payments, playing a key role in reducing poverty levels up until 2009.

Table 3.7: The role of social welfare (SW) payments in addressing poverty

	2001	2005	2007	2009	2011	2013
Poverty pre SW	35.6	40.1	41.0	46.2	50.7	49.8
Poverty post SW	21.9	18.5	16.5	14.1	16.0	15.2
The role of SW	**-13.7**	**-21.6**	**-24.5**	**-32.1**	**-34.7**	**-34.6**

Source: CSO SILC Reports (various years) using national equivalence scale.

As social welfare payments do not flow to everybody in the population, it is interesting to examine the impact they have on alleviating poverty among certain groups, such as older people, for example. Using data from SILC 2009, the CSO found that without any social welfare payments 88 per cent of all those aged over 65 years would have been living in poverty. Benefit entitlements reduce the poverty level among this group to 9.6 per cent in 2009. Similarly, social welfare payments (including child benefit) reduce poverty among those under 18 years of age from 47.3 per cent to 18.6 per cent – a 60 per cent reduction in poverty risk (CSO, 2010:47).[7] These findings, combined with the social welfare impact data in table 3.7, underscore the importance of social transfer payments in addressing poverty; a point that needs to be borne in mind as Government forms policy and priorities in the years to come.

Analysis in Annex 3 (see table A3.1 and the subsequent analysis) shows that many of the groups in Irish society which experienced increases in poverty levels over the last decade have been dependent on social welfare payments. These include pensioners, the unemployed, lone parents and those who are ill or have a disability. Table 3.8 presents the results of an analysis of five key welfare recipient groups performed by the ESRI using poverty data for five of the years between 1994 and 2001. These are the years that the Irish economy grew fastest and the core years of the famed 'Celtic Tiger' boom. Between 1994 and 2001 all categories experienced large growth in their poverty risk. For example, in 1994 only five out of every 100 old age pension recipients were in poverty. In 2001 this had increased ten-fold to almost 50 out of every 100. The experience of widow's pension recipients is similar.

Table 3.9: Percentage of persons in receipt of welfare benefits/assistance who were below the 60 per cent median income poverty line, 1994/1997/1998/2000/2001

	1994	1997	1998	2000	2001
Old age pension	5.3	19.2	30.7	42.9	49.0
Unemployment benefit/assistance	23.9	30.6	44.8	40.5	43.1
Illness/disability	10.4	25.4	38.5	48.4	49.4
Lone Parents allowance	25.8	38.4	36.9	42.7	39.7
Widow's pension	5.5	38.0	49.4	42.4	42.1

Source: Whelan et al (2003: 31)

---

[7] This data has not been updated in subsequent SILC publications.

Table 3.8 highlights the importance of adequate social welfare payments to prevent people becoming at risk of poverty. Over the period covered by these studies, groups similar to *Social Justice Ireland* repeatedly pointed out that these payments had failed to rise in proportion to earnings and incomes elsewhere in society. The primary consequence of this was that recipients slipped further and further back and as a consequence more and more fell into poverty. It is clear that adequate levels of social welfare need to be maintained to ensure that the mistakes of the past are not repeated. These are important lessons that should not be forgotten as the economy recovers from its recent crisis. We outline our proposals for this later in the chapter.

The poverty gap

As part of the 2001 Laeken indicators, the EU asked all member countries to begin measuring their relative "at risk of poverty gap". This indicator assesses how far below the poverty line the income of the median (middle) person in poverty is. The size of that difference is calculated as a percentage of the poverty line and therefore represents the gap between the income of the middle person in poverty and the poverty line. The higher the percentage figure, the greater the poverty gap and the further people are falling beneath the poverty line. As there is a considerable difference between being 2 per cent and 20 per cent below the poverty line this approach is significant

Table 3.19: The Poverty Gap, 2003-2013

	2003	2005	2008	2009	2011	2012	2013
Poverty gap size	21.5	20.6	19.2	16.2	19.6	20.3	17.5

Source: CSO SILC Reports (various years).

The *SILC* results for 2013 show that the poverty gap was 17.5 per cent, compared to 20.3 per cent in 2012 and 16.2 per cent in 2009. Over time, the gap had decreased from a figure of 21.5 per cent in 2003. The 2013 poverty gap figure implies that 50 per cent of those in poverty had an equivalised income below 82.5per cent of the poverty line. Watson and Maitre (2013:39) compared the size of the market income poverty gap over the years 2004, 2007 and 2011. Adjusting for changes in prices, they found that in 2011 terms the gap was €261 for households below the poverty line, an increase from a figure of €214 in 2004. They also found that after social transfers, those remaining below the poverty line were further from that threshold in 2011 than in 2004.

As the depth of poverty is an important issue, we will monitor closely the movement of this indicator in future editions of the *SILC*. It is crucial that, as part of Ireland's approach to addressing poverty, this figure further declines in the future.

Poverty and deprivation

Income alone does not tell the whole story concerning living standards and command over resources. As we have seen in the NAPS definition of poverty, it is necessary to look more broadly at exclusion from society because of a lack of resources. This requires looking at other areas where 'as a result of inadequate income and resources people may be excluded and marginalised from participating in activities that are considered the norm for other people in society' (NAPS, 1997). Although income is the principal indicator used to assess wellbeing and ability to participate in society, there are other measures. In particular, these measures assess the standards of living people achieve by assessing deprivation through use of different indicators. To date, assessments of deprivation in Ireland have been limited and confined to a small number of items. While this is regrettable, the information gathered is worth considering.

Deprivation in the SILC survey

Since 2007 the CSO has presented 11 measures of deprivation in the *SILC* survey, compared to just eight before that. While this increase was welcome, *Social Justice Ireland* and others have expressed serious reservations about the overall range of measures employed. We believe that a whole new approach to measuring deprivation should be developed. Continuing to collect information on a limited number of static indicators is problematic in itself and does not present a true picture of the dynamic nature of Irish society. However, given these reservations, the trends are informative and offer some insight into the impact of the recent recession on households and living standards across the state.

The results presented in table 3.10 shows that in 2013 the rates of deprivation recorded across the set of 11 items varied between 4 and 26 per cent of the Irish population. Overall 55.1 per cent of the population were not deprived of any item, while 14.3 per cent were deprived of one item, 9.7 per cent were without two items and 20.9 per cent were without three or more items. Among those living on an income below the poverty line, more than half (53.9 per cent) experienced deprivation of 2 or more items.

Table 3.10: Levels of deprivation for eleven items among the population and those in poverty, 2013 (%)

	Total Pop	Those in Poverty
Without heating at some stage in the past year	15.7	30.8
Unable to afford a morning, afternoon or evening out in the last fortnight	25.1	41.7
Unable to afford two pairs of strong shoes	5.2	10.0
Unable to afford a roast once a week	8.1	15.9
Unable to afford a meal with meat, chicken or fish every second day	4.2	7.4
Unable to afford new (not second-hand) clothes	10.6	22.6
Unable to afford a warm waterproof coat	3.9	10.2
Unable to afford to keep the home adequately warm	10.0	19.4
Unable to replace any worn out furniture	25.8	42.5
Unable to afford to have family or friends for a drink or meal once a month	18.7	33.3
Unable to afford to buy presents for family or friends at least once a year	7.2	15.4

Source: CSO (2015: table 5)
Note: Poverty as measured using the 60 per cent median income poverty line.

It is of interest that from 2007 onwards, as the economic crisis unfolded, the proportion of the population which experienced no deprivation has fallen steadily from 75.6 per cent in 2007 to 55.1 per cent in 2013. Simultaneously, the proportion of the population experiencing deprivation of two or more items (the deprivation rate) has steadily increased from 11.8 per cent in 2007 to 30.5 per cent in 2013 – see Chart 3.1. There are now more than 1.4 million people (30.5 per cent of the population) experiencing deprivation at this level. Most notable have been increases in the numbers: going without heating at some stage in the year; unable to afford a morning, afternoon or evening out in the last fortnight; unable to afford to replace any worn out furniture; and unable to replace any worn out furniture.

Chart 3.1: Deprivation Rate, 2005-2013

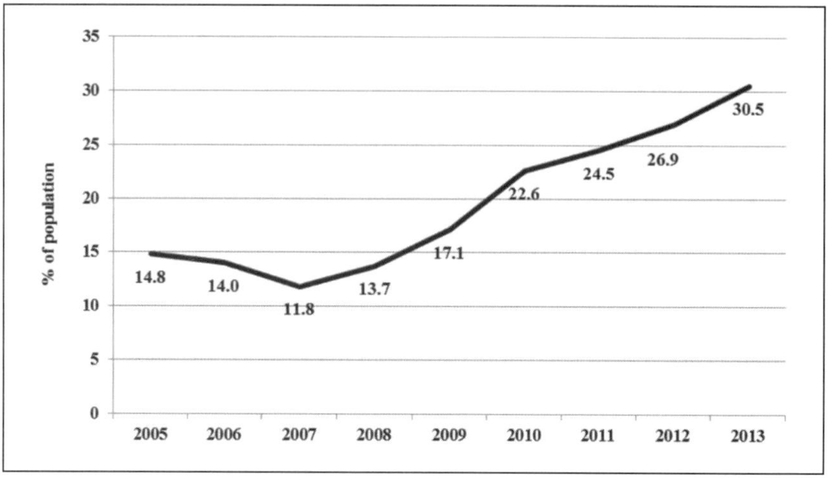

Year	% of population
2005	14.8
2006	14.0
2007	11.8
2008	13.7
2009	17.1
2010	22.6
2011	24.5
2012	26.9
2013	30.5

Source: CSO SILC Reports (various years).

Deprivation and poverty combined: consistent poverty
'Consistent poverty' combines deprivation and poverty into a single indicator. It does this by calculating the proportion of the population simultaneously experiencing poverty and registering as deprived of two or more of the items in table 3.11. As such, it captures a sub-group of those who are poor.

The 2007 *SILC* data marked an important change for this indicator. Coupled with the expanded list of deprivation items, the definition of consistent poverty was changed. From 2007 onwards, to be counted as experiencing consistent poverty individuals must be both below the poverty line and experiencing deprivation of at least two items. Up to 2007 the criteria was below the poverty line and deprivation of at least one item. The *National Action Plan for Social Inclusion 2007-2016* (*NAPinclusion*) published in early 2007 set its overall poverty goal using this earlier consistent poverty measure. One of its aims was to reduce the number of people experiencing consistent poverty to between 2 per cent and 4 per cent of the total population by 2012, with a further aim of totally eliminating consistent poverty by 2016. A revision to this target was published as part of the Government's *National Reform Programme 2012 Update for Ireland* (2012). The revised poverty target is to reduce the numbers experiencing consistent poverty to 4 per cent by 2016 and to 2 per cent or less by 2020. *Social Justice Ireland* participated in the consultation process on the revision of this and other poverty targets. While we agree with the revised 2020 consistent poverty target (it is not possible to measure below this 2 per cent level using survey data) we have proposed that this target should be accompanied by other targets focused on the overall population and vulnerable groups.[8] These are outlined at the end of this chapter.

Using these new indicators and definition, the 2013 *SILC* data indicates that 8.2 per cent of the population experience consistent poverty, an increase from 4.2 per cent in 2008 and 5.5 per cent in 2009 (CSO, 2015: table 5). In terms of the population, the 2013 figures indicate that just over 375,000 people live in consistent poverty. The legacy of the recent recession and its austerity measures are pushing Ireland further away from these targets.

Annex 3 also examines the experience of people who are in food poverty, fuel poverty alongside an assessment of the research on minimum incomes standards in Ireland.

Moving to Persistent Poverty

Social Justice Ireland is committed to using the best and most up-to-date data in its ongoing socio-economic analysis of Ireland. We believe that to do so is crucial to the emergence of accurate evidence-based policy formation. It also assists in establishing appropriate and justifiable targeting of state resources.

As part of the EU structure of social indicators, Ireland has agreed to produce an indicator of persistent poverty. This indicator measures the proportion of those living below the poverty line in the current year and for two of the three preceding years. It therefore identifies those who have experienced sustained exposure to poverty which is seen to harm their quality of life seriously and to increase levels of deprivation.

To date the Irish *SILC* survey has not produced any detailed results and breakdowns for this measure. We regret the unavailability of this data and note that there remains some sampling and technical issues impeding its annual publication.

Social Justice Ireland believes that this data should be used as the primary basis for setting poverty targets and monitoring changes in poverty status. Existing measures of relative and consistent poverty should be maintained as secondary indicators. If there are impediments to the annual production of this indicator, they should be addressed and the SILC sample augmented if required. A measure of persistent poverty is long overdue and a crucial missing piece in society's knowledge of households and individuals on low income.

---

[8] See also Leahy et al (2012:61).

Poverty: a European perspective

It is helpful to compare Irish measures of poverty with those elsewhere in Europe. Eurostat, the European Statistics Agency, produces comparable 'at risk of poverty' figures (proportions of the population living below the poverty line) for each EU member state. The data is calculated using the 60 per cent of median income poverty line in each country. Comparable EU-wide definitions of income and equivalence scale are used.[9] The latest data available for all member states is for the year 2013.

As table 3.11 shows, Irish people experience a below average risk of poverty when compared to all other EU member states. Eurostat's 2008 figures marked the first time Ireland's poverty levels fell below average EU levels. This phenomenon was driven, as outlined earlier in this review, by sustained increases in welfare payments in the years prior to 2008. Ireland's poverty levels have remained below average EU levels since then to 2013. In 2013, across the EU, the highest poverty levels were found in the recent accession countries of Romania, Bulgaria and Lithuania and the two countries caught up in the EU-wide economic crash - Spain and Greece. The lowest levels were in Denmark, Finland, the Netherlands and the Czech Republic.

Table 3.11: The risk of poverty in the European Union in 2013

Country	Poverty Risk	Country	Poverty Risk
Greece	23.1	Cyprus	15.3
Romania	22.4	Belgium	15.1
Bulgaria	21.0	Sweden	14.8
Lithuania	20.6	Slovenia	14.5
Spain	20.4	Austria	14.4
Croatia	19.5	Hungary	14.3
Latvia	19.4	**IRELAND**	**14.1**
Italy	19.1	France	13.7
Portugal	18.7	Slovakia	12.8
Estonia	18.6	Denmark	12.3
Poland	17.3	Finland	11.8
Germany	16.1	Netherlands	10.4
Luxembourg	15.9	Czech Rep	8.6
UK	15.9		
Malta	15.7	EU-28 average	16.6

Source: Eurostat online database

---

[9] Differences in definitions of income and equivalence scales result in slight differences in the poverty rates reported for Ireland when compared to those reported earlier which have been calculated by the CSO using national definitions of income and the Irish equivalence scale.

The average risk of poverty in the EU-28 for 2013 was 16.6 per cent. Chart 3.2 further develops the findings of table 3.11 and shows the difference between national poverty risk levels and the EU-28 average. While there have been some reductions in poverty in recent years across the EU, the data does suggest that poverty remains a large and ongoing EU-wide problem. In 2013 the average EU-28 level implied that 83.3 million people are in poverty across the EU.

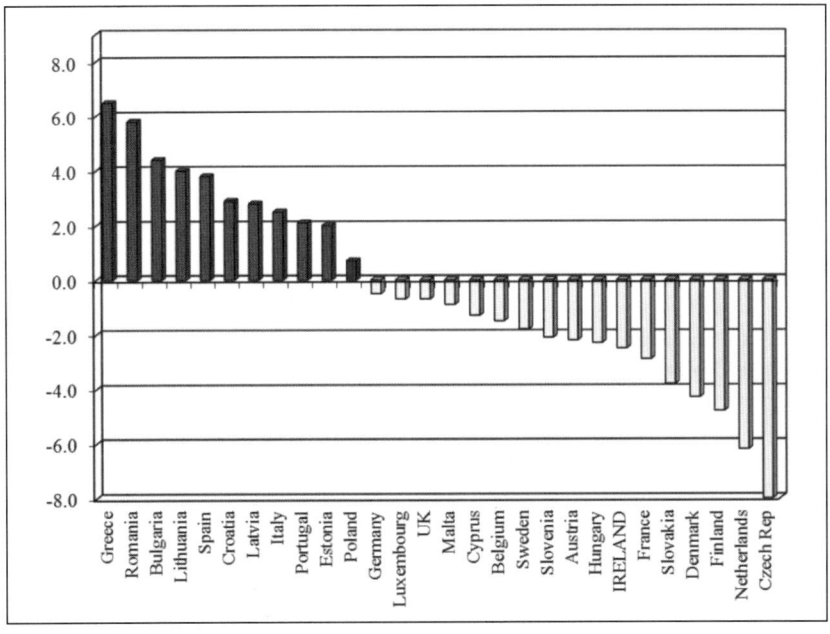

Chart 3.2: Percentage difference in National Poverty risk from EU-28 average

Source: Eurostat online database

Europe 2020 Strategy – Risk of Poverty or Social Exclusion

As part of the Europe 2020 Strategy, European governments have begun to adopt policies to target these poverty levels and are using as their main benchmark the proportion of the population at risk of poverty or social exclusion. This indicator has been defined by the European Council on the basis of three indicators: the aforementioned 'at risk of poverty' rate after social transfers; an index of material deprivation;[10] and the percentage of people living in households with very low work

---

[10] Material deprivation covers indicators relating to economic strain and durables. Severely materially deprived persons have living conditions severely constrained by a lack of resources. They experience at least 4 out of 9 listed deprivations items. (Eurostat 2012)

intensity.[11] It is calculated as the sum of persons relative to the national population who are at risk of poverty or severely materially deprived or living in households with very low work intensity, where a person is only counted once even if recorded in more than one indicator.[12]

Table 3.12: People at risk of poverty or social exclusion, Ireland and the EU 2007-2013

	2007	2009	2011	2013
Ireland % Population	23.1	25.7	29.4	29.5
Ireland 000s people	1,005	1,150	1,319	1,358
EU % Population*	24.4	23.3	24.3	24.5
EU 000s people*	119,360	114,560	121,314	122,897

Source: Eurostat online database
Note: *EU data for 2007 and 2009 is for the EU-27, 2011 and 2013 data are for the EU-28 (including Croatia)

Chart 3.3: Population at risk of poverty, severely deprived or in low work intensity households Ireland 2013

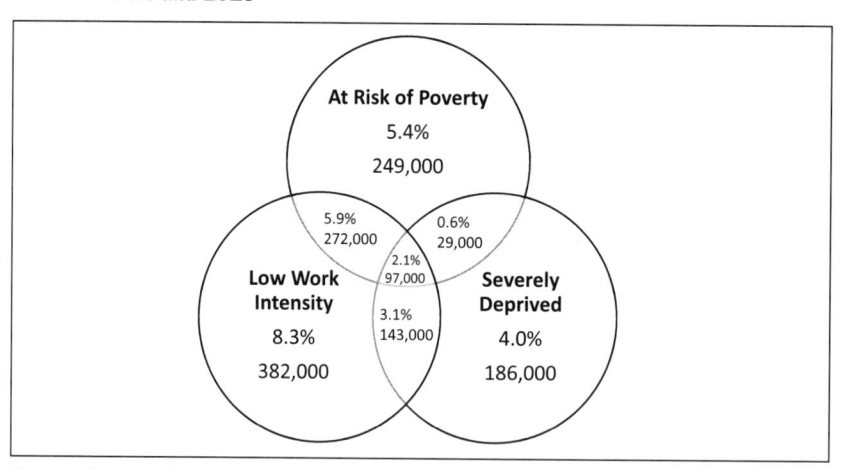

At Risk of Poverty
5.4%
249,000

5.9%
272,000

0.6%
29,000

2.1%
97,000

Low Work Intensity
8.3%
382,000

3.1%
143,000

Severely Deprived
4.0%
186,000

Source: Compiled from Eurostat online database

---

[11] People living in households with very low work intensity are those aged 0-59 living in households where the adults (aged 18-59) work less than 20% of their total work potential during the past year (Eurostat, 2012)
[12] See European Commission (2011) for a more detailed explanation of this indicator.

Table 3.12 summarises the latest data on this indicator for Europe and chart 3.3 summarises the latest Irish data (which is for 2013). While *Social Justice Ireland* regrets that the Europe 2020 process shifted its indicator focus away from an exclusive concentration on the 'at risk of poverty' rate, we welcome the added attention at a European level to issues regarding poverty, deprivation and joblessness. Together with Caritas Europa, we have initiated a process to monitor progress on this strategy over the years to come (Mallon and Healy, 2012, Leahy et al, 2012, Social Justice Ireland, 2015). However, it is clear already that the austerity measures which have been pursued in many EU countries will result in the erosion of social services and lead to the further exclusion of people who already find themselves on the margins of society. This is in direct contradiction to the inclusive growth focus of the Europe 2020 Strategy. It is reflected in the figures in table 3.12 which show an increase in risk levels in 2011 and 2013.

3.2 Income Distribution

As previously outlined, despite some improvements poverty remains a significant problem. The purpose of economic development should be to improve the living standards of all of the population. A further loss of social cohesion will mean that large numbers of people continue to experience deprivation and the gap between that cohort and the better-off will widen. This has implications for all of society, not just those who are poor, a reality that has begun to receive welcome attention recently.

Analysis of the annual income and expenditure accounts yields information on trends in the distribution of national income. However, the limitations of this accounting system need to be acknowledged. Measures of income are far from perfect gauges of a society. They ignore many relevant non-market features, such as volunteerism, caring and environmental protection. Many environmental factors, such as the depletion of natural resources, are registered as income but not seen as a cost. Pollution is not registered as a cost but cleaning up after pollution is seen as income. Increased spending on prisons and security, which are a response to crime, are seen as increasing national income but not registered as reducing human well-being.

The point is that national accounts fail to include items that cannot easily be assigned a monetary value. But progress cannot be measured by economic growth alone. Many other factors are required, as we highlight elsewhere in this review.[13] However, when judging economic performance and making judgements about how well Ireland is really doing, it is important to look at the distribution of national income as well as its absolute amount.[14]

---

[13] We return to critique National Income statistics in chapter 11. There, we also propose some alternatives.
[14] We examine the issue of the world's income and wealth distribution in chapter 13.

Ireland's income distribution: latest data

The most recent data on Ireland's income distribution, from the 2013 SILC survey, is summarised in chart 3.4. It examines the income distribution by household deciles starting with the 10 per cent of households with the lowest income (the bottom decile) up to the 10 per cent of households with the highest income (the top decile).

The data presented is equivalised meaning that it has been adjusted to reflect the number of adults and children in a household and to make it possible to compare across different household sizes and compositions. It measures disposable income which captures the amount of money available to spend after receipt of any employment/pension income, payment of all income taxes and receipt of any welfare entitlements.

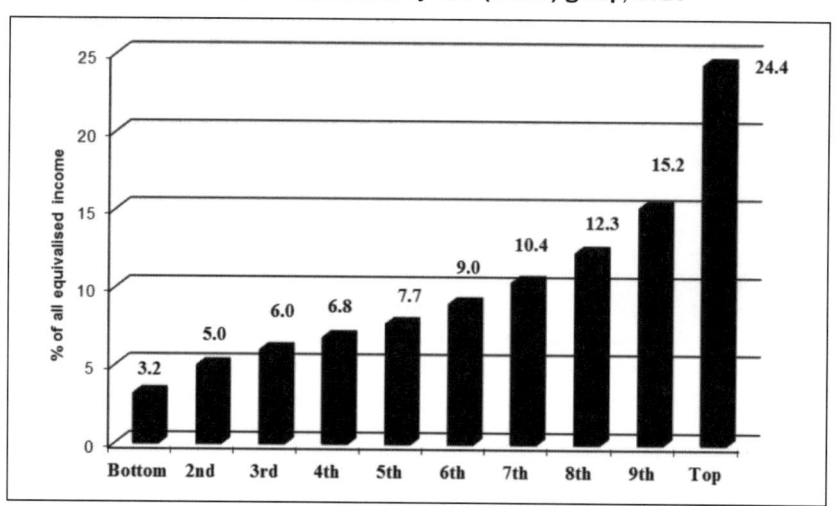

Chart 3.4: Ireland's Income Distribution by 10% (decile) group, 2013

Decile	% of all equivalised income
Bottom	3.2
2nd	5.0
3rd	6.0
4th	6.8
5th	7.7
6th	9.0
7th	10.4
8th	12.3
9th	15.2
Top	24.4

Source: Calculated from CSO SILC 2015 release In 2013, the top 10 per cent of Irish households received 24.4 per cent of the total income while the bottom decile received 3.2 per cent. Collectively, the poorest 60 per cent of households received a very similar share (37.7 per cent) to the top 20 per cent (39.6 per cent). Overall the share of the top 10 per cent is almost 8 times the share of the bottom 10 per cent.

Income distribution data for the last few decades suggested that the overall structure of that distribution has been largely unchanged. One overall inequality measure, the Gini coefficient, ranges from 0 (no inequality) to 100 (maximum inequality) and has stood at approximately 29-32 for Ireland for some time. In 2013 it stood at 31.3.

Chart 3.5 compares the change in income between 2008 and 2013. 2008 represented the year when average incomes in Ireland peaked. Since then incomes have fallen for all, but the impact of the recession has been felt in different ways by different people/households.

Over that period, the changes to the income shares received by deciles has been small; between + and -0.5 per cent. The decline in the share of the bottom two deciles highlights the reality that if we wish to address and close these income divides, future Government policy must prioritise those at the bottom of the income distribution. Otherwise, these divides will persist for further generations and perhaps widen. A further examination of income distribution over the period 1987-2013 is provided in annex 3.

Chart 3.5: Change in Decile Shares of Equivalised Disposable Income, 2008-2013

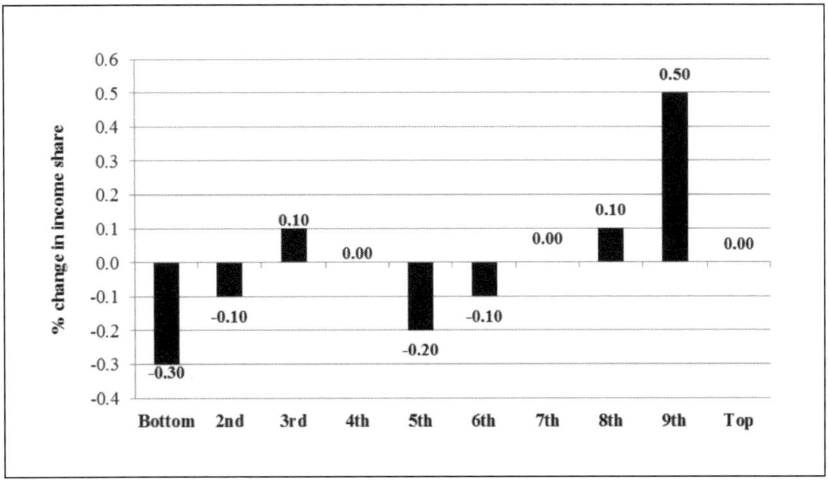

Decile	% change in income share
Bottom	-0.30
2nd	-0.10
3rd	0.10
4th	0.00
5th	-0.20
6th	-0.10
7th	0.00
8th	0.10
9th	0.50
Top	0.00

Source: Calculated from CSO SILC Reports (various years).

Income distribution: a European perspective

Another of the indicators adopted by the EU at Laeken assesses the income distribution of member states by comparing the ratio of equivalised disposable income received by the bottom quintile (20 per cent) to that of the top quintile. This indicator reveals how far away from each other the shares of these two groups are – the higher the ratio, the greater the income difference. Table 3.13 presents the most up-to-date results of this indicator for the 28 EU states. The data indicate that the Irish figure increased to 4.5 from a ratio of 4.2 in 2009, reflecting the already noted increase in income inequality since then. Ireland now has a ratio just below the EU average and, given recent economic and budgetary policy, this looks likely to persist and may even worsen. Overall, the greatest differences in the shares of those at the top and bottom of income distribution are found in many of the newer and poorer member states. However, some EU-15 members, including the Spain, Greece, Portugal and Italy also record large differences.

Table 3.13: Ratio of Disposable Income received by bottom quintile to that of the top quintile in the EU-28, 2013

Country	Ratio	Country	Ratio
Bulgaria	6.6	IRELAND	4.5
Greece	6.6	France	4.5
Romania	6.6	Denmark	4.3
Spain	6.3	Hungary	4.2
Latvia	6.3	Malta	4.1
Lithuania	6.1	Austria	4.1
Portugal	6.0	Belgium	3.8
Italy	5.7	Sweden	3.7
Estonia	5.5	Netherlands	3.6
Croatia	5.3	Slovenia	3.6
Cyprus	4.9	Slovakia	3.6
Poland	4.9	Finland	3.6
Germany	4.6	Czech Republic	3.4
Luxembourg	4.6		
UK	4.6	**EU-28 average**	**5.0**

Source: Eurostat online database

A further measure of income inequality is the Gini coefficient, which ranges from 0 to 100 and summarises the degree of inequality across the entire income distribution (rather than just at the top and bottom).[15] The higher the Gini coefficient score the greater the degree of income inequality in a society. As table 3.14 shows, over time income inequality has been reasonably static in the EU as a whole, although within the EU there are notable differences. Countries such as Ireland cluster around or just above the average EU score and differ from other high-income EU member states which record lower levels of inequality. As the table shows, the degree of inequality is at a notably lower scale in countries like Finland, Sweden and the Netherlands. For Ireland, the key point is that despite the aforementioned role of the social transfer system, the underlying degree of direct income inequality dictates that our income

---

[15] See Collins and Kavanagh (2006: 159-160) who provide a more detailed explanation of this measure.

distribution remains much more unequal than in many of the EU countries we wish to emulate in term of economic and social development.

Table 3.14: Gini coefficient measure of income inequality for selected EU states, 2005-2013

	2005	2007	2009	2011	2012	2013
EU-27/28	30.6	30.6	30.5	30.8	30.4	30.5
IRELAND	31.9	31.3	28.8	29.8	29.9	30.0
UK	34.6	32.6	32.4	33.0	31.3	30.2
France	27.7	26.6	29.9	30.8	30.5	30.1
Germany	26.1	30.4	29.1	29.0	28.3	29.7
Sweden	23.4	23.4	24.8	24.4	24.8	24.9
Finland	26.0	26.2	25.9	25.8	25.9	25.4
Netherlands	26.9	27.6	27.2	25.8	25.4	25.1

Source: Eurostat online database
Notes: The Gini coefficient ranges from 0-100 with a higher score indicating a higher level of inequality.
EU data for 2005-2009 is for the EU-27, 2011 onwards data are for the EU-28 (including Croatia)

Income Distribution and Recent Budgets

Budget 2015, delivered in October 2014, was the fourth regressive Budget in a row. Taken together, the measures announced in the Budget, alongside those due for implementation following Budget decisions (e.g. water charges), carry a disproportionate impact on lower income households across the state.

The regressive nature of Budget 2015 follows that of Budget 2014 (e.g. doubling of property tax, cuts to household benefits package, cuts to youth welfare payments and increases in prescription charges for medical card holders), Budget 2013 (e.g. abolition of PRSI allowance, cuts to child benefit and increases in prescription charges for medical card holders) and Budget 2012 (e.g. increase in standard VAT rate from 21% to 23%, cuts to 3rd and 4th child benefit payments, cuts to fuel allowance). Each of these Budgets also orientated their adjustments towards cuts in public services, further increasing their regressive impact.

In this section, we first review the distributive impact of Budget 2015 before presenting the results of our analysis of the series of austerity driven budget adjustments since 2008.

Impact of Budget 2015
When assessing the change in people's incomes following any Budget, it is important that tax changes be included as well as changes to basic social welfare payments. In our calculations we have not included any changes to welfare allowances and secondary benefits as these payment do not flow to all households. Similarly, we have not included changes to other taxes (including property taxes) as these are also experienced differently by households. Chart 3.6 sets out the implications of the Budget announcements on various household groupings in 2015.

Single people who are unemployed will benefit from the Christmas bonus which equates to 90c per week (€47 per year) after Budget 2015.

Those on €25,000 a year will see an increase of €3.34 a week (€174 a year) in their take home pay while those on €50,000 will be €10.47 a week (€546 a year) better off this year and those on €75,000 a year will be €14.30 a week (€746 a year) better off.

Couples with one income on €25,000 a year will be €3.34 a week (€174 a year) better off while those on €50,000 will be €8.74 a week (€456 a year) better off. Couples with two incomes on €25,000 a year will be €5.31 a week (€277 a year) better off while those on €50,000 will be €6.63 a week (€346 a year) better off in 2014 compared to 2014.

The impact of Budget 2015 on the distribution of income in Ireland can be further assessed by examining the rich-poor gap. This measures the gap between the disposable income of a single unemployed person and a single person on €50,000 per annum. Budget 2015 widened the rich-poor gap by €9.57 per week (€499 a year).

Chart 3.6: Impact of Tax and Headline Welfare Payment Changes from Budget 2015

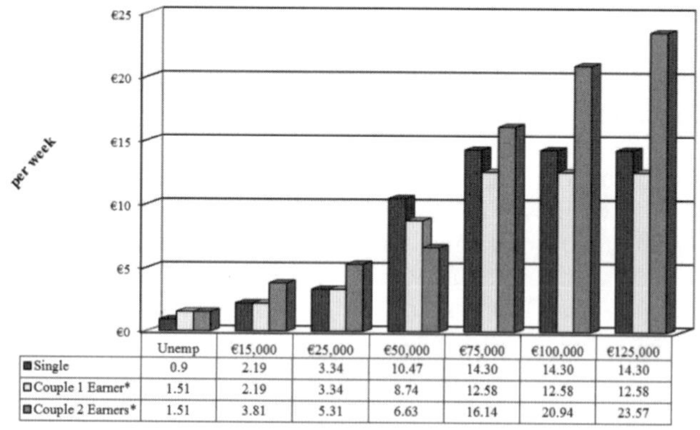

per week	Unemp	€15,000	€25,000	€50,000	€75,000	€100,000	€125,000
Single	0.9	2.19	3.34	10.47	14.30	14.30	14.30
Couple 1 Earner*	1.51	2.19	3.34	8.74	12.58	12.58	12.58
Couple 2 Earners*	1.51	3.81	5.31	6.63	16.14	20.94	23.57

Source: Social Justice Ireland (2014:8)
Notes: * Except in case of the unemployed where there is no earner
Couple with 2 earners are assumed to have a 65%/35% income division.

Impact of Tax and Benefit Changes, 2008-2015
Since 2008 a series of ten budgetary adjustments have been introduced by Government impacting on taxation, welfare and other areas of public spending. Overall, these adjustments totalled just over €30 billion.

Over the past year *Social Justice Ireland* has developed its ability to track changes to taxes and benefits over time, so that we can further deepen our annual analysis of Budgets. Following Budget 2015, we assessed the cumulative impact of changes to income taxation and welfare since the start of the crisis in 2008. At the outset it is important to stress that our analysis does not take account of other budgetary changes, most particularly to indirect taxes (VAT), other charges (such as prescription and water charges) and property taxes. Similarly, it does not capture the impact of changes to the provision of public services – changes which as we highlight elsewhere in this review, have been severe given the scale of the expenditure reductions introduced since 2008 (approximately €20 billion). As the impact of these measures differs between households it is impossible to quantify these household impacts and include them here. However, as we have demonstrated in previous publications these changes have been predominantly regressive – impacting hardest on households with the lowest incomes.

The households we examine are spread across all areas of society and capture those with a job, families with children, those unemployed and pensioner households. In households which are earning income from a job, we include workers on the minimum wage, on the living wage, workers on average earnings and multiples of this benchmark, and families with incomes ranging from €25,000 to €200,000.

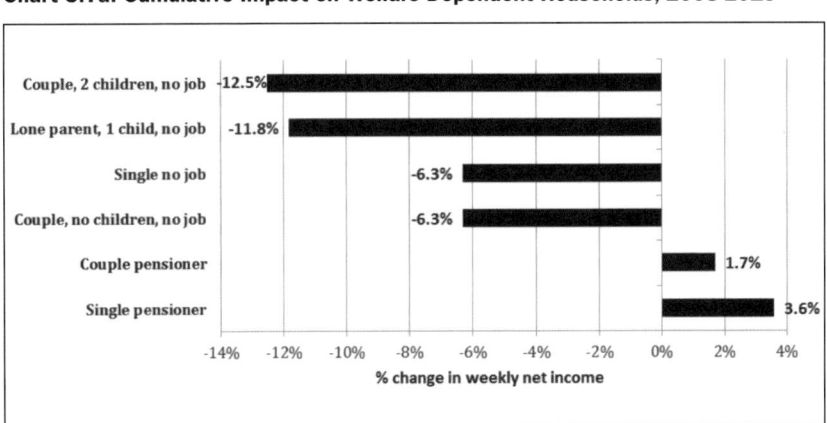

Chart 3.7a: Cumulative Impact on Welfare Dependent Households, 2008-2015

Household	% change in weekly net income
Couple, 2 children, no job	-12.5%
Lone parent, 1 child, no job	-11.8%
Single no job	-6.3%
Couple, no children, no job	-6.3%
Couple pensioner	1.7%
Single pensioner	3.6%

3. Income Distribution

Over the years examined (2008-2015) almost all households recorded notable decreases in their disposable income (after taxes and welfare payments). These changes have been driven by increases in income taxes, increases in social insurance contributions and reductions in welfare payments including child benefit. Measured as a proportion of household income, the decrease experienced by welfare dependent and working poor households are the largest. While other low income households record smaller percentage decreases in income, it should be noted that these decreases have had to be absorbed by households with little or no spare capacity. This differs from higher income households recording similar percentage declines.

Only one household type, those dependent on the old age pension, experienced a small increase in income. Of course, this group has also been exposed to notable reductions in public services, indirect benefits and measures such as the multiple increases in prescription charges. Charts 3.7a and 3.7b present the results of this analysis.

Chart 3.7b: Cumulative Impact on Households with Jobs, 2008-2015

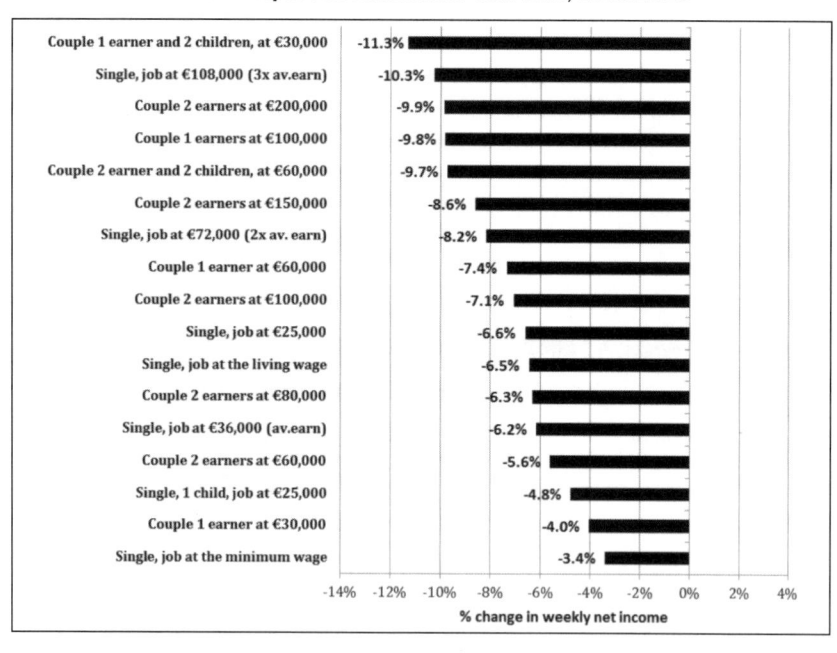

Household type	% change in weekly net income
Couple 1 earner and 2 children, at €30,000	-11.3%
Single, job at €108,000 (3x av.earn)	-10.3%
Couple 2 earners at €200,000	-9.9%
Couple 1 earners at €100,000	-9.8%
Couple 2 earner and 2 children, at €60,000	-9.7%
Couple 2 earners at €150,000	-8.6%
Single, job at €72,000 (2x av. earn)	-8.2%
Couple 1 earner at €60,000	-7.4%
Couple 2 earners at €100,000	-7.1%
Single, job at €25,000	-6.6%
Single, job at the living wage	-6.5%
Couple 2 earners at €80,000	-6.3%
Single, job at €36,000 (av.earn)	-6.2%
Couple 2 earners at €60,000	-5.6%
Single, 1 child, job at €25,000	-4.8%
Couple 1 earner at €30,000	-4.0%
Single, job at the minimum wage	-3.4%

Ireland's Wealth Distribution

While data on income and poverty levels has improved dramatically over the past 15 years, a persistent gap has been our knowledge of levels of wealth in Irish society. Data on wealth is important, as it provides a further insight into the distribution of resources and an insight into some of the underlying structural components of inequality.

A welcome development in early 2015 was the publication by the CSO of the first Household Finance and Consumption Survey (HFCS). The HFCS is part of a European initiative to improve countries knowledge of the socio-economic and financial situations of households across the EU. For the first time, its results offer robust information on the types and levels of wealth that households in Ireland possess. The data was collected for 2013 across 5,545 households.[16]

The result of the survey showed that the level of household net wealth in Ireland amounts to €378 billion. The CSO's net wealth measure includes the value of all assets (housing, land, investments, valuables, savings and private pensions) and removes any borrowings (mortgages, loans, credit card debt etc) to give the most informative picture of households wealth. On average the results imply that Irish households have a net wealth of almost €225,000 each. However, averages are very misleading for wealth data, as they are skewed upwards by high wealth households. Looking closer at the data, the CSO illustrates that the bottom 50 per cent of households have a net wealth of less than €105,000.

Chart 3.8 presents the distribution of net wealth across the income distribution – the CSO has only presented data for quintiles (20 per cent groups). The HFCS results show that those in the top 20 per cent of the income distribution possess 39.7 per cent of all the wealth – this is the same share as those in the bottom 60 per cent of the income distribution. Across the various household types that the CSO examined, those with the lowest wealth were single parents, the unemployed and those under 35 years. Detailed data has yet to be released on the distribution of wealth across households given their wealth status – i.e. what percentage of all the net wealth in Ireland do the wealthiest 10 per cent of households possess.

---

[16] The data is reviewed by Collins here: www.nerinstitute.net/blog/2015/02/18/wealth-in-ireland-at-last-some-robust-data/

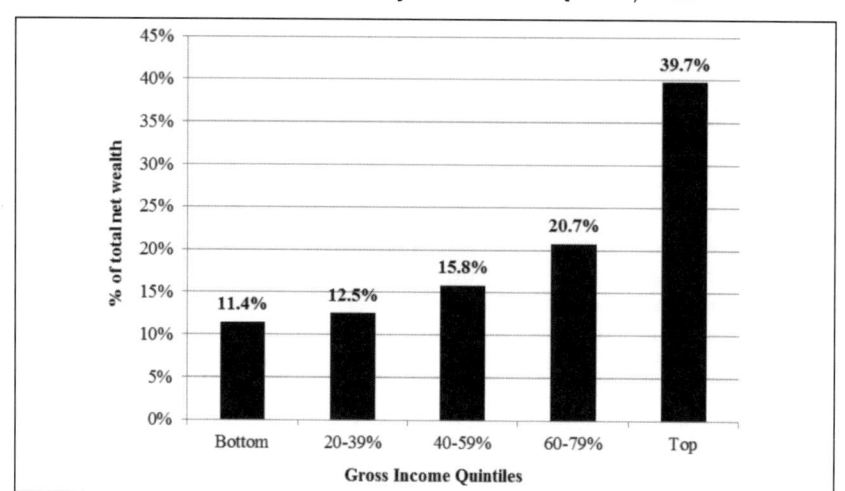

Chart 3.8: Distribution of Net Wealth by Gross Income Quintile, 2013

Gross Income Quintile	% of total net wealth
Bottom	11.4%
20-39%	12.5%
40-59%	15.8%
60-79%	20.7%
Top	39.7%

Source: CSO HFCS (2014: 40). Over the year to come, there is considerable potential for this new data to be analysed further and more detailed insights to be obtained. The composition and distribution of wealth points towards policy issues to be considered, concerning inheritance taxes (capital acquisitions tax), gift taxes and capital gains taxes – some of which are addressed in the next chapter. The arrival of this new data also allows, for the first time, an opportunity for informed consideration of policy options around wealth, as well as income, inequality. As further details emerge, Social Justice Ireland looks forward to contributing to that debate.

3.3 The Living Wage

During the past year *Social Justice Ireland* and a number of other organisations came together to form a technical group which researched and developed a Living Wage for Ireland.[17] In July 2014 the group launched a new website (www.livingwage.ie), a technical paper outlining how the concept is calculated and a figure for the Living Wage in 2014, which was €11.45 per hour.

What is a Living Wage?

The establishment of a Living Wage for Ireland adds to a growing international set of similar figures which reflect a belief across societies that individuals working full-

---

[17] The members of the group were Social Justice Ireland, the Vincentian Partnership for Social Justice, the Nevin Economic Research Institute, TASC, Unite the Union and SIPTU.

time should be able to earn enough income to enjoy a decent standard of living. The Living Wage is a wage which makes possible a minimum acceptable standard of living. Its calculation is evidence based and built on budget standards research which is grounded in social consensus. The new figure is:

- based on the concept that work should provide an adequate income to enable individuals to afford a socially acceptable standard of living;
- the average gross salary which will enable full time employed adults (without dependents) across Ireland to afford a socially acceptable standard of living;
- a living wage which provides for needs not wants;
- an evidence based rate of pay which is grounded in social consensus and is derived from Consensual Budget Standards research which establishes the cost of a Minimum Essential Standard of Living in Ireland;
- unlike the National Minimum Wage which is not based on the cost of living.

In principle, a living wage is intended to establish an hourly wage rate that should provide employees with sufficient income to achieve an agreed acceptable minimum standard of living. In that sense it is an income floor; representing a figure which allows employees to afford the essentials of life. Earnings below the living wage suggest employees are forced to do without certain essentials so they can make ends meet.

How is the Living Wage Calculated?

The Living Wage for Ireland is calculated on the basis of the Minimum Essential Standard of Living research in Ireland, conducted by the Vincentian Partnership for Social Justice (VPSJ). This research establishes a consensus on what members of the public believe is a minimum standard that no individual or household should live below. Working with focus groups, the minimum goods and services that everyone needs for a Minimum Essential Standard of Living (MESL) are identified. With a focus on needs not wants, the concern is with more than survival as a MESL is a standard of living which meets physical, psychological and social needs, at a minimum but acceptable level. Where necessary the core MESL data has been complemented by other expenditure costs for housing, insurance and transport.

The Living Wage Technical Group decided to focus the calculation of a Living Wage for the Republic of Ireland on a single-adult household. In its examination of the methodological options for calculating a robust annual measure, the group concluded that a focus on a single-adult household was the most practical approach. However, in recognition of the fact that households with children experience additional costs which are relevant to any consideration of such households standards of living, the group has also published estimates of a Family Living Income each year.[18]

The calculations established a Living Wage for the country as a whole, with cost examined in four regions: Dublin, other Cities, Towns with a population above 5,000, and the rest of Ireland. The expenditure required varied across these regions and reflecting this so too did the annual gross income required to meet this expenditure. To produce a single national rate, the results of the gross income calculation for the four regions were averaged; with each regional rate being weighted in proportion to the population in the labour force in that region. The weighted annual gross income is then divided by the number of weeks in the year (52.14) and the number of working hours in the week (39) to give an hourly wage. Where necessary, this figure is rounded up or down to the nearest five cent.[19] It is planned to update this number on an annual basis.

The Merits of a Living Wage

Social Justice Ireland believes that concepts such as the Living Wage have an important role to play in addressing the persistent income inequality and poverty levels outlined earlier in this chapter. As shown in tables 3.4 to 3.6, there are many adults living in poverty despite having a job – the working poor. Improvements in the low pay rates received by many employees offers an important method by which levels of poverty and exclusion can be reduced. Paying low paid employees a Living Wage offers the prospect of significantly benefiting the living standards of these employees and we hope to see this new benchmark adopted across many sectors of society in the years to come.

3.4 Maintaining an Adequate Level of Social Welfare

Since 2010 the minimum social welfare payment has remained at €188. However, as chart 3.9 illustrates, since then consumer prices have not stood still and inflation increases have eroded the value of the basic jobseekers payment. Between 2010 and 2015 inflation was 3.46 per cent - implying that a buying power of €188 in 2010 was equivalent to €194.50 by January 2015. This suggests that a jobseekers payment at this level is required in 2015 to protect the basic living standards of welfare recipients.

---

[18] See Living Wage Technical Group (2014:4).
[19] A more detailed account of the methodology used to calculate the Living Wage has been published by the Living Wage Technical Group and is available on the website.

Social Justice Ireland believes that Budget 2016 should address this unacceptable decrease in the living standards of those on the lowest incomes in society. An increase of €6.50 per week to the basic payment would address the gap and it should be a priority for Government in the year ahead.[20]

Chart 3.9 CPI Price Changes, January 2010-January 2015

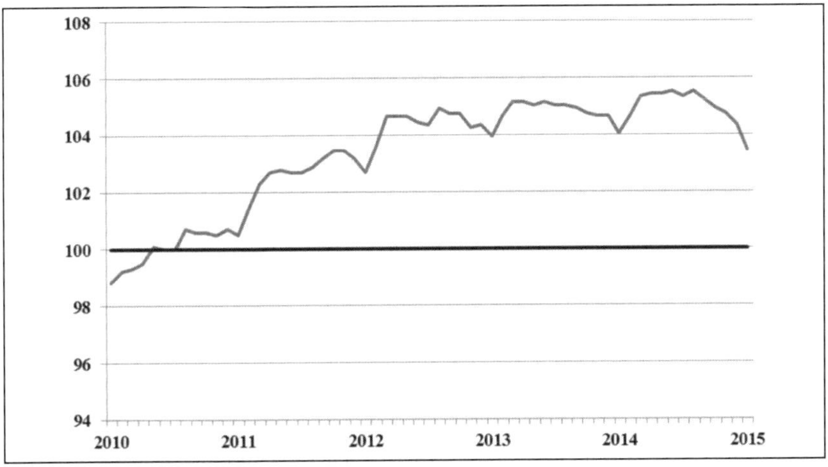

Source: CSO CPI online database
Note: Average price levels in 2010 = 100

Individualising social welfare payments

The issue of individualising payments so that all recipients receive their own social welfare payments has been on the policy agenda in Ireland and across the EU for several years. *Social Justice Ireland* welcomed the report of the Working Group, *Examining the Treatment of Married, Cohabiting and One-Parent Families under the Tax and Social Welfare Codes*, which addressed some of these individualisation issues.

At present the welfare system provides a basic payment for a claimant, whether that be, for example, for a pension, a disability payment or a job-seeker's payment. It then adds an additional payment of about two-thirds of the basic payment for the second person. For example, following Budget 2015, a couple on the lowest social welfare rate receives a payment of €312.80 per week. This amount is approximately 1.66 times the payment for a single person (€188). Were these two people living separately they would receive €188 each; giving a total of €376. Thus by living as a household unit such a couple receive a lower income than they would were they to live apart.

---

[20] We will develop this policy position further in our pre-Budget submission in mid-2015.

Social Justice Ireland believes that this system is unfair and inequitable. We also believe that the system as currently structured is not compatible with the Equal Status Acts. People, more often than not, women, are disadvantaged by living as part of a household unit because they receive a lower income. We believe that where a couple is in receipt of welfare payments, the payment to the second person should be increased to equal that of the first. Such a change would remove the current inequity and bring the current social welfare system in line with the terms of the Equal Status Acts (2000-2004). An effective way of doing this would be to introduce a basic income system which is far more appropriate for the world of the 21st century.

3.5 Basic Income

Over the past 13 years major progress has been achieved in building the case for the introduction of a basic income in Ireland. This includes the publication of a *Green Paper on Basic Income* by the Government in September 2002 and the publication of a book by Clark entitled *The Basic Income Guarantee* (2002). A major international conference on basic income was held in Dublin during Summer 2008 at which more than 70 papers from 30 countries were presented. These are available on *Social Justice Ireland*'s website. More recently, Healy et al (2012) have provided an initial set of costing for a basic income and new European and Irish Basic Income networks have emerged.[21]

The case for a basic income

Social Justice Ireland has consistently argued that the present tax and social welfare systems should be integrated and reformed to make them more appropriate to the changing world of the 21st century. To this end we have sought the introduction of a basic income system. This proposal is especially relevant at the present moment of economic upheaval.

A basic income is an income that is unconditionally granted to every person on an individual basis, without any means test or work requirement. In a basic income system every person receives a weekly tax-free payment from the Exchequer while all other personal income is taxed, usually at a single rate. The basic-income payment would replace income from social welfare for a person who is unemployed and replace tax credits for a person who is employed.

---

[21] These networks are the European Citizens' Initiative for Unconditional Basic Income and Basic Income Ireland.

Basic income is a form of minimum income guarantee that avoids many of the negative side-effects inherent in social welfare payments. A basic income differs from other forms of income support in that:

- It is paid to individuals rather than households;
- t is paid irrespective of any income from other sources;
- It is paid without conditions; it does not require the performance of any work or the willingness to accept a job if offered one; and
- It is always tax free.

There is real danger that the plight of large numbers of people excluded from the benefits of the modern economy will be ignored. Images of rising tides lifting all boats are often offered as government's policy makers and commentators assure society that prosperity for all is just around the corner. Likewise, the claim is often made that a job is the best poverty fighter and consequently priority must be given to securing a paid job for everyone. These images and claims are no substitute for concrete policies to ensure that all members of society are included. Twenty-first century society needs a radical approach to ensure the inclusion of all people in the benefits of present economic growth and development. Basic income is such an approach.

As we are proposing it, a basic income system would replace social welfare and income tax credits. It would guarantee an income above the poverty line for everyone. It would not be means tested. There would be no 'signing on' and no restrictions or conditions. In practice, a basic income recognises the right of every person to a share of the resources of society.

The Basic Income system ensures that looking for a paid job and earning an income, or increasing one's income while in employment, is always worth pursuing, because for every euro earned the person will retain a large part. It thus removes poverty traps and unemployment traps in the present system. Furthermore, women and men would receive equal payments in a basic income system. Consequently the basic income system promotes gender equality because it treats every person equally.

It is a system that is altogether more secure, rewarding, simple and transparent than the present tax and welfare systems. It is far more employment friendly than the present system. It also respects other forms of work besides paid employment. This is crucial in a world where these benefits need to be recognised and respected. It is also very important in a world where paid employment cannot be permanently guaranteed for everyone seeking it. There is growing pressure and need in Irish society to ensure recognition and monetary reward for unpaid work. Basic income

3. Income Distribution

is a transparent, efficient and affordable mechanism for ensuring such recognition and reward.

Basic income also lifts people out of poverty and the dependency mode of survival. In doing this, it restores self-esteem and broadens horizons. Poor people, however, are not the only ones who should welcome a basic income system. Employers, for example, should welcome it because its introduction would mean they would not be in competition with the social welfare system. Since employees would not lose their basic income when taking a job, there would always be an incentive to take up employment.

Costing a basic income

During 2012 Healy et al presented an estimate for the cost of a basic income for Ireland. Using administrative data from the Census, social protection system and taxation system, the paper estimated a cost where payments were aligned to the existing social welfare payments (children = €32.30 per week; adults of working age = €188.00 per week; older people aged 66-80 = €230.30 per week; and older people aged 80+ = €240.30 per week). The paper estimated a total cost of €39.2 billion per annum for a basic income and outlined a requirement to collect a total of €41 billion in revenue to fund this. It is proposed that the revenue should be raised via a flat 45 per cent personal income tax and the continuance of the existing employers PRSI system (renamed a 'social solidarity fund'). It is important to remember that nobody would have an effective tax rate of 45 per cent in this system as they would always receive their full basic income and it would always be tax-free. Healy et al also outlined further directions for research in this area in the future and are likely to contribute future inputs into the evolving Irish and European basic income networks.

Ten reasons to introduce basic income

- It is work and employment friendly.
- It eliminates poverty traps and unemployment traps.
- It promotes equity and ensures that everyone receives at least the poverty threshold level of income.
- It spreads the burden of taxation more equitably.
- It treats men and women equally.
- It is simple and transparent.
- It is efficient in labour-market terms.

- It rewards types of work in the social economy that the market economy often ignores, e.g. home duties, caring, etc.
- It facilitates further education and training in the labour force.
- It faces up to the changes in the global economy.

Key policy priorities on income distribution

- If poverty rates are to fall in the years ahead, *Social Justice Ireland* believes that the following are required:
    - Increase in social welfare payments.
    - equity of social welfare rates.
    - adequate payments for children.
    - refundable tax credits.
    - a universal state pension.
    - a cost of disability payment.

Social Justice Ireland believes that in the period ahead Government and policy-makers generally should:

- Acknowledge that Ireland has an on-going poverty problem.
- Adopt targets aimed at reducing poverty among particular vulnerable groups such as children, lone parents, jobless households and those in social rented housing.
- Examine and support viable, alternative policy options aimed at giving priority to protecting vulnerable sectors of society.
- Carry out in-depth social impact assessments prior to implementing proposed policy initiatives that impact on the income and public services that many low income households depend on. This should include the poverty-proofing of all public policy initiatives.
- Provide substantial new measures to address long-term unemployment. This should include programmes aimed at re-training and re-skilling those at highest risk.
- Recognise the problem of the 'working poor'. Make tax credits refundable to address the situation of households in poverty which are headed by a person with a job.
- Support the widespread adoption of the Living Wage so that low paid workers

receive an adequate income and can afford a minimum, but decent, standard of living.

- Introduce a cost of disability allowance to address poverty and social exclusion of people with a disability.
- Recognise the reality of poverty among migrants and adopt policies to assist this group. In addressing this issue also replace direct provision with a fairer system that ensures adequate allowances are paid to asylum seekers.
- Accept that persistent poverty should be used as the primary indicator of poverty measurement and assist the CSO in allocating sufficient resources to collect this data.
- Move towards introducing a basic income system. No other approach has the capacity to ensure all members of society have sufficient income to live life with dignity.

4.
TAXATION

CORE POLICY OBJECTIVE: TAXATION
To collect sufficient taxes to ensure full participation in society for all, through a fair tax system in which those who have more, pay more, while those who have less, pay less.

The fiscal adjustments of recent years highlight the centrality of taxation in budget deliberations and to policy development at both macro and micro level. Taxation plays a key role in shaping Irish society through funding public services, supporting economic activity and redistributing resources to enhance the fairness of society. Consequently, it is crucial that clarity exist with regard to both the objectives and instruments aimed at achieving these goals. To ensure the creation of a fairer and more equitable tax system, policy development in this area should adhere to our core policy objective outlined above. In that regard, *Social Justice Ireland* is committed to increasing the level of detailed analysis and debate addressing this area.[22]

This chapter first considers Ireland's present taxation position and outlines the anticipated future taxation needs of the country. Given this, we outline approaches to reforming and broadening the tax base and proposals for building a fairer tax system. The issues addressed in this chapter include a number of the elements of *Social Justice Ireland's* Core Policy Framework (see Chapter 2) including: 'Macroeconomic Stability', 'Just Taxation' and 'Decent Services'.

Ireland's total tax-take: current and future needs

The need for a wider tax base is a lesson painfully learnt by Ireland during the past number of years. A disastrous combination of a naïve housing policy, a failed regulatory system and foolish fiscal policy and economic planning caused a collapse

---
[22] We present our analysis in this chapter and in the accompanying annex 4.

in exchequer revenues. It is only through a determined effort to reform Ireland's taxation system that these mistakes can be addressed and avoided in the future. The narrowness of the Irish tax base resulted in almost 25 per cent of tax revenues disappearing, plunging the exchequer and the country into a series of fiscal policy crises. As shown in table 4.1, tax revenues collapsed from over €60 billion in 2007 to €46 billion in 2009; it has since increased to just over €50 billion in 2013.

Table 4.1: The changing nature of Ireland's tax revenue (€m)

	2007	2008	2009	2011	2013
Taxes on income and wealth					
Income tax	15872	15668	14681	15271	16661
Corporation tax	6393	5071	3889	3751	4272
Motor tax - households*	723	800	793	758	859
Local Property Tax	0	0	0	0	318
Other taxes	0	0	201	185	180
Various Levies on income	411	414	369	319	315
Social Insurance	7745	7932	7168	7268	7299
Total taxes on income and wealth	**31144**	**29885**	**27101**	**27552**	**29904**
Taxes on capital					
Capital gains tax	3097	1424	545	416	369
Capital acquisitions tax	405	349	258	242	278
Pension Fund Levy	0	0	0	460	536
Total taxes on capital	**3502**	**1773**	**803**	**1118**	**1183**
Taxes on expenditure					
Excise duties including VRT	6139	5402	4877	4866	5024
Value added tax	14355	13084	10324	9755	10371
Rates	1267	1353	1471	1527	1564
Motor tax- businesses**	239	265	264	253	284
Stamps (excluding fee stamps)	3219	1768	972	933	776
Other fees and levies	193	242	224	264	681
Total taxes on expenditure	**25412**	**22114**	**18132**	**17598**	**18700**
EU Taxes	**273**	**247**	**209**	**240**	**247**
Total Taxation*	**60331**	**54019**	**46245**	**46508**	**50034**
Total Taxation as % GDP#	**30.7**	**28.9**	**27.5**	**27.2**	**28.6**

Source: CSO on-line database tables N1322:T22 and N1302: T02.
Notes: *Motor tax is an estimate of the portion paid by households.
**Motor tax is an estimate of the portion paid by business.
*** Total taxation is the sum of the rows in bold.
# Total taxation expressed as a % of published CSO GDP at current prices.

While a proportion of this decline in overall taxation revenue is related to the recession, a large part is structural and requires further policy reform. As detailed in chapter 2, *Social Justice Ireland* believes that over the next few years policy should focus on increasing Ireland's tax-take to 34.9 per cent of GDP, a figure defined by Eurostat as 'low-tax' (Eurostat, 2008:5). Such increases are certainly feasible and are unlikely to have any significant negative impact on the economy in the long term. As a policy objective, Ireland should remain a low-tax economy, but not one incapable of adequately supporting the economic, social and infrastructural requirements necessary to support our society and complete our convergence with the rest of Europe.

Looking to the years immediately ahead, Budget 2015 provided some insight into the expected future shape of Ireland's current taxation revenues and this is shown in table 4.2. The Budget provided a detailed breakdown of current taxes for 2014 and 2015 and overall projections for 2016-2017. Over the next three years, assuming these policies are followed, overall current revenue will climb to almost €45.5 billion.

Table 4.2: Projected current tax revenues, 2014-2017

	2014 €m	2015 €m	2016 €m	2017 €m
Customs	260	285		
Excise Duties*	5,080	5,245		
Capital Gains Tax	400	415		
Capital Acquis. Tax	330	400		
Stamp Duties	1,675	1,185		
Income Tax **	17,180	17,980		
Corporation Tax	4,525	4,575		
Value Added Tax	11,070	11,775		
Local Property Tax	520	440		
Total#	41,040	42,300	44,430	45,490

Source: Department of Finance, Budget 2015: C19, C24.
Notes: * Excise duties include carbon tax and motor tax revenues.
**Including USC.
#These figures do not incorporate other tax sources including revenues to the social insurance fund and local government charges. These are incorporated into the totals reported in table 4.3 below.

The documentation accompanying Budget 2015 also set out projections for the overall scale of the national tax-take (as a proportion of GDP) out to 2018. These figures are reproduced in table 4.3 and have been used to calculate the cash value of the overall levels of tax revenue expected to be collected. While the estimates in the table are based on the tax-take figures from Budget 2015 and its projections of national income, the document provides limited detail on the nature and composition of these figures.

It should also be borne in mind that over recent years the Department's projections for the overall taxation burden have continually overstated the actual figures subsequently reported by the CSO.[23] However, taking the Department's projections as the likely outcome, Chart 4.1 highlights just how far below average EU levels (assuming these remain at the 2012 level of 36.3 per cent of GDP) and the *Social Justice Ireland* target (34.9 per cent of GDP) these taxation revenue figures are. Table 4.3's Tax Gap, the difference between the 34.9% benchmark and Government's planned level of taxation, stands at €9 billion in 2015 and averages at €10.9 billion per annum over the next four years (2015-2018). Were Government to maintain overall taxation levels at their 2014 level (30.9% of GDP), rather than pursuing the planned reductions highlighted in Chart 4.1, the state would collect an average of €2.5 billion per annum in additional taxation revenue between now and 2018.

Table 4.3: Ireland's projected total tax take and the tax gap, 2013-2018

Year	Tax as % GDP	Total Tax Receipts	The Tax Gap
2013	30.5%	53,311	7,691
2014	30.9%	56,794	7,352
2015	30.2%	58,429	9,093
2016	29.8%	60,613	10,373
2017	29.5%	63,108	11,552
2018	29.3%	65,910	12,597

Source: Calculated from Department of Finance (2014:c55).
Notes: Total tax take = current taxes (see table 4.1 and 4.2) + Social Insurance Fund income + charges by local government + EU taxes.
The Tax Gap is calculated as the difference between the projected tax take and that which would be collected if total tax receipts were equal to 34.9% of projected GDP.
The 2013 Department of Finance estimate for the total tax take (30.5% GDP) differs from the corresponding CSO figure (28.6% GDP) reported in table 4.1.

---

[23] Compare the outcomes for 2013 as reported by the CSO in table 4.1 and those estimated by the Department of Finance as reported in table 4.3.

Chart 4.1: Ireland's Projected Taxation Levels to 2018 and comparisons with EU-28 averages and Social Justice Ireland target

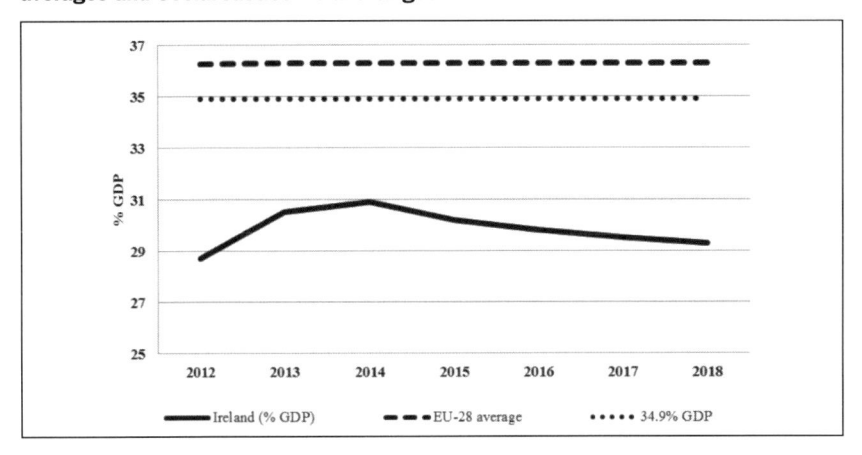

Source: Calculated from Eurostat (2014: 174) and Department of Finance (2014: c55).
Note: The EU-28 average was 36.3% of GDP in 2012 and this value is used for all years.

Future taxation needs
Government decisions to raise or reduce overall taxation revenue needs to be linked to the demands on its resources. These demands depend on what Government is required to address or decides to pursue. The effects of the recent economic crisis, and the way it was handled, carry significant implications for our future taxation needs. The rapid increase in our national debt, driven by the need to borrow both to replace disappearing taxation revenues and to fund emergency 'investments' in the failing commercial banks, has increased the on-going annual costs associated with servicing the national debt.

National debt has increased from a level of 25 per cent of GDP in 2007 - low by international standards - to peak at 123.3 per cent of GDP in 2013. Documents from the Department of Finance, to accompany Budget 2015, project that the national debt will decrease to 108 per cent of GDP in 2015 and to 95 per cent by 2018 (2014: C29). Despite favourable lending rates and payback terms, there remains a recurring cost to service this large national debt – costs which have to be financed by current taxation revenues. The estimated debt servicing cost for 2015 is €7.38 billion (Department of Finance, 2014: C57). Furthermore, the erosion of the National Pension Reserve Fund (NPRF) through using it to fund various bank rescues (over €20 billion) has transferred the liability for future public sector pensions onto future exchequer expenditure. Although there may be some return from a number of the rescued banks, it is likely to be small relative to the funds committed and therefore will require additional taxation resources.

These new future taxation needs are in addition to those that already exist for funding local government, repairing and modernising our water infrastructure, paying for the health and pension needs of an ageing population, paying EU contributions and funding any pollution reducing environmental initiatives that are required by European and International agreements. Collectively, they mean that Ireland's overall level of taxation will have to rise significantly in the years to come – a reality Irish society and the political system need to begin to seriously address.

As an organisation that has highlighted the obvious implications of these long-terms trends for some time, *Social Justice Ireland* welcomes the development over the past few years where the Government has published a section of the April Stability Programme Update (SPU) focused on the 'long-term sustainability of public finances'.

Table 4.4: Projected Age Related Expenditure, as % GDP 2015-2060

Expenditure areas	2015	2025	2035	2045	2055	2060
Gross Public Pensions	8.3	9.0	9.4	10.6	11.7	11.7
of which:						
Social protection pensions	6.0	6.5	7.0	7.9	8.5	8.3
Public service pensions	2.3	2.5	2.4	2.7	3.2	3.3
Health care	7.1	7.5	7.9	8.2	8.3	8.3
Long-term care	1.2	1.3	1.6	2.1	2.5	2.6
Education	6.9	7.0	6.1	6.2	6.6	6.4
Other age-related (JA etc)	3.6	2.5	1.7	1.4	1.3	1.3
Total age-related spending	27.0	27.3	26.8	28.5	30.3	30.3

Source: European Commission (2012: 400-401)

Research by Bennett et al (2003), the OECD (2008) and the ESRI (2010) have all provided some insight into future exchequer demands associated with healthcare and pensions in Ireland in the decades to come. The Department of Finance has used the European Commission publication entitled *'The 2012 Ageing Report: Economic and budgetary projections for the EU27 Member States (2010-2060)'*. Table 4.4 summarises some of its baseline projections for Ireland. Over the period the report anticipates an increase in the elderly population (65 years +) from 13 per cent of the population in 2015 to 21.9 per cent in 2060 while the 'very elderly population', those aged more than 80 years, will triple from 3 per cent in 2015 to 9.1 per cent in 2060. Over the same period, the proportion of those of working age will decline as a percentage of the population and the old-age dependency ratio will increase from approximately five people of working age for every elderly person today to less than three for every elderly person in 2060 (EU Commission, 2012: 399-401).[24] While these increases imply a range of necessary policy initiatives in the decades to come, there is an inevitability that an overall higher level of taxation will have to be collected.

Is a higher tax-take problematic?
Suggesting that any country's tax take should increase normally produces negative responses. People think first of their incomes and increases in income tax, rather than more broadly of reforms to the tax base. Furthermore, proposals that taxation should increase are often rejected with suggestions that they would undermine economic growth. However, a review of the performance of a number of economies over recent years sheds a different light on this issue. For example, in the years prior to the current international economic crisis, Britain achieved low unemployment and higher levels of growth compared to other EU countries (OECD, 2004). These were achieved simultaneously with increases in its tax/GDP ratio. In the decade to 2004 it increased by 2.3 percentage points of GDP (it stands at 35.4 per cent in the latest figures, see Annex 4). Furthermore, in his March 2004 Budget the then British Chancellor Gordon Brown indicated that this ratio would reach 38.3 per cent of GDP in 2008-09 (2004:262); it subsequently reached 37.1 per cent in 2008 before the economic crisis took hold. His announcement of these increases was not met with predictions of economic ruin or doom for Britain and its economic growth remained high compared to other EU countries (IMF, 2004 & 2008).

Taxation and competitiveness
Another argument made against increases in Ireland's overall taxation levels is that it will undermine competitiveness. However, the suggestion that higher levels of taxation would damage our position relative to other countries is not supported by international studies of competitiveness.

Annually the World Economic Forum publishes a *Global Competitiveness Report* ranking the most competitive economies across the world.[25] Table 4.5 outlines the top fifteen economies in this index for 2014-15 as well as the ranking for Ireland (which comes 25th). It also presents the difference between the size of the tax-take in these, the most competitive, economies in the world, and Ireland, for 2013.[26]

---

[24] The European Commission plan to update these projections in May 2015.
[25] Competitiveness is measured across 12 pillars including: institutions, infrastructure, macroeconomic environment, health and primary education, higher education and training, goods markets efficiency, labour market efficiency, financial market development, technological readiness, market size, business sophistication and innovation. See WEF (2014: 537-545) for further details on how these are measured.
[26] This analysis updates that first produced by Collins (2004: 15-18).

Table 4.5: Differences in taxation levels between the world's 15 most competitive economies and Ireland.

Competitiveness Rank	Country	Taxation level versus Ireland
1	Switzerland	-1.2
2	Singapore	*not available*
3	United States	-2.9
4	Finland	+15.7
5	Germany	+8.4
6	Japan	+1.2
7	Hong Kong SAR	*not available*
8	Netherlands	+8.0
9	United Kingdom	+4.6
10	Sweden	+14.5
11	Norway	+12.5
12	United Arab Emirates	*not available*
13	Denmark	+20.3
14	Taiwan, China	*not available*
15	Canada	+2.3
28	**IRELAND**	-

Source: World Economic Forum (2014: 13)
Notes: a) Taxation data from OECD (2014) for the year 2013 except for the Netherlands and Japan where the taxation data is for 2012.
b) For some non OECD countries comparable data is *not available*.
c) The OECD's estimate for Ireland in 2013 = 28.29 per cent of GDP

Only two of the top fifteen countries, for which there is data available, report a lower taxation level than Ireland: Switzerland and the US. All the other leading competitive economies collect a greater proportion of national income in taxation. Over time Ireland's position on this index has varied, most recently rising from 31st to 25th, although in previous years Ireland had been in 22nd position. When Ireland has slipped back the reasons stated for Ireland's loss of competitiveness included decreases in economic growth and fiscal stability, poor performances by public institutions and a decline in the technological competitiveness of the economy (WEF, 2003: xv;

2008:193; 2011: 25-26; 210-211). Interestingly, a major factor in that decline is related to underinvestment in state funded areas: education; research; infrastructure; and broadband connectivity. Each of these areas is dependent on taxation revenue and they have been highlighted by the report as necessary areas of investment to achieve enhanced competitiveness.[27] As such, lower taxes do not feature as a significant priority; rather the focus is on increased and targeted efficient government spending.

A similar point was expressed by the Nobel Prize winning economist Professor Joseph Stiglitz while visiting Ireland in June 2004. Commenting on Ireland's long-term development prospects, he stated that "all the evidence is that the low tax, low service strategy for attracting investment is short-sighted" and that "far more important in terms of attracting good businesses is the quality of education, infrastructure and services." Professor Stiglitz added that "low tax was not the critical factor in the Republic's economic development and it is now becoming an impediment".[28]

Reforming and broadening the tax base

Social Justice Ireland believes that there is merit in developing a tax package which places less emphasis on taxing people and organisations on what they earn by their own useful work and enterprise, or on the value they add or on what they contribute to the common good. Rather, the tax that people and organisations should be required to pay should be based more on the value they subtract by their use of common resources. Whatever changes are made should also be guided by the need to build a fairer taxation system, one which adheres to our already stated core policy objective.

There are a number of approaches available to Government in reforming the tax base. Recent Budgets have made some progress in addressing some of these issues while the 2009 Commission on Taxation Report highlighted many areas that require further reform. A short review of the areas we consider a priority are presented below across the following subsections:

Tax Expenditures / Tax Reliefs
Minimum Effective Tax Rates for Higher Earners
Corporation Taxes
Site Value Tax
Second Homes, Empty Houses and Underdeveloped Land
Taxing Windfall Gains
Financial Transactions Tax
Carbon Taxes

---

[27] A similar conclusion was reached in another international competitiveness study by the International Institute for Management Development (2007).
[28] In an interview with John McManus, Irish Times, June 2nd 2004.

Tax Expenditures / Tax Reliefs

A significant outcome from the Commission on Taxation is contained in part eight of its Report which details all the tax breaks (or "tax expenditures" as they are referred to officially). Subsequently, two members of the Commission produced a detailed report for the Trinity College Policy Institute which offered further insight into this issue (Collins and Walsh, 2010). Since then, the annual reporting of the costs of tax expenditures has improved considerably with much more detail than in the past being published annually by the Revenue Commissioners.[29]

The most recent tax expenditure data published by the Revenue Commissioners covers the tax year 2012. In total it provides data for 62 tax breaks ranging from those associated with tax credits for earners (Personal, PAYE, Couple, Lone Parent etc) to reliefs on capital investment and films. 17 per cent of tax breaks did not report any data either on account of delays or non-collection. These include the tax breaks for various pension reliefs which are only available for 2011 and before. Overall, the tax breaks with available data involve revenue forgone of €15.8 billion.

Some progress has been made in addressing and reforming these tax breaks in recent Budgets, and we welcome this progress. However, despite this, recent Budgets and Finance Bills have introduced new tax breaks targeted at high earning multinational executives and research and development schemes and extended tax breaks for film production and the refurbishment of older building in urban areas. For the most part, there has been no or limited accompanying documentation evaluating the cost, distributive impacts or appropriateness of these proposals.

Both the Commission on Taxation (2009:230) and Collins and Walsh (2010:20-21) have also highlighted and detailed the need for new methods for evaluation/introducing tax reliefs. We strongly welcomed these proposals, which were similar to those made by the directors of *Social Justice Ireland* to the Commission in written and oral submissions. The proposals focused on prior evaluation of the costs and benefits of any proposed expenditure, the need to collect detailed information on each expenditure, the introduction of time limits for expenditures, the creation of an annual tax expenditures report as part of the Budget process and the regular scrutiny of this area by an Oireachtas committee. Over the past year there has been some progress in this direction with a report for the Department of Finance, accompanying Budget 2015, proposing a new process for considering and evaluating tax breaks. We welcome this development and believe it is important to further develop this work, to deepen the proposed analysis and to further improve the ability of the Oireachtas to regularly review all of the tax expenditures in the Irish taxation system.

---

[29] See http://www.revenue.ie/en/about/statistics/index.html

Social Justice Ireland believes that reforming the tax break system would make the tax system fairer. It would also provide substantial additional resources which would contribute to raising the overall tax take towards the modest and realistic target we outlined earlier.[30]

Minimum Effective Tax Rates for Higher Earners

The suggestion that it is the better-off who principally gain from the provision of tax exemption schemes is underscored by a series of reports published by the Revenue Commissioners entitled *Effective Tax Rates for High Earning Individuals* and *Analysis of High Income Individuals' Restriction*. These reports provided details of the Revenue's assessment of the top earners in Ireland and the rates of effective taxation they incur.[31] The reports led to the introduction of a minimum 20 per cent effective tax rate as part of the 2006 and 2007 Finance Acts for all those with incomes in excess of €500,000. Subsequently, Budgets have revised up the minimum effective rate and revised down the income threshold from where it applies – reforms we have welcomed as necessary and long-overdue. Most recently, the 2010 Finance Bill introduced a requirement that all earners above €400,000 pay a minimum effective rate of tax of 30 per cent. It also reduced from €250,000 to €125,000 the income threshold where restrictions on the use of tax expenditures to decrease income tax liabilities commence.

Table 4.6: The Distribution of Effective Income Tax Rates among those earning in excess of €125,000 in 2012 (% of total)

Effective Income Tax Rate	Individuals with incomes of €400,000+	Individuals with incomes of €125,000 - €400,000
0%-5%	0%	1.14%
5% < 10%	0%	0.38%
10% < 15%	0%	2.91%
15% < 20%	0.77%	11.77%
20% < 25%	1.15%	16.96%
25% < 30%	14.23%	19.62%
30% < 35%	83.84%	20.76%
35% < 40%	0%	18.86%
> 40%	0%	7.6%
Total Cases	260	790

Source: Revenue Commissioners (2015).
Notes: Effective rates are for income taxation only as the reliefs are off-set against these liabilities. They do not include tax paid under the USC and PRSI.

---

[30] See section later in this chapter on the standard rating of tax expenditures.
[31] The effective taxation rate is calculated as the percentage of the individual's total pre-tax income that is liable to income tax and that is paid in taxation.

The latest Revenue Commissioners analysis of the operation of these new rules is for the tax year 2012 (Revenue Commissioners, 2015). Table 4.6 gives the findings of that analysis for the 260 individuals subject to the restriction with income in excess of €400,000. The report also includes information on the distribution of effective income tax rates among the 790 earners subject to the restriction and with incomes between €125,000 and €400,000.

Social Justice Ireland welcomed the introduction of this scheme which marked a major improvement in the fairness of the tax system. The published data indicate that is seems to be working well for those above an income of €400,000. However, between €125,000 and €400,000 there are still surprisingly low effective income taxation rates being reported; half of these individuals pay less than 30 per cent of their liable income in income taxes. Such an outcome may be better than in the past, but it still has some way to go to reflect a situation where a fair contribution is being paid.

The report also includes average effective taxation rates paid by these individuals where both income taxes and USC are included. It states that the average effective tax rate faced by earners above €400,000 in 2012 was 40.8 per cent, equivalent to the amount of income tax and USC paid by a single PAYE worker with a gross income of €150,000 in that year. Similarly, the average income tax and USC effective tax rate faced by people earning between €125,000 - €400,000 in 2012 (29.4 per cent) was equivalent to the amount of income tax paid by a single PAYE worker with a gross income of approximately €58,500 in that year. The contrast in these income levels for the same overall rate of income taxation brings into question the fairness of the taxation system as a whole.

Social Justice Ireland believes that it is important that Government continues to raise the minimum effective tax rate so that it is in-line with that faced by PAYE earners on equivalent high-income levels. Following Budget 2015 a single individual on an income of €125,000 gross will pay an income tax and USC effective tax rate of 38.7 per cent (down from 39.3 per cent in 2014); a figure which suggests that the minimum threshold for high earners has potential to adjust upwards over the next few years. We also believe that Government should reform the High Income Individuals' Restriction so that all tax expenditures are included within it. The restriction currently does not apply to all tax breaks individuals avail of, including pension contributions. This should change in Budget 2016.

Corporation Taxes
Over the past three years, a growing international focus on the way multi-national corporations (MNC) manage their tax affairs has lead to the OECD commencing a major examination of the system known as the Base Erosion and Profits Shifting (BEPS) process (OECD, 2013). It is intended to establish the manner and methods

by which MNC exploit international tax structures to minimise the tax they pay. It is important that this work leads to the emergence of a transparent international corporate finance and corporate taxation system where multinational firms pay a reasonable and credible effective corporate tax rate – to date the OECD's BEPS publications have been welcome and focused on this objective.[32] In tandem with this international reform process, the European Commission has begun a series of investigations into the tax management and tax minimisation practices of a number of large MNCs operating within the EU, including Ireland.

Despite a low headline rate (12.5%), there is limited data on the effective rate of corporate taxation in Ireland. A report from the Department of Finance in 2014 pointed towards four methods of calculating that rate. Although each were valid methods, it favoured one which reported an effective rate of 11.9 per cent on 'taxable income'. As 'taxable income' excludes income removed or offset from taxation through various tax breaks, it is unsurprising that the measure is close to the headline rate. However, in practical terms, the provision of tax breaks and exemptions is likely to imply corporations enjoy a substantial reduction in their tax liability. Data from Eurostat estimate an implicit corporate tax rate on business income of between 6% and 8.6% although it is likely to be as low as 3% for many large corporations while Small and Medium Enterprises (SMEs) pay close to 12.5% for the most part.[33]

Social Justice Ireland believes that an EU wide agreement on a minimum effective rate of corporation tax should be negotiated and this could evolve from the ongoing discussions around a Common Consolidated Corporate Tax Base (CCCTB). We believe that the minimum rate should be set well below the 2014 EU-28 average headline rate of 22.9 per cent but above the existing low Irish level.[34] A headline rate of 17.5 per cent and a minimum effective rate of 10 per cent seems appropriate. This reform would simultaneously maintain Ireland's low corporate tax position and provide additional revenues to the exchequer. Were such a rate in place in Ireland in 2014, corporate tax income would have been between €1 billion and €1.8 billion higher – a significant sum given the socio-economic challenges outlined throughout this publication. Rather than introducing this change overnight, agreement may need to be reached at EU level to phase it in over three to five years. Reflecting this, we proposed prior to Budget 2015 that the effective rate be adjusted to a minimum of 6 per cent – an opportunity regrettably missed in Budget 2015.

Social Justice Ireland believes that the issue of corporate tax contributions is principally one of fairness. Through the recent recession, the contrast between a

---

[32] See www.oecd.org/ctp/beps.htm
[33] See Eurostat online database, code: gov_a_tax_itr
[34] Data from Eurostat (2014:36-37).

static corporate tax rate and the increases to almost all other areas of taxation was stark. From a societal perspective, it is important that corporations contribute in a reasonable and credible way to the costs of running the state in which they operate in and benefit from.

Site Value Tax

Taxes on wealth are minimal in Ireland. Revenue is negligible from capital acquisitions tax (CAT) because it has a very high threshold in respect of bequests and gifts within families and the rates of tax on transfers of family farms and firms are very generous (see tax revenue tables at the start of this chapter). While recent increases in the rate of CAT are welcome, the likely future revenue from this area remains limited given the tax's current structure. The requirement, as part of the EU/IMF/ECB bailout agreement, to introduce a recurring property tax led Government in Budget 2012 to introduce an unfairly structured flat €100 per annum household charge and a value based Local Property Tax in Budget 2013. While we welcome the overdue need to extend the tax base to include a recurring revenue source from property, we believe that a Site Value Tax, also known as a Land Rent Tax, would be a more appropriate and fairer approach.

In previous editions of this publication we have reviewed this proposal in greater detail.[35] There has also been a number of research papers published on this issue over the past decade.[36] Overall they point towards a recurring site value tax that is fairer and more efficient than other alternatives. *Social Justice Ireland* believes that the introduction of a site value tax would be a better alternative than the current Government value based local property tax. A site value tax would lead to more efficient land use within the structure of social, environmental and economic goals embodied in planning and other legislation.

Second Homes, Empty Houses and Underdeveloped Land

A feature of the housing boom of the last decade was the rapid increase in ownership of holiday homes and second homes. For the most part these homes remain empty for at least nine months of the year. It is a paradox that many were built at the same time as the rapid increases in housing waiting lists (see chapter 7).

Results from Census 2011 indicated that since 2006 there had been a 19 per cent increase in the number of holiday homes, with numbers rising from 49,789 in 2006 to 59,395 in 2011. The Census also found that overall, the number of vacant houses on Census night was 168,427 (April 2011) – some of which are also likely to be second homes.

---

[35] See for example the 2013 edition of the Socio-Economic Review pages 132-134.
[36] These include O'Siochru (2004:23-57), Dunne (2004:93-122), Chambers of Commerce of Ireland (2004), Collins and Larragy (2011), and O'Siochru (2012).

What is often overlooked when the second home issue is being discussed is that the infrastructure to support these houses is substantially subsidised by the taxpayer. Roads, water, sewage and electricity infrastructure are just part of this subsidy which goes, by definition, to those who are already better off as they can afford these second homes in the first place. *Social Justice Ireland* supports the views of the ESRI (2003) and the Indecon report (2005:183-186; 189-190) on this issue. We believe that people purchasing second houses should have to pay these full infrastructural costs, much of which is currently borne by society through the Exchequer and local authorities. There is something perverse in the fact that the taxpayer subsidies the owners of these unoccupied houses while many people do not have basic adequate accommodation.

The introduction of the Non Principal Private Residence (NPPR) charge in 2009 was a welcome step forward. However, notwithstanding subsequent increases, the charge was very low relative to the previous and on-going benefits that are derived from these properties. It stood at €200 in 2013 and was abolished under the 2014 Local Government Reform Act. While second homes are liable for the local property tax, as are all homes, *Social Justice Ireland* believes that second homes should be required to make a further annual contribution in respect of the additional benefits these investment properties receive. We believe that Government should re-introduce this charge and that it should be further increased and retained as a separate substantial second homes payment. An annual charge of €500 would seem reasonable and would provide additional revenue to local government of approximately €170 million per annum.

In the context of a shortage of housing stock (see chapter 7), building new units is not the entire solution. There remains a large number of empty units across the country, something reflected in the aforementioned 2011 Census data. *Social Justice Ireland* believes that policy should be designed to reduce the number of these units and penalise those who own units and leave them vacant for more than a six month period. We propose that Government should introduce a levy on empty houses of €200 per month with the revenue from this charge collected and retained by local authorities.

Local authorities should also be charged with collecting a new site value tax on underdeveloped land - such as abandoned urban centre sites and land-banks of zoned land on the edges of urban areas. This tax should be levied at a rate of €2,000 per hectare (or part thereof) per annum. Income from both measures should reduce the central fund allocation to local authorities by €75m per annum.

Taxing Windfall Gains
The vast profits made by property speculators on the rezoning of land by local authorities was a particularly undesirable feature of the recent economic boom. For

some time *Social Justice Ireland* has called for a substantial tax to be imposed on the profits earned from such decisions. Re-zonings are made by elected representatives supposedly in the interest of society generally. It therefore seems appropriate that a sizeable proportion of the windfall gains they generate should be made available to local authorities and used to address the ongoing housing problems they face (see chapter 7). In this regard, *Social Justice Ireland* welcomed the decision to put such a tax in place in 2010 and strongly condemned its removal as part of Budget 2015. Its removal has been one of the most retrograde policy initiatives in recent years.

A windfall tax level of 80 per cent is appropriate and, as table 4.7 illustrates, this still leaves speculators and land owners with substantial profits from these rezoning decisions. The profit from this process should be used to fund local authorities. In announcing his Budget 2015 decision, the Minister for Finance noted that the tax was not currently raising any revenue and so justified its abolition on this basis. However, as the property market recovers and as the population continues to grow in years to come, there will be many beneficiaries of vast unearned speculative windfalls.

Social Justice Ireland believes that this tax should be re-introduced. Taxes are not just about revenue, they are also about fairness.

Table 4.7: Illustrative examples of the Operation of an 80% Windfall Gain Tax on Rezoned Land

Agricultural Land Value	Rezoned Value	Profit	Tax @ 80%	Post-Tax Profit	Profit as % Original Value
€50,000	€400,000	€350,000	€280,000	€70,000	140%
€100,000	€800,000	€700,000	€560,000	€140,000	140%
€200,000	€1,600,000	€1,400,000	€1,120,000	€280,000	140%
€500,000	€4,000,000	€3,500,000	€2,800,000	€700,000	140%
€1,000,000	€8,000,000	€7,000,000	€5,600,000	€1,400,000	140%

Note: Calculations assume an eight-fold increase on the agricultural land value upon rezoning.

Financial Transactions Tax

As the international economic chaos of the past few years has shown, the world is now increasingly linked via millions of legitimate, speculative and opportunistic financial transactions. Similarly, global currency trading increased sharply throughout recent decades. It is estimated that a very high proportion of all financial transactions traded are speculative currency transactions which are completely free of taxation.

An insight into the scale of these transactions is provided by the Bank for International Settlements (BIS) Triennial Central Bank Survey of Foreign Exchange and Derivatives Market Activity (December 2013). The key findings from that report were:

- In April 2013 the average daily turnover in global foreign exchange markets was US$5.3 trillion; an increase of almost 35 per cent since 2010 and 331 per cent since 2001.
- The major components of these activities were: $2.046 trillion in spot transactions, $680 billion in outright forwards, $2.228 trillion in foreign exchange swaps, $54 billion currency swaps, and $337 billion in foreign exchange options and other products.
- 58 per cent of trades were cross-border and 42 per cent local.
- The vast majority of trades involved four currencies: US Dollar, Euro, Japanese Yen and Pound Sterling.
- Most of this activity (60 per cent) occurred in the US and UK.
- The estimated daily foreign exchange turnover for Ireland was US$11 billion.

Social Justice Ireland regrets that to date Government has not committed to supporting recent European moves to introduce a Financial Transactions Tax (FTT) or Tobin Tax. The Tobin tax, first proposed by the Nobel Prize winner James Tobin, is a progressive tax, designed to target only those profiting from speculation. It is levied at a very small rate on all transactions but given the scale of these transactions globally, it has the ability to raise significant funds. In September 2011 the EU Commission proposed an FTT and its proposal has evolved since then through a series of revisions and updates. Current plans are for the tax to commence under the EU's enhanced co-operation procedure in at least 11 EU members states in January 2016. It suggested that an FTT would be levied on transactions between financial institutions when at least one party to the transaction is located in the EU. Although the final structure of rates has yet to be agreed, the initial rates reflect the concept's focus on charging small rates on financial flows. These included the taxing of the exchange of shares and bonds at a rate of 0.1% and derivative contracts, at an even lower rate of 0.01%. The rates are minimums as countries within the EU retain the right to set individual tax rates and could choose higher levels if desired.

To date 11 of the 27 EU member states have signed up to this tax and *Social Justice Ireland* believes that Ireland should also join this group. In our opinion, the tax offers the dual benefit of dampening needless and often reckless financial speculation and generating significant funds. We believe that the revenue generated by this tax should be used for national economic and social development and international development co-operation purposes, in particular assisting Ireland and other developed countries to fund overseas aid and reach the UN ODA target (see chapter

13). According to the United Nations, the amount of annual income raised from a Tobin tax would be enough to guarantee to every citizen of the world basic access to water, food, shelter, health and education. Therefore, this tax has the potential to wipe out the worst forms of material poverty throughout the world.

Social Justice Ireland believes that the time has come for Ireland to support the introduction of a financial transactions tax.

Carbon Taxes

Budget 2010 announced the long-overdue introduction of a carbon tax. This had been promised in Budget 2003 and committed to in the *National Climate Change Strategy* (2007). The tax has been structured along the lines of the proposal from the Commission on Taxation (2009: 325-372) and is linked to the price of carbon credits which was set at an initial rate of €15 per tonne of CO_2 and subsequently increased in Budget 2012 to €20 per tonne. Budget 2013 extended the tax to cover solid fuels on a phased basis from May 2013 with the full tax applying from May 2014. Products are taxed based on the level of the emissions they create.

While *Social Justice Ireland* welcomed the introduction of this tax, it regrets the lack of accompanying measures to protect those most affected by it, in particular low income households and rural dwellers. *Social Justice Ireland* believes that as the tax increases the Government should be more specific in defining how it will assist these households. Furthermore, we are concerned that the effectiveness of the tax is being undermined as there is limited focus on the original intention of encouraging behavioural change and greater emphasis on simply raising revenue.

Building a fairer taxation system

The need for fairness in the tax system was clearly recognised in the first report of the Commission on Taxation 33 years ago. It stated:

> "...in our recommendations the spirit of equity is the first and most important consideration. Departures from equity must be clearly justified by reference to the needs of economic development or to avoid imposing unreasonable compliance costs on individuals or high administrative costs on the Revenue Commissioners." (1982:29)

The need for fairness is just as obvious today and *Social Justice Ireland* believes that this should be a central objective of the current reform of the taxation system. Below we outline a series of necessary reforms that would greatly enhance the fairness of Ireland's taxation system. This section is structured in six parts:

Standard rating discretionary tax expenditures
Keeping the minimum wage out of the tax net
Favouring fair changes to income taxes
Introducing Refundable Tax Credits
Reforming individualisation
Making the taxation system simpler

Standard rating discretionary tax expenditures
Making all discretionary tax reliefs/expenditures only available at the standard 20 per cent rate would represent a crucial step towards achieving a fairer tax system. If there is a legitimate case for making a tax relief/expenditure available, then it should be made available in the same way to all. It is inequitable that people on higher incomes should be able to claim certain tax reliefs at their top marginal tax rates while people with less income are restricted to claim benefit for the same relief at the lower standard rate of 20 per cent. The standard rating of tax expenditures, otherwise known as reliefs, offers the potential to simultaneously make the tax system fairer and fund the necessary developments they are designed to stimulate without any significant macroeconomic implications.[37]

Recent Budgets have made substantial progress towards achieving this objective and we welcome these developments. However, there remains considerable potential to introduce further reform. A recent paper, Collins (2013:17) reported that in 2009 (the latest Revenue data available) there were €2.3 billion of tax breaks made available at the marginal rate and that if these were standardised the estimated saving was just over €1 billion.

Keeping the minimum wage out of the tax net
The decision by the Minister for Finance to remove those on the minimum wage from the tax net was a major achievement of Budget 2005. This had an important impact on the growing numbers of working-poor and addressed an issue about which *Social Justice Ireland* is highly concerned.

The fiscal and economic crisis of 2008-13 led to Government reversing this policy, first via the income levy in second Budget 2009, then via the Universal Social Charge (USC) in Budget 2011 and via a PRSI increase in Budget 2013. Following Budget 2015 the USC is charged on all the income of those who earn more than €12,012 per annum. Using the unadjusted minimum wage of €8.65 per hour, the threshold implies that a low-income worker on the minimum wage and working more than 27 hours per week (earning €234 per week) is subject to the tax. *Social Justice Ireland* believes that this threshold remains too low and unnecessarily depresses the income and living standards of the working poor. Budget 2012 raised the entry point for the

---
[37] See O'Toole and Cahill (2006:215) who also reach this conclusion.

USC from €4,004 per annum to €10,036 per annum and Budget 2015 raised it further to €12,012; moves welcomed by Social *Justice Ireland*. However, the imposition of the USC at such low income levels raises a very small amount of funds for the exchequer. Forthcoming Budgets should continue to raise the point at which the USC commences and in the years to come, as more resources become available to the Exchequer, *Social Justice Ireland* will urge Government to restore the policy of keeping the minimum wage fully outside the tax net.

Favouring fair changes to income taxes

Reducing income taxes is not a priority for *Social Justice Ireland* either in the forthcoming Budget 2016 or any future plans for taxation policy reform. We believe that any available money should be used to improve Ireland's social services and infrastructure, reduce poverty and social exclusion and increase the number of jobs – policy priorities detailed throughout this publication. However, discussion and policy considerations often focuses on income taxation reductions, and as a consequence, we have recently published a document examining, from the perspectives of fairness, various reform choices. The document is entitled *Fairness in Changing Income Tax: 7 Options Compared* (Social Justice Ireland, 2015).[38] As a minimum, the analysis highlights the distributive impact taxation policy choices can have and the potential policy has to pursue both fair and unfair outcomes.

Table 4.8 presents a comparison of the reforms to tax rates, tax credits, tax bands and the USC as examined in the document. In all cases the policy examined would carry a full year cost of between 1% and 1.5% of the total income taxation yield (€184m-€268m).[39] The reforms examined are for changes to the 2015 income taxation system and are:

- a decrease in the top tax rate from 40% to 39% (full year cost €226m)
- a decrease in the standard rate of tax from 20% to 19.5% (full year cost €268m)
- an increase in the personal tax credit of €110 with commensurate increases in couple, widowed parents and the single person child carer credit (full year cost €235m)
- an increase in the standard rate band (20% tax band) of €1,500 (full year cost €234m)
- a 1% point decrease in the 1.5% USC rate – that applied to income below €12,012 (full year cost €235m)
- a 2% point decrease in the 3.5% USC rate (so that it merges with the 1.5% rate) – that applied to income between €12,012 and €17,576 (full year cost €202m)
- a 0.5% point decrease in the 7% USC rate – that applied to income above €17,576 (full year cost €184m)

---

[38] The document is available on our website.
[39] The cost estimates are based on the most recent taxation ready reckoner available from the Revenue Commissioners (post-Budget 2015).

Table 4.8: Comparing gains under seven possible income tax reforms (€ per annum)

Gross Income	€15,000	€25,000	€50,000	€75,000	€100,000	€125,000
Decrease in the top tax rate from 40% to 39% (full year cost €226m)						
Single earner	0	0	162	412	662	912
Couple 1 earner	0	0	72	322	572	822
Couple 2 earners	0	0	0	74	324	574
Decrease in the standard tax rate from 20% to 19.5% (full year cost €268m)						
Single earner	0	125	169	169	169	169
Couple 1 earner	0	50	214	214	214	214
Couple 2 earners	0	0	250	338	338	338
Increase in the personal tax credit of €110 (full year cost €235 million)						
Single earner	0	110	110	110	110	110
Couple 1 earner	0	20	220	220	220	220
Couple 2 earners	0	0	220	220	220	220
Increase in the standard rate band of €1,500 (full year cost €234 million)						
Single earner	0	0	300	300	300	300
Couple 1 earner	0	0	300	300	300	300
Couple 2 earners	0	0	0	600	600	600
A 1% point decrease in the 1.5% USC rate (full year cost €235m)						
Single earner	120.12	120.12	120.12	120.12	120.12	120.12
Couple 1 earner	120.12	120.12	120.12	120.12	120.12	120.12
Couple 2 earners	0.00	120.12	240.24	240.24	240.24	240.24
A 2% point decrease in the 3.5% USC rate (full year cost €202m)						
Single earner	59.76	111.28	111.28	111.28	111.28	111.28
Couple 1 earner	59.76	111.28	111.28	111.28	111.28	111.28
Couple 2 earners	0.00	84.76	221.04	222.56	222.56	222.56
A 0.5% point decrease in the 7% USC rate (full year cost €184m)						
Single earner	0.00	37.12	162.12	262.33	262.33	262.33
Couple 1 earner	0.00	37.12	162.12	262.33	262.33	262.33
Couple 2 earners	0.00	0.00	74.62	199.24	324.24	393.20

Notes: All workers are assumed to be PAYE workers. For couples with 2 earners the income is assumed to be split 65%/35%. Cost estimates are based on the latest available Revenue Commissioners taxation ready reckoner and are applied to the structure of the 2015 income taxation system. The increase in the personal tax credit assumes a commensurate increase in the couple, widowed parents and the single person child carer credit. USC calculations assume earners pay the standard rate of USC.

Although all of the income taxation options have similar costs (1%-1.5% of the income taxation yield), they each carry different effects on the income distribution. Overall, three of the changes would produce a fair outcome:

- increasing the personal tax credit;
- reducing the 1.5% USC rate by 1 percentage point; and
- reducing the 3.5% USC rate by 2 percentage points.

Four of the changes would produce an unfair outcome:

- reducing the top tax rate to 39%;
- reducing the standard tax rate to 19%;
- increasing the standard rate band; and
- reducing the 7% USC rate.

Each of the three fair options would provide beneficiaries with an improvement in their annual income of around €110-120. Each of the four unfair options would skew benefits towards those with higher incomes.

Introducing refundable tax credits

The move from tax allowances to tax credits was completed in Budget 2001. This was a very welcome change because it put in place a system that had been advocated for a long time by a range of groups. One problem persists however. If a low income worker does not earn enough to use up his or her full tax credit then he or she will not benefit from any income tax reductions introduced by government in its annual budget.

Making tax credits refundable would be a simple solution to this problem. It would mean that the part of the tax credit that an employee did not benefit from would be "refunded" to him/her by the state.

The major advantage of making tax credits refundable lies in addressing the disincentives currently associated with low-paid employment. The main beneficiaries of refundable tax credits would be low-paid employees (full-time and part-time). Chart 4.2 displays the impacts of the introduction of this policy across various gross income levels. It clearly shows that all of the benefits from introducing this policy would go directly to those on the lowest incomes.

With regard to administering this reform, the central idea recognises that most people with regular incomes and jobs would not receive a cash refund of their tax credit because their incomes are too high. They would simply benefit from the tax credit as a reduction in their tax bill. Therefore, as chart 4.2 shows, no change is proposed for these people and they would continue to pay tax via their employers, based on their net liability after deduction of tax credits by their employers on behalf of the Revenue Commissioners. For other people on low or irregular incomes, the refundable tax credit could be paid via a refund by the Revenue Commissioners at the end of the tax year. Following the introduction of refundable tax credits, all subsequent increases in the level of the tax credit would be of equal value to all employees.

Chart 4.2: How much better off would people be if tax credits were made refundable?

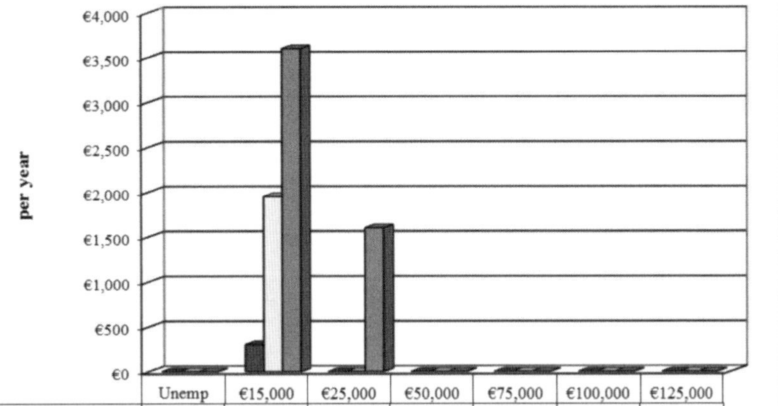

per year	Unemp	€15,000	€25,000	€50,000	€75,000	€100,000	€125,000
■ Single	-	300	-	-	-	-	-
□ Couple 1 Earner*	-	1,950	-	-	-	-	-
■ Couple 2 Earners*	-	3,600	1,600	-	-	-	-

Note: * Except where unemployed as there is no earner

To illustrate the benefits of this approach, charts 4.3 and 4.4 compare the effects of a €100 increase in the personal tax credit before and after the introduction of refundable tax credits. Chart 4.3 shows the effect as the system is currently structured – an increase of €100 in credits, but these are not refundable. It shows that the gains are allocated equally to all categories of earners above €50,000. However, there is no benefit for those workers whose earnings are not in the tax net.

Chart 4.4 shows how the benefits of a €100 a year increase in personal tax credits would be distributed under a system of refundable tax credits. This simulation demonstrates the equity attached to using the tax-credit instrument to distribute budgetary taxation changes. The benefit to all categories of income earners (single/couple, one-earner/couple, dual-earners) is the same. Consequently, in relative terms, those earners at the bottom of the distribution do best.

Chart 4.3: How much better off would people be if tax credits were increased by €100 per person?

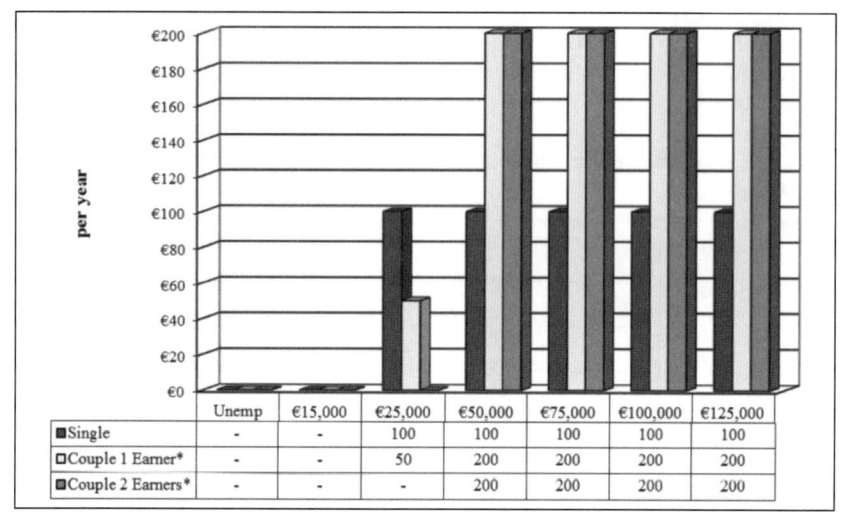

	Unemp	€15,000	€25,000	€50,000	€75,000	€100,000	€125,000
■ Single	-	-	100	100	100	100	100
□ Couple 1 Earner*	-	-	50	200	200	200	200
▣ Couple 2 Earners*	-	-	-	200	200	200	200

Note: * Except where unemployed, as there is no earner

Chart 4.4: How much better off would people be if tax credits were increased by €100 per person and this was refundable?

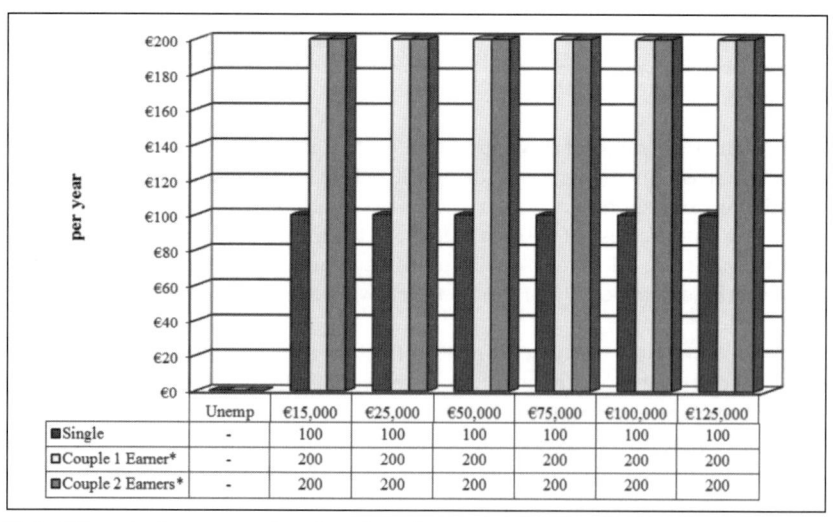

	Unemp	€15,000	€25,000	€50,000	€75,000	€100,000	€125,000
■ Single	-	100	100	100	100	100	100
□ Couple 1 Earner*	-	200	200	200	200	200	200
▣ Couple 2 Earners*	-	200	200	200	200	200	200

Note: * Except where unemployed, as there is no earner

Overall the merits of adopting this approach are: that every beneficiary of tax credits would receive the full value of the tax credit; that the system would improve the net income of the workers whose incomes are lowest, at modest cost; and that there would be no additional administrative burden placed on employers.

Outside Ireland, the refundable tax credits approach has gained more and more attention, including a detailed Brooking Policy Briefing on the issue published in the United States in late 2006 (see Goldberg et al, 2006). In reviewing this issue in the Irish context the late Colm Rapple stated that "the change is long overdue" (2004:140).

During late 2010 *Social Justice Ireland* published a detailed study on the subject of refundable tax credits. Entitled *'Building a Fairer Tax System: The Working Poor and the Cost of Refundable Tax Credits'*, the study identified that the proposed system would benefit 113,000 low-income individuals in an efficient and cost-effective manner.[40] When children and other adults in the household are taken into account the total number of beneficiaries would be 240,000. The cost of making this change would be €140m. The *Social Justice Ireland* proposal to make tax credits refundable would make Ireland's tax system fairer, address part of the working poor problem and improve the living standards of a substantial number of people in Ireland. The following is a summary of that proposal:

Making tax credits refundable: the benefits
- Would address the problem identified already in a straightforward and cost-effective manner.
- No administrative cost to the employer.
- Would incentivise employment over welfare as it would widen the gap between pay and welfare rates.
- Would be more appropriate for a 21st century system of tax and welfare.

Details of Social Justice Ireland proposal
- Unused portion of the Personal and PAYE tax credit (and only these) would be refunded.
- Eligibility criteria in the relevant year.
- Individuals must have unused personal and/or PAYE tax credits (by definition).
- Individuals must have been in paid employment.
- Individuals must be at least 23 years of age.
- Individuals must have earned a minimum annual income from employment of €4,000.

---
[40] The study is available from our website: www.socialjustice.ie

- Individuals must have accrued a minimum of 40 PRSI weeks.
- Individuals must not have earned an annual total income greater than €15,600.
- Married couples must not have earned a combined annual total income greater than €31,200.
- Payments would be made at the end of the tax year.

Cost of implementing the proposal
- The total cost of refunding unused tax credits to individuals satisfying all of the criteria mentioned in this proposal is estimated at €140.1m.

Major findings
- Almost 113,300 low income individuals would receive a refund and would see their disposable income increase as a result of the proposal.
- The majority of the refunds are valued at under €2,400 per annum, or €46 per week, with the most common value being individuals receiving a refund of between €800 to €1,000 per annum, or €15 to €19 per week.
- Considering that the individuals receiving these payments have incomes of less than €15,600 (or €299 per week), such payments are significant to them.
- Almost 40 per cent of refunds flow to people in low-income working poor households who live below the poverty line.
- A total of 91,056 men, women and children below the poverty threshold benefit either directly through a payment to themselves or indirectly through a payment to their household from a refundable tax credit.
- Of the 91,056 individuals living below the poverty line that benefit from refunds, most, over 71 per cent receive refunds of more than €10 per week with 32 per cent receiving in excess of €20 per week.
- A total of 148,863 men, women and children above the poverty line benefit from refundable tax credits either directly through a payment to themselves or indirectly (through a payment to their household. Most of these beneficiaries have income less than €120 per week above the poverty line.
- Overall, some 240,000 individuals (91,056 + 148,863) living in low-income households would experience an increase in income as a result of the introduction of refundable tax credits, either directly through a refund to themselves or indirectly through a payment to their household.

Once adopted, a system of refundable tax credits as proposed in this study would result in all future changes in tax credits being equally experienced by all employees in Irish society. Such a reform would mark a significant step in the direction of building a fairer taxation system and represent a fairer way for Irish society to allocate its resources.

Reforming individualisation
Social Justice Ireland supports individualisation of the tax system. However, the process of individualisation followed to date has been deeply flawed and unfair. The cost to the exchequer of this transition has been in excess of €0.75 billion, and almost all of this money has gone to the richest 30 per cent of the population. A significantly fairer process would have been to introduce a basic income system that would have treated all people fairly and ensured that a windfall of this nature did not accrue to the best off in this society (see chapter 3).

Given the current form of individualisation, couples with one partner losing his/her job end up even worse off than they would have been had the current form of individualisation not been introduced. Before individualisation was introduced, the standard-rate income-tax band was €35,553 for all couples. Above that, they would start paying the higher rate of tax. Now, the standard-rate income-tax band for single-income couples is €42,800 while the band for dual-income couples covers a maximum of a further €24,800 (up to €67,600). If one spouse (of a couple previously earning two salaries) leaves a job voluntarily or through redundancy, the couple loses the value of the second tax band.

Making the taxation system simpler
Ireland's tax system is not simple. Bristow (2004) argued that "some features of it, notably VAT, are among the most complex in the world". The reasons given to justify this complexity vary but they are focused principally around the need to reward particular kinds of behaviour which is seen as desirable by legislators. This, in effect, is discrimination either in favour of one kind of activity or against another. There are many arguments against the present complexity and in favour of a simpler system.

Discriminatory tax concessions in favour of particular positions are often very inequitable, contributing far less to equity than might appear to be the case. In many circumstances they also fail to produce the economic or social outcomes which were being sought and sometimes they even generate very undesirable effects. At other times they may be a complete waste of money, since the outcomes they seek would have occurred without the introduction of a tax incentive. Having a complex system has other down-sides. It can, for example, have high compliance costs both for taxpayers and for the Revenue Commissioners.

For the most part, society at large gains little or nothing from the discrimination contained in the tax system. Mortgage interest relief, for example, and the absence of any residential or land-rent tax contributed to the rise in house prices up to 2007. Complexity makes taxes easier to evade, invites consultants to devise avoidance schemes and greatly increases the cost of collection. It is also inequitable because those who can afford professional advice are in a far better position to take advantage of that complexity than those who cannot. A simpler taxation system would better serve Irish society and all individuals within it, irrespective of means.

Key Policy Priorities on Taxation

Social Justice Ireland believes that Government should:
- increase the overall tax take
- adopt policies to broaden the tax base
- develop a fairer taxation system

Policy priorities under each of these headings are listed below.

Increase the overall tax take
- Move towards increasing the total tax take to 34.9 per cent of GDP (i.e. a level below the high tax threshold identified by Eurostat).

Broaden the tax base
- Continue to reform the area of tax expenditures and put in place procedures within the Department of Finance and the Revenue Commissioners to monitor on an on-going basis the cost and benefits of all current and new tax expenditures.
- Continue to increase the minimum effective tax rates on very high earners (those with incomes in excess of €125,000) so that these rates are consistent with the levels faced by PAYE workers.
- Move to negotiate an EU wide agreement on minimum corporate taxation rates (a rate of 17.5 per cent would seem fair in this situation).
- Adopt policies to ensure that corporations based in Ireland pay a minimum effective corporate tax rate of 10 per cent.
- Impose charges so that those who construct or purchase second homes pay the full infrastructural costs of these dwellings.
- Restore the 80 per cent windfall tax on the profits generated from all land re-zonings.
- Join with other EU member states to adopt a financial transactions tax (FTT).
- Adopt policies which further shift the burden of taxation from income tax to eco-taxes on the consumption of fuel and fertilisers, waste taxes and a land rent tax. In doing this, government should avoid any negative impact on people with low incomes.

Develop a fairer taxation system
- Apply only the standard rate of tax to all discretionary tax expenditures.
- Adjust tax credits and the USC so that the minimum wage returns to falling outside the tax net.
- Make tax credits refundable.
- Accept that where reductions in income taxes are being implemented, they should favour fair options which do not skew the benefits towards higher earners.
- Ensure that individualisation in the income tax system is done in a fair and equitable manner.
- Integrate the taxation and social welfare systems.
- Begin to monitor and report tax levels (personal and corporate) in terms of effective tax rates.
- Develop policies which allow taxation on wealth to be increased.
- Ensure that the distribution of all changes in indirect taxes discriminate positively in favour of those with lower incomes.
- Adopt policies to simplify the taxation system.
- Poverty-proof all budget tax packages to ensure that tax changes do not further widen the gap between those with low income and the better off.

5.
WORK, UNEMPLOYMENT AND JOB CREATION

CORE POLICY OBJECTIVE:
WORK, UNEMPLOYMENT AND JOB CREATION
To ensure that all people have access to meaningful work

The scale and severity of the 2008-2010 economic collapse saw Ireland revert to the phenomenon of widespread unemployment. Since then, despite the attention given to the banking and fiscal collapse, the transition from near full-employment to high unemployment was the most telling characteristic of that recession. The implications for individuals, families, social cohesion and the exchequer's finances have been serious and the effects are likely to be felt for many years to come. CSO data and economic forecasts for the remainder of 2015 indicate that unemployment will reach an annual rate of between 10.2 and 9.6 per cent of the labour force in 2015, having been 4.7 per cent before the recession in 2007. Significant improvements have been achieved over the past three years, but there can be little doubt but that we are in a very challenging period in which a high level of long-term unemployment has once again become a characteristic of Irish society.

This chapter reviews the evolution of this situation and considers the implications and challenges which arise for Government and society.[41] It also looks at the impact on various sectors of the working-age population and outlines a series of proposals for responding to this unemployment crisis. To date, *Social Justice Ireland* considers that the policy response has been limited. As the chapter shows, the scale and nature of our unemployment crisis deserves greater attention, in particular given the scale of long-term unemployment. The chapter concludes with some thoughts on the narrowness of how we consider and measure the concept of 'work'. The issues addressed in this chapter principally focus on one pillar of *Social Justice Ireland's* Core Policy Framework (see Chapter 2), 'Enhance Social Protection'.

---
[41] The analysis complements information on the measurement of the labour market and long-term trends in employment and unemployment detailed in annex 5.

Recent trends in employment and unemployment

The nature and scale of the recent transformation in Ireland's labour market is highlighted by the data in table 5.1. Over the eight years from 2007-2014 the labour force decreased by just over 4.5 per cent, participation rates dropped, full-time employment fell by almost 15 per cent, representing some 272,700 jobs, while part-time employment increased by almost 14 per cent. By the end of 2014 the number of underemployed people, defined as those employed part-time but wishing to work additional hours, stood at 115,500 people – almost 5.5 per cent of the labour force. Over this period unemployment increased by almost 110,000 people, bringing the unemployment rate up from 4.6 per cent to 9.9 per cent; although the 2014 figure represents a dramatic improvement on the levels experiences during the height of the economic crisis in 2010.

Table 5.1: Labour Force Data, 2007 – 2014

	2007	2010	2014	Change 07-14
Labour Force	2,260,600	2,168,200	2,152,500	-108,100
LFPR %	63.8	60.2	59.8	-4.0%
Employment %	68.8	59.0	62.6	-6.2%
Employment	2,156,000	1,857,300	1,938,900	-217,100
Full-time	1,765,300	1,422,800	1,492,600	-272,700
Part-time	390,700	434,400	446,400	+55,700
Underemployed	n/a	116,800	115,500	-
Unemployed %	4.6	14.3	9.9	+5.3%
Unemployed	104,600	310,900	213,600	+109,000
LT Unemployed %	1.4%	7.9%	5.7%	+4.3%
LT Unemployed	31,700	172,100	123,400	+91,700

Source: CSO, QNHS on-line database.
Notes: All data is for Quarter 4 of the reference year.
LFPR = Labour force participation rate and measures the percentage of the adult population who are in the labour market.
Underemployment measures part-time workers who indicate that they wish to work additional hours which are not currently available.
Comparable underemployment data is not available for 2007.
LT = Long Term (12 months or more).

This transformation in the labour market has significantly altered the nature of employment in Ireland when compared to the pre-recession picture in 2007. Overall, employment fell by 10 per cent (217,000 jobs) between 2007-2014 and table 5.2 traces the impact of this fall across various sectors, groups and regions. Within the CSO's broadly defined employment sectors, industrial employment has seen the biggest fall of over 35 per cent while there has been a smaller fall in both services and agricultural employment. However, compared to 2010, overall employment has been growing, representing a welcome recovery.

Overall, job losses have had a greater impact on males than females with male employment down 14 per cent since 2007 while female employment decreased by 5 per cent. The proportional impact of the crisis has hit employment levels for employees and self-employed in much the same way; although there are many more of the former and the actual job losses among employees is significantly higher.

Table 5.2: Employment in Ireland, 2007 – 2014

	2007	2010	2014	Change 07-14
Employment	2,156,000	1,857,300	1,938,900	-217,100
Sector				
Agriculture	114,300	85,400	105,900	-8,400
Industry	551,600	355,300	361,300	-190,300
Services	1,482,900	1,409,900	1,468,200	-14,700
Gender				
Male	1,221,800	994,100	1,053,100	-168,700
Female	934,200	863,200	885,900	-48,300
Employment Status				
Employees*	1,775,900	1,548,900	1,605,500	-170,400
Self Employed	364,300	298,000	320,300	-44,000
Assisting relative	15,800	10,300	13,200	-2,600
Region				
Border	221,100	187,400	185,800	-35,300
Midland	126,100	103,400	113,700	-12,400
West	206,400	181,500	181,100	-25,300
Dublin	640,000	552,600	587,500	-52,500
Mid-West	173,200	151,000	152,800	-20,400
South-East	226,600	185,800	204,500	-22,100
South-West	310,600	269,300	275,600	-35,000
Mid-East	251,900	226,300	237,900	-14,000

Source: CSO, QNHS on-line database.

Notes: * Numbers recorded as employed include those on various active labour market policy schemes. See also notes to table 5.1.

The consequence of all these job losses has been the sharp increase in unemployment and emigration. Dealing with unemployment, table 5.3 shows how it has changed between 2007 and 2014, a period when the numbers unemployed increased by over 100 per cent. As the table shows, male unemployment increased by 69,000 and female unemployment by 40,000. Most of the unemployed, who had been employed in 2007 and before it, are seeking to return to a full-time job with approximately 10 per cent of those unemployed in 2014 indicating that they were seeking part-time employment. The impact of the unemployment crisis was felt right across the age groups and it is only over the past two years that there has been a decrease in the numbers aged above 34 years that are unemployed. Younger age groups have seen their numbers unemployed consistently fall since 2011 – a phenomenon not unrelated to the return of high emigration figures over recent years.[42]

The rapid growth in the number and rates of long-term unemployment are also highlighted in table 5.3 and in chart 5.1. The number of long-term unemployed was less than 32,000 in 2007 and has increased since, reaching 172,100 in 2010 before falling again to 123,400 at the end of 2014. For the first time on record, the QNHS data for late 2010 indicated that long-term unemployment accounted for more than 50 per cent of the unemployed and by the end of 2014 the long-term unemployed represented 58 per cent of the unemployed. The transition to these high levels since 2007 has been rapid – see chart 5.1. The experience of the 1980s showed the dangers and long-lasting implications of an unemployment crisis characterised by high long-term unemployment rates. It remains a major policy failure that Ireland's level of long-term unemployment has been allowed to increase so rapidly in recent years. Furthermore, it is of serious concern that to date Government policy has given limited attention to the issue.

Addressing a crisis such as this is a major challenge and we outline our suggestions for immediate policy action later in the chapter. However, it is clear that reskilling many of the unemployed, in particular those with low education levels, will be a key component of the response. Using the latest data, for 2011, almost 60 per cent of the unemployed had no more than second level education with 30 per cent not having completed more than lower secondary (equivalent to the junior certificate). At the other extreme, the scale and severity of the recession has resulted in high levels of third-level graduates becoming unemployed.[43] While Government should not ignore any group in its overdue attempts to address the unemployment crisis, major emphasis should be placed on those who are most likely to become trapped in long term unemployment – in particular those with the lowest education levels.

---

[42] See chapter 10 for more information on recent migration trends.
[43] The CSO has not updated its profile of unemployment by completed education level since this data.

Table 5.3: Unemployment in Ireland, 2007 - 2014

	2007	2010	2014	Change 07-14
Unemployment	104,600	310,900	213,600	+109,000
Gender				
Male	66,700	211,100	135,500	+68,800
Female	37,900	99,800	78,100	+40,200
Employment sought				
Seeking FT work	85,900	272,600	185,000	+99,100
Seeking PT work	16,200	23,700	21,400	+5,200
Age group				
15-19 years	9,400	18,300	12,100	+2,700
20-24 years	21,700	54,200	26,700	+5,000
25-34 years	33,000	96,800	60,100	+27,100
35-64 years	40,400	140,700	113,800	+73,400
Region				
Border	14,000	29,200	20,600	+6,600
Midland	6,500	20,300	17,200	+10,700
West	8,400	33,000	20,600	+12,200
Dublin	30,200	82,400	55,500	+25,300
Mid-West	9,500	31,100	17,300	+7,800
South-East	12,100	41,700	27,700	+15,600
South-West	14,400	40,200	32,700	+18,300
Mid-East	9,400	33,100	22,000	+12,600
Duration				
Unemp. less than 1 yr	72,000	136,700	85,300	+13,300
Unemp. more than 1 yr	31,700	172,100	123,400	+91,700
LT Unemp. as % Unemp	30.3%	55.4%	57.8%	

Source: CSO, QNHS on-line database
Note: See also notes to table 5.1.

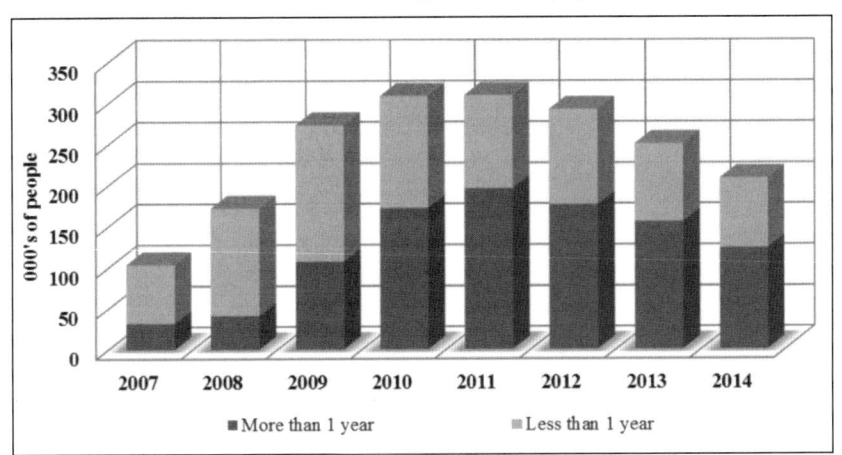

Chart 5.1: The Increased Presence of Long-Term Unemployed in Ireland, 2007-2014

```
350
300
250
200
150
100
 50
  0
     2007  2008  2009  2010  2011  2012  2013  2014
         ■ More than 1 year    ■ Less than 1 year
```
(000's of people)

Source: CSO, QNHS on-line database
Note: Data is for Q4 of each year

Previous experiences, in Ireland and elsewhere, have shown that many of those under 25 and many of those over 55 find it challenging to return to employment after a period of unemployment. This highlights the danger of the aforementioned large increases in long-term unemployment and suggests a major commitment to retraining and re-skilling will be required. In the long-run Irish society can ill afford a return to the long-term unemployment problems of the 1980s. In the short-run the new-unemployed are adding to the numbers living on low-income in Ireland and this, in turn, will continue to have a negative impact on future poverty figures (see chapter 3).

Two further themes arise from the employment and unemployment data and we address these over the next two subsections: youth unemployment and the increase in precarious work. We then conclude this section by examining trends on the live register.

Youth unemployment
While the increase in unemployment has been spread across all ages and sectors (see table 5.3), chart 5.2 highlights the very rapid increase in the numbers unemployed under 25 years-of-age. The numbers in this group more than doubled between 2007 and 2009 peaking at 83,100 in quarter 2 2009. Since then decreases have occurred, reaching 38,000 in late 2014. Although we have limited empirical knowledge of the reasons for these decreases, a large part of the decrease is probably due to emigration.

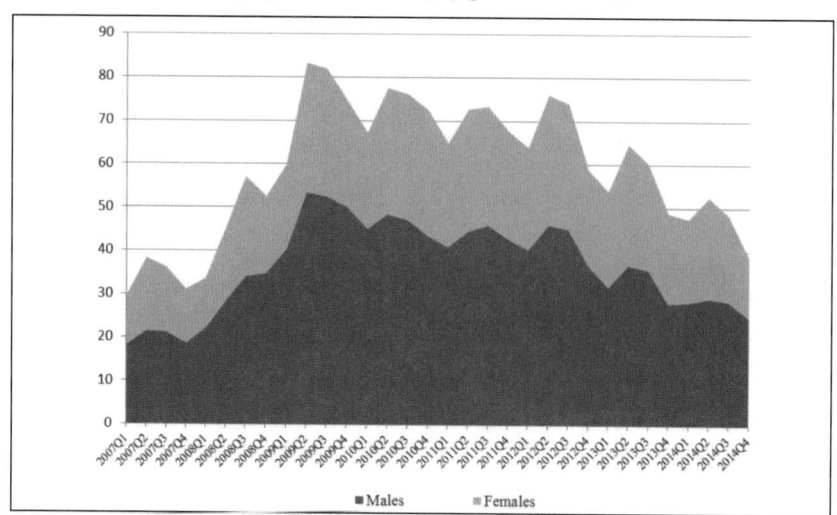

Chart 5.2: Youth Unemployment in Ireland, by gender 2007-2014

Source: CSO, QNHS on-line database.

Although youth unemployment represents about 18 per cent of the total population that are unemployed, there is merit in giving it particular attention. Experiences of unemployment, and in particular long-term unemployment, alongside an inability to access any work, training or education, tends to leave a 'scaring effect' on young people. It increases the challenges associated with getting them active in the labour market at any stage in the future. The latest data on the number of young people aged 18-24 years in Ireland who are not in education, employment or training (NEETs) is 20.5 per cent in 2012 (NERI, 2014).

In the short-term it makes sense for Government to invest in the 'youth unemployed' and *Social Justice Ireland* considers this to be a central priority of any programme to seriously address the unemployment crisis. At a European level, this issue has been receiving welcome attention over the past two years; driven by high levels of youth unemployment in other crisis countries.

Under-employment, Part-time employment and Precarious Work

The figures in table 5.1 also point towards the growth of various forms of precarious work over recent years. Since 2007 employment has fallen by 10 per cent; but this figure masks a bigger decline in full-time employment (15 per cent) and a growth in part-time employment (+14 per cent). Within those part-time employed there has also been an increase in the numbers of people who are underemployed, that is working part-time but at less hours than individuals are willing to work. By the end of 2014 the numbers underemployed stood at 115,500 people, about 5.5 per cent of the total labour force and almost one-quarter of all part-time workers.

While an element of these figures can be explained by the recession, and the suppressed levels of activity in some sectors, they also suggest the emergence of a greater number of workers in precarious employment situations. The growth in the number of individuals with less work hours than ideal, as well as those with persistent uncertainties on the number and times of hours required for work, is a major labour market challenge. Aside from the impact this has on the well-being of individuals and their families, it also impacts on their financial situation and adds to the working-poor challenges we outlined in chapter 3. There are also impacts on the state given that Family Income Supplement (FIS) and the structure of jobseeker payments tends to lead to Government subsidising these families incomes; and indirectly subsidising some employers who create persistent precarious work patterns for their workers.

As the labour market improves, *Social Justice Ireland* believes that now is the time to adopt measures to address and eliminate these problems. Our commitment to the development of a Living Wage (see section 3.3) reflects this. Also in that context, the recent establishment of the Low Pay Commission is a welcome development. It is important that that group provides credible solutions to these labour market challenges and that those proposals are implemented.

The Live Register
While the live register is not an accurate measure of unemployment, it is a useful barometer of the nature and pace of change in employment and unemployment. Increases suggest a combination of more people unemployed, more people on reduced employment weeks and consequently reductions in the availability of employment hours to the labour force. Conversely, reductions signal signs of improvements in job opportunities and/or longer working weeks. Table 5.4 shows that the number of people signing on the live register increased rapidly since the onset of the economic crisis in 2007. The numbers peaked in July 2011 and by January 2015 the numbers signing-on the live register had increased by almost 200,000 compared to seven years earlier.

Table 5.4: Numbers on the Live Register (unadjusted), Jan 2007 - 2015

Year	Month	Males	Females	Total
2007	January	95,824	62,928	158,752
2008	January	116,160	65,289	181,449
2009	January	220,412	105,860	326,272
2010	January	291,648	145,288	436,936
2011	January	292,003	150,674	442,677
2011	July (peak)	297,770	172,514	470,284
2012	January	283,893	155,696	439,589
2013	January	273,627	155,769	429,396
2014	January	248,723	150,907	399,630
2015	January	218,678	139,994	358,672

Source: CSO Live Register on-line database.

The live register data offers a useful insight into the skills and experience of those signing on. Table 5.5 presents a breakdown of the January 2015 live register number by people's last occupation and also examines the differences between those over and under 25 years. The figures once again highlight the need for targeted reskilling of people who hold skills in sectors of the economy that are unlikely to ever return to the employment levels of the early part of the last decade.

Table 5.5: Persons on Live Register by last occupation – January 2015

Occupational group	Overall	Under 25 yrs	Over 25 yrs
Managers and administrators	15,731	404	15,327
Professional	19,773	1,350	18,423
Associate prof.& technical	10,082	1,040	9,042
Clerical and secretarial	33,697	2,245	31,452
Craft and related	71,640	5,411	66,229
Personal and protective service	46,470	6,290	40,180
Sales	38,771	8,536	30,235
Plant and machine operatives	59,316	7,337	51,979
Other occupation	43,032	8,398	34,634
Never worked / not stated	20,160	8,278	11,882
Total	358,672	49,289	309,383

Source: CSO Live Register on-line database.

Responding to the unemployment crisis

Despite recent improvements, the scale of the increases in unemployment since the outset of the economic crisis in 2007 is enormous and it is crucial that Government, commentators and society in general remember that each of these numbers represent people who are experiencing dramatic and, in many cases, unexpected turmoil in their lives and their families' lives. As Irish society comes to terms with the enormity of this issue, we believe that this perspective should remain central.

To date, the policy response to this crisis has been limited, comprising announcements of apprenticeship schemes, 'Job Initiative' reforms, annual Action Plans, the 'Pathways to Work' programme and a few other small policy initiatives. Each of these has targeted minor reforms and had limited success given the scale of the unemployment crisis – for the most part the long-term unemployment, skill deficits, under-employment and precarious work issues have been given limited attention.

In responding to this situation *Social Justice Ireland* believes that Government needs to formulate a clear and integrated set of policy priorities. We set these out in detail in the final section of this chapter.

Even the most optimistic economic and labour market projections for the years to come suggest that unemployment will remain a major factor. The Department of Finance's estimates in Budget 2015 point towards a rate 9.4 per cent in 2016; we anticipate this figure will be revised down during 2015 towards 9 per cent. As recovery emerges, it is important that policy focuses on those furthest from being able to rejoin the numbers employed and assist those within employment but struggling as the working poor.

Work and people with disabilities

Results from Census 2011 have provided new data on the scale and nature of disability in Ireland. In a report published in November 2012, the CSO reported that a total of 595,335 people had a disability in Ireland; equivalent to 13 per cent of the population. The most common disability overall was a difficulty with pain, breathing or other chronic illness or condition which was experienced by 46.2 per cent of all people with a disability; this was followed by a difficulty with basic physical activities, experienced by 41.1 per cent. The report found that both of these disabilities were strongly age-related. It also showed that 1.1 per cent of the population were blind or had a sight related disability (51,718 people); 1.3 per cent of the population suffered from an intellectual disability (57,709 people); 2 per cent of the population were deaf or had a hearing related disability (92,060 people); 2.1 per cent of the population had a psychological or emotional condition (96,004 people); 3 per cent of the population had a difficulty with learning, remembering or concentrating (137,070 people); 5.3 per cent of the population had a difficulty with basic physical activities (244,739 people); and 6 per cent of the population had a disability connected with pain, breathing or another chronic illness or condition (274,762 people) (CSO, 2012: 45, 51-53).[44]

The Census 2011 data also revealed that there was 162,681 persons with a disability in the labour force representing a participation rate of 30 per cent, less than half that for the population in general. These findings reflect earlier results from the 2006 National Disability Survey (CSO, 2008 and 2010) and a 2004 QNHS special module on disability (CSO, 2004). This low rate of employment among people with a disability is of concern. Apart from restricting their participation in society it also ties them into state dependent low-income situations. Therefore, it is not surprising that Ireland's poverty figures reveal that people who are ill or have a disability are part of a group at high risk of poverty (see chapter 3).

Social Justice Ireland believes that further efforts should be made to reduce the impediments faced by people with a disability to obtain employment. In particular, consideration should be given to reforming the current situation in which many such people face losing their benefits, in particular their medical card, when they take up employment. This situation ignores the additional costs faced by people with a disability in pursuing their day-to-day lives. For many people with disabilities the opportunity to take up employment is denied to them and they are trapped in unemployment, poverty or both.

Some progress was made in Budget 2005 to increase supports intended to help people with disabilities access employment. However, sufficient progress has not been made and recent Budgets have begun to reduce these services. New policies, including that outlined above, need to be adopted if this issue is to be addressed successfully. It is even more relevant today, given the growing employment challenges of the past few years.

Asylum seekers and work

Social Justice Ireland is very disappointed that the government continues to reject any proposal that recognises the right to work for asylum seekers. Along with others, we have consistently advocated that where government fails to meet its own stated objective of processing asylum applications in six months, the right to work should be automatically granted to asylum seekers. Detaining people for an unnecessarily prolonged period in such an excluded state is completely unacceptable. Recognising

---

[44] Note, some individuals will experience more than one disability and feature in more than one of these categories.

asylum seekers' right to work would assist in alleviating poverty and social exclusion in one of Ireland's most vulnerable groups.[45]

The need to recognise all work

A major question raised by the current labour-market situation concerns assumptions underpinning culture and policy making in this area. The priority given to paid employment over other forms of work is one such assumption. Most people recognise that a person can be working very hard outside a conventionally accepted "job". Much of the work carried out in the community and in the voluntary sector comes under this heading. So too does much of the work done in the home. *Social Justice Ireland*'s support for the introduction of a basic income system comes, in part, because it believes that all work should be recognised and supported (see chapter 3).

The need to recognise voluntary work has been acknowledged in the Government White Paper, *Supporting Voluntary Activity* (Department of Social, Community and Family Affairs, 2000). The report was prepared to mark the UN International Year of the Volunteer 2001 by Government and representatives of numerous voluntary organisations in Ireland. The report made a series of recommendations to assist in the future development and recognition of voluntary activity throughout Ireland. A 2005 report presented to the Joint Oireachtas Committee on Arts, Sport, Tourism, Community, Rural and Gaeltacht Affairs also provided an insight into this issue. It established that the cost to the state of replacing the 475,000 volunteers working for charitable organisations would be at least €205 million and could be as high as €485 million per year.

Social Justice Ireland believes that government should recognise in a more formal way all forms of work. We believe that everyone has a right to work, to contribute to his or her own development and that of the community and wider society. However, we believe that policy making in this area should not be exclusively focused on job creation. Policy should recognise that *work* and a *job* are not always the same thing.

The Work of Carers

The work of Ireland's carers receives minimal recognition despite the essential role their work plays in society. Results from the 2011 Census offer a new insight into the scale of these commitments, which save the state large costs that it would otherwise have to bear.

---

[45] We examine this issue in further detail in chapter 10.

Census 2011 found that 4.1 per cent of the population aged over 15 provided some care for sick or disabled family members or friends on an unpaid basis. This figure equates to 187,112 people. The dominant caring role played by women was highlighted by the fact that 114,113 (61 per cent) of these care providers were female.[46] When assessed by length of time, the census found that a total of 6,287,510 hours of care were provided by carers each week, representing an average of 33.6 hours of unpaid help and assistance each. Two thirds of this volume of care was provided by female carers (CSO, 2012: 71-77). Using the minimum wage as a simple (an unrealistically low) benchmark to establish the benefit which carers provide each year suggests that Ireland's carers provide care valued at more than €2.8bn per annum.

Social Justice Ireland welcomed the long overdue publication of a *National Carers Strategy* in July 2012 (Department of Health, 2012). The document included a 'roadmap for implementation' involving a suite of actions, and associated timelines and identifies the Government Department responsible for their implementation. However, these actions were confined to those that could be achieved on a cost neutral basis. Two annual progress reports of the strategy have been published by Minister Kathleen Lynch (Department of Health, 2014, 2015). They point towards some progress on the actions set out, but these are, as a group, limited given the unwillingness of Government to allocate sufficient resources to supporting those in this sector.

Social Justice Ireland believes that further policy reforms should be introduced to reduce the financial and emotional pressures on carers. In particular, these should focus on addressing the poverty experienced by many carers and their families alongside increasing the provision of respite care for carers and for those for whom they care. In this context, the 24 hour responsibilities of carers contrast with the improvements over recent years in employment legislation setting limits on working-hours of people in paid employment.

Key policy priorities on work, unemployment and job creation

- Adopt the following policy positions in responding to the challenges on unemployment arising from the recession:
    - Launch a major investment programme focused on creating employment and prioritise initiatives that strengthen social infrastructure, including a comprehensive school building programme and a much larger social housing programme.
    - Resource the up-skilling of those who are unemployed and at risk of

---

[46] A CSO QNHS special module on carers (CSO, 2010) and a 2008 ESRI study entitled '*Gender Inequalities in Time Use*' found similar trends (McGinnity and Russell, 2008:36, 70).

- becoming unemployed through integrating training and labour market programmes.
- Maintain a sufficient number of active labour market programme places available to those who are unemployed.
- Adopt policies to address the worrying trend of youth unemployment. In particular, these should include education and literacy initiatives as well as retraining schemes.
- Recognise that many of the unemployed are skilled professionals who require appropriate support other than training.
- Resource a targeted re-training scheme for those previously unemployed in the construction industry, recognising that this industry is never likely to recover to the level of employment it had prior to 2007.
- Recognise the scale of the evolving long-term unemployment problem and adopt targeted policies to begin to address this.
- Ensure that the social welfare system is administered such that there is minimal delays in paying the newly unemployed the social welfare benefits to which they are entitled.

• Funded programmes supporting the community should be expanded to meet the growing pressures arising as a result of the recent economic downturn.

• A new programme should be put in place targeting those who are very long-term unemployed (i.e. 5+ years).

• Policy should seek at all times to ensure that new jobs have reasonable pay rates and adequately resource the labour inspectorate.

• As part of the process of addressing the working poor issue, reform the taxation system to make tax credits refundable.

• Develop employment-friendly income-tax policies which ensure that no unemployment traps exist. Policies should ease the transition from unemployment to employment.

• Adopt policies to address the obstacles facing women when they return to the labour force. These should focus on care initiatives, employment flexibility and the provision of information and training.

• Reduce the impediments faced by people with a disability in achieving employment. In particular, address the current situation in which many face losing their benefits when they take up employment.

• Recognise the right to work of all asylum seekers whose application for asylum is at least six months old and who are not entitled to take up employment.

• Recognise that the term "work" is not synonymous with the concept of "paid employment". Everybody has a right to work, i.e. to contribute to his or her own development and that of the community and the wider society. This, however, should not be confined to job creation. *Work* and a *job* are not the same thing.

- Request the CSO to conduct an annual survey to discover the value of all unpaid work in the country (including community and voluntary work and work in the home). Publish the results of this survey as soon as they become available.
- Give greater recognition to the work carried out by carers in Ireland and introduce policy reforms to reduce the financial and emotional pressures on carers. In particular, these should focus on addressing the poverty experienced by many carers and their families as well as on increasing the provision of respite opportunities to carers and to those for whom they care.

6.
PUBLIC SERVICES

CORE POLICY OBJECTIVE: PUBLIC SERVICES
To ensure the provision of, and access to, a level of public services regarded as acceptable by Irish society generally

Later chapters will analyse a range of public services such as healthcare, education and housing. This Chapter, however, looks at public services in a range of areas not addressed elsewhere. These include public transport, library services, financial services, information and communications technology, telecommunications, free legal aid, sports facilities and regulation.

Public Transport

Access to adequate public transport is a key component of modern society. In the wake of the economic collapse, many households remain on the commuter belt of urban centres in properties with negative equity mortgages that were originally intended to be 'starter homes' for young professionals. These families need proper access to local and regional amenities, including schools and hospitals, as well as a cost-effective way to maintain social networks with family and friends. While great improvements have been made to motorways connecting urban centres, the country's national roads remain in a state of disrepair. This in turn leads to isolation in many rural areas where access to social outlets is more difficult. Social isolation, which is highest among the elderly, poor and minorities, has an adverse effect on health, in particular stress related disorders and anxiety (Cacioppo and Hawkley, 2003) and has been compared to other major health risks such as smoking (House, 2001). In addition, research also suggests that an increase in the use of public transport would have the effect of increasing physical activity by between an additional eight and 33 minutes of walking per day, leading to increased population health overall (Rissel et al, 2012).

The National Roads Authority *National Road Network Indicators 2013* (National Roads Authority, 2014) segregates road types into five categories, depending on type of pavement construction, age, and traffic volumes carried. A large proportion of roads in rural areas are classified as legacy pavement with low or very low traffic (2014:20). These roads are 'typically constructed without formal geometric or pavement design' and tend to be in the poorest condition. It is not surprising then that the rural single carriageways had the highest rate of fatal collisions per 100 million kilometres over the period 2007-11 and the second highest rate of serious injuries per 100 million kilometres in the same period (although these rates are in decline). Motorways, where the majority of improvements have been made, consistently have the lowest fatality and injury rates. The apparent correlation between road repair and road accidents is argument alone for expenditure to be allocated to improve the country's road networks, in addition to addressing the unseen damage of social isolation and related issues.

A profile from Census 2011 (CSO, 2012) found that the number of commuters using public transport (bus or train) declined by over 20 per cent in the intercensal period 2006-11. There was, however, an increase of 40,000 on the number of people commuting by train, DART or LUAS between 1981 and 2011, doubling the share of commuters using the train (2012:9). Dublin had the highest percentage of users (21 per cent), compared with 6.8 per cent in Cork, 6.4 per cent in Galway, 4.4 per cent in Limerick and 1.8 per cent in the aggregate rural areas (2012:11). This stark contrast between Dublin and the rest of the country only highlights the disparity of functioning public transport between urban and rural locations. In 2013, the Department of Transport, Tourism and Sport issued plans for restructuring the Rural Transport Programme (2013). These plans build on the Rural Transport Initiative of 2002 and Rural Transport Programme of 2007 which work with a collective of private rural transport companies which supplement the national network and seeks to address the high administrative costs of providing rural transport. However, costs cannot be the only consideration when reviewing how public transport operates in rural areas. Accessibility, end-user costs and frequency must also be considerations.

Library Services

Libraries provide an important social and educational outlet in Ireland, with 17.1 million visits annually[47]. They are run by 32 library authorities assisted by An Chomhairle Leabharlanna (the Library Council) to develop library services. The services provided by libraries have evolved to include internet access, online journals and according to the latest figures there are 1.9 million internet sessions provided every year in libraries and 19.3 million books, audio books, CDs and DVDs are borrowed.

---

[47] http://www.askaboutireland.ie/libraries/public-libraries/fast-facts-and-figures/

Libraries play an important role in Irish society, performing a valuable community and educational service and ensuring access to reading, information and learning. 'They provide a focal point for community and intergenerational contact, and enable access to learning and an ever-expanding range of information for a wide constituency through an increasingly broad and varied range of media' (McGrath et al, 2010: 6). Recent research by the Carnegie Trust (2012) indicated that overall more than three quarters (79 per cent) of those in Ireland said that libraries were 'very important' or 'essential' for communities. This was higher than any other jurisdiction included in this research.

The last available statistics from the Public Library Authority (2011) further underscore the important function that libraries play in Ireland. In that year registered membership of libraries increased by 11.3per cent from 809,169 to 900,811. Fractionally under one in five of the population (19.6 per cent) are registered as members of the public library service, up from 19.1 per cent in 2010. Visits to full-time branches increased by 11.9 per cent from 14.7 million to 16.45 million and estimated visits to all branches increased by 1.1 million over 2010 (Public Library Authority, 2011). In 2012 Local authorities invested €137 million of their revenue budgets on public library services, a 2.6 per cent decrease on 2011. Although this figure represents a decrease, library expenditure as a proportion of overall local authority expenditure remains at 3.3 per cent. Total local authority expenditure on library stock decreased by 12.1 per cent in 2012 and this is of particular concern in light of the growing demand for the service and the need to preserve quality (An Comhairle Leabharlanna, 2012).

'Branching Out' (Department of Environment, Heritage and Local Government, 2008) was a major review of library services in Ireland and built on a publication of the same name published in 1998 (Department of Environment, Heritage and Local Government, 1998). Between 1998 and 2008, when this review of policy was published, there were significant improvements in the services provided by libraries. These included improvements in book collections, ICT infrastructure and electronic services and building infrastructure. According to the review, it is imperative that the improvements made in the library service to date are maintained. This is particularly important given the continued growth in demand on library services.

While, great improvements have been made and a vision of a vibrant library service is articulated in the new strategy, *Opportunities for All: A Strategy for Public Libraries 2013-2017* there have been reductions in regard to funding for libraries over the past number of years. One of its key recommendations in this strategy concerns the need for public libraries to 'explore the potential to secure additional funding through philanthropy, enterprise, public-private partnership and other alternative sources' (Department of Environment, Community and Local Government 2013:35). The securing of additional funding should not be utilised as a means to further reduce funding to public libraries. This is particularly pertinent in light of the role of public libraries as the public face of local government in the community and Government's vision that they promote active citizenship, lifelong learning and support the needs of both entrepreneurs and those seeking employment (Department of Environment, Community and Local Government 2013).

The issue of fees is viewed as a barrier to use, with An Chomhairle Leabharlanna's 2010 annual report concluding that the benefits of free access outweigh the value of the money gained. This is a particularly important point in terms of social inclusion, promoting active citizenship and lifelong learning. *Social Justice Ireland* urges local authorities to reconsider this measure; indeed, one of the aims in the new strategy indicates that libraries will attempt to ensure equity of access for all through the provision of free core services by 2017.

Public libraries play a crucial role in Irish society and have the potential to play an even more important role into the future. *Social Justice Ireland* believes that, as part of our commitment to providing a continuum of education provision from early childhood to third level and throughout the life-cycle, Ireland needs to recognise the potential that the library service offers. This requires ready availability and easy access to information. Coupled with this is the need for easy access to modern means of communication. Libraries are obvious centres with potential to support these objectives. To play this potential role, continued support for, and expansion of, the library service is essential.

Financial Services

Access to finance, particularly in today's cashless society, is key to inclusion in society generally. Collard and Kempson (2005) found that those on low incomes are often restricted from accessing mainstream credit, turning instead to subprime and high-cost credit alternatives. While a low income does not always mean over-indebtedness, the report found that there was a significantly higher instance of over-indebtedness among households with gross annual incomes of under £10,000 (23 per cent) than households of more than £35,000 (5 per cent). Corr (2006), expanded on Korczak's (2004) findings, enumerating a number of barriers to financial inclusion relating to both access to financial services and use thereof. She also found, in line with Collard and Kempson (2005) that a low income is the most significant influence on financial exclusion. The result of this financial exclusion, according to Corr, is that over-indebted and low income consumers are excluded from banking services on the basis of charges and conditions attaching; affordable credit on the basis of conditions attaching and difficulty of the application process; and insurance, as low-income consumers are more likely to live in disadvantaged areas, incurring a higher premium.

Gloukoviezoff (2011) defines the process of financial exclusion as (2011:12):

...the process whereby people face such financial difficulties of access or use that they cannot lead a normal life in the society to which they belong.

This differs from Russell et al. (2011:20) who, in considering the impact of financial exclusion and over-indebtedness, finds that it is possible for over-indebtedness to be both a cause and effect of financial exclusion, particularly where access to credit is hindered by a poor credit record.

In their vision for financial inclusion, Kempson and Collard (2012) focused part of their research on the influence of financial capability and over-indebtedness on financial inclusion. As in the case of Russell et al. (2011), they found that an increased number of debtors accessing high-cost credit were doing so as a result of already being financially impaired 'with either a history of bad debt...or an adverse credit rating' (2011:12).

In their 2011 study, Russell et al (2011) found that there were connections between financial exclusion and over-indebtedness and that both may be causally related (2011:20), with causation running either way. They found that Ireland had the highest instance of banking exclusion among the EU15 States and that those who are economically and socially disadvantaged, and those on low incomes, are at most risk of financial exclusion (2011:29). Using the Household Budget Survey (HBS) 2004-2005 Russell et al. measured the level of access to bank accounts with reference to income quintile, finding a direct linear relationship between increased access and higher income (2011:31). The HBS 2009-2010 shows an increase in the level of bank account ownership in the State, from 80 per cent in 2004-2005 to 91 per cent in 2009-2010 (2011:254), however the linear relationship remains.

The Report of the Steering Group on Financial Inclusion recognised the social and economic consequences of financial exclusion (Department of Finance, 2011:11) and recommended as a 'first necessary step' the introduction of a BPA to enable users to 'move from managing their affairs entirely in cash to electronic money management' (2011:23). The BPA would also facilitate better budgeting, and provide an access point to other financial services (2011:24).

The BPA was introduced by an amendment to the Finance Act, 2012 (section 104), as an account meeting certain conditions, including the user not having had access to a card account (or using an account he/she had access to) in the last three years; all Social Welfare payments must be made to the BPA; and the balance in any two consecutive quarters must not exceed €2,000.

To date, there is no information regarding the use of the BPA among the financially excluded or any evaluation of the impact it may have had in returning to mainstream financial services.

Financial literacy, the ability to understand the financial options available, including the pros and cons, is an important component of financial inclusion. *Social Justice Ireland* welcomes the initiatives of the Competition and Consumer Protection Commission in tackling this important issue and making available resources for all ages and abilities.

Information and Communications Technology

In 2014 an estimated 82 per cent of households had access to the internet at home. This was an increase of 19 percentage points since 2008. Portable computers (including netbooks and tablets) were the most popular devices used to access the internet in the household. There has been strong growth each year in internet connections. 80 per cent of individuals used the internet in the 3 months prior to the survey, with 86 per cent of the 16-29 age category using the internet every day (CSO, 2014). However, almost one in five Irish adults have never used the internet, with over half of people aged 60 to 74 having never used the internet (Department of Communication, Energy, Natural Resources, 2013).

These figures underscore the progressively important role that ICT plays in modern society and the level of progress being made in regard to access to digital technology in Ireland. 'Digital literacy is increasingly becoming an essential life competence and the inability to access or use ICT has effectively become a barrier to social integration and personal development. Those without sufficient ICT skills are disadvantaged in the labour market and have less access to information to empower themselves as consumers, or as citizens saving time and money in offline activities and using online public services (European Commission, 2008: 4). Digital competence is also one of the competencies highlighted as part of the key competencies required for lifelong learning by the European Commission in 2006. Factors such as disability, age and social disadvantage all have significant roles to play in increasing digital exclusion. Apart from the impact on the individual, there are also losses to the business community and the economy at large (McDaid & Cullen, 2008). The OECD Adult Skills Survey (PIAAC - discussed in more detail in chapter 9) examined adult competency in problem solving in technology rich environments. The results show that 10 per cent of Irish adults stated they had no computer experience, 5 per cent failed the assessment and 42 per cent scored at or below Level 1 on the assessment. These figures highlight the gaps in digital literacy and digital skills that remain in Ireland.

In 2012 the Government published its digital strategy for delivering public services. Covering the period 2012 to 2015, this strategy encourages greater sharing of data between Government public bodies, wider adoption of online payments and the use of smartphone optimised sites and apps. It also identified a number of services which may be particularly suitable for electronic delivery, such as the renewal of adult passports, planning applications and objections and welfare applications. With this increasing focus on digital communication and a move to the delivery of services via electronic formats, Government needs to show sustained commitment to counteract the issue of digital exclusion in particular for the more vulnerable sectors of society. The Government in 2013 committed to getting 288,000 people "on line" over the period to 2016. Delivering a new scheme [BenefIT 4] which targets specific groups most likely to be non-internet users for digital skills training-- funding of €1.4m was provided in 2013 for training 24,000 citizens at multiple locations across Ireland (Department of Communication, Energy, Natural Resources, 2013). The scheme was expanded in late 2014 to provide digital skills training to a further 12,000 people. This continued rollout is critical as only 53 per cent of the population have sufficient digital skills to operate effectively online, down from 56 per cent in 2012 (European Commission, 2015).

At an economic level this is essential to promote competitiveness and effectiveness, while at a social services level it is essential to ensure digital exclusion does not become another form of exclusion being experienced by those who are already vulnerable. This is particularly pertinent for rural dwellers, who having experienced the removal of some public services are now expected to access public services via digital and electronic format. Government has committed to the roll out of the fibre infrastructure for rural broadband (see chapter 12 for details) – this will be essential to ensure that people living in rural areas have the same access to public services electronically as their counterparts in urban areas.

Telecommunications

Two issues are of note in this area. Firstly, the Commission for Communications Regulation (ComReg) has put in place a system to ensure that a basic set of telecommunications services is available to all consumers throughout the country. This is known as a Universal Service Obligation (USO). The services to be provided include: meeting reasonable requests for connections at a fixed location to the public communications network and access to publicly available telephone service; provision of directory services and maintenance of the national directory database; public telephone provision; specific services for disabled users; affordability of tariffs and options for consumers to control expenditure (ComReg, 2011: 13). Eircom is the designated Universal Service Provider (USP) and has a number of obligations regarding the supply of these services. *Social Justice Ireland* welcomes the vigilance of ComReg in maintaining the quality of the service provided under this obligation, taking into account any potential negative effects on disadvantaged members of the community were these obligations not to be met. Eircom was re-designated as the Universal Service Provider in July 2014 with the term set to last until 31 December 2015 (ComReg, 2014).

Secondly, as part of the Digital Agenda for Europe, the European Commission has set targets of 30mbps broadband for all citizens and 50 per cent of citizens subscribing to 100mbps by 2020. While there have been substantial increases in the numbers of people connecting to the internet and subscribing to high speed broadband, Ireland is still performing badly in relation to the roll-out and take-up of advanced broadband services, particularly in rural areas. Ireland now ranks 9th out of the 28 EU member states with subscriptions for high speed broadband increasing to 40 per cent in 2014. Ireland now falls into the cluster of medium-performance countries on the European Digital Economy and Society Index. Prices for fixed broadband in Ireland are almost double the EU average when measured as a proportion of income, and while 96 per cent of Irish households are covered by fixed broadband take up is only 62 per cent (European Commission, 2015). The European commission also notes that prices for fixed broadband in Ireland rose in 2014. Such disparities between Ireland and the rest of the European Union in terms of the price for fixed broadband means that those living on low incomes are in danger of being left behind. This is particularly worrying at a time when there is a drive to get people to access public services electronically.

Ireland still has a long way to go to ensure all households and businesses have access to quality high speed broadband. 'Given the weak telecommunications investment climate in Ireland, our dispersed population patterns and the recession, there is a strong risk, if appropriate action is not taken, that Ireland is likely to fall even further behind as other countries are moving ahead to deploy advanced telecoms networks' (Forfas, 2011:27).

Government has recognised the need to address Ireland's performance in regard to advanced broadband technology, The National Broadband Plan was published in August 2012 committing to the role-out of:

- 70Mbps – 100Mbps to more than half of the population by 2015;

- at least 40Mbps, and in many cases much faster speeds, to at least a further 20 per cent of the population and potentially as much as 35 per cent around smaller towns and villages; and

- a minimum of 30Mbps for every remaining home and business in the country – no matter how rural or remote (Department of Communications, Energy and Natural Resources, 2012:1).

Government has published maps which identify which areas of the country will be provided with broadband by a commercial operator and which parts of the country will require direct state intervention (broadband.gov.ie). The commercial telecoms industry intends to deliver high-speed broadband access to 68 per cent of premises in the state – 1.6 million homes and businesses by the end of 2016. The remaining

600,000 homes and 100,000 businesses will require direct State intervention in order to access high-speed broadband access. This will require a major infrastructural programme. The tender process for the fibre infrastructure roll-out is due to be completed by December 2015. Government aims to ensure that all homes and premises have access to high-speed broadband by 2020[48]. The roll-out and delivery of high quality broadband particularly to rural areas will need to be monitored carefully, in terms of cost and quality; this is vital to ensure access for all.

Free Legal Aid

The function of laws in democratic society is to protect the rights of citizens from unjust attack. While the distribution of rights is not explicitly discriminatory, access to their protection for those on low income can be difficult to secure. The Legal Aid Board provides advice and representation for those on low income on civil legal matters. Those in need of civil legal aid are subject to means testing and pay a nominal fee of between €30 and €150 for this service. Their case is also subject to a merits test to ascertain if the case has a chance of success.

The range of civil legal services provided by the Legal Aid Board includes those relating to family law matters (including separation and divorce and custody), debt and wills and inheritance. While not directly providing criminal legal aid, the Legal Aid Board is also responsible for the management and administration of three criminal legal aid schemes – the Garda Station Legal Advice Revised Scheme, the Legal Aid – Custody Issues Scheme, and the Criminal Assets Bureau Ad-hoc Legal Aid Scheme.

According to the website of the Legal Aid Board, most law centres operate on the basis that the applicant will receive a first consultation within three to four months. If further advice is required after this initial consultation, the applicant will be placed back on the waiting list and may have to wait another number of months for a second appointment. Figures available for December 2014 show the highest maximum waiting time for a first appointment of 46 weeks in Tallaght, Dublin, with the lowest maximum waiting time of eight weeks in Letterkenny, Nenagh and Portlaoise. Maximum waiting times for second appointments vary between a high of 65 weeks in Tallaght and Francis St. in Galway, and a low of four weeks in Newbridge[49]. The 2013 Annual Report of the Legal Aid Board (Legal Aid Board, 2014)

---

[48] http://www.dcenr.gov.ie/Press+Releases/2014/Minister+Alex+White+publishes+national+broadband+coverage+map+and+consultation+in+significant+step+t.htm

[49] Where a law centre operates a different waiting list scheme to that outlined by the Legal Aid Board and restated above, the maximum waiting time for a second appointment is listed as 0. This is the case for Blanchardstown, Dundalk, Monaghan, Tralee, Waterford and Wicklow.

shows that the number of applicants on waiting lists for its service more than doubled in the period 2009-13 (from 2228 in 2009 to 5067 in 2013) (2014:20).

The majority of funding for the Legal Aid Board is derived from an annual Grant in Aid received from the Department of Justice. In 2013, this Grant in Aid amounted to €33.759 million, an increase from €32.922 million in the previous year. While funding has increased in recent years, so too has the number in need of the services provided by the Legal Aid Board and so, in turn, has the length of the waiting lists.

In its report on legal aid in Ireland, the Law Society (2012) surmised that the delays in accessing legal aid was 'potentially a breach of a person's fundamental human rights where they are denied access to legal services and ultimately denied effective access to the legal system.' (2012:9). The report found that delay in accessing legal aid were having a detrimental impact on applicants and their families and personal circumstances.

Social Justice Ireland calls on the Government to ensure adequate resources are allocated to the Legal Aid Board to allow them reduce the waiting times and ensure access to justice for all.

Sports Facilities

Sport is an important part of Ireland's social and cultural heritage. Research has also found that youth involvement in sport has helped combat social problems and antisocial behaviours such as drug and alcohol addictions, truancy and petty crime (Jarrett, Sullivan and Watkins, 2005).

Under the Department of Transport, Tourism and Sport, the Sports Capital Programme aims to support local communities to engage in sports programmes that benefit those communities, prioritises the needs of disadvantaged areas in the provision of sports facilities and encourages the multi-use of sports facilities by local community groups by providing grants to individual organisations. Between 17th January 2014 and 10th March 2014 (the applications deadline), 2036 applications were made for grants, with a total of €34,129,280 allocated in respect of local sports capital allocations, €6,356,852 allocated in respect of non-local sports capital allocations (including active retirement programmes), €1,026,000 allocated in respect of special NGB (National Government Body) equipment grants and €3,565,648 allocated in respect of other sports programmes, a total of €45,077,780. This compares to €1,990,745 in Sports Capital Allocations in 2013, and €35,435,879 in Sports Capital Programme and Special Allocations in 2012 (Department of Transport, Tourism and Sport, 2015).

While funding is available in respect of sports facilities, no specific funding is allocated to participation initiatives to motivate people to engage in sport and to reduce the rate of those dropping out of sporting activities. A recent report from the ESRI (Lunn, Kelly and Fitzpatrick, 2013) identified a number of policy implications aimed at retaining participation rates post-primary school (when participation rates in sporting activities are at their highest, at almost 90 per cent), which include making physical education an examinable subject to combat drop-out rates at secondary school level, particularly in exam years; increased participation programmes involving local community organisation to encourage adult participation; and consideration by the GAA of ways in which participation post-second level education might be continued. The first of these policy implications was supported by a survey undertaken by a major health insurance provider which found that 80 per cent of teachers believed that physical education should be examinable. However, with straitened resources in schools and education policy currently under pressure for other reasons it is unlikely to happen in the coming years. Small initiatives such as the Go for Life Small Grant Scheme, which awarded almost €300,000 in grants to older persons' groups in 2014, and local Sports Partnerships are encouraging adult participation in sport at local level, however in order to be effective regular and sufficient funding is required.

The role of the GAA in local communities cannot be overstated. It not only provides a physical outlet for those playing the game, but also a social and recreational space for communities to get involved in fundraising and volunteering activities. The Strategic Report 2015-2017 (GAA, 2014) of the GAA has as a primary strategic goal 'to increase player and member participation and to support the continued growth of the Association'. The strategies for achieving this goal include the development of a recruitment programme; implementing new participation models in communities, including development of participation centres in each county; increasing participation in recreational games across the Association targeted at specific groups; targeted retention programmes for the 12 to 20 year age group (the group identified as most at risk of drop-out by the ESRI); review coaching and fixture programmes; and establishing the Respect Programme as a core element of the game.

In September 2014 the Government introduced an exemption for Community Sports Clubs from rates on those facilities used solely for sports, with those parts of the buildings used for commercial purposes (such as bars, shops, cafes and so on) being subject to rates. While *Social Justice Ireland* welcomes this exemption as increasing the revenue available to sports clubs, it is not enough to address the overarching need to increase participation throughout the lifecycle. The Government must be cognisant of the health, societal and economic benefits of sports and social outlets and provide sufficient ring-fenced funding for the promotion and retention of participation.

Regulation

Regulatory policy has been lacking in Ireland for decades. While financial regulation is probably to the forefront of people's minds in this context, a lack of vision and direction in the areas of energy, communications and healthcare has created the position whereby regulation is used as a means to protect competiveness in an increasingly privatised marketplace rather than a method of consumer protection *Social Justice Ireland* believes that regulation has a place in protecting the rights of the vulnerable in addressing the balance of power when engaging with corporations, but not be so involved as to increase bureaucracy, creating a barrier rather than a safety net.

A recent working paper on the history and future of regulation in Ireland (Brown and Scott, 2010) credits EU liberalist policies for the transition of the regulatory structure from one of State ownership, to one of a single open market. This had a knock-on effect on public perception of State-owned entities as inefficient, poor quality and highly subsidised with no incentive to reduce cost or improve services (2010:7). Increasing privatisation, while not as extensive as in other countries, saw the State divest itself of organisations in areas including telecommunications, finance and air travel, areas that did not benefit from lack of State intervention. Where the State retained an interest in companies, such as VHI, Bord na Mona, regulation was separated from total State control to provide for competition from private operators.

Ireland has also seen a steady rise in the number of State agencies, which has peaked in the last number of years. Brown and Scott (2010) attribute this to a 'taken for granted-ness' that regulatory agencies will solve all regulatory problems, however given the fractious nature of the establishment of these agencies, and their diverse reporting requirements to their governing Departments, increased agencification has not had the effect of creating a unified regulatory platform, but of creating a panacea of divergent agencies with varying levels of political involvement.

The OECD, in its report on regulation in Ireland (2010), acknowledged the work undertaken by the Irish Government since the downturn in seeking to address the regulatory issues that attributed to the crash, but found that progress in this area was slow and the structures and communications needed to be simplified.

Social Justice Ireland believes that regulation should not have at its centre the aim of increasing market participation over consumer protection. Before engaging in any new regulatory processes, the Government should ensure that the rights of its citizens are protected, including the right to a reasonable standard of living with access to basic services at a reasonable cost.

Key policy priorities for public services

- Develop an integrated public transport network ensuring that commuters can access local, regional and national transport services.
- Ensure adequate support for the Rural transport Initiative.
- Ensure adequate support and funding of public library services including the provision of open-access information technology.
- Ensure the roll out of rural broadband to all households and premises across the State.

7.
HOUSING AND ACCOMMODATION

CORE POLICY OBJECTIVE: HOUSING & ACCOMMODATION
To ensure that adequate and appropriate accommodation is available for all people and to develop an equitable system for allocating resources within the housing sector.

For too long housing was looked upon as a commodity rather than a home, with policy benefiting those who could afford to speculate on the 'property market' and leaving behind those in need of basic shelter. The right to adequate housing should be a basic human right recognised and respected by every State. Unfortunately, there is no legal entitlement to housing in Ireland. The Constitutional Convention called for the right to housing to be listed among those economic, social and cultural rights to be expressly stated in any revision of the Constitution of Ireland (Constitutional Convention, 2014:4). However, no constitutional or legislative change has been forthcoming. In its Summary of Social Housing Assessments 2013, the Housing Agency identified 89,872 households which were assessed as qualifying for social housing (Housing Agency, 2013). Of these 60% (54,045) were on the housing list for more than two years and 55% (49,179) were families. While the figure of 89,872 appears to represent a reduction on previous years, it should be noted that different methodology was used to carry out housing assessments, as discussed in greater detail in *Social Justice Ireland*'s Socio-Economic Review 2014.

Housing Supply and Adequacy

Housing Supply
According to Census 2011 (CSO, 2012(a)) there were 1,994,845 permanent dwelling units in the State in April of that year, of which 83 per cent were occupied on Census night. While this figure represents an increase on Census 2006, it shows a clear

reduction in the rate of housing stock growth with only 12.7 per cent in the intercensal period 2006-11, down from 21 per cent in the 2002-6 period. Recent statistics available from the Department of Environment, Community and Local Government put total housing stock to over two million dwellings for the year ending 2013 (Department of the Environment, Community and Local Government, 2014(a)). Table 7.1 shows house completions in the various sectors from 2001 to date. While the rate of private housing completions has seen a moderate increase in the first three quarters of 2014, local authority and voluntary/non-profit housing remains low.

Table 7.1: House Completions, 2001-14

Year	Local Authority Housing	Voluntary /Non Profit Housing	Private Housing	Total
2001	3,622	1,253	47,727	52,602
2002	4,403	1,360	51,932	57,695
2003	4,516	1,617	62,686	68,819
2004	3,539	1,607	71,808	76,954
2005	4,209	1,350	75,398	80,957
2006	3,968	1,240	88,211	93,419
2007	4,986	1,685	71,356	78,027
2008	4,905	1,896	44,923	51,721
2009	3,362	2,011	21,076	26,420
2010	1,328	741	12,533	14,602
2011	486	745	9,295	10,480
2012	363	653	7,472	8,488
2013	293	211	7,797	8,301
2014 up to Q3	56	178	7,555	7,789

Source: Department of Environment, Community and Local Government Housing Statistics (2015). Note: Local authority house completions do not include second-hand houses acquired by them. New units acquired under Part V, Planning & Development Acts 2000-2006 for local authority rental purposes are included. Voluntary and co-operative housing consists of housing provided under the capital loan & subsidy and capital assistance schemes.

A report carried out on behalf of the Housing Agency indicates that an average of 15,932 units per annum will be required across urban settlements in the period 2014-18 (Future Analytics, 2014), with an average of 7500 of these being required in Dublin. These projections were based on natural population growth and migration patterns and are not cumulative, presuming that expectations have been met for housing supply year on year and further project that 57 per cent of all properties in Dublin over the period 2014-18 will be occupied by one and two person households. An analysis by the ESRI (Duffy et al, 2014) found that the number of households in Ireland increased by 12.6 per cent in the intercensal period 2006-11 and, taking into account increased population age and migration factors, project annual household growth of between 19,000 and 33,300 (2014:16).

How then are these increased households to be accommodated? In 2006, 93,149 housing units were constructed in Ireland, with 19,470 of these in Dublin. Since then this number has fallen year on year, with only 8301 new units constructed in 2013, 1360 of which were in Dublin. While figures released up to October 2014 indicate a slight rise in construction activity (8796) (Department of the Environment, Community and Local Government, 2014(a)), construction remains far below demand.

The number of unfinished housing developments currently stands at 992, reduced from over 3000 in 2010. It is anticipated that a further 74 developments will be resolved with the use of the Special Resolution Funding Scheme (SRF), a €10 million fund established to complete sites which would not otherwise be completed through the usual way because of financial constraints. Of the 992 unfinished developments, 776 are part-occupied, with 681 of these having no active construction activity to complete them. These 681 developments are intended to be prioritised in the next phase of funding (Housing Agency, 2014(a)). A breakdown of the 992 developments indicate that 4,453 units are currently complete and vacant, with a further 12,027 still under construction (2014(a):2). Of the 86 developments approved for SRF funding, only 4 are in Dublin where demand for housing supply is highest (Fig.7.1), however it is acknowledged that Dublin developments are a more attractive option for financing than those in less lucrative areas.

Social and affordable housing stock is delivered through local authorities, Housing Associations and the private rented sector with the support of the Rent Supplement payment from the Department of Social Protection. In 2013, the last year for which data is available, the number of dwellings in local authority stock was just over 125,000 units (LGMA, 2014).

Fig. 7.1: Number of developments approved for SRF funding

Region	No. of developments initially approved	Total Funding initially approved	Funding Leveraged including 3rd Party & Bond amount available
Greater Dublin Area	4	€493,090.00	€1,738,329.00
Rest of Leinster	28	€3,165,301.95	€1,744,242.35
Munster	17	€1,833,457.01	€2,736,406.22
Connaught/Ulster	37	€4,378,631.62	€5,871,269.64

Source: Progress Report on Actions to Address Unfinished Housing Developments, Housing Agency, (2014:14)

Housing Adequacy

The Housing (Standards for Rented Houses) Regulations 2008 and 2009 enumerate minimum requirements for the adequacy of rented accommodation in areas such as sanitation, heating, structural repair, ventilation and light and heating supply. These Regulations were supplemented by a Guide to Minimum Standards in Rented Accommodation issued by the Department of Environment, Community and Local Government as an explanatory note to landlords of their obligations. These Regulations came into effect in 2009 for newly rented accommodation and 2013 for dwellings rented before the introduction of the Regulations to allow landlords time to comply. Local authorities are tasked with inspecting rented properties for compliance with the Regulations. In 21,223 inspections were carried out in respect of 17,613 dwellings (LGMA, 2014:46). Inspections are not consistently carried out across local authorities, with some taking a pro-active approach, devising strategic plans and implementing target inspection quotas, while others respond to RAS requests for inspections only (2014:92). Between May 2012 and April 2014, Dublin City Council carried out inspections of 4700 units under the Regulations, of which 93 per cent were found to be in breach and served with enforcement notices. 60 per cent of those in breach remedied the defect by the time follow up inspections were issued by Dublin City Council (DKM et al, 2014). In their Annual Report 2013, Threshold reported receiving 2098 queries relating to accommodation standards, including damp, lack of proper heating facilities and hot and cold water (Threshold, 2014:18) and proposed a 'NCT for housing', a certification system requiring the landlord to prove compliance with minimum standards under the regulations. The subsidiary report of the Independent Assessment Panel included in the Service Indicators in Local Authorities further recommended a more pro-active approach by local authorities to private rental inspections following the example of those local authorities which currently exercise best practice in this regard and the establishing of a common set of standards applicable to all local authorities in the carrying out of this statutory function (LGMA, 2014:92). Inadequate living standards have been linked with ill health, with cardiovascular and respiratory illnesses attributable to

7. Housing and Accommodation

poor thermal efficiency in households a particular concern in Ireland (WHO, 2011). With almost half a million rented properties in the State (CSO, 2012(a)) the rate of inspection, and inability of some local authorities to properly comply with a statutory obligation to inspect, is a grossly inadequate response.

Social Justice Ireland calls on the Government to put in place appropriate resources to equip local authorities to undertake sufficient numbers of inspections and enforcement actions to ensure that private rented accommodation is of an adequate and habitable standard.

Of the households currently on the housing list, 23 per cent (20,349) are living in unsuitable accommodation due to a particular household circumstance, 11 per cent (9587) have a reasonable requirement for separate accommodation, three per cent (2808) are living in an institution, emergency accommodation or hostel and three per cent (2896) are living in overcrowded accommodation (Housing Agency, 2013). The total overcrowding rate in Ireland in 2012 was reported as 3.4 per cent, which increases to 7.1 per cent when considering those below 60 per cent of the median income, compared to 2.8 per cent for those above this threshold (Eurostat, 2014). General household satisfaction rates were recorded in the SILC Housing Module 2007 (CSO, 2009). 17 per cent of respondents to the survey reported dissatisfaction with their accommodation, with the highest dissatisfaction rates among those in the lowest income quintile, those renting below the market rate and those in the Border, Midlands and West regions. In all cases where dissatisfaction, inadequate facilities or inadequate local utilities were reported, households had a below average annual income and had above average at risk of poverty and consistent poverty rates. One third of households reported inadequate facilities, the most prevalent being a shortage of space (reported by 18 per cent). Shortage of space was a particular issue for those renting at market rate (31 per cent) and those living in apartments (44 per cent). It is clear that those on low income experience a disproportionate amount of inadequate housing difficulties. In developing a response to the current housing crisis, the Government must take cognisance of the needs of households as a whole, building not only dwelling units but ensuring adequate social and infrastructural resources to maintain sustainable communities.

Construction 2020

In May 2014, the Government published its strategy for creating a sustainable construction sector, Construction 2020 (Government of Ireland, 2014). This document proposes to provide a measured approach to housing supply, while addressing legacy issues arising from the economic downturn, such as ghost estates, pyrite and non-compliant developments such as Prior Hall (2014:9). A Housing Supply Coordination Task Force will be established to monitor supply of market-ready dwellings in Dublin working closely with industry to address issues emerging.

Construction 2020 further proposes, from a supply perspective, that economic opportunities may arise with purpose built dwellings for students and older people. A commitment was also made to 'actively review' the social and affordable elements of Part V of the Planning and Development Act 2000 (2014:15).

Planning is a key part of development of supply, requiring a community approach which ensures not only a sufficient number of dwelling units, but also adequate infrastructure and amenities. Construction 2020 commits to the publication of a Planning Bill and Policy Statement implementing the recommendations of the Mahon Tribunal. The Final Report of the Mahon Tribunal contained 64 recommendations (Mahon Tribunal, 2012:2516) including control of conflicts of interest, increased transparency in the planning process, the facilitation of documentation of the Regional Authority considerations in making draft Planning Guidelines, providing for advance notice of material contravention of development plans, providing documentation on submissions / interventions made by elected representatives in the planning process, and a transfer of the Minister's enforcement powers to an independent Planning Regulator. It is intended that the current Regional Planning Guidelines will be replaced by Regional Spatial and Economic Strategies from 2016 to allow local authorities and key stakeholders to coordinate and progress key development opportunities (Government of Ireland, 2014:22). In consideration of some developers currently retaining planning permission on development lands for speculative purposes, Construction 2020 introduces the use of a 'use it or lose it' approach by local authorities requiring developers to provide a schedule of work on application for permission and face penalties, such as a reduction in the term of the permission, should that schedule not be adhered to. While this is a positive move going forward, it does nothing to address the current stock of development lands in this category.

Social Justice Ireland welcomes this approach to construction, to be based on comprehensive centralised datasets relating to all housing aspects, in developing a framework for housing supply, however this framework must be underpinned by adequate resources allocation within the various stakeholders providing the datasets to ensure that construction policy is made on the basis of accurate and up to date data.

Housing Tenure

Since the introduction of the Housing Act 1966, there was a significant shift towards home ownership in Ireland (Norris, 2013). Figures from Census 2011 (CSO, 2012(a)) indicate that while the majority of properties were owner occupied, the growth rate of owner occupancy is in decline at 5.3 per cent compared to the rapid growth in the rental sector (47 per cent) in the period 2006-11. The overall rate of home ownership decreased by five per cent to 69.7 per cent in that time. In its report on housing tenure,

NESC (2014(a)) attributed the changing tenure pattern to changes in Irish society and economy (2014(a):9), with the acceleration in rent growth rates between the 1990s and 2002 linked with a larger workforce, dual and increased incomes, greater access to credit and Government schemes which increased the supply of rental units facilitating greater choice for those who did not wish to buy. The rapid expansion and contraction in the housing market from 2006-11 mirrored that in the economy as a whole, and owner occupancy rates fell as rent plummeted and access to credit reduced along with job security and the introduction of the Private Residential Tenancies Act, 2004. Age was a relevant factor in this study, with those under 24 most likely to rent, those between 35 and 44 most likely to have a mortgage, and those over 55 most likely to own a home. In terms of current and future tenure patterns, it is interesting to note that the number of over-65s who own has been increasing since 1991, while the ownership of those between 35 and 44 is in decline. Rental rates for all age groups in increasing (2014(a):13, Fig.2.1). The rates of home ownership among those between the ages of 35 and 44 in unskilled / semi-skilled employment was 49 and 63.8 per cent respectively in 2011, down from a high of 65.5 and 77.1 per cent in 2002. This demographic is more likely to be renting privately or in social housing, which is significant in the context of an aging population and rising costs to the State. It should also have a bearing on any proposal under Construction 2020 to provide specific accommodation for older people as referred to earlier.

The increase in renters was also noted in an ESRI Working Paper earlier this year (Byrne et al, 2014) as attributable to an increase in household formations. In their analysis of 2012 occupancy patterns, they noted that while traditionally only the 20-24 age group had renting as the main occupancy, the last decade has seen a rise in rent across all age groups, with those 25-29 also having a rented majority (2014:6). While the ESRI study concerns age groups from 20 to 39, the tenure patterns identified are similar to those identified by NESC (2014(a)), with renters increasing, while owner occupation decreases (Fig.7.2).

Rented Accommodation

Private Rented Accommodation
Whether by choice or circumstance, there has been a significant shift towards private property in recent years (NESC, 2014(a), Byrne et al, 2014). With increased demand and a shortage of supply, rent prices are rising, particularly in urban areas. The most recent report on rent prices from Daft.ie (Daft, 2014(a)) saw rents continuing to rise between August and October 2014, with an average increase of €150 nationwide, significantly affected by the market in Dublin which saw rents rise by €300 per month since 2012. In the period covered by the report, inflation rates in Dublin decreased slightly while rising in other areas. A comparison of rents with their peak in 2007 and trough in 2012 shows that Dublin rent is now less than 10 per cent below the highest amount and almost 30 per cent above the lowest

(2014(a):2). This pattern is not followed for other areas, with other cities less than 20 per cent below the highest amount and less than 15 per cent above the lowest. A lack of supply in Dublin is a factor in the higher rent costs, with the number of new listings falling from 47,000 in the first nine months of 2011 to 27,000 for the same period in 2014. With an anticipated rise in household formations (Duffy et al, 2014) and an increase in renters to the market, indicates that construction activity needs to focus on the provision of sustainable and affordable rented accommodation.

Fig. 7.2: Proportion of Household Heads (all Private Households) in Each Age Group that Own*, and Rent Privately^, 1991, 2002, 2006 and 2011

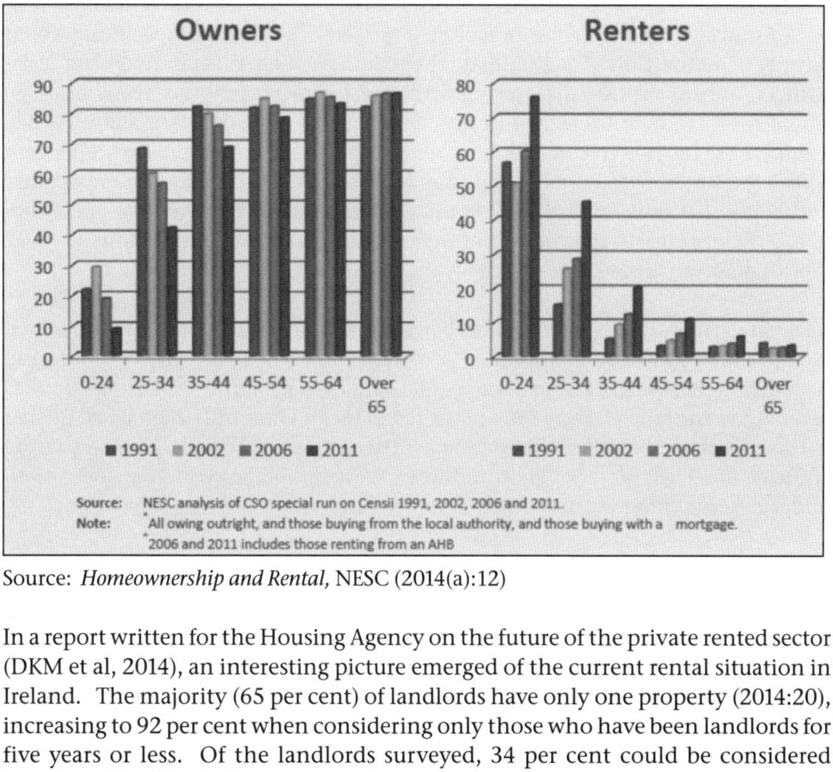

Source: *Homeownership and Rental*, NESC (2014(a):12)

In a report written for the Housing Agency on the future of the private rented sector (DKM et al, 2014), an interesting picture emerged of the current rental situation in Ireland. The majority (65 per cent) of landlords have only one property (2014:20), increasing to 92 per cent when considering only those who have been landlords for five years or less. Of the landlords surveyed, 34 per cent could be considered 'accidental landlords', having moved out of a property carrying too much negative equity to sell it (19 per cent), moved in with a partner and rented their property (eight per cent) or inherited a property (seven per cent). Of these 'accidental landlords', 55 per cent became landlords in the past five years with 82 per cent having only one property. 71 per cent of all landlords surveyed said that their rent does not cover their mortgage payments (with eight per cent of these reported to be in arrears of over 90 days), however only 16 per cent have increased their rent in the past 12 months. While the majority of landlords (61 per cent) intend to continue as landlords in the future, but not increase their property portfolios, 29 per cent said they intended to sell their property as soon as they could, increasing to 31 per cent of 'accidental landlords'. On this basis, security of tenure and rent costs for some tenants, particularly those who are renting from accidental landlords with negative equity mortgages / rent not covering the mortgage instalment (not to mention service charges, property tax and income tax), is a major concern.

This concern is borne out in the responses by tenants contained in the report (2014:22). Almost half of tenants (44 per cent) were unhappy with their landlords, 55 per cent were unhappy with the security of their rental situation and 52 per cent were dissatisfied with the condition of their property. When asked specifically about security of tenure, only 17 per cent said they could see themselves renting long-term, with 33 per cent strongly disagreeing with this statement and 72 per cent said they would prefer to own their own home. The report found that rent stability may induce more tenants to consider long-term renting as an option, with 45 per cent agreeing that they would rent long term if there was a possibility of rent stability and 29 per cent agreeing that they would rent long-term if there was the possibility of a long term lease (the most common rental agreement in Ireland is for 7-12 month duration (2014:30)).

In general, there appears to be a number of immediate issues in the private rented sector: the supply of adequate, affordable accommodation, security of tenure and rent for tenants, the instability of accidental landlords and, with increasing numbers of renters in the market, regulation of the sector (Regulation will be discussed further in this Chapter). Neither Construction 2020 nor, as we will discuss, Social Housing Strategy 2020 go far enough to address these problems which will serve to undermine any progress made by the implementation of these policies.

Social Justice Ireland calls on Government to implement specific policies aimed at protecting the rights of tenants to a secure home while addressing the issue of accidental landlords.

Social Housing

Social housing is delivered either directly through local authorities and AHBs or through the private rented sector through Rent Allowance payments. In its review of the provision of social and affordable housing in Ireland, NESC found that Ireland lagged behind other European countries in its provision of social housing, with just eight per cent of its housing stock and one third of the rental sector consisting of social housing (NESC, 2014(b):7). Local authorities and the private rented sector currently provide the bulk of social housing, with AHBs accounting for only 11 per cent of social housing stock (2014(b):8, interpretation of Table 1).

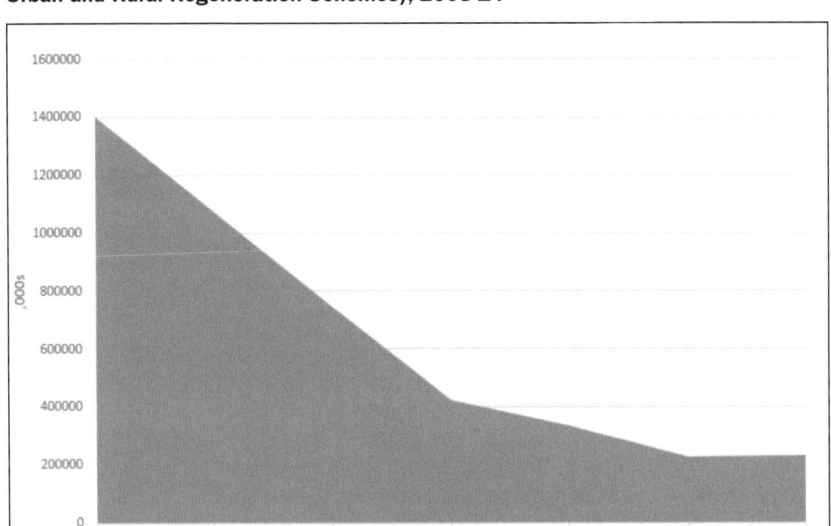

Fig.3: Capital Expenditure Provision, Social and Affordable Housing (including Urban and Rural Regeneration Schemes), 2008-14*

Source: Extracted from Dáil Debates, Written Answers, Tuesday 17 June 2014, www.oireachtas.ie
*2014 includes €50 million provision included in Budget 2014

With the exception of private rented tenants in receipt of Rent Allowance, social housing rents tend to be below the private market rate. According to Census 2011, the average cost of renting from the local authority in 2011 was €59 per week (CSO, 2012(a)), although this figure was reported by the Department of Environment, Community and Local Government as €50.26 (Department of the Environment, Community and Local Government, 2014). Total rental income for 2011 (the last year for which data is available) (Department of the Environment, Community and Local Government, 2014) was just over €329 million, or approximately €2633 per unit. This is not enough for the management and maintenance of these units, particularly the older ones and those with a high tenant turnover, resulting in units being left vacant for extended periods of time. A concern about the availability of funding to meet repairs and maintenance was expressed in the most recent Service Indicators for Local Authorities (LGMA, 2014:85). Furthermore, local authority tenants tend to be the poorest and most marginalised and are unlikely to be in a position to absorb a rent increase. In fact, rent arrears at year end 2011 were in excess of €58.5 million, an increase of 9.7 per cent on the previous year. This problem is further compounded by the use of differential rents throughout the local authority areas which are not only based on the tenants ability to pay, but on where the

7. Housing and Accommodation

property is situated, meaning a family in Dublin could be paying a higher differential rent than a family in a rural location in similar circumstances for a similar property.

Any rent paid to local authorities becomes part of overall local authority funds and is not ring-fenced for the provision of social and affordable housing. Capital funding for new social housing projects has been in decline since 2008 (Fig.7.3) (Dáil Debates, 2014), and while there are proposals to increase the funding potential of AHBs to position them to increase their share of housing stock and to reform the means of supporting low income households to access accommodation through the private rented sector (Department of the Environment, Community and Local Government, 2014), progress has been slow and is far short of meeting demand.

Part V of the Planning Acts, 2000 provides that planning permissions granted to property developers for large scale developments (that is, over four properties or in excess of 0.2 hectares) would include special conditions for the transfer to the local authority of up to 20 per cent of the development lands for the provision of social and affordable housing at 'existing use value', that is, the value of the greenfield site without planning permission. The aim of the legislation was to increase the stock of social and affordable housing and ensure a societal mix within larger developments. An alternative to the transfer of lands, should the development be unsuitable for social housing, was the payment by the developer to the local authority of an amount equivalent to the value of the lands that would have been transferred. From 2002-11, 15,114 units were delivered through Part V, with only 38 per cent of this being allocated as social housing and local authorities received financial contributions of €122.4 million (NESC, 2014(b):11). With a decline in construction and reduced capital for social housing, it is not surprising that Part V would become of little value to the sector in recent years. One of the options put forward in the review of Part V (DKM et al, 2012) was to remove it from the legislation. While these options are still under consideration by stakeholders, Construction 2020 cites Part V as 'having the potential to again be significant contributor to social housing in the context of a recovering housing market' (Government of Ireland, 2014:15). NESC also questions the wisdom of reducing Part V obligations, citing it as one of the 'few mechanisms available...which might increase the stock of social housing owned by local authorities and/or housing associations' (NESC, 2014(b):13) and views a reduction of Part V as a conduit for reducing local authority housing supply.

While Part V currently provides for more integrated developments, an insufficient number of transfers coupled with policies aimed at converting ghost estates and currently unsuitable units into temporary social housing runs the risk of segregating the poor, creating a wider societal problem.

The private rented sector is currently providing a large proportion (79,788 units) of social housing (NESC, 2014(b):8). These households are supported through Rent Supplement payments and while the number of households renting has increased in recent years, Rent Supplement expenditure has been in decline since 2010 (Fig.7.4). The increase in rent and insecurity of tenure discussed previously is likely to have the most detrimental effect on this cohort of renters.

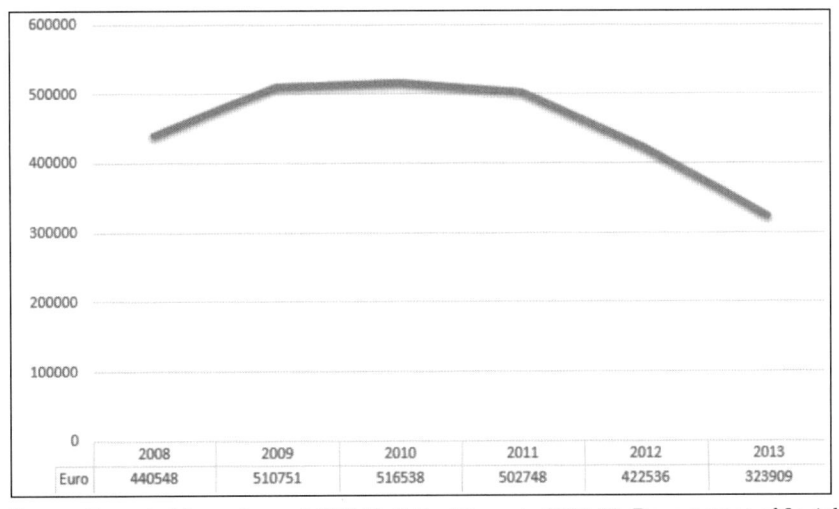

Fig.7.4: Rent Supplement, 2008-13

	2008	2009	2010	2011	2012	2013
Euro	440548	510751	516538	502748	422536	323909

Source: Extracted from Annual SWS Statistical Reports 2008-13, Department of Social Protection, www.welfare.ie

What is required is an adequate supply of social housing, with rents controlled through a central housing body with capacity to manage the maintenance of properties, resolve tenant disputes and secure finance for the ongoing provision of housing into the future.

Social Justice Ireland believes that NAMA could be such a housing body, having built a cache of experience in housing since its inception and having sufficient staff numbers to actively undertake the role required.

Regulation

In its Housing Policy Statement, 2011 (Department of the Environment, Community and Local Government, 2011), the Government acknowledged that 'A balanced housing sector requires a strong, vibrant and well regulated private rented sector'. In its report on behalf of the Housing Agency, DKM et al found that 42 per cent of the landlords surveyed (DKM et al, 2014) felt that the sector was becoming too regulated in favour of the tenant (2014:21). This could be a reflection of the number of 'accidental landlords' with one property who are unwillingly engaged in this sector. Landlords were, overall, more knowledgeable about existing regulations, with 90 per cent stating that their only dealing with the PRTB was to register their tenancies. On the other hand, one third of tenants surveyed said they were not fully aware of their rights and only 64 per cent had heard of the PRTB.

The Residential Tenancies Act, 2004, which established the PRTB (Private Residential Tenancies Board), provided some security of tenure for tenants who had been in situ for 6 months or more by introducing statutory notice periods for the determination of a tenancy, providing an exhaustive list of grounds on which a tenancy could be terminated by the landlord, requiring compulsory registration of all tenancies, and providing a mechanism for disputes (Oireachtas, 2004). According to a NESC report (NESC, 2014(b)), 281,000 tenancies were registered in 2013 which, based on Census 2011 data, indicates a gap of approximately 12 per cent in the actual number of tenancies, although allowances must be made for tenancies which are exempt from registration, such as landlord occupied rent a room schemes. The number of new disputes referred to the PRTB jumped between 2008 and 2010 rose by 550 per cent, reaching a high of 589 in 2011 (Fig.7.5).

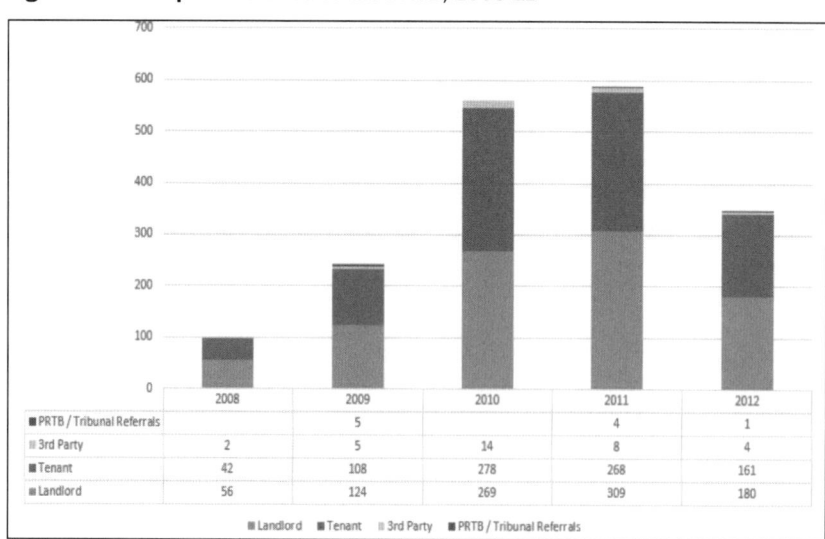

Fig.7.5: New Disputes referred to the PRTB, 2008-12

	2008	2009	2010	2011	2012
PRTB / Tribunal Referrals		5		4	1
3rd Party	2	5	14	8	4
Tenant	42	108	278	268	161
Landlord	56	124	269	309	180

Source: Extracted from PRTB Annual Reports 2008-12, www.prtb.ie

Likely reflecting the downturn in the economy, the majority of landlord dispute requests across all years concern rent arrears and overholding (that is, the tenant not leaving the property when served with a notice to quit), while tenant dispute requests involve deposit retention and unlawful termination.

An amendment to this Act, the Residential Tenancies (Amendment) (No.2) Bill, 2012 was passed by the Dáil on the 18th July 2013 but has not yet been signed into law (Oireachtas, 2013). This Bill seeks to include local authorities and AHBs within the ambit of the regulation and removing all references to 'private' tenancies, introduces a deposit protection mechanism, and transfers the functions of the Rent Tribunal to the Residential Tenancies Board (as it is proposed to be called). As previously discussed, there is much room for improvement in the implementation of the standards regulations in rented accommodation, having the regulation is not enough if there is not capacity to implement it effectively and insufficient knowledge among tenants of their enforceable rights.

Social Justice Ireland welcomes a strengthening of the regulation in favour of tenants and its expansion to include social tenants and calls on Government to ensure that adequate resources are allocated for its effective implementation.

Owned through Mortgage

Census 2011 recorded an owner occupier rate of 69.7 per cent. Of this, just over half had a loan or mortgage on the property (CSO, 2012(a):12).

During the Celtic Tiger era, testing the affordability of housing loans moved away from the traditional loan to value ratio (LTV), to a more complex series of ratios concentrated on income, mortgage, house price and loan data, which could be split into two over-arching categories: those that considered access to the housing market, and those that measured the affordability of housing debt (Duffy, 2004). In the Financial Stability Report, 2006, the Financial Regulator argued that the demand for housing was 'a function of the amount that could be borrowed based on current disposable income and the existing mortgage interest rate' (Financial Regulator, 2006) and proceeded, on application of a number of stress-testing models, to conclude that the banking system had 'adequate capacity to absorb first-round losses from a moderate fall in house prices because the banks report that a significant proportion of their loan books have relatively low LTV ratios'. A report by the ESRI (Duffy, 2012) questioned what happened to Loan to Value rates in Ireland, which increased dramatically between 2004 and 2009 and refers to a 2010 report in which the now Governor of the Central Bank revealed that LTV measures were thought to 'dampen the property boom' and denounced high LTV loans considered 'out of tune with the principles based approach and with international regulatory fashion of the time'.

Ever-increasing house prices, low interest rates and regulatory policy aimed at maintaining the boom meant an increase in those accessing credit, even to those who were traditionally excluded from financial services (Gloukoviezoff, 2006). The pressure was on income levels and interest rates to grow, or at least not decrease. In his analysis of the Financial Stability Report 2006, Power (2007) surmised that the risks were clearly apparent (2007:10). This burden was realised in 2008 in the wake of a global economic crisis. Disposable incomes decreased as unemployment increased along with interest rates on variable rate loans and the rate of lending to Irish households went into decline (Fig.7.6).

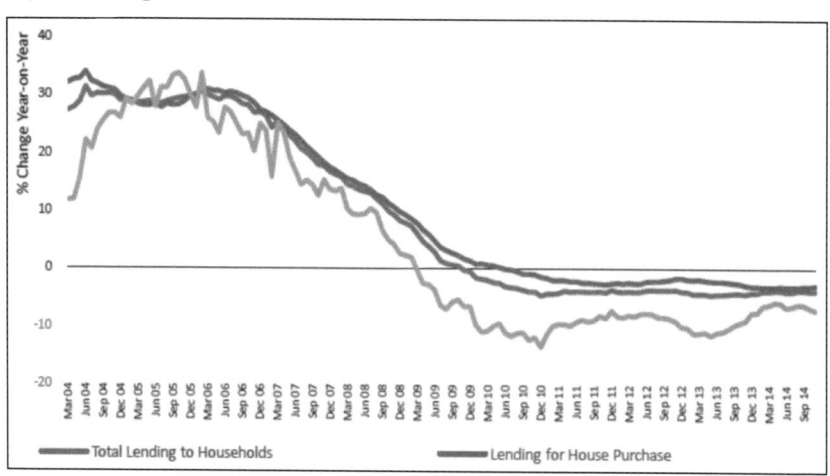

Fig.6: Lending to Irish Resident Households

Source: Financial Statistics Summary Chart Pack, Central Bank of Ireland, www.centralbank.ie (Central Bank (2014(a))

Notwithstanding restricted lending, property prices began to rise from 2011, with an average increase of 14 per cent nationally (highest in Dublin with almost 20 per cent) reported in Q.4 2014 (Daft, 2014(b)). In response to this, the Central Bank introduced prudential lending criteria for housing mortgages (Central Bank, 2015). The criteria aim to limit banking risk on house mortgages by restricting loans for more than 80 per cent LTV to 15 per cent or less of the total housing loan book and loans with a Loan to Income (LTI) ratio of 3.5 times to 20 per cent or less. With Buy-to-Let (BTL) mortgages experiencing particular difficulty, the consultation paper proposes more stringent LTV requirements, with loans for more than 70 per cent LTV to account for no more than 10 per cent of an institution's BTL loan book. Exemptions exist for homeowners in negative equity on their primary residence who wish to trade up without increasing the principal amount borrowed, borrowers in arrears who wish to enter an alternative payment arrangement and residual debt from discharging negative equity mortgages on a switcher mortgage. The new standards will be considered on an individual property basis and include equity releases on existing mortgaged property. Mortgage insurance and high-level guarantees, while considered within the consultation document issued by the Central Bank in October 2014 as an additional security measure, were thought to 'weaken the effectiveness of the macroprudential measure as a tool to dampen the pro-cyclical credit-price dynamics'. These measures were supported by research undertaken by the Central Bank (Clancy and Merola, 2014) which found that they were helpful in 'smoothing economic fluctuations' (2014:42). However, in an address made to MABS National Conference in November 2014 (Honohan, 2014). Census 2011 recorded a decrease of 5 per cent in the overall home ownership rate between 2006 and 2011 due to the increase in the number of renters.), the Governor of the Central Bank appeared more in favour of the use of mortgage insurance instruments to circumvent the limits. It is notable that property prices declined slightly in the final quarter of 2014 (Daft, 2014(b)), possibly in response to this consultation paper.

Social Justice Ireland welcomes the introduction of macroprudential mortgage lending rules and an increase of regulation in the residential mortgage sector. However, a balance must be struck to ensure that while lender and borrower risk is managed, there is still movement in the housing sector, particularly for those currently living in accommodation that does not meet the needs of the household.

While access to credit and affordability remain issues for those wishing to enter the market, the comparison between current rents and mortgage instalment amounts for first time buyers contained in the Daft Rent Report (Daft, 2014(a):10), based on a standard variable rate of 4.3 per cent over 30 years with a LTV of 80 per cent shows that rents are higher than the cost of borrowing for one to three bedroom units, where such lending is available, the Daft.ie House Price Report (Daft, 2014(b)) sentiment survey reported that supply was the main concern for those active in the housing market. Less than 30,000 properties were placed on the market in Q.4 2014, the lowest number in almost 8 years. Again, it is apparent that sustainable supply across housing sectors is needed, requiring leadership, direction and regulation to stimulate the construction sector.

Mortgage Arrears

Mortgage arrears increased steadily since September 2009, standing at a record high of over 12.9 per cent in Q.3 2013 before gradually declining to 11.2 per cent in Q.3 2014 (Central Bank, 2014(c)) (Fig.7.7).

The main policy measures introduced by the Central Bank to deal with mortgage arrears were the Code of Conduct on Mortgage Arrears (CCMA) and the Mortgage Arrears Resolution Targets (MARTs).

Fig.7: Mortgage Arrears 2009-14

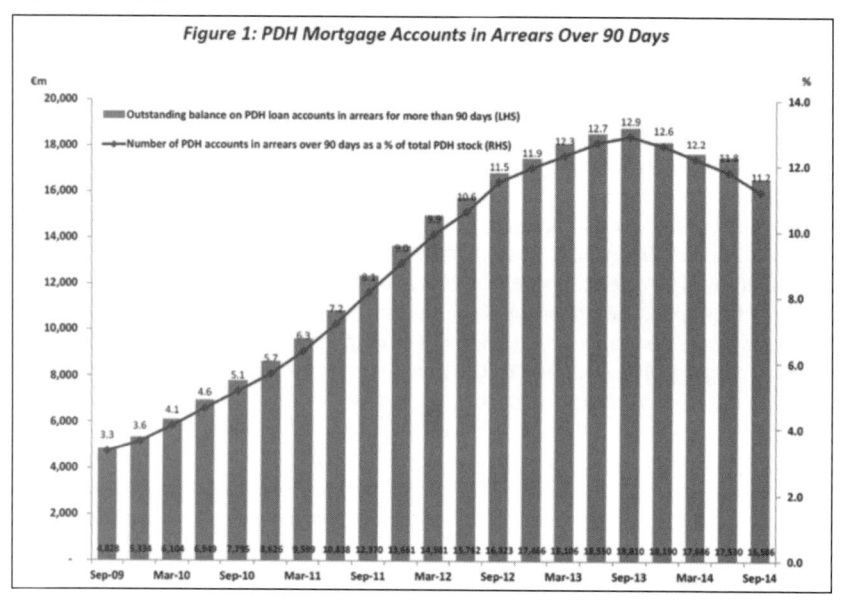

Figure 1: PDH Mortgage Accounts in Arrears Over 90 Days

Source: Residential Mortgage Arrears and Repossession Statistics: Q.3 2014, Central Bank of Ireland, www.centralbank.ie

The first CCMA was introduced in February 2009 in respect of consumers with a principal private residence in the State. The CCMA aimed to provide lenders with a framework with which to address mortgage debt difficulties. The framework provided was relatively light in detail and commenced from the date the arrears were first incurred. In February 2010 an amendment was introduced which imposed on lenders a moratorium on legal action for 12 months from the date the arrears were first incurred. Following the recommendations of the Mortgage Arrears and Personal Debt Group (Mortgage Arrears and Personal Debt Group, 2010), a further CCMA was issued in December 2010, which took effect from 01 January 2011. This CCMA was far more prescriptive in its approach to lenders' treatment of a borrower's case, as it implemented the recommendations almost entirely. The protection afforded by the new CCMA meant that borrowers and their agents had a clear process for dealing with mortgage arrears, including pre-arrears cases (that is, where the borrower was not yet in arrears but had experienced a change in circumstances that would result in an arrears situation arising imminently), with an internal appeals mechanism to the lender's Appeals Board and externally to the Financial Services Ombudsman. The most recent CCMA was introduced, not in response to the needs of borrowers, but in response to Troika recommendations following the Ninth Review (IMF, 2013:19) which saw an increase in the communications provisions for lenders, a reduction in the protection of tracker mortgages, a narrowing of the definition of 'not co-operating' and a reduction in the moratorium on legal action to eight months from the date the arrears first arose or two months from the date the borrower was deemed by the lender to be 'not co-operating'. This iteration further reduces the term of the moratorium on legal action to eight months from the date the arrears first arose or two months from the date the lender deems the borrower to be uncooperative; removes the right of appeal for non-compliance with the CCMA or the treatment of the borrower's case to the complaints procedures in the Consumer Protection Code 2012; removes the Appeals procedure from the MARP; and reduces the information requirements of the lender in initiating communication with the borrower. The experience of borrowers engaging with the CCMA was the subject of two recent reports (Bennett, 2013; Central Bank, 2013). The experiences reported varied significantly between the two, with MABS clients experiencing delays at each stage of the process and money advisers reporting confusion on the part of their clients in understanding the procedures, while the Central Bank research reported a majority of satisfied customers. The Central Bank will undertake a review of the CCMA in the second half of 2015 (Honohan, 2014(b)).

Mortgage Arrears Resolution Targets

In March 2013, the Central Bank published its MART for the six main mortgage lenders[50] in Ireland. This document set 'common public targets' aimed at resolving arrears cases which were 90 days or more overdue. The resolutions offered take the form of 'sustainable solutions' offered by lenders to distressed borrowers, and acknowledges that, in some cases, this may mean repossession of the principal dwelling house. In addition to the public targets, each institution also had specific quarterly targets to 'manage operational milestones at granular level', primarily monitoring early arrears cases as well as the operational effectiveness of the lender. The definition of a sustainable solution is with reference to the CCMA, which leaves to the lender's own Arrears Support Unit, the task of assessing a borrower's circumstances and making a proposal, and includes repossession of a family home. As the options provided by each lender differ in their composition, a mortgage which may be considered sustainable by one lender may be regarded as unsustainable to another. While the Central Bank reserves the right to impose sanctions on lenders for non-compliance with the MART, having tested only a sample of the solutions provided, the solutions themselves are at the individual discretion of the lender who then reports its compliance to the Central Bank.

---

[50] ACC Bank plc, Allied Irish Bank plc (including AIB Mortgage Bank, EBS Limited and EBS Mortgage Finance), The Governor and Company of the Bank of Ireland (including Bank of Ireland Mortgage Bank and ICS Building Society), KBC Bank Ireland plc, Permanent Tsb plc and Ulster Bank Ireland Limited

From the perspective of tacking over-indebtedness, the requirement that the MART be based on both 'actual and prospective borrower affordability' together with the guiding principles to be applied to each sustainable solution proposed are welcome departures from the strict case-by-case approach taken previously, which led to lenders creating different solutions for each borrower, with no consistency of approach across the sector. The Mortgage Arrears Resolution Measures further support this consistent approach by requiring that lenders have effective strategies in place to deal with pre-arrears, arrears and loan modifications / resolutions; a robust framework for the fair treatment of customers; and a sustainable framework for lenders and borrowers which tests the sustainability of resolution mechanisms. However, the definition of 'sustainable solution' allows lenders to apply a subjective approach in formulating proposals, particularly where such solution is the repossession of the family home which includes 'any situation where a Specified Credit Institution takes possession of the property' which, if based on the lender's subjective assessment that the mortgage is unsustainable allows the lender to meet the targets specified while affording no protection to the borrower.

In his address to the Joint Oireachtas Committee on Finance, Public Expenditure and Reform, Governor Patrick Honohan outlined the main issues emerging from the Central Bank's review of the MART (Honohan, 2014(b)) which included lack of clear written communication with borrowers, over-use of short-term arrangements with borrowers in arrears, lack of evidence of affordability assessments being carried out on borrowers and breaches of the CCMA.

Repossessions

The number of properties taken into possession by lenders has increased by almost 500 per cent in the period Q.3 2010 to Q.4 2014, with the largest rise occurring following the introduction of the MARTs in 2013 (Fig.7.8). The rate of voluntary surrenders / abandonments to court ordered repossessions was highest in Q.4 2014 at 5:1.

This increase in repossessions has an obvious knock-on effect on social housing provision, with borrowers whose mortgages have been deemed 'unsustainable' by their lenders entitled, under the Social Housing Assessment (Amendment) (No.2) Regulations 2011, to be included on the social housing list. The most recent figures indicate that 154 households were placed on the housing list due to having an unsustainable mortgage (Housing Authority, 2013). With the rise in repossessions in 2014 it is likely that this number has increased.

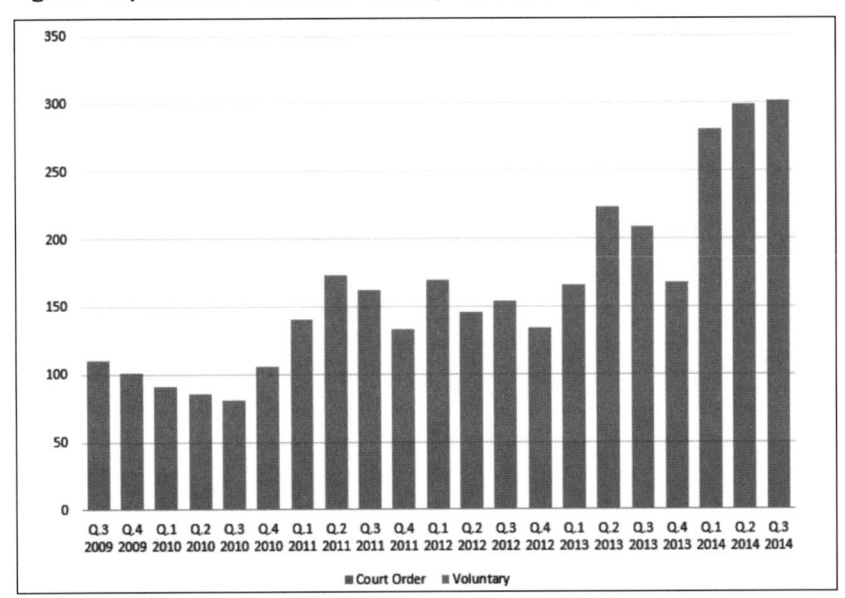

Fig.7.8: Repossession Statistics, Voluntary and Court Ordered, 2009-14

Source: Extracted from Mortgage Arrears and Repossession Statistics, 2009-14, Central Bank, www.centralbank.ie

Local Authority Mortgages

It is hardly surprising that local authority mortgages are following a similar arrears trajectory to private mortgages, increasing steadily from 2010, with a minor decrease in the level of mortgage arrears over 90 days from Q.1 2014 (Fig.7.9) (Department of the Environment, Community and Local Government, 2014(b)).

In March 2010, the Department of Environment published the first CCMA for Local Authorities which mirrored that of the Central Bank almost entirely. With the introduction of the Central Bank's revised CCMA in December 2010, the Department of Environment was keen to follow suit and provided for the development of a more comprehensive code in their Housing Policy Statement (Department of the Environment, Community and Local Government, 2011:4). In August 2012, the Department of Environment published their revised code in the form of a 'Guide for Local Authorities' which introduced a MARP-style system for all local authorities. While the nature of such guidance issued by the Department of Environment tends to allow for voluntary participation by local authorities, this Guide was accompanied by a circular which made its application compulsory. The

Guide, which became effective in October 2012, replaced the voluntary Code of Conduct within a compulsory framework and places obligations on local authorities to show a willingness to work with borrowers to address their arrears situation. The provisions of the Guide not only seek to protect the borrower, but also take account of individual circumstances, affording greater support to the most disadvantaged. Although the Guide does not appear to have had an effect on the amount of mortgages going into arrears of more than 90 days, which remains relatively stable since Q.3 2012, repossessions of local authority mortgaged properties appear to have peaked at 129 in 2012 before declining slightly in 2013 (Fig.7.10) (Department of the Environment, Community and Local Government, 2014(b)).

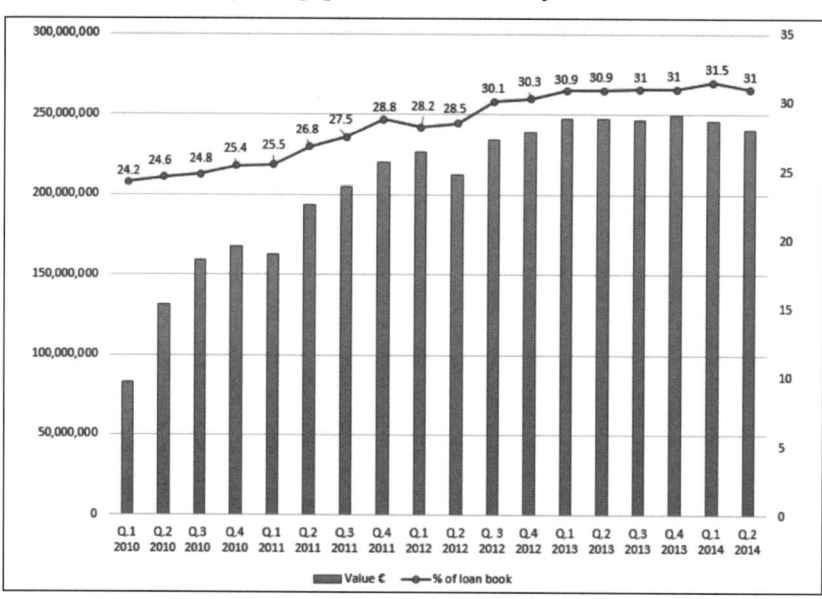

Fig.7.9: Local Authority Mortgage Arrears Over 90 Days

Source: Extracted from Housing Statistics, Housing Loans, Mortgage Data/Arrears in Local Authorities, www.environ.ie

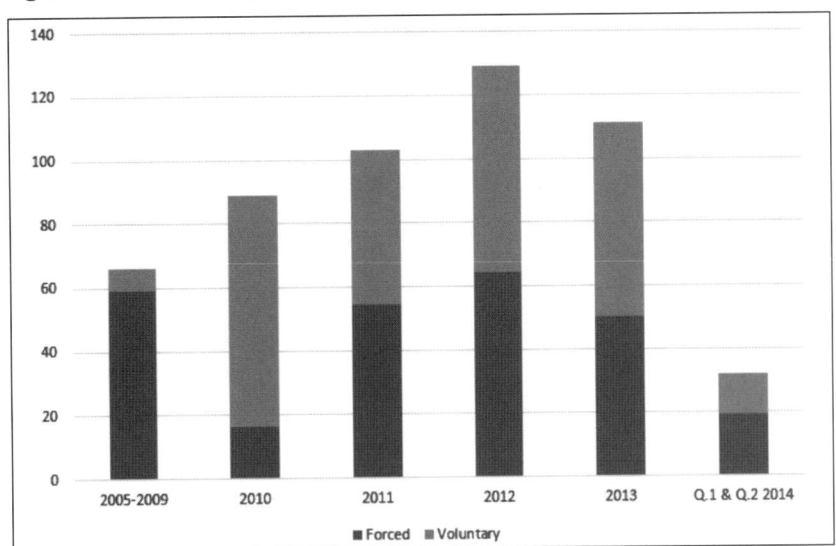

Fig.7.10: Local Authority Repossessions, 2005 to Q.2 2014

Source: Extracted from Housing Statistics, Housing Loans, Local Authority Mortgage Repossession Data, www.environ.ie

It is interesting to note the change in pattern of the type of repossession over time, with forced repossessions dominating the period 2005-9 giving way to voluntary possession in 2010 and a more even distribution between the two in the following 3.5 years. It is unclear what has caused this change, but what is clear is that these households need to be rehoused in an affordable and sustainable way.

Homelessness

The most recent figures indicate that 2499 households on the housing list are recorded as having a specific accommodation need due to homelessness (Housing Agency, 2013). A special report from Census 2011 counted 3808 persons as homeless on Census night (10 April 2011) (CSO, 2012(b)). As homelessness tends to be hidden, these numbers are not necessarily indicative of the actual number of homeless individuals and families in Ireland today. Since April 2014, lead housing authorities have been asked to report to the Department of Environment, Community and Local Government on the numbers of homeless persons in emergency accommodation in each region. This information provides the most comprehensive picture of homelessness in Ireland to date. Between April and November 2014, an average of 2500 persons accessed emergency homeless accommodation. In November that figure was 2720, of which 887 were dependents in 396 families

(Fig.7.11) (Department of the Environment, Community and Local Government, 2014(c)). Dublin has the highest reported instances of homeless persons accessing emergency accommodation for this period, accounting for more than 60 per cent of the overall amount each month.

Fig.7.11: Homeless accessing Emergency Accommodation, April to November 2014*^

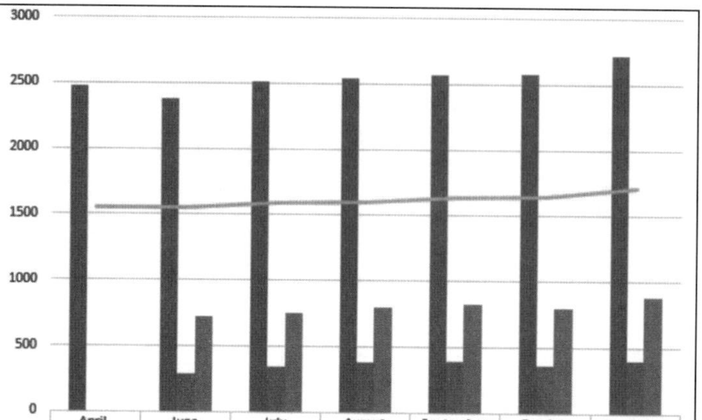

	April	June	July	August	September	October	November
All Homeless Persons	2477	2385	2509	2539	2574	2580	2720
Families		291	344	385	387	361	396
Dependents		727	749	796	828	798	887
Dublin Only	1551	1548	1592	1598	1633	1648	1709

Source: Extracted from Breakdown of Homeless Persons in Emergency Accommodation tables, April to November 2014, Department of Environment, Community and Local Government, www.environ.ie
*Family breakdown not available for April
^No data available for May

The most prevalent accommodation type nationally is 'Supported Temporary Accommodation' (STA) - hostel accommodation with onsite supports from NGOs such as Focus Ireland, Simon Community Crosscare and others, followed by 'Private Emergency Accommodation' (PEA) - accommodation rented directly from landlords, B&Bs and hotels. When taking Dublin on its own the reverse is true, with slightly more people accessing PEAs than STAs. This could be explained with reference to the breakdown of families accessing services in the Dublin region included in the November tables (DEJLG, 2014(c)). An average of 163 families per month resided in commercial hotels during April to November 2014 (highest in November, with 192). The average number of new families presenting for access to homeless services in the Dublin region between January and November 2014 is 33 (with highs of 42 in January and October and 41 in July). A Briefing Note focussing on family homelessness issued by Focus Ireland to all TDs in mid-2014 (Focus Ireland, 2014) identifies a combination of structural / economic reasons and individual reasons for family homelessness, but places the burden of the underlying cause on the lack of suitable social housing supply. It found that the overwhelming majority (almost 100 per cent) of homeless families presenting to their service had no previous experience of homelessness and had a lack of awareness of prevention services available to them (2014:5). The 'Implementation Plan on the State's Response to Homelessness May 2014 to December 2016' (the Plan) (Department of the Environment, Community and Local Government, 2014(d)) proposes to engage with all stakeholders to secure accommodation for the housing of homeless families, to prioritise homeless families on the Rent Supplement Initiative, while also increasing the rent thresholds for these families, launch a public awareness campaign on preventative services and to establish an assessment centre to re-locate homeless families currently living in hotels and other private temporary accommodation. While the two Progress Reports on the Plan (Department of the Environment, Community and Local Government, 2014(e)) indicate that progress has been made on many of these actions, negotiations are continuing in an effort to secure a hotel for use as an assessment centre for families in unsuitable temporary accommodation.

Social Justice Ireland supports the call for increased resources for frontline homeless services, a focus on preventative measures and information for persons at risk of homelessness, and an increase in adequate social housing supply prioritised for those who are homeless or at risk of homelessness with appropriate supports to ensure a reasonable standard of living.

Of course, not all homeless persons access emergency accommodation. 'Rough sleepers' are the face of homelessness, being the visible presence on the streets of Ireland's cities. A 'Rough Sleeper Count' is conducted in Dublin twice each year, in Spring and Winter, and is based on staff and volunteers of homeless services finding persons who are sleeping rough on a given night. The Winter 2014 rough sleeper count was carried out in November 2014 and found 168 people sleeping rough, an increase of 32 per cent on the Spring 2014 count (127) and 20 per cent on the Winter 2013 count (139) (Dublin City Council, 2014). Of the 168 counted:

- 130 were male, 16 were female and 22 were unknown.

- 36 were aged between 18-30 years, 40 were aged between 31-40 years, 17 were aged 41-50 years, 10 were aged 51-60 years, three were aged 60+ and 62 were of unknown age.

- 81 had previously accessed homeless services, 10 were not known to homeless services and 77 were unknown.

On the night of the count, 1526 people accessed emergency accommodation. The Plan also outlined the actions to be taken in respect of rough sleepers, namely the provision of beds pending the establishment by Dublin City Council of its Housing First service, the delivery of at least 100 households to independent living with support, the identification and support of rough sleepers outside of the Dublin area, the engagement with the Department of Justice and Equality in respect of non-national rough sleepers who have residency issues (the Winter 2014 count recorded 39 persons not from Ireland and 70 of unknown nationality), and the engagement of stakeholders to repatriate or house non-national rough sleepers as appropriate. The Progress Report for Q.3 2014 (Department of the Environment, Community and Local Government, 2014(e)) indicated that half of these actions had been addressed, with the Housing First service established in October 2014 and supporting 35 tenancies, and an additional 80 beds being brought into use under the Cold Weather Initiative. The identification of rough sleepers outside of Dublin has not been addressed due to cost implications and differences in identification methods, and those actions proposed for non-national rough sleepers have come into difficulty with Data Protection issues.

Other actions contained in the Plan (Department of the Environment, Community and Local Government, 2014(d)) include the delivery of an estimated 2700 units at 900 per year by ensuring that vacant units are brought into viable stock, giving priority to homeless persons in the Allocation Schemes of each local authority, ensuring that other vacant units under Government ownership are brought into use, such as those owned by the OPW, and ensuring that other properties being secured by local authorities and AHBs are prioritised for homeless persons. In addition, actions were proposed to tackle issues of mental health, provide financial assistance and the development of a multi-annual funding mechanism. The Plan is ambitious in its remit and work is underway on many of the actions proposed, however of those designated as currently completed / underway / on time for delivery in the Progress Reports, many are still at the concept stages. *Social Justice Ireland* is concerned that those actions which are not on schedule are those mainly concerned with securing adequate accommodation and continuing resources to support homeless persons.

Specific Purpose Accommodation

Persons with Disability
Of the almost 90,000 households on the housing list, 3938 are reported as having a stated disability, with a further 2909 in need of housing due to 'unsuitable accommodation due to exceptional medical or compassionate grounds' (Housing Agency, 2013).

Article 19 of the UN Convention on the Rights of Persons with Disabilities directs that signatory countries ensure that 'persons with disabilities have the opportunity to choose their place of residence and where and with whom they live on an equal basis with others and are not obliged to live in a particular arrangement'. As the needs of persons with disabilities are diverse and wide-ranging, there is no 'one size fits all' solution to the provision of adequate housing. Indeed, 'adequate housing' is that which takes account of the individual need, with supports and modifications made in accordance with the person's ability / disability. Housing for persons with disability is usually provided by way of adaptation grants issued by local authorities to modify existing dwellings. The Housing Adaptation Grant for People with a Disability is available on application to local authorities. The grant covers a maximum of 95 per cent of the cost of the work required, up to a maximum value of €30,000, and is subject to a means test. In January 2014, the eligibility criteria were amended to include the income of all persons in a household for the purpose of means-testing and proof of compliance with property tax, while the maximum income limit on the means test was reduced from €65,000 to €60,000 (that is, no grant is payable where the combined income of the entire household is more than €60,000). The Mobility Aids Grant Scheme is also available to cover works carried out to address mobility needs. This grant is usually provided to older people, but is capable of being accessed by people with a disability. The maximum grant is €6000 (to cover 100 per cent of the work) and is subject to a means test, the maximum household income not exceeding €30,000. The average waiting time for the receipt of grants varies between local authorities. According to the 2013 Service Indicators Report (LGMA, 2014), the range of averages was between 1 week in Dublin City Council and 69 weeks in Offaly County Council. There is similar disparity in the processing of the Mobility Aids Grant, ranging from 3 weeks in each of Kildare, Louth and Wexford County Councils and 47 weeks in Kilkenny County Council.

According to Census 2011 (CSO, 2012(c)) 17.9 per cent (106,270) of persons with a disability were living alone, accounting for over a quarter (27.3 per cent) of all persons living alone on Census night. 52.8 per cent of these were over 65 years old. A further 7.6 per cent (44,952) of all persons with a disability lived in communal establishments, with the majority (55 per cent) being older people in nursing homes. The labour force participation rate of persons with a disability was less than half that of the rest of the population (30 per cent and 61.9 per cent respectively). Even when those over 65 years old are removed from the equation, the labour force participation rates remain at least 20 percentage points lower than for the rest of the population. The latest SILC data (CSO, 2015) showed that households where the principal economic status of the head of the household was 'Not at work due to disability' earned the least of all economic groups, behind the unemployed, students and retired persons. The median income of this group for 2013 was €20,989, while this represents the highest per cent increase on 2012 figures, at 16.2 per cent, it is still less than half the median income of those at work. Persons with a disability also have the second highest deprivation rate at 53.1 per cent, less than two percentage points lower than the unemployed.

7. Housing and Accommodation

A reduction in the availability of grants for home modifications coupled with low income and a prevalence of poverty means that those with a disability are unlikely to be able to afford adequate accommodation to support independent or assisted living. The National Housing Strategy for People with a Disability 2011-2016 (Department of the Environment, Community and Local Government, 2011) and the National Implementation Framework that supports it contains an ambitious plan for development of adequate and supportive accommodation for persons with disabilities. The Government must ensure that funding is allocated for the successful implementation of this plan while maintaining a sufficient level of support for home modifications.

Travellers
According to Census 2011, the number of people identifying as being members of the Traveller community in Ireland was 29,573, an increase of 32 per cent on 2006 figures. Figures released from the Department of the Environment, Community and Local Government (2015) show that the most prevalent accommodation for Traveller families is by or with the assistance of local authorities, with a consistent annual figure of approximately 5500 in the three years from 2011-13. Private rented accommodation also features prominently with approximately 2700 families living housed through private accommodation, however there has been a slight decrease between 2012 (2829) and 2013 (2717). The remaining three accommodation types reported – On Unauthorised Sites, Own Resources (Estimates) and Sharing Housing – combined account for roughly half of each of the other two.

A report carried out on behalf of the National Traveller Accommodation Consultative Committee and the Housing Agency (KW Research and Associates, 2014) found that the use of unauthorised sites fell by 26 per cent from 2010-12, while shared accommodation rose by 34 per cent. As with other household types, there has been a rise in the use of private rented accommodation among Traveller households also, increasing by 15 per cent in this period (2014:7). The use of local authority halting sites also decreased by eight per cent in this period, the largest decrease within the subgroup of local authority accommodation. The research also found that almost one third of local authority Traveller specific accommodation was more than 25 years old, with all sites in need of some refurbishment and 20 per cent in need of complete redevelopment. Almost 20 per cent of all Traveller sites are voids, with the highest number of these being in the Basic Service Sites category (32 per cent). When asked why Traveller families were leaving Traveller specific accommodation, the most cited response (50 per cent) from local authorities was internal tension between Traveller families. There was also the view that some younger Travellers preferred the private rented sector and moved for that purpose, a view that was not shared by the Traveller representatives interviewed. When asked the same question, Travellers interviewed also cited feuding between families as a reason for the voids in Traveller specific accommodation, however they were also able to provide insight into why this feuding may occur, with some citing a lack of training and supports due to the closure of Senior Traveller Training Centres in 2012 as making it difficult to transition to work and adult life. The report concludes with a series of recommendations, many of which seek greater intervention by local authorities to tackle identified issues. The experience of Travellers contained in this report further supports the findings of the All-Ireland Traveller Health study (2010), which linked substandard accommodation with a high rate of ill health amongst Traveller communities. However, while consecutive reports have called for greater Government intervention to provide a quality of life for Traveller communities, figures released in a parliamentary question of 10 June 2014 (Dáil Debates, 2014(b)) show that capital allocations to local authorities to fund Traveller specific accommodation has decreased by over 90 per cent in the years 2010-14 (Fig. 7.12).

Fig.7.12: Capital Allocations to Local Authorities for the provision of Traveller specific accommodation

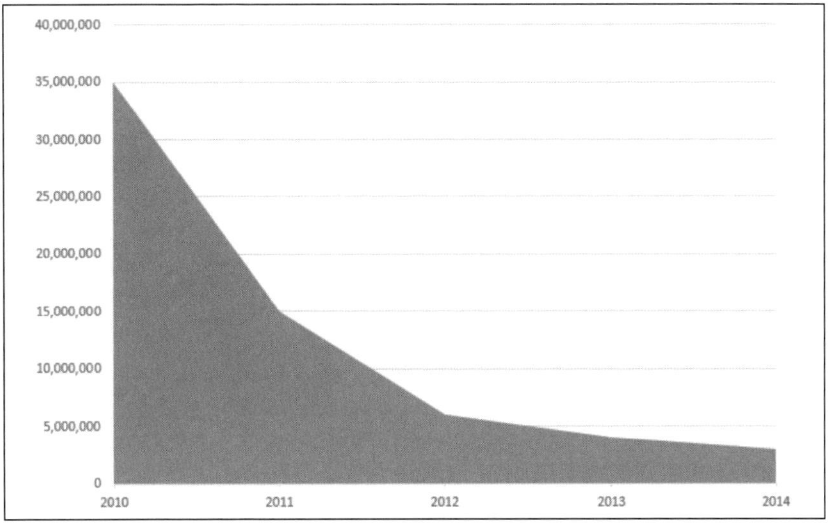

Source: Parliamentary Question, 10th June 2014, http://www.nascireland.org/campaign-for-change/roma-in-ireland/pq-traveller-accommodation-5/

Social Justice Ireland calls on the Government to ensure that the culture and status of Traveller communities in Ireland, being extricably linked with adequate accommodation, is protected.

Social Housing Strategy 2020

On the 26th November 2014, the Department of Environment, Community and Local Government published its Social Housing Strategy, 2020 'Support, Supply and Reform' approved by the Government the previous day. The stated aim of the Strategy is to 'fully meet our obligations to those who need assistance to provide a home for themselves'. *Social Justice Ireland* welcomes this initiative and its ambition to address the social housing need, however it is immediately clear (2014:iv) that the number of accommodation units proposed (a maximum of 110,000) foresees the number of households currently on waiting lists rising by only 10 per cent in the next six years. Furthermore, these 110,000 units will only be delivered provided the other stakeholders meet the Government's challenge to 'respond in a positive and proactive way'.

A reliance on the private rental sector to form the second of the three housing Pillars provided for in the Strategy seems misplaced. The Strategy admits that there has been overreliance in recent years on the private rental sector (2014:1), however again places an expectation on that sector to provide 75,000 units with the assistance of a package of benefit schemes (reviewed in more detail later in this section). While it is correct to say that the overall tenure mix is changing, and the private rental sector provides a larger proportion of housing than may have historically been the case, this is not necessarily a product of choice. Restrictions on mortgage lending since 2008, reduced income capacity to finance deposits and mortgage payments and a lack of suitable, affordable accommodation on the market has driven many households to turn to private landlords. With rents increasing by €150 per month nationally (double this in Dublin) (Daft, 2014(a)), the security of this accommodation for those on low income is uncertain.

Social Justice Ireland welcomes the goal of the Strategy to provide affordable, sustainable and inclusive homes. However the reliance on a private rental market to provide the majority of the units, with little incentive to move away from market rent, makes it unlikely to succeed in doing so. Provision of social housing must be driven by Government action, with robust regulation and policy with clearly defined parameters to streamline social housing provision across the various stakeholders.

Progress to date has been slow, with retrenchment in expenditure on housing provision in successive Budgets since 2008. In 2014, the Government anticipated 6,000 households having their needs met, with a further 3000 being met through 'normal relettings' (Department of the Environment, Community and Local Government, 2014:10). Those tenants whose lettings will be renewed as a matter of course are not included in the housing list statistics of 89,872 households (as of May 2013), and accordingly, in 2014, less than seven per cent of households are expected to have been accommodated.

Pillar 1 – Provision of New Social Housing

The Strategy's first Pillar is presented as a commitment to the provision of 35,000 new social housing units by 2020 in an effort to kickstart supply. At a rate of approximately 6000 per annum, this provision is clearly inadequate to meet the needs of almost 90,000 households currently awaiting support, even when taken in conjunction with the other delivery mechanisms outlined in Pillar 2 of the Strategy and discussed in more detail later in this Chapter.

NAMA SPV as housing provider
NAMA reported identifying 5482 residential properties as being potentially suitable for social housing (NAMA, 2014), of which demand was confirmed for 2121 by local authorities, 2854 are no longer under consideration, being unsuitable or sold, and 507 are awaiting determination of demand. A special purpose vehicle (SPV), the National Asset Residential Property Services (NARPS) was established in April 2013 to acquire residential properties to where there is demand and to enter into long-term leases with AHBs or local authorities. According to the NAMA website 669 properties (12 per cent of those identified) were delivered to social housing through AHBS or local authorities. The Housing Agency reports a further 257 properties have been contracted from NAMA by local authorities or AHBs and 1702 are under negotiation or consideration (www.housing.ie/NAMA). The Strategy proposes to expand the remit of NARPS to fund Part V units though its residential delivery programme in Dublin (2014:32) with capital funding available for an estimated 450 units and potential for 2250 should NAMA's Dublin residential delivery reach its upper limit of 22,500 in the next 5 years. Given that less than half of the units identified by NAMA were unsuitable or sold and only 12 per cent have actually been delivered, this target appears optimistic.

PPP Model
The use of public private partnerships (PPP) to procure capital infrastructure projects in Ireland has been in place since 1999 using a standard 'design, build, finance and maintain' (DBFM) model. The Strategy proposes to use the DBFM model once again for the provision of social housing, investing €300 million for the development and maintenance of up to 1500 housing units over a 25 year period following which the units will be returned. In a paper delivered to the Nevin Economic Research Institute in 2013, Eoin Reeves, the Director of Privatisation & Public Private Partnership Research Group with the University of Limerick (Reeves, 2013) reviewed the use of DBFM PPPs for State infrastructure and found not only is there no evidence to suggest that it has delivered value for money for Irish taxpayers (2013:19), there are also significant governance issues inherent in the model such as high transaction costs, conflict of interest between the Ministerial role of 'guardian of the public purse' and 'advocate for PPP', the exclusion of alternative options, the management of PPP contracts without the necessary breathe of skills required and the long-term

nature of the contract which creates a potential conflict between managing an ongoing relationship while enforcing contractual obligations (2013:12). Accountability is also a concern where more accountability (although less liability through the use of exclusion of liability clauses) is held by private operators, removing the direct line between citizen and responsible public representative and creating an information gap. The paper concludes with a quote from Vining and Boardman (2008) which attempts to answer the question of what criteria should be used by society to judge the best way to provide infrastructure. In the context of critiquing the Strategy's commitment of €300 million of public money to a questionable procurement process, it is worth transcribing that quote in its entirety here for consideration:

From a normative perspective, one potential criterion is that governments should seek to minimize the sum of total social costs....this means that governments should minimize the sum of the production costs they incur (including payment to third parties), plus their transaction costs, plus (net) negative externalities, holding quality constant. As some of these costs, especially for major infrastructure projects, can occur over an extensive time period, government should seek to minimize the present value of these costs. This criterion emphasizes that in assessing the consequences of alternative ways to provide infrastructure, one should include all government transaction costs that derive from the project even if they do not appear in the project's budget. Also one should include all externalities and account for quality differences; these costs rarely show up in any budget (2008:150).

Financial Vehicle
Budget 2015 announced the establishment of a special purpose finance vehicle for the social housing sector to allow Approved Housing Bodies greater access to long-term private capital funding. This funding will be incentive-linked to encourage AHBs to be more proactive in the provision of housing. It is acknowledged in the Strategy that AHBs alone will be unable to adequately meet the full extent of housing need, and so consideration is also to be given to allowing local authorities, either individually or collectively, to establish AHBs for the purpose of accessing this funding for the provision of housing. The plan for the future of this financial vehicle to act as a Social Housing Body is dependent on its ability to become financially self-sufficient, charging cost-based rents, which admittedly will require mixed tenure developments and supplementary payments from local authorities to address the shortfall between costs and differential rents. *Social Justice Ireland* has previously proposed the use the skills and resources of NAMA as a housing agency with the ability to access and distribute appropriate off-balance sheet funding and to take an active role in the direction and support of AHBs in the provision of social housing.

It would also seem prudent at this stage for the Government to review the inherently unfair differential rent system, which is not fully reflective of the tenant's income, but also of locations with local authority tenants in Dublin and other urban areas paying more than those in rural communities (Department of the Environment, Community and Local Government, 2009:98) while living on the same basic income.

Existing Housing Stock
Each local authority will be required to provide plans for the refurbishment and ongoing maintenance of vacant units, in addition to existing maintenance plans, in order to access funding for vacant stock. This funding coincides with that provided for under the National Regeneration Plan requiring social housing to meet generally accepted standards under the Convention on Economic Social and Cultural Rights.

Investment by AHBs
Funding of social housing is discussed in greater detail in this Chapter, however as the repositioning of AHBs to take a more central role in the provision of social housing is a key tenet of the Strategy and funding will play a large part in achieving this goal, it is important to note some of the points mentioned. Where once fully State funded, in 2011 a new funding model was developed to enable AHBs to access private funds for social housing development in an effort to increase the lending capacity of AHBs, the borrowing of which do not add to Government debt. The uptake to date has been minimal as while it allows AHBs more independence in funding and supply of social housing, it carries greater risk, particularly where rents are insufficient to cover maintenance and funding costs, without a multi-annual commitment, which AHBs are understandably reticent to undertake. Some commentators (NESC, 2014(b)) have also cautioned against a transfer of properties from local authorities to AHBs as to do so removes the rental income from the local authority, which would be cause difficulty in smaller, particularly rural, local authorities reliant on rental income (2014(b):13).

The Strategy encourages the engagement of AHBs with non-State funding models while committing to introduce regulation to mitigate the risk. No detail is provided as to what form this regulation might take, however with 27,000 units provided in 30 years and a commitment to 5000 more over three years, it is clear that the sector requires a greater level of regulatory support and financial protection if it is to play a significant role in addressing the current housing crisis.

Pillar 2 – The Private Rented Sector

HAP Scheme
As referenced earlier in this Chapter, the majority of social housing units (75,000) promised by the Strategy are intended to be supplied by the private rented sector. However Pillar 2 of the Strategy does not commit to the provision of an additional

75,000 rental units, but rather a nominal transfer of 50,000 households in receipt of long term Rent Allowance from the Department of Social Protection to a new benefit, the Housing Assistance Payment (HAP) paid by the local authorities, or the Rental Accommodation Scheme (RAS) and a projected 25,000 more households with similar housing needs who will access HAP directly over time. The HAP Scheme is essentially a modified Rent Allowance, with benefit being retained should the recipient find employment and differential rent reflecting any increase in income that recipient might enjoy as a result of this employment and payment being made directly to the landlord by the local authorities. HAP recipients may apply to transfer from HAP to local authority or AHB housing which suggests that, while these households are in receipt of a long term housing benefit, they are not automatically placed on the housing list or reflected in the national statistics on housing need. There is also vague reference in the Strategy to HAP contributing to better oversight of the private rental sector, however there is no detail as to what this oversight might entail or how it might arise in a market-driven economy. *Social Justice Ireland* welcomes the retention of the HAP payment for recipients who gain employment as support to the working poor, however adequate resources and support will be required to ensure the efficacy of this new support.

The Rent Allowance scheme will be retained for those with a short term housing need, who will not be part of the housing list. As no assessment of housing need will be undertaken in respect of Rent Allowance recipients and the criteria for accessing HAP have not yet been defined, there is a real risk that households with a long term housing need will instead be placed on a short term benefit and not reflected in the overall picture of housing deficit. Rent Allowance itself requires a greater review as it is entirely dependent on the private sector, does not impose a minimum standard of living accommodation and is paid to the tenant rather than the landlord directly. In addition, there is evidence to suggest that approximately half of tenants in receipt of Rent Allowance are making supplementary payments above the statutory threshold, leaving tenants with little income for the provision of basic necessities or payment of other household expenses (Threshold, 2014).

The Government's commitment to the new HAP scheme appears to be wavering from the beginning, with reference made to the possibility of instead utilising HAP funding for off-balance sheet acquisition instead (2014:46). If the new schemes under the Strategy are not afforded proper focus they are doomed to failure from inception.

Cost Rental
Cost rental is a mechanism by which a housing provider, rather than private landlords, develop accommodation and charge rent on the basis of covering capital and maintenance costs only. While these costs would likely increase over time in line with inflation, it is proposed that such increases would still be less than a rise

in market rents. In its paper on cost-effective, sustainable housing models, NESC (2014(a)) reported that current social housing rents are set at a level below costs, creating a reliance on State capital expenditure. When this expenditure is cut, as has been the case in consecutive Budgets since 2008, the provision of social housing falls dramatically (2014:52).

From the tenant's perspective, cost rental will at least initially mean higher rents than are currently being paid to AHBs and local authorities. However, as previously referred, successive surveys carried out by Threshold (2014) indicate that approximately half of tenants in receipt of Rent Allowance are making 'top up' payments to private landlords (2014:12) and would welcome greater stability of rental costs. From the provider's perspective, in order to implement a cost rental sector there must be available capital to acquire and refurbish new and existing social housing units. The NESC report (2014(a):44) clearly states that a healthy level of supply is needed to make cost based rental effective. The level of supply proposed in Pillar 1 of the Strategy is insufficient to meet existing demand and in order to create conditions in which cost rental would be effective, this shortage must be addressed. The Strategy refers to an annual cost to the Exchequer of funding private rented accommodation of €500 million which could be used more effectively. This figure includes Rent Allowance which accounted for almost €393 million in 2013 (DOSP, 2013:87). As mentioned previously, the introduction of the HAP scheme will see 50,000 households (of the approximately 80,000 households in receipt of Rent Allowance) transferred from Rent Allowance with funding to be provided to the local authorities from central sources, accordingly it is likely that only a very small proportion of that €500 million may be available for other schemes.

In the absence of immediately available funding, it is unlikely that a single housing provider would be able to acquire sufficient housing stock to have the steadying impact on market rents required. In the event that the local authorities and AHBs could pool their portfolios under an umbrella agency, there are questions of competition in the market that may need to be addressed. This pooling of resources seems unlikely however as the Strategy foresees a variety of cost rental schemes across the social housing providers, making any collective impact on the private market questionable.

The Strategy commits to a pilot cost rental segment with Approved Housing Bodies (AHBs) and local authorities. The terms of reference of this pilot are yet to be agreed.

Buy-to-Lets
There is vague reference within the Strategy of dealing with Buy-to-Let (BTL) properties so as to reduce the demand for social housing. This is primarily an area of concern for the Central Bank and Department of Finance in structuring lending and credit control policy in relation to BTL mortgages so as to lend themselves more

favourably to reduced rents for tenants. The Executive Summary of the Strategy commits to ongoing collaboration with the Department of Finance and the Central Bank to consider the scope to 'devise effective means of managing the transition of encumbered Buy-to-Let Properties'. The impact of this transition needs thorough examination to ensure that the taxpayer will not be expected to bear the cost of any write-down of the lenders' bad debts. Reference within the Strategy to the Government's Mortgage to Rent scheme is unhelpful in this regard, which is a scheme for mortgage holders in unsustainable mortgages borrowed on foot of their family homes and not available in respect of investment properties.

Pillar 3 – Reform

Local Authority Reform
Social Justice Ireland welcomes the Strategy's commitment to reform of the social housing sector. With so many diverse agencies involved this is no easy task and the targets set out in the Strategy may be optimistic. For reform in this sector to be effective it must be streamlined and clear. It is therefore disappointing to note that the first reference to implementing a new framework for rent payments involves each local authority devising its own rents policy, albeit under an overarching regulatory structure to be determined by the Minister. Statutory Instruments are rarely directive in their language and allow for flexibility within wide parameters. The success of any reform of local authority social housing provision will depend on the scope of the regulation and the interpretation by local authorities of the parameters in which they operate.

The Strategy imposes a high volume of change on local authorities within a relatively short timeframe. The capacity of local authorities to take on these additional responsibilities, assimilate the requirements of each scheme and manage the influx of new service users with existing staff at diminished levels since the beginning of the downturn is highly questionable and risks exacerbating the issues experienced by those in need of social housing.

Tenant Purchase Scheme
A new Tenant Purchase Scheme was introduced by the Housing (Miscellaneous Provisions) Act 2014 enabling a social housing tenant to purchase their rental property for a reduced rent. The housing authority will create a charge over the property for the percentage difference between the market price and the sale price of the property to the tenant. This percentage will be reduced by two per cent per annum over five years unless the property is sold in the meantime and/or the shortfall is paid by the tenant to the housing authority in the meantime. Universal tenant purchase was introduced in 1966 with the Housing Act 1966 which extended the rural right to buy under the Labourers Act of 1936 to urban housing authority tenants. Following the introduction of this legislation, owner occupancy rose from

59.8 per cent in 1961 to a peak of 80 per cent in 1990 (NESC, 2014(a)). Normalising home ownership contributed to rapid market growth with Government policies focusing on expansion and facilitation of private ownership (Norris, 2013). Increased availability of credit and a relaxation of lending regulation culminated in the over-inflation of a highly leveraged market. Renewing the tenant purchase legislation to enable more low income households to become owner occupiers with private mortgages without robust regulation of the mortgage market puts these households at risk of losing, rather than increasing, their security of tenure.

Choice based Lettings and the Housing passport
Social Justice Ireland welcomes choice based lettings empowering tenants to choose the most appropriate accommodation for their household while maintaining priority allocation for those in most need. This system of allocation must be monitored to ensure that social housing allocations are being properly made, that abuses to the system are minimised and that those who cannot access the web-based system are catered for to ensure equality of opportunity. The provision of a housing passport may prove more problematic, however, as assessments for housing need vary between local authority functional areas hindering movement between these areas.

Regulation of AHBs
Increased regulation of AHBs is an important step in streamlining access to social housing and standards of housing provision, particularly if AHBs are to play the central role envisaged by the Strategy. The Department of the Environment, Community and Local Government published its Voluntary Regulation Code (VRC) in July 2013 which sought to implement a three-tiered approach to regulation of the AHB sector, taking size of housing portfolio and availability of development plans into consideration to determine the level of regulation required by each entity (Department of the Environment, Community and Local Government, 2013). At time of writing, less than one third (32.9 per cent) of all AHBs had signed up to the VRC (Housing Agency, 2014). It is of critical importance to the social housing sector that robust compulsory regulation and governance is implemented before AHBs undertake a more central role in social housing provision. With implementation scheduled for mid-2016, it is unclear how the increased funding capacity envisaged by Pillar 1 of the Strategy to be in place by mid-2015 can be properly monitored.

Planning and Supply
In order to provide an adequate number of social housing units, more units need to be built. Part V of the Planning and Development Act, 2000 (Part V) provides that a developer must either transfer units to the local authority for social and affordable housing or 'where site attributes preclude an agreement on the transfer of land' (DELG, 2000) make a financial contribution to the local authority equal in value to the transfer value. In reality, developers' financial contributions became widespread and Part V delivered only 15,114 units between 2002 and 2011 which, when

excluding one off developments, accounted for only 2.6 per cent of all houses built in that period, of which only 38 per cent were social housing (Downey, 2014). When transfers and financial contributions are taken into account, approximately 19,245 units were delivered through Part V in the period 2002-11, a total of 4.8 per cent of all housing units delivered within that period.

A review of Part V undertaken on behalf of the Housing Agency in November 2012 (DKM et al, 2012) found that the tendency for local authorities to opt for financial contributions over land was a 'major concern' and 'an inhibitor of social integration' (2012:47). The report concluded that Part V was no longer fit for purpose with depressed land values reducing the benefit to local authorities, it then provided six alternative options proposed for consultation amongst stakeholders. The Strategy makes reference to a forthcoming Planning Bill, however insufficient detail is available at this time to comment on the likely impact of any amendments.

The Strategy appears ambitious in its objectives, citing the provision of 110,000 social housing supports and a radical reform of the sector, however in reality it commits to only 35,000 additional units over a five year period and the adoption of wide-ranging reform requiring multi-stakeholder buy-in which, within the timeframes allowed, seem overly optimistic.

Housing Finance

While Budget 2015 increased funding for social housing by €210 million to €800 million, this is still less than half the 2008 expenditure of €1.7 billion. The two main financing mechanisms for the provision of social housing were the Local Authority Construction and Acquisition Programme and the Capital Acquisition Scheme. Table 7.2 and 7.3 demonstrate how, in the period 2010-13, funding was cut by almost 80 per cent and over 50 per cent respectively to these two programmes.

Table 7.2: Local Authority Housing Construction and Acquisition Programme, 2010-13

Local Authority	2010 €	2011 €	2012 €	2013 €
Carlow County Council	4,220,000	1,069,097	1,900,711	1,046,542
Cavan County Council	3,694,879	1,116,877	1,360,702	1,947,374
Clare County Council	5,620,420	1,420,897	979,207	1,404,067
Cork County Council	42,822,737	6,585,702	8,389,441	3,808,461
Cork City Council	22,257,380	1,546,225	1,871,352	1,051,597
Donegal County Council	12,490,305	5,744,975	1,902,596	1,453,503
Dublin City Council	53,384,302	20,929,685	9,861,345	17,910,771
Dun Laoghaire/Rathdown County Council	19,716,708	4,611,178	12,673,635	3,253,979
Fingal County Council	6,434,304	8,355,797	4,808,767	6,110,592
Galway City Council	6,614,733	1,593,731	2,587,123	835,238
Galway County Council	6,972,073	4,035,823	1,939,128	2,853,496
Kerry County Council	9,700,950	2,396,769	1,304,258	1,356,402
Kildare County Council	15,795,789	2,901,449	4,114,913	3,801,389
Kilkenny County Council	10,104,029	4,566,591	6,090,448	1,888,413
Laois County Council	6,466,501	2,738,481	1,567,167	604,893
Leitrim County Council	1,429,056	116,308	304,954	902,126
Limerick City Council	11,873,208	3,586,290	1,216,646	1,400,028
Limerick County Council	7,003,199	1,616,243	869,055	752,635
Longford County Council	3,820,875	758,309	1,227,029	576,033
Louth County Council	13,279,097	5,375,852	10,203,632	1,942,919
Mayo County Council	5,423,522	1,101,258	804,563	295,791
Meath County Council	9,960,630	4,962,456	2,377,523	4,960,841
Monaghan County Council	4,539,127	3,256,000	1,731,686	1,159,804
Offaly County Council	13,171,128	2,478,979	1,708,186	797,832
Roscommon County Council	3,255,095	847,340	1,044,332	656,348
Sligo County Council	6,365,034	2,750,919	2,052,179	906,040
South Dublin County Council	18,069,760	6,292,681	6,461,093	10,295,596
Tipperary North County Council	8,938,683	2,176,078	956,844	618,979
Tipperary South County Council	5,541,249	725,829	780,778	598,592
Waterford City Council	5,507,854	1,394,419	3,303,585	904,103
Waterford County Council	3,832,007	564,485	3,683,959	669,850
Westmeath County Council	6,022,684	2,249,432	2,916,450	531,658
Wexford County Council	10,379,914	3,333,130	2,947,720	1,049,837
Wicklow County Council	11,624,095	4,800,000	8,741,271	3,442,935
Total	376,331,327	117,999,285	114,682,278	81,788,664

Source: Dáil Debates, Written Answers, 21 January 2015, www.oireachtas.ie

Table 7.3: Capital Assistance Scheme, 2010-13

Local Authority	2010 €	2011 €	2012 €	2013 €
Carlow County Council	812,609	658,320	1,488,727	2,168,748
Cavan County Council	1,284,593	14,378	664,288	348,563
Clare County Council	1,738,589	787,153	885,309	2,827,788
Cork County Council	3,689,618	1,245,460	871,091	1,628,254
Cork City Council	4,904,190	547,937	1,222,763	844,687
Donegal County Council	820,518	515,591	871,158	448,236
Dublin City Council	15,717,826	4,968,484	10,258,397	9,327,326
Dun Laoghaire/Rathdown County Council	4,988,449	385,573	1,512,349	457,141
Fingal County Council	5,815,961	2,132,123	4,969,304	1,625,163
Galway City Council	6,118,835	360,538	3,984,938	475,026
Galway County Council	1,044,027	27,067	764,980	229,188
Kerry County Council	3,876,327	2,789,529	242,052	63,308
Kildare County Council	5,921,801	1,956,675	1,891,864	842,708
Kilkenny County Council	2,623,400	681,185	984,044	1,028,692
Laois County Council	1,920,539	345,665	695,291	142,447
Leitrim County Council	1,335,000	10,000	22,115	10,000
Limerick City Council	58,691	2,286,271	3,772,811	1,827,945
Limerick County Council	1,811,184	550,183	1,431,786	887,751
Longford County Council	4,054,104	802,912	1,123,017	212,308
Louth County Council	5,159,568	0	728,437	760,433
Mayo County Council	1,948,301	281,063	1,054,003	2,499,474
Meath County Council	4,199,940	21,108	685,743	961,298
Monaghan County Council	415,175	86,636	1,125,300	1,191,568
Offaly County Council	812,508	178,248	1,139,322	539,520
Roscommon County Council	655,576	357,098	928,590	511,376
Sligo County Council	2,850,214	4,319,357	3,537,274	251,134
South Dublin County Council	11,822,349	3,096,552	4,367,485	1,229,114
Tipperary North County Council	2,177,126	234,817	1,280,339	193,490
Tipperary South County Council	3,774,142	1,089,300	485,615	338,374
Waterford City Council	2,691,671	4,578,871	2,005,274	885,346
Waterford County Council	2,028,058	176,359	1,448,472	409,222
Westmeath County Council				
Wexford County Council	1,161,563	254,723	269,551	229,384
Wicklow County Council	1,883,455	2,086,839	742,351	1,180,675
Total	3,045,018	2,341,562	1,011,902	1,410,059

Source: Dáil Debates, Written Answers, 21 January 2015, www.oireachtas.ie

It is clear that the Exchequer cannot provide the funding necessary to deal with the current demand and more sustainable solutions are required. Ireland cannot continue to borrow using traditional methods as an increase in borrowing to fund local authority social housing adds to the Government deficit, which is already too high.

In their report, *Social Housing at the Crossroads: Possibilities for Investment, Provision and Cost Rental* (2014(c)), NESC reviewed current social housing policy in Ireland and selected European countries and made a series of recommendations towards a 'more unified, cost-effective and sustainable model in Ireland'. In order to achieve this, NESC outlines three main goals for Irish housing in the coming years (2014(c):42):

1. Affordable house purchase in a stable market that prioritises housing for occupation rather than speculation;

2. Affordable and secure rental accommodation available to a significant share of the population;

3. Future supply and a growing stock of homes, in well-designed sustainable neighbourhoods, available to those on lower incomes.

In order to achieve the latter two goals, a fourth requirement was identified, that is, the need for new institutional arrangements for housing finance, planning and land management, development, construction and housing management. The report proceeds to identify an interdependent three-strand approach for achieving the ultimate goals, based on supply, finance and cost rental. There needs to be an adequate supply of housing for those on low incomes, financed by way of new off-balance sheet mechanisms relying on public policy interventions on development. That supply is required to stabilise the rental market and enable cost-based rental to work with the market, which in turn will require initial subsidies to allow housing bodies to service available loans.

In considering available finance structures, the report discusses (2014(c):48) using a portion of the An Post savings deposits, which would be available through the NTMA to the Housing Finance Agency which would then lend to housing bodies at a moderate fixed mark-up on the rate paid to savers with An Post. Other structures found worthy of further consideration were Real Estate Investment Trusts (REITs) as a vehicle for generating investment in social housing, investment by pension funds and retirement schemes, cooperative equity shares with householders who have the option to take an equity stake in the property, and impact investments in which investors seek to create both financial return and measurable positive social or environmental impact. (2014(c):50).

Social Justice Ireland has been in discussion with Key Capital Investments in relation to one such impact investment which would see the creation of a €35 million social housing fund, backed by Key Capital, partnered with a major Irish housing charity who would ultimately take ownership of the housing stock. If successful, this initiative could then be replicated for other projects, reducing the reliance on Government backed securities and injecting sufficient capital into social housing to help regulate the market rate.

Social Justice Ireland believes that mechanisms are available to increase the stock of social housing to address the current need and calls on Government to implement policy to support this increase in supply by way of off-balance sheet funding and initial subsidisation to support the framework required.

Policy Priorities on Housing and Accommodation in Ireland

- Resource local authorities to undertake sufficient numbers of inspections and enforcement actions to ensure that private rented accommodation is of an adequate and habitable standard.
- Ensure adequate resources are allocated within the various stakeholders involved in Construction 2020 providing the datasets to ensure that construction policy is made on the basis of accurate and up to date data.
- Implement specific policies aimed at protecting the rights of tenants to a secure home while addressing the issue of accidental landlords.
- Ensure that adequate resources are allocated for the effective implementation of tenancy regulation to protect the rights of tenants.
- Ensure that a balance is struck in the determination of mortgage regulation to ensure that while lender and borrower risk is managed, there is still movement in the housing sector, particularly for those currently living in accommodation that does not meet the needs of the household.
- Provide increased resources for homeless services, focusing on preventative measures and information for persons at risk of homelessness, and an increase in adequate social housing supply prioritised for those who are homeless or at risk of homelessness with appropriate supports to ensure a reasonable-standard of accommodation.
- Ensure that the culture and status of Traveller communities in Ireland, being inextricably linked with adequate accommodation, is protected.
- Explore the utilisation of the skills and resources of NAMA as a housing agency with the ability to access and distribute appropriate off-balance sheet funding and to take an active role in the direction and support of AHBs in the provision of social housing.

- Provide adequate resources and support for the implementation of the HAP payment.
- Monitor any implementation of a choice based lettings scheme to ensure that social housing allocations are being properly made, that abuses to the system are minimised and that those who cannot access the web-based system are catered for to ensure equality of opportunity.
- Explore off-balance sheet financing structures aimed at generating sufficient capital to adequately finance the social housing need.

8.
HEALTHCARE

CORE POLICY OBJECTIVE: HEALTHCARE
To provide an adequate healthcare service focused on enabling people to attain the World Health Organisation's definition of health as a *state of complete physical, mental and social wellbeing and not merely the absence of disease or infirmity.*

Healthcare services are fundamental to wellbeing and thus are important in themselves and are also important as a factor in economic success in a range of ways, including improving work participation and productivity. Provision of decent services is one of the key policy areas that must be addressed urgently as part of the Core Policy Framework we set out in Chapter 2 under the heading of Enhancing Social Protection. This is one of five priority areas identified by *Social Justice Ireland* which must be addressed in order to realise the vision for Ireland articulated there.

Healthcare is a social right that every person should enjoy. People should be assured that care is guaranteed in their times of illness or vulnerability. The standard of care is dependent to a great degree on the resources made available, which in turn are dependent on the expectations of society. The obligation to provide healthcare as a social right rests on all people. In a democratic society this obligation is transferred through the taxation and insurance systems to government and other bodies that assume or contract this responsibility. These are very important issues in Ireland today as our health services come under increasing financial pressure and fundamental changes are envisaged. This chapter outlines some of the major considerations *Social Justice Ireland* believes Government should bring to bear on such decision-making.

Poverty and Health

Health is not just about healthcare. The link between poverty and ill-health has been well established by international and national research. A World Health Organization Commission that reported in 2008 on the social determinants of health found that health is influenced by factors such as poverty, food security, social exclusion and discrimination, poor housing, unhealthy early childhood conditions, poor educational status and low occupational status.

A more recent report by the World Health Organization into 53 European countries highlights how people have not shared equally in Europe's social, economic and health development and that in fact health inequalities are not diminishing but are increasing in many countries (WHO, Regional Office for Europe, 2013). In Ireland, studies conducted by the Irish Public Health Alliance (IPHA) detail striking differences in life expectancy and premature death between people in different socio-economic groups. The Pfizer Health Index showed that those from a lower socio-economic background are more likely to be affected by a wide range of medical conditions (including heart disease, cancer, depression and arthritis) than middle class people (ABC1) (Pfizer, 2012).

Analysis of Census 2011 data by the CSO confirms the relationship between social class and health. While 95 per cent of people in the top social class enjoyed good or very good health, this proportion fell across the social groups to below 75 per cent in social class 7 (CSO, 2012).

Poverty directly affects the incidence of ill-health; it limits access to affordable healthcare and reduces the opportunity for those living in poverty to adopt healthy lifestyles. In summary, poor people get sick more often and die younger than those in the higher socio-economic groups. The crisis of recent years has reduced access to healthcare for many people across the EU (Eurofound 2014). This is attributed to reduced availability of healthcare services and reduced coverage as well as to reduced access due to households' increased need for certain services and reduced disposable income. A study by Eurofound (European Foundation for the Improvement of Living and Working Conditions) showed that regarding chronic diseases the health status of Europeans deteriorated during the economic crisis and that the gap between the self-reported health of low-income earners and that of the highest income earners is increasing (Eurofound, 2012).

A number of recent studies provide evidence that is of great concern relative to inequality and health in Ireland especially for children:

- A survey measuring the response of Irish households to the economic downturn showed that a large majority reduced their spending and that more than half cut back spending on groceries (CSO 2013).

- Research funded by the Department of Social Protection in 2012 found that 10 per cent of the population in Ireland was living in food poverty; the rate of food poverty increased to 18 per cent for households with three or more children and 23 percent for lone parent families (Carney & Maitre, 2012).

- The latest report from a study that has tracked a large cohort of Irish children from birth highlights a widening health and social gap by the time they are just 5 years old. Children from the highest social class (professional/ managerial) are more likely than those from the lowest socio-economic group to report that their children are very healthy and have no problems. The socio-economic background of the child is also shown to be associated with being overweight or obese (Growing Up in Ireland, 2013).

- The position of Ireland in an international study (published in the Lancet in 2015) across 34 countries is of particular concern; this study, carried out between 2002 and 2004 has shown widening health inequalities among adolescents (aged 11 to 15). The study confirms that adolescents from the most impoverished socioeconomic groups are more likely to suffer from poor health due to diminished physical activity and larger body mass indices. In relation to the amount of physical activity taken by poorer adolescents, Ireland was ranked worst of 34 countries for socioeconomic inequalities. It ranked second worst for body mass index, meaning the difference in size between poor adolescents and their better-off peers is greater in Ireland than almost anywhere else (Cullen 2015).

These findings are of particular concern in respect of the future health and life-chances of disadvantaged children.

Life Expectancy

According to Eurostat's figures for 2012, Irish males had life expectancies at birth of 78.7 years while Irish females were expected to live 4.5 years longer, reaching 83.2 years (See Table 8.1). These figures have gradually but consistently improved in recent years and there has been an increase of almost 3 years since 2003 (Department of Health 2014). This improvement is largely attributed to better survival from conditions such as heart disease and cancer affecting older age groups (Department of Health 2014).

Ireland's life expectancy performance is slightly above the European average. It must be acknowledged, however, that the EU average is decreased by low life expectancies, especially among men, in such countries as Bulgaria, Latvia and Lithuania (see Table 8.1). Relative to the older member states of the EU, the Irish figures are somewhat less impressive. Furthermore, life expectancy at birth for both men and women in Ireland is lower in the most deprived geographical areas than in the most affluent (CSO, 2010). For example, life expectancy at birth of men living in the most deprived areas was 73.7 years (in 2006/07) compared with 78 years for those living in the most affluent areas. For women the corresponding figures were 80 and 82.7 years (CSO, 2010).

Ireland's life expectancy figures should be considered in the context of many of the findings of reports on health inequalities referred to above and the poverty figures discussed earlier (see Chapter 3). Ireland's poverty problem has serious implications for health, because of the link between poverty and ill health. Thus, those in lower socio-economic groups have a higher percentage of both acute and chronic illnesses.

Table 8.1 - Life Expectancy at Birth by sex, 2012

	Males	Females	Gender difference
EU (28 countries)	77.5	83.1	5.6
Belgium	77.8	83.1	5.3
Bulgaria	70.9	77.9	7
Czech Republic	75.1	81.2	6.1
Denmark	78.1	82.1	4
Germany	78.6	83.3	4.7
Estonia	71.4	81.5	10.1
Ireland	**78.7**	**83.2**	**4.5**
Greece	78	83.4	5.4
Spain	79.5	85.5	6
France	78.7	85.4	6.7
Croatia	73.9	80.6	6.7
Italy	79.8	84.8	5
Cyprus	78.9	83.4	4.5
Latvia	68.9	78.9	10
Lithuania	68.4	79.6	11.2
Luxembourg	79.1	83.8	4.7
Hungary	71.6	78.7	7.1
Malta	78.6	83	4.4
Netherlands	79.3	83	3.7
Austria	78.4	83.6	5.2
Poland	72.7	81.1	8.4
Portugal	77.3	83.6	6.3
Romania	71	78.1	7.1
Slovenia	77.1	83.3	6.2
Slovakia	72.5	79.9	7.4
Finland	77.7	83.7	6
Sweden	79.9	83.6	3.7
United Kingdom	79.1	82.8	3.7

Source: Eurostat 2014, tsp00025

Access to Healthcare: Medical Cards, Health Insurance and Waiting Lists

In a report from 2012, international experts noted that Ireland is the only EU health system that does not offer universal coverage of primary care (World Health Organisation & European Observatory on Health Systems and Policies, 2012). People without medical or GP visit cards (approximately 60 per cent of the population) must pay the full cost of almost all primary care services and outpatient prescriptions. Thus Ireland is considered to have a very under developed system of primary care and 60 per cent of the population have to pay €40-60 for each GP visit, and up to €144 a month for prescription drugs (Burke *et al* 2014). The international report, already mentioned, also noted that gaps in population and cost coverage distinguish Ireland from other EU countries as does an element of discretion and lack of clarity about the scope of some services, especially community care services, in which there are service and regional differences (World Health Organisation & European Observatory on Health Systems and Policies, 2012). Our complex system involving a two-tier approach to access to public hospital care means that private patients have speedier access to both diagnostics and treatment (Burke et al 2014).

In Ireland out-of-pocket spending on medical expenses as a share of household consumption is above the European (EU28) average and it increased by over 2 percentage points between 2007 and 2012 (OECD 2014). Out-of-pocket expenses – such as prescription charges - in healthcare tend to operate as a much bigger barrier for poorer people who may defer visits or treatment as a result. A study by the Centre for Health Policy and Management, TCD, shows that while the numbers of people covered by medical cards, drug payment, long term illness and high tech drugs schemes went up from 2005 on, the costs of the schemes went down from 2009 on – partly driven by better deals with the pharmaceutical industry. However, in the case of the drugs payment scheme this is also driven by declining numbers using the scheme due to hefty increases on the reimbursement threshold;[51] as the study concludes this was in effect a direct transfer of costs from the State onto patients (Burke et al 2014).

According to the Health Insurance Authority, in September 2014 there were 2,018,000 people insured with inpatient health insurance plans (2014). This represents an increase in the number of insured people of 1,000 over the latest quarter, but a decrease of 29,000 over the past twelve months. Overall this figure has been declining since the end of 2008 when 2.3 million were insured. The percentage of the population with inpatient health insurance plans stands at 43.8% down from the 2008 peak of 50.9% (Health Insurance Authority 2014). A report on 37 European

---

[51] In 2008 the State paid out over €311 million under the Drugs Payment Scheme whereas by 2012 this had more than halved to €127 million (Burke et al 2014)

countries queries if Ireland's very high reliance on healthcare insurance can be regarded as an extreme case of dissatisfaction with the public health system (Health Consumer Powerhouse, 2015). One puzzling part of this situation from a funding point of view is that, notwithstanding the fact that so many people are insured, private health insurance contributes relatively little to Ireland's overall spending on healthcare – between 7-10 percent of current public revenue (Normand 2015).

Statistics published on the Department of Health web site suggest that in April 2014, 1,800,182 people had a medical card (Department of Health, 2014); the number projected to have one at 31 December 2014 is 1,782,395 (Health Service Executive 2014). This represents a significant decrease on the position in 2013 when 1,849,380 people (40.3 per cent of the population) had a medical card. Some 125,166 people had a GP Visit card in April 2014 and a large increase in this number is now envisaged as a result of Government's decision to issue them to those under 6's and those over 70 years ((Department of Health, 2014; Health Service Executive 2014).

The number of people benefitting from Discretionary Medical Cards fell by just under 24,000 or over 30 per cent between 2011 and 2013 – that is, from 74,281 people benefitting at the end of 2011 to 50,294 in December 2013 (Health Service Executive, 2012; Health Service Executive, 2013). Many people suffered unnecessary stress as a result of a review of discretionary medical cards that took place in 2014, although this policy was discontinued and revised guidelines on their operation are awaited. However, there are still reports in the media of difficulties and delays in accessing medical cards for adults and children with serious long-term illnesses.

Social Justice Ireland believes that healthcare is a social right that every person should enjoy and that people should be assured that care is guaranteed in their times of illness or vulnerability. Thus full medical card coverage is necessary for all people in Ireland who are vulnerable. Timely access to quality healthcare services can also prevent higher healthcare costs in the long run (Eurofound 2014).

Between January and October 2014 there was an overall increase of 5,539 (1.7 per cent) in the number of emergency (or unscheduled) admissions to hospitals compared to the same period in 2013 (Health Service Executive 2014). Particular problems with overcrowding in emergency departments are being highlighted in the media in early 2015. For example, figures from the INMO (Irish Nurses and Midwives Organisation) suggested that there were just over 600 people on trolleys on 6th January 2015 and the figure on 23 January remained relatively high (at 388 people) (Irish Nurses and Midwives Organisation, 2014). By contrast, in 2006, a former health Minister was forced to declare a national emergency when the number of patients on trolleys hit 495, well below the levels that were reached in January 2015 (Cullen, Irish Times, 2015). Behind these figures there is unnecessary human suffering as many patients, often older patients, are left waiting on trolleys or chairs for hours or even days before they are admitted to hospital, to say nothing about the risk to patient safety which is much greater in cramped conditions.

This situation is exacerbated by problems accessing support in the community as well as access to nursing homes – in October 2014, 2,135 people were waiting on funding to allow them to avail of a residential bed through the Nursing Home Support Scheme (Fair Deal) with an average waiting time of 15 weeks (Health Service Executive, 2014). In November the figure was reduced somewhat but was still 1,898 people (Health Service Executive 2014).

In addition to the issue of emergency admissions, the length of waiting lists is a cause of major concern in the Irish healthcare system. Overall, towards the end of 2012 and through 2013 and 2014, there has been a decrease in inpatient activity and a levelling off of day cases despite increased demand (Burke *et al* 2014).

According to monthly trends published by the Department of Health, there have been very significant increases during 2014 in the numbers waiting for elective procedures (in-patient and day-case) both for adults (waiting more than 8 months) and children (waiting more than 20 weeks) (Department of Health, 2014, Figure 3.2). This continues a trend in recent years: in October 2012 the number of adults waiting more than 8 months was under 3,000; in September 2013 it was approximately 5,000, and by September 2014 it was approaching 10,000 (Department of Health 2013; 2014).

There have also been increases (from Jan 2014 to September 2014) in the numbers on the outpatient waiting list and in those waiting longer than 52 weeks for an outpatient appointment (Department of Health, 2014). There are extremely long wait times for an initial appointment with a specialist. According to a study by the Centre for Health Policy and Management, TCD, in November 2013, there were 384,632 people waiting for public outpatient appointments, of these 846 were waiting over four years, 3,138 were waiting between three and four years, 12,861 were waiting between two and three years, while 39,425 people were waiting between one and two years (Burke *et al* 2014).

The above statistics illustrate how many of those dependent on the public system may spend very lengthy periods waiting for a first appointment with a specialist and also for treatment. These waiting times are totally unacceptable and demonstrate the lack of fairness within our current system in which people with private health insurance do not have to wait. The 2001 health strategy, *Quality and Fairness*, set a target of a maximum wait of three months for treatment following referral from an out-patient department. A subsequent Government target was that no one would wait over one year for a first specialist appointment by December 2013. The most recently announced target is that no one will wait longer for treatment or an outpatient appointment than 18 months by mid-2015 and no longer than 15 months by end 2015 (Department of Health Priorities published in January 2015). These are extremely unambitious targets.

In a survey of 36 countries from a consumer perspective, the Euro Health Consumer Index, Ireland was ranked 22nd, down from 14th the previous year (Health Consumer Powerhouse, 2015). The report expresses doubts about Irish official statistics on waiting times and, for the latest report (relating to 2014), the authors took account of feedback from patient organisation, which accounts for the drop in the ranking. By contrast, the health system in the Netherlands topped this ranking (with the authors concluding that their system 'does not seem to have any weak spots') and is the only country that has consistently been among the top three in the total ranking of any European index published by the Health Consumer Powerhouse since 2005 (Health Consumer Powerhouse, 2015). As can be seen from Table 8.2 below, the Netherlands also tops the European table in terms of health spending as a proportion of GDP. It may also be worth noting that the Netherlands has an overall tax to GDP ratio that is considerably higher than Ireland's: at 39 per cent in 2012, the level in the Netherlands is similar to the EU-28 average rate (of 39.4) but over 10 percentage points above the Irish level (of 28.7 per cent) (Eurostat 2014).

Health expenditure

Healthcare is a social right for everyone and a move to a rights based approach is a key action under the heading of Governance Reform in the Core Policy Framework set out in Chapter 2 - one of five priority areas identified by *Social Justice Ireland* which must be addressed in order to realise its vision for Ireland. For this right to be upheld, governments must provide the funding needed to ensure that the relevant services and care are available when required.

Comparative statistics are available for total expenditure on health (i.e. public plus private) across the EU. Changes in the ratio of health spending to GDP are the result of the combined effects of growth/reductions in both GDP and health expenditure. Table 8.2 shows that, at 8.1 per cent, Ireland's spending on healthcare as a percentage of GDP, was similar to the EU average in 2012 (the latest comparable data available). In Gross National Income (GNI) terms this expenditure translates into a figure of 9.9 per cent (in 2012).

Table 8.2 - EU 27 Expenditure on Health as a percentage of GDP, 2010- 2012

Country	2010	2011	2012
Netherlands	12.1	11.9	12.4
France	11.7	11.6	11.7
Austria	11.6	11.3	11.5
Germany	11.5	11.3	11.3
Denmark	11.1	10.9	11.2
Belgium	10.5	10.5	10.8
Ireland (% of GNI)	11.1	10.8	9.9
Spain	9.6	9.3	9.6
Sweden	9.5	9.5	9.6
Portugal	10.8	10.2	9.4
United Kingdom	9.6	9.4	9.4
Greece	9.4	9.0	9.3
Italy	9.4	9.2	9.2
Finland	9.0	9.0	9.1
Malta	8.5	8.7	9.1
Slovenia	8.9	8.9	8.8
EU			8.7 (EU28)
Ireland (% of GDP)	9.3	8.8	8.1
Hungary	8.0	7.9	7.8
Slovakia	9.0	7.9	7.8
Czech Republic	7.4	7.5	7.7
Bulgaria	7.6	7.3	7.4
Cyprus	7.4	7.4	7.3
Luxembourg	7.2	6.7	6.9
Croatia	7.8	6.8	6.8
Poland	7.0	6.8	6.7
Lithuania	7.0	6.7	6.7
Latvia	6.5	6.0	6.0
Estonia	6.3	5.8	5.9
Romania	5.9	5.6	5.1

Source: Ireland: CSO: 2015; EU: OECD 2014, Table 6.2.1. Includes public and private spending.

Ireland's public spending on healthcare has reduced in recent years as Table 8.3 shows – using the latest data published by the CSO. However, healthcare costs tend to be higher in countries that have larger populations of older people. This is not yet a significant issue for Ireland as, at 17.3 (Department of Health 2014), the old age dependency ratio[52] is low compared to the much higher EU average.

Table 8.3 Ireland: Public expenditure on health care, 2002-2013

Year	Total (€m)	% of GNI	% of GDP	Per capita at constant 2012 prices (€)
2002	7,933	7.3	6.1	2,645
2003	8,853	7.4	6.3	2,755
2004	9,653	7.2	6.2	2,773
2005b	11,160	7.6	6.6	3,026
2006	12,248	7.6	6.7	3,092
2007	13,736	8.0	7.0	3,223
2008	14,588	9.0	7.8	3,193
2009	15,073	10.7	9.0	3,269
2010	14,452	10.3	8.8	3,249
2011	13,728	9.8	8.0	3,044
2012	13,787	9.7	8.0	3,007
2013	13,492	9.1	7.7	2,973

CSO, 2014 (2002/2004); CSO 2015 (2004-2013). b=break in series

The decline in expenditure that took place between 2009 and 2012 was particularly rapid in the opinion of international experts (WHO & European Observatory on Health Systems and Policies, 2012).

In 2012, health spending has started to increase again in real terms. But in the view of the OECD, this is at a very modest rate (OECD 2014). In Ireland, 68 per cent of health spending was funded by public sources in 2012, which is slightly less than the average of 72% in OECD countries (OECD 2014) – but is considerably less than the Netherlands, the U.K and most Nordic countries which have levels of public financing exceeding 80 per cent (OECD 2014) and they also tend to have higher levels of overall tax revenue than Ireland (that is, taxation as a ratio of GDP) (Eurostat 2014, Graph 3). In fact the trend in Ireland's public expenditure on health has been consistently downwards in recent years (as a percentage of total expenditure on health) – the

---

[52] The old age dependency Ratio refers to the number of persons aged 65 years and over as a percentage of those aged 15-64 years.

percentage in 2005 was 76 per cent (OECD Stat Extracts). This means that the rate has dropped by 8 percentage points between 2005 and 2012. See Table 8.4.

Table 8.4 Public expenditure on health as a percentage of total expenditure on health

	2005	2006	2007	2008	2009	2010	2011	2012
Ireland	76.0	75.4	75.7	75.4	72.6	69.6	67.0	68

Source: OECD online database (2005-2011); 2012: OECD 2014.

Approximately €4 billion was cut from the Irish healthcare system between 2008 and 2014 (Health Service Executive 2013); there were over 12,000 fewer Health Service Executive staff in December 2013 than there were at the height of public health sector employment in 2007 (Burke et al 2014). The Department of Health reports that there has been a 16 per cent reduction in total public health expenditure between 2009 and 2014 (Department of Health, 2014). Capital expenditure was 42 per cent lower in 2013 than in 2008 (Department of Health, 2014).

These changes took place during a period of rapidly rising unemployment and consequently growth in the numbers of people qualifying for medical cards, and of population ageing. A study by the Centre for Health Policy and Management, TCD, concludes that, from 2013 on, the health system has been under increasing pressure and has had no choice but to do 'less with less' (Burke et al 2014, p.7). Given that the Health Service Executive cannot control emergency admissions to hospitals, what could be expected this to result in is reduced access to medical cards, day and inpatient hospital treatment, as well as social care in the home. While these strictures may result in short-term savings, they may work out more expensive in the longer term if they result in hospital admissions that could have been avoided (Burke et al 2014) – to say nothing of the cost in human suffering.

The amount allocated in Budget 2015 for the health services was €13,079 billion, and involved a modest increase (€635m). However, according to the Health Service Executive National Service Plan for 2015, this only allows net costs to increase by €115million when account is taken of the 2014 projected net expenditure deficit (the deficit being €510million). Simultaneously there is a minimum savings target of €130million set by the Department of Health for 2015 and an increased income collection target of €10million (Health Service Executive 2014). This comes after seven consecutive years of budget cuts resulting, as stated already, in a 16 per cent reduction in total public health expenditure between 2009 and 2014 according to the Department of Health (2014).

Budget 2015 also envisaged a move to multi-annual planning, with the health budget now envisaged to be developed over a two-year period, something that *Social Justice Ireland* has welcomed.

Successive budget cuts in recent years have also occurred while simultaneously a major system transformation was being pursued (including major organizational change such as the abolition of the HSE, the establishment of separate Directorates and a reconfiguration toward a universal primary care system). International evidence from the World Health Organization and others suggests that significant year-on-year variations in the level of statutory funding available for health services is disruptive to the sustained delivery of services of a given quality and desired level of access (World Health Organization & European Observatory on Health Systems and Policies, 2012). These international experts who reviewed the Irish healthcare system in 2012 concluded that continuing budgetary cuts and consequent adjustments raise 'serious concerns whether this can be achieved without damaging access to necessary services for certain groups' (World Health Organization & European Observatory on Health Systems and Policies, 2012, p.47). Barriers to access to healthcare are highlighted, especially among those just above the threshold for a medical or GP visit card (World Health Organisation & European Observatory on Health Systems and Policies, 2012).

Social Justice Ireland believes that, overall, the cutbacks over seven years (resulting in measures like high prescription charges, increased thresholds for the Drug Repayment Scheme and other measures) are most adversely affecting people on low-incomes. Very long waiting times are impacting on poorer people without private health insurance. This is not compatible with a health-service designed to included safety, high-quality and equity. Furthermore, *Social Justice Ireland* is seriously concerned that there is no evidence that funding has been provided to address the ageing of the population that will result in a steady increase in older people and people with disabilities accessing services. For example, those over 65 are increasing in number annually by approximately 20,000. Those over 80 years, who have the greatest healthcare needs, are growing by some 4% annually. This ageing of the population is the most dramatic anticipated change in the future structure of the Irish population (Department of Health 2014). See below for more discussion of population ageing and its consequences.

One would have to conclude that overall the thrust of recent policy is disjointed, lacks coherence and involves levels of expenditure reduction within a short space of time that are not compatible with a well-managed system.

Current capacity on community services is insufficient to meet growing demands associated with demographic pressure and which are reflected in the inappropriate levels of admission to and delayed discharges from acute hospitals referenced above. The acute hospital system, which is already under some considerable pressure, will be unable to operate effectively unless there is a greater shift towards primary and community services as a principal means of meeting home support and continuing care needs and enabling people to live in the community for as long as possible.

The short-comings in resourcing of community services can be illustrated in figure 8.1 below.

Social Care: Fair Deal, Home Helps, Home Care Packages

A review of the funding across the Social Care services of Fair Deal, Home Help and Home Care Packages relative to the over65 population from the period 2006-2014 indicates that while the population continues to grow year on year, the allocated funding for each service was reduced in 2011 (see Figure 8.1 below). It is acknowledged that pay savings and productivity measures arising from national agreements and associated measures have contributed to control of staffing costs in the public system, but the benefits in this regard are not sufficient to offset the growth in demand.

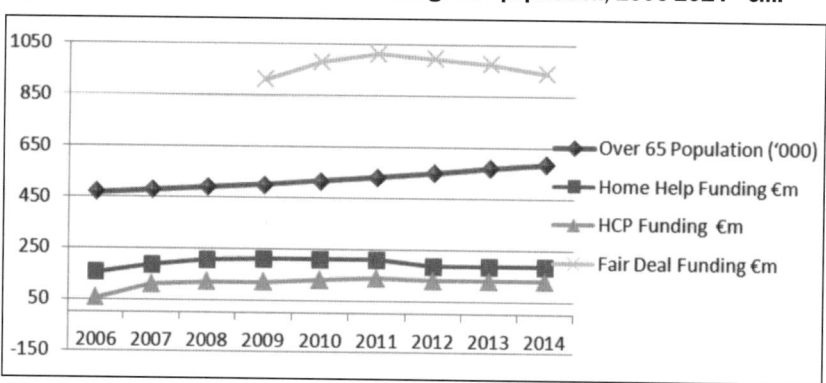

Figure 8.1 Fair Deal and Home Care Funding: 65+ population, 2006-2014 - €m.

Source: Health Service Executive Reports – Various years

Key points in relation to Figure 8.1:

- **Home Help:** the level of Home Help service has reduced from a high of 12.64m hours delivered to 55,000 people in 2008 to a current level of 10.3m hours delivered to 47,000 people, a reduction of 14% being supported by the service. The funding level was reduced from a high of €211m to €185m over this period.

- **Home CarePackages:** While the numbers being supported by HCPs have increased year on year to the current position of 13,199, the average value of each HCP has fallen as the funding available has remained relatively static since 2008.

- **Fair Deal:** Since the inception of NHSS, the number of clients supported in long-stay residential care has remained relatively static despite the increase in population of older people.

Public Residential care beds are key resources in the continuum of care, as short-stay beds serve as an intermediate care provision across hospital and community, providing respite, assessment and step-down care. The long-stay residential care is the resource which provides for residents with highly complex requirements that may not be able to be supported in private beds.

Figure 8.2 Public Residential Long-stay & Short-stay beds, 2008-2014

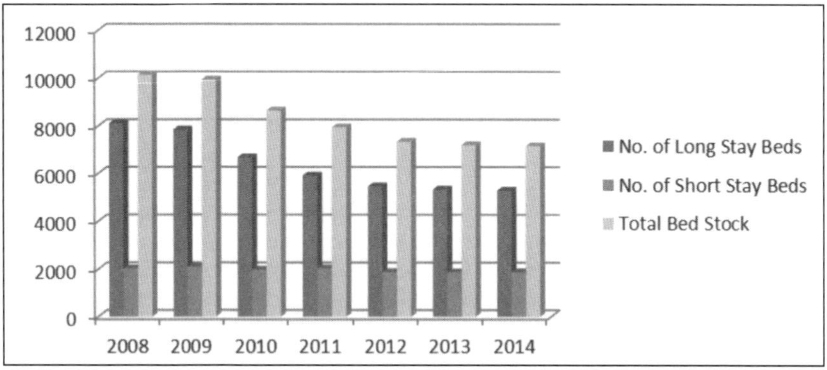

Source: Health Service Executive Reports – various years

Key points in relation to Figure 2:

- Despite the steady growth in population, the public bed stock capacity has reduced significantly from a high of over 10,000 beds in 2008 to a current capacity of 7,157 beds in 2014, which represents a 29% bed stock reduction since 2008 inclusive of:

    - a reduction in short-stay from a high of over 2,000 to the current capacity of 1,868 (11% reduction);
    - a reduction in long-stay beds from over 8,000 to the current capacity of 5,289 (35% reduction);
    - In addition to the funding issues, HIQA requirements in relation to the standards of long-stay accommodation has deemed certain facilities or parts of facilities to be unsuitable or required reduced occupancy levels in others. This is a continuing issue for the sustainability of current levels of public bed provision. There has been some major and minor capital provision to address this issue, but not on a scale which would allow for the planned improvement or replacement of all facilities in need of upgrading.

The above information underlines the reduction that has been a feature of the available resource across these key areas of service provision at a time of increasing population of older people. What is of interest is that the provision of community based service, albeit at lower capacity over the past 5-6 years, has 'stretched' the service provision in order to match the needs as far as possible. Also, a key indicator of value is that the NHSS (Nursing Homes Support Scheme) at this point supports 3.9% of the population aged over-65 in residential care. In planning norms identified in the mid-2000s, the key target figure was 4%.

However, it is clear that there is a link between the diminished levels of services as outlined above and the ongoing increasing activity experienced by the Acute Services in terms of presentations of older people and subsequent delayed discharge numbers while the current configuration of services are in place. We will return to some of the issues highlighted in this section below when we discuss the situation relating to older people.

An open and transparent debate on funding of healthcare services is needed. Ireland must decide what services are expected and how these should be funded and prioritized. In terms of government's overall expenditure, healthcare accounted for 27 per cent in 2011 and 24 per cent in 2015, the second largest area of expenditure (after social protection) (Department of Expenditure & Reform, 2011; 2014). Despite expenditure of 8 per cent of GDP on healthcare (in 2012), and a relatively young population, there are recurring problems illustrated above and in the rest of this Chapter in areas that include access to specialists, waiting lists, access to accident and emergency care, mental health services, long-term care and community care. However, this debate must acknowledge the enormous financial expenditure on healthcare. Public healthcare expenditure grew rapidly over the decade 2000 to 2010, from €5.334bn to €14.165bn. This was an increase of 160 per cent over a period in which inflation increased by 33 per cent. The difference is attributed in part to improved and expanded services, as well as to organisational changes (such as home-helps, for example, becoming salaried members of staff within the HSE). Medical inflation was inevitably also an issue. International experts have noted that, despite increased investment during the previous decade, when the financial crisis occurred in 2008 Ireland still had poorly developed primary and community care services (WHO & European Observatory on Health Systems and Policies, 2012).

Clearly significant efficiencies are possible within healthcare system – not least due to improvements in technologies. Experts in this area conclude that good versions of universal health care are affordable where services are provided efficiently (Norman 2015). Obtaining value for money is essential. However, these efforts should be targeted at areas in which efficiencies can be delivered without compromising the quality of the service and without disproportionately disadvantaging poorer people. *Social Justice Ireland* continues to argue that there is a need to be specific about the efficiencies that are needed and how they are to be delivered.

As well as a debate on the overall budget for healthcare, there should be discussion and transparency on the allocation to each of the services. Currently nearly 60% per cent of the budget is allocated to Primary, Community and Continuing Care, which includes the medical card services schemes (Department of Health, 2014 figure 6.2). *Social Justice Ireland* recommends an increase in this percentage and greater clarity about the budget lines.

The model of healthcare

Community-based health and social services require a model of care that:

- is accessible and acceptable to the communities they serve;
- is responsive to the particular needs and requirements of local communities;
- is supportive of local communities in their efforts to build social cohesion; and
- accepts primary care as the key component of the model of care, affording it priority over acute services as the place where health and social care options are accessed by the community;
- provides adequate resources across the full continuum of care, including primary care, social care as well as specialist acute hospital service to fully meet the needs of our ageing population.

There are a number of key areas requiring action if the basic model of care that is to underpin the health services is not to be undermined. There areas include:

Older people's services
Primary care, primary care teams and primary care networks
Children and family services
Disability, and
Mental health

Older people's services

Although Ireland's population is young in comparison to those of other European countries, it is still ageing. Between 2006 and 2011, those over 65 years of age increased by 14.4 per cent and those aged over 85 years increased by 22 per cent (CSO, 2012). The most dramatic anticipated change in the future structure of the Irish population is the increase in the numbers of older people. See Figure 8.3. Some facts recently published by the Department of Health (2014) relative to population ageing:

- Those over 65 are increasing in number annually by approximately 20,000 per year;
- By 2026 the number of those over 85 years will have almost doubled;
- While there were approximately 530,000 people aged 65 and over in 2011, there will be nearly 1 million by 2031 – an increase of 86.4 per cent;
- There were 58,000 people aged 85 or over in 2011 and this number will increase to some 136,000 people by 2031, and this represents an increase of 132.8 per cent;
- The old age dependency ratio (the ratio of those aged 65 years and over to those aged 15-64) was 17.3 in 2011 and it is projected to rise to 30 by 2031.

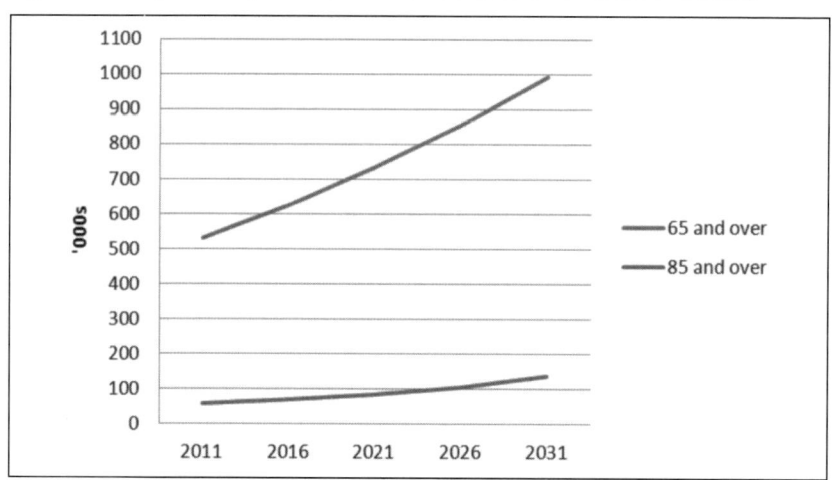

Figure 8.3 Projected Population, 2011 to 2031; ages 65+ and 85+ ('000s)

Source: Department of Health 2014, Table 1.4. Actual figure for 2011

Statistics from the 2011 Census (CSO, 2012) demonstrate a strong link between disability and increased age:

- The disability rate is less than 10 per cent for those in their 20s;
- The rates is 20 per cent by the age of 60, and from age 70 on the rates increase more sharply
- The percentage of the population aged 85 and over who have a disability is 72.3 per cent – the rate is higher (at 75.1 per cent) for females aged 85 or over
- There were 56,087 disabled persons who lived alone and were 65 years or over.

Thus very striking increases in the numbers of older people are now projected, particularly of those who are over 85. While there is some evidence that the care needs of older people will not overwhelm the health system and that the changes will happen gradually and slowly (Normand 2015), there is also evidence to the contrary which suggests that the current experience of challenges within the acute hospital system around trolley waits, delayed discharges, increased waiting lists for elective surgery as well as significant HIQA reports indicating a system under pressure provides strong evidence that the reducing budgets since 2008, allied to the increasing ageing population and related demands, are indeed overwhelming the system. This level of population ageing will be associated with higher levels of disability and long-term ill-health and this requires planning and investment which will provide a resource not just for demographic growth from 2015 onwards but the deficits which have grown from 2008 onwards to achieve a stabilised healthcare system across hospital and community services. It requires health promotion measures and action to facilitate the full participation of people with disabilities – including older disabled people - in social life. It also requires a comprehensive approach to care services that would include integrated services across the areas of GP care, public health nursing, home care supports, acute hospital care, rehabilitation and long-term care.

The 2015 HSE National Service Plan envisages an approach to delayed hospital discharges that involves an allocation of an additional €25million (Health Service Executive 2014). This is to be used on, amongst other things, increased provision of long stay places under the Nursing Homes Support Scheme (€10million), increased provision of short-stay beds intended to provide transitional and rehabilitation services in the Dublin area (€8million), and additional Home Care Packages (400 additional packages benefiting 600 people in course of the year, cost €5 million). However, the Service Plan acknowledges that this allocation has 'limited potential' to deal with the increased demand due to rising levels of chronic disease and dependency on health and other social services associated with people living longer than even a decade ago (Health Service Executive 2014 p.6). Thus the level of funding allocated to address population ageing is not adequate.

For example, the HSE Service Plan for 2015 envisages making 300 new places available under the Nursing Home Support Scheme (NHSS or 'Fair Deal' scheme) and a reduction in waiting times to eleven weeks from January 2015 (Health Service Executive, 2014). These are not ambitious targets, given that there were almost 2,000 people waiting for funding approval under the scheme in November 2014 (Health Service Executive 2014). This appears to represent a huge increase in those waiting to access the scheme – as there were fewer than 500 people on the placement list in December 2013 (Health Service Executive, 2013). The number of people projected to be funded by the scheme in 2015 is 22,016 (Health Service Executive, 2014) but this is some 1,000 fewer places from the total at end Dec 2013 (23,007) (Health

Service Executive (2014). The National Service Plan for 2015 acknowledges the risk that there is insufficient capacity to meet current and additional requirements. This approach risks leading to more older people remaining in inappropriate care facilities such as acute hospitals, an outcome in the best interests of neither the individual nor the health services. This is not an appropriate response when the number of people aged over 85 is increasing rapidly as many of them rely on public services to continue to live with dignity. It is crucial that funding be released in a timely manner when a person is deemed in need of a 'Fair Deal' bed and that sufficient capital investment is provided to ensure that enough residential care beds are available to meet the growing demand for them.

Support for people to remain in their own homes is a key and appropriate policy objective and coincides with the wish of most older people. But this commitment does not appear to be supported in practice when we note the significant decrease in the provision of home help hours in recent years[53] especially at a time of population ageing. As Table 8.5 shows, there were approximately 8,300 fewer people in receipt of home help support in 2014 than there had been in 2008 (a decrease of approximately 14.5 per cent) and there was a decrease of 2.34million in the hours delivered (a decrease of some 18.5 per cent). Looking at the years after 2008 there was a steady decrease in the number of hours delivered and people receiving hours especially from 2011, and although there has been a slight increase in 2014, both the number of hours delivered and those served by the scheme are still considerably less than in 2008 or indeed in 2011. During the period 2008-2014, the number of people in receipt of Home Care Packages grew (by 4,200 people), representing an increase of some 47 per cent, but, as already mentioned, the funding for this scheme has remained static. The 2015 Health Service Executive National Service Plan envisages additional spending in this area (including on Home Care Packages for 600 people) but also acknowledges the risk that overall the amount allocated for older people is not sufficient to address increasing demand.

---

[53] HSE reports make it clear that older people are the main beneficiaries of Home Help services and Home Care Packages.

Table 8.5 - HSE Support to Older People in the Community, 2007 - 2013

	2007	2008	2009	2010	2011	2012	2013	2014
Home Help: People in receipt	54,736	55,366	53,971	54,000	50,986	44,387	46,454	47,061
Home Help: Hours delivered	12.35m	12.64m	11.97m	11.68m	11.09m	9.8m	9.73m	10.3m
Home Care Packages People in receipt	8,035	8,990	8,959	9,941	10,968	10,526	11,873	13,199

December Performance Reports, 2008, 2009, 2011, 2012; 2013;2014.
November Performance Report, 2010 and HSE Annual Report 2010.

Another issue that is relevant is the impending closure of public nursing home beds due to failure to meet the standards set by the Health Information and Quality Authority (HIQA). The Health Service Executive Director General has indicated that there is currently insufficient funding to bring accommodation standards in thirty large public nursing homes up to the levels required by HIQA. Closure of these units would have a number of consequences for their individual residents and also a knock-on effect on hospital overcrowding due to increasing the numbers of people needlessly occupying hospital beds for want of a suitable alternative.

Over the past six or so years, changes in public services (such as in home help hours and community nursing units, reductions in the Fuel Allowance, cuts in the Household Benefits Package, abolition of the Christmas bonus, and increases in prescription charges as well as decreased frontline staff and services within the healthcare sector) have all adversely affected older people, falling most heavily on poorer groups without the income to compensate and especially, of course, on poorer people with disabilities or illness. International experts have identified that in relation to public health spending alone, the reduction in Ireland's spending on over 65s will have fallen by approximately 32 per cent per head between 2009 and 2016 (World Health Organization & European Observatory on Health Systems and Policies, 2012).

Supports that enable people to live at home need to be part of a broader integrated approach that ensures appropriate access to, and discharge from, acute services when required. To achieve this, the specific deficits in infrastructure that exist across the country need to be addressed urgently. There should be an emphasis on replacement and/or refurbishment of facilities. If this is not done the inappropriate admission of older people to acute care facilities will continue, along with the consequent negative effects on acute services and unnecessary stress on older people and their families. A related issue is the shortage of appropriately resourced and staffed geriatric rehabilitation units. The National Clinical Programme for Older People (2012) recommended that every hospital receiving acutely ill older adults have a dedicated specialist geriatric ward and a designated multi-disciplinary team, as well as access to onsite and off-site rehabilitation beds delivering a structured rehabilitation programme for older people. This document recognises that it is a fundamental right of an older person to receive an adequate period of rehabilitation before a decision with regard to long-term care is made. But implementation of these recommendations is lacking and there continues to be a shortage of appropriately resourced and staffed geriatric rehabilitation units in the country (O'Neill 2015).

The stated focus on the development of community based services to support older people in their own homes/communities for as long as possible is welcome. But an Expert Group described Ireland's under-resourced community health services as 'perhaps the greatest deficiency in the current provision of public health services in Ireland' (Ruane, 2012, p.48). A commitment to supporting people at home is only aspirational if funding is not provided for home help services, day care centres and home care packages – some of which have received serious and unwelcome cuts in recent Budgets at a time when they should, on the contrary, be the subject of investment to address population ageing.

Social Justice Ireland believes that on the capital side, an investment in the order of a total of €500 million over five years, (i.e. €100 million each year), is required to meet this growing need. This would enable some 12 to 15 community nursing facilities with about 50 beds each to be replaced or refurbished each year. In addition to supporting the needs of older people, this proposal would also stimulate economic activity and increase employment in many local communities during the construction periods.

Social Justice Ireland also believes that, on the revenue side, funding in excess of €100m is required at a minimum to bring core community services for HCPs, Home Help as well as residential care supports through the Fair Deal scheme to more sustainable levels. This funding will assist in stabilising the current system and allow for a progressive development towards an integrated model of service over a period of years based on an appropriate allocation for demographic growth each year.

Primary care

Primary care is one of the cornerstones of the health system something acknowledged in the strategy document *Primary Care – A New Direction* (2001). Its importance was recognised in subsequent strategies, *Future Health* (2012) and *Healthy Ireland* (2013). Between 90 and 95 per cent of the population is treated by the primary care system. The model of a primary care needs to be flexible so that it can respond to the local needs assessment. Paying attention to local people's own perspective on their health and understanding the impact of the conditions of their lives on their health is essential to community development and to community orientated approaches to primary care. A community development approach is needed to ensure that the community can define its own health needs, work out collectively how these needs can best be met, and decide on a course of action to achieve this in partnership with service providers. This will ensure greater control over the social, political, economic and environmental factors that determine the health status of any community. The principle underlining this model should be a social model of health, in-keeping with the World Health Organization's definition of health as a 'state of complete physical, mental and social well-being and not merely the absence of disease or infirmity'. Ireland's *Healthy Ireland* strategy describes health as 'a personal, social and economic good'.

Universal access is needed to ensure that a social model of health can become a reality. Government's commitment to introduce universal health insurance is currently postponed if not entirely shelved[54] and indeed the timeframe for its introduction always seemed ambitious. Delays and challenges are associated with government's approach to extending free GP care to all children under six. Another issue that has to be addressed in any planning for the future is how to deliver an integrated system of care, especially for people with complex or chronic conditions, if what is proposed is that primary and hospital care would be funded through the insurance system, but social care services, including long-term care, would not be. For the approach outlined in *Future Health* to be implemented there is a clear need for an increase in the proportion of the total healthcare budget being allocated to primary care and a more comprehensive and integrated approach to social care services to support people living at home.

Ireland's healthcare system has struggled to provide an efficient response to the health needs of its population. Despite a huge increase in investment in recent years great problems persist. The development of primary care teams (PCTs) across the country could have a substantial positive impact on reducing these problems.

Developing PCTs and primary care networks is intended as the basic building block of local public health care provision. The Primary Care Team (PCT) is intended to be a team of health professionals that includes GPs and Practice Nurses, community

---

[54] As of January 2015, a costing analysis is to be completed and the Minister for Health is preparing a 'roadmap' for next steps. Furthermore, current changes to the rules on community rating which incentivise people at younger ages to buy insurance directly contradict the plan to move to a single tier universal insurance system for everyone within the next few years (Normand 2015).

nurses (i.e. public health nurses and community RGNs), physiotherapists, occupational therapists and home-care staff. PCTs are expected to link in with other community-based disciplines to ensure that health and social needs are addressed. These include speech and language therapists, dieticians, area medical officers, community welfare officers, addiction counsellors, community mental health nurses, consultant psychiatrists and others.

It was envisaged that 530 Primary Care Teams supported by 134 Health and Social Care Networks would cover the country by 2011. According to the HSE, there were 486 PCTs in place by the end of 2012 (Department of Health, 2012) but some of these have now been merged, and, at the end of December 2013, 419 Primary Care Teams were operating (Department of Health, 2014). Thirty-four primary care centres have opened and the development of a further 48 are underway (Department of Health, 2014). The Health Service Executive Service Plan for 2015 envisages establishment of new organisational structures including nine Community Healthcare Organisations and 90 Primary Care Networks intended, inter alia, to support Primary Care Teams. The work done on existing teams is very welcome but much more is needed to ensure they command the confidence and trust of local communities. Greater transparency about their planning and roll-out is also needed.

The recent establishment of seven Directorates to run the health system is of concern because this approach may obstruct the delivery of an integrated healthcare system for service users at local level. There are real concerns that the new approach will increase rather than reduce costs and bureaucracy. Instead of an integrated system based on primary care teams at local level, seven 'silos' could emerge, competing for resources and producing a splintered system that is not effective, sustainable or viable in the long term.

Social Justice Ireland believes that reform of the healthcare system is necessary but is seriously concerned that the proposed new structure will see each Directorate establish its own bureaucracy at national, regional and local levels. An important first step to address these concerns would be the publication of a comprehensive plan for the implementation of the new community healthcare organisations and the 90 primary care networks envisaged. This plan should clearly outline how the Primary Care Teams and networks will link with mental health and social care services and how collectively these community services will be integrated with acute hospital services as well as other important services at local government, education and wider community level. It will also be necessary that this work be linked to the new GP contract which it is intended will focus on chronic disease management, prevention and community involvement.

Children and family services

There is a need to focus on health and social care provision for children and families in tandem with the development of primary care team services. The 2006 Concluding Observations of the UN Committee on the Rights of the Child noted the lack of a comprehensive legal framework and the absence of statutory guidelines safeguarding the quality of, and access to, health care services, particularly for children in vulnerable situations (Children's Rights Alliance, 2014). The Committee also raised concerns about the practice of treating children with mental health issues in adult in-patient facilities.

Social Justice Ireland welcomed the announcement of free GP care for under-fives several years ago. However, implementation of this scheme (now to apply to under 6's) is still awaited and it will require negotiation with providers and legislative changes. Policy in this area appears fragmented and lacking transparency as the withdrawal of discretionary medical cards from some children with high levels of medical need during 2014 shows, and - although this policy has officially been reversed - there are still media reports of difficulties for families in this situation. A universal approach to primary care of under 6's should not be accompanied by a harder line being taken to children with high levels of medical need.

Many community and voluntary services are being provided in facilities badly in need of refurbishment or rebuilding. Despite poor infrastructure, these services are the heart of local communities, providing vital services that are locally 'owned'. There is a great need to support this activity and, in particular, to meet its infrastructural requirements. *A Vision for Change* (revised as per Census 2011 data) recommended the establishment of 107 specialist Child and Adolescent Mental Health teams, but by the end of 2012 there were 63 teams operating and staffing was at just 38 per cent of what had been recommended (Children's Rights Alliance, 2014).

Social Justice Ireland has welcomed the extra €6million allocation for therapy services in the Children and Young People programme provided in Budget 2015, and believes that a total of €250 million is required over a five year period to address the infrastructural deficit in Children and Family Services. This amounts to €27 million per area for each of the nine Children Services Committee areas and a national investment of €7 million in Residential and Special Care.

As well as the issue of child protection, current key issues include waiting times for treatment (see above), policy on early childhood care and education, child poverty, youth homelessness, addressing disability issues among young people and the issue of young carers.

Disability

A total of 595,335 persons, accounting for 13 per cent of the population, had a disability in April 2011 (CSO 2012). Disability policy remains largely as set out in the National Disability Strategy from 2004 and its Implementation Plan published in 2013. There are many areas within the disability sector in need of further development and core funding and an ambitious implementation process needs to be pursued now.[55]

People with disabilities have been cumulatively affected by a range of policies introduced in successive Budgets in recent years. These include cuts to disability allowance, changes in medical card eligibility criteria and increased prescription charges, cuts in respite services, cuts to home help and personal assistant hours and other community-based supports such as the Housing Adaptation Grants Scheme as well as the non-replacement of front-line staff providing services to people with disabilities. A modest additional allocation provided for in the Health Service Executive Plan, 2015, while welcome, is not sufficient for 'additional new service developments' (Health Service Executive 2014). The cumulative effect of the changes made in recent years makes it more difficult for some people to continue to live in their communities. Furthermore, people with disabilities experience higher everyday costs of living because of their disabilities and one study suggests that the estimated long-term cost of disability is about one third of an average weekly income (cited in Watson and Nolan 2011). As Chapter 3 discusses, they are one of the groups in Irish society at greatest risk of poverty.

The Value for Money (VFM) & Policy Review of Disability Services in Ireland 2012 recommends a complete and radical transformation of disability services in Ireland. The HSE Service Plans in 2014 and 2015 indicates some progress in putting in place the structures and processes necessary to implement the type of comprehensive change programme envisaged by Government. However, *Social Justice Ireland* is concerned that the pace of change is too slow and that additional targeted resources will need to be provided to ensure a comprehensive and lasting system of change initiative is delivered to the benefit of service users and local communities. *Social Justice Ireland* welcomes the establishment of a high level Steering Group to oversee the change programme, reporting to the Minister. However, given the scale of infrastructural development required to move away from communal settings, towards a community based, person-centred model of service, a dedicated reform fund will need to be put in place to support the transition to a new model of service. People with disability will need to be supported, not only by the health service, but by the Department of the Environment through Local Authorities in terms of

---

[55] Other disability related issues are addressed throughout this review.

housing need and through the Department of Social Protection in terms of income supports as well as by the Department of Education in terms education and training requirements. A dedicated reform fund supported by government departments would assist in achieving the type of radical change required.

Mental health

The Expert Group on Mental Health Policy published a report entitled *A Vision for Change – Report of the Expert Group on Mental Health Policy* (2006). This report offered many worthwhile pathways to adequately address mental health issues in Irish society. Unfortunately, to date little has been implemented to achieve this vision. In 2009, the Mental Health Commission expressed concern about the slow pace of implementation and consequent impacts on the quality of mental health services available to those with mental health issues (2009).

A study on the impact of the recession on men's health, especially mental health, showed that employment status was the most important predicator of psychological distress, with 30.4 per cent of those unemployed reporting mental health problems (The Institute for Public Health, 2011).

According to a study from Eurofound, between 2008 and 2012, there was almost no increase in the transfer of either budget or staff from hospitals to the community resulting in the under-provision of community services and the overmedication and increased hospitalisation of people with mental health problems (Eurofound, 2014). Readmission rates were also found to have increased.

There is an urgent need to address this whole area in the light of the World Health Report (2001) *Mental Health: New Understanding, New Hope.* This estimated that in 1990 mental and neurological disorders accounted for 10 per cent of the total Disability-Adjusted Life Years (DALYs) lost due to all diseases and injuries. This estimate increased to 12 per cent in 2000. By 2020, it is projected that these disorders will have increased to 15 per cent. This has serious implications for services in all countries in coming years.

Social Justice Ireland welcomed the allocations in Budgets 2014 and 2015 for mental health services, but there have been delays in spending previous allocations due it appears mainly to recruitment difficulties. According to the HSE's divisional plan for mental health for 2015, staffing levels are still at approximately 75% of what was recommended in *A Vision for Change* (HSE 2015). The mental health services are going through a significant change process at a time when demands on services are growing, as the HSE has noted, in line with population increases and the effects of the economic crisis (2014). It is vital that ongoing reductions in inpatient beds are matched by adequate and effective alternative provision in the community.

Areas of concern in mental health

There is a need for effective outreach and follow-up programmes for people who have been in-patients in institutions upon their discharge into the wider community. These should provide:

- sheltered housing (high, medium and low supported housing);
- monitoring of medication;
- retraining and rehabilitation; and
- assistance with integration into community.

In the development of mental health teams there should be a particular focus on people with an intellectual disability and other vulnerable groups, including children, the homeless, prisoners, Travellers, asylum seekers, refugees and other minority groups. People in these and related categories have a right to a specialist service to provide for their often complex needs. A great deal remains to be done before this right could be acknowledged as having been recognised and honoured in the healthcare system.

The connection between disadvantage and ill health when the social determinants of health (housing, income, childcare support, education etc.) are not met is well documented. This is also true in respect of mental health issues.

Older people and Mental Health

Mental health issues affect all groups in society and people of all ages. Dementia is not the only mental health issue to affect older people. It is not an inevitable part of ageing nor is it solely a disease of older age, but older people with dementia are a particularly vulnerable group whose average length of stay in long-stay residential care far exceeds that of others, for example (Cahill *et al* 2015). It is estimated that 47,000 people in Ireland have dementia (based on 2011 Census) and that number is projected to rise with the ageing of the population and could be as high as 132,000 by 2041 (Pierce, Cahill & O'Shea 2014).

A co-ordinated service needs to be provided for people with dementia. The uncoordinated and fragmented provision of specialist care units for people with dementia has recently been highlighted and offers an example of a lack of planning and coherence. It is generally agreed that the needs of people with dementia are unmet within long-term-care and that unmet needs are a source of reduced quality of life and increased disruptive behaviours: many symptoms are estimated to be caused, not by the dementia itself, but from the quality of care people with dementia receive in inappropriate settings (Cahill *et al* 2015). As a consequence, specialist care units are required which offer care in relatively small household-type settings with specially trained staff and meaningful activities provided. However, a recent study found that, where they exist in Ireland, they account for only 11 per cent of the long term care facilities (54 units), and accommodate only 7 per cent of long term care residents[56] – this being the case when it is estimated that over 60 per cent of residents living in long-term care facilities have dementia in middle and high-income countries (Cahill *et al* 2015). A high proportion of the specialist units that do exist were also found to be caring for people in groups that are larger than the small group living arrangements that are recommended, and there were significant inequities regarding their location, with over 50 per cent of all specialist units in only four counties and long waiting lists for access to units in many areas.

A National Dementia Strategy was published at the end of December 2014 and funding has been promised for three priority areas over the next few years – intensive home care supports, GP education and training and dementia awareness. This is welcome. However, the strategy's publication is only a first step and there are many other areas that also require investment – day centres, respite services and other supports for carers, quality long-term care (at home and in care settings) and specialist care units, and evaluation and monitoring of all services.

Research and development in all areas of mental health are needed to ensure a quality service is delivered. Providing good mental health services should not be viewed as a cost but rather as an investment in the future. Public awareness needs to continue to be raised to ensure a clearer understanding of mental illness so that the rights of those with mental illness are recognised.

Suicide – a mental health issue

Suicide is a problem related to mental health issues. For many years the topic was rarely discussed in Irish society and, as a consequence, the healthcare and policy implications of its existence were limited. There was a downward trend in the rate from 2003, which stopped in 2007, something partly attributed to the change in the economy by the National Office of Suicide Prevention (2011). There has been a subsequent reduction in 2010 followed by an increase in the rate in 2011 and a decrease in 2012.

Over time Ireland's suicide rate has risen significantly, from 6.4 suicides per 100,000 people in 1980 to a peak of 13.9 in 1998 and to 11.7 suicides per 100,000 people in 2008 (National Office of Suicide Prevention, 2011).

---

[56] By contrast, in the Netherlands for example, approximately 25% of all long-stay care is small-scale dementia specific, and this proportion is intended to be increased to 33% by 2015

As Table 8.6 shows, according to the latest figures available from the National Suicide Research Foundation, there were 507 recorded suicides in 2012, of which 413 were males and 94 were females. Table 8.6 shows that suicide is predominantly a male phenomenon, accounting for approximately 80 per cent of such deaths. Young males in particular, are the group most at risk, although the rate for men remains consistently high at all ages up to mid-sixties (National Office for Suicide Prevention, 2014).

Identification of overall trends in suicide rates is a complex process particularly using international comparisons. Statistics from Eurostat suggest that where overall rates of suicide are concerned, Ireland ranked 11th lowest in the EU (based on the 2010 rate). However, where younger age-groups are concerned (15-19), Ireland ranked fourth highest for deaths by suicide at 10.5 per 100,000 population (National Office of Suicide Prevention, 2014).

Table 8.6   Suicides in Ireland 2003-2012

Year	No.	Overall Rate	No.	Males Rate	No.	Females Rate
2003	497	12.5	386	19.5	111	5.5
2004	493	12.2	406	20.2	87	4.3
2005	481	11.6	382	18.5	99	4.8
2006	460	10.9	379	17.9	81	3.8
2007	458	10.6	362	16.7	96	4.4
2008	506	11.4	386	17.5	120	5.4
2009	552	12.4	443	20.0	109	4.9
2010	490	11	405	18.3	90	4.0
2011	554	12.1	458	20.2	96	4.1
2012	507	11.1	413	18.2	94	4.1

Rate is rate per 100,000 of the population.

National Suicide Research Foundation (2015)

The sustained high level of suicides in Ireland is a significant healthcare and societal problem. Of course, the statistics only tell one part of the story. Behind each of these victims are families and communities devastated by these tragedies. Likewise, behind each of the figures is a personal story which leads to victims taking their own lives. *Social Justice Ireland* believes that further attention and resources need to be devoted to researching and addressing Ireland's suicide problem.

Future healthcare needs

A number of the factors highlighted elsewhere in this review will have implications for the future of our healthcare system. The projected increases in population forecast by the CSO imply that there will be more people living in Ireland in 10 to 15 years' time and many of them will be older people. One clear implication of this will be additional demand for healthcare services and facilities. In the context of our past mistakes it is important that Ireland begins to plan for this additional demand and begins to train staff and construct the needed facilities.

The system of Universal Health Insurance envisaged in the health reform strategy, 2012-2015, *Future Health,* was intended to facilitate access to healthcare based on need not income. Access to healthcare based on need, not income, is an important aim for Ireland's healthcare system. While steps toward a universal health service have been announced by way of the extension of free GP services to those aged under six and those aged over 70, the timescale for their implementation is less clear. The timeframe for the introduction of Universal Health Insurance has always seemed optimistic (given the level of change involved to an already very complex system) and its development appears to be currently on hold while a costing analysis is completed and while the Minister for Health prepares a 'roadmap' for next steps (as of January 2015).

We share the concerns of the Council for Justice and Peace of the Irish Episcopal Conference (2012) about a lack of focus on health outcomes in Irish public policy on health. We agree with it that the: 'public health strategy should … not only spell out goals for public health but also set out the role that each major field of intervention is expected to perform in achieving those goals, the implications for resource allocation that arise from such roles, and the mechanisms that will be used to ensure that spending actually goes to the areas where it will achieve greatest benefit'.

Key policy priorities on healthcare

- Roll out the nine Community Healthcare Organisations and 90 Primary Care Networks intended, inter alia, to support Primary Care Teams as envisaged in the 2015 HSE Service Plan.
- Recognise the considerable health inequalities present within the Irish healthcare system, develop strategies and provide sufficient resources to tackle them.
- Give far greater priority to community care and restructure the healthcare budget accordingly so as to make the commitment to enable groups like older people to live in their own homes for as long as possible. Care should be taken

to ensure that the increased allocation does not go to the GMS or the drug subsidy scheme.

- Increase the proportion of the health budget allocated to health promotion and education in partnership with all relevant stakeholders, targeting, in particular, people who are economically disadvantaged in recognition of the health inequalities that exist.
- Provide the childcare services with the additional resources necessary to effectively implement the Child Care Act.
- Provide additional respite care and long stay care for older people and people with disabilities and proceed to develop and implement all aspects of the dementia strategy.
- Develop and resource mental health services, recognising that they will be a key factor in determining the health status of the population.
- Continue to facilitate and fund a campaign to give greater attention to the issue of suicide in Irish society. In particular, focus resources on educating young people about suicide.
- Enhance the process of planning and investment so that the healthcare system can cope with the increase and diversity in population and the ageing of the population projected for the next few decades.
- Ensure any new healthcare structure is fit for purpose and publish detailed evidence of how the decisions taken will meet healthcare goals.

9.
EDUCATION AND EDUCATIONAL DISADVANTAGE

CORE POLICY OBJECTIVE:
EDUCATION AND EDUCATIONAL DISADVANTAGE
To provide relevant education for all people throughout their lives, so that they can participate fully and meaningfully in developing themselves, their community and the wider society.

Education can be an agent for social transformation. *Social Justice Ireland* believes that education can be a powerful force in counteracting inequality and poverty while recognising that, in many ways, the present education system has quite the opposite effect. The primary focus of education is to prepare students for life enabling them to participate in and to contribute to society. Education allows people to live a full life. Living a full life requires both knowledge and skills appropriate to age, environment, and social and economic roles, as well as the ability to function in a world of increasing complexity and to adapt to continuously changing circumstances without sacrificing personal integrity (Department of Education and Skills, 1995). Education makes a fundamentally important contribution to the quality and well-being of our society. It is a right for each individual and a means to enhancing well-being and quality of life for the whole of society (ibid). Investment in education at all levels can deliver a more equal society and prepare citizens to participate in a democracy. Education is one of the key policy areas that must be addressed urgently as part of the Policy Framework for a Just Ireland we set out in Chapter 2 under the pillar Social Services. Education must also be available as a right as envisaged in Governance pillar of our policy framework, set out in the same chapter.

Education in Ireland – the numbers

There are just over one million full-time students in the formal Irish education system. Of these, 536,317 are at primary level, 367,178 at second level and 168,982 at third level. The numbers at primary level have been increasing since 2001 and this will have knock on implications for provision at second and third level. (CSO 2012:100). This demographic growth and the knock-on pressure on the education system and the need to develop long-term policies to cater for increased demand have been acknowledged by the Minister for Education and Skills.[57] By 2017 there will be an extra 105,000 extra students in education in Ireland; 64,000 at primary level, 25,000 at second level and 16,000 at third-level[58]. By 2026 the secondary school aged population is projected to increase by between 31 and 34 per cent (CSO, 2013) with the fastest increase expected between 20120 and 20206. This projected increase will require long-term planning in terms of both capital and current expenditure between now and 2026. It will require a significant increase in expenditure during the period. Such planning will require policy coherence across the framework areas of social infrastructure and investment as set out in chapter 2.

Table 9.1: Ireland: Real current public expenditure on education, 2003-2012

Year	First Level* €	Second Level* €	Third Level* €	Real Current Public Expenditure** €m
2003	5,390	7,825	10,539	6,687
2004	5,794	7,914	10,332	6,893
2005	5,898	8,262	10,689	7,133
2006	6,103	8,625	11,206	7,498
2007	6,246	9,085	11,078	7,822
2008	6,361	9,207	10,866	8,061
2009	6,605	9,307	10,314	8,343
2010	6,493	9,010	9,898	8,293
2011	6,455	8,911	9,161	8,326
2012	6,272	8,735	8,417	8,005

*€ per student at 2012 prices **€m at 2012 prices
Source: Department of Education and Skills, CSO (2014)

---

[57] See address by Minister Quinn at Nordic Education Seminar 12/09/2012 http://www.education.ie/en/Press-Events/Speeches/2012-Speeches/SP2012-09-17.html
[58] ibid

Ireland's expenditure on education equalled 6.2 per cent of GDP in 2011, an increase of almost two percentage points since 2008. This is due mainly to the decrease of GDP in Ireland over this period (CSO 2014). However, education accounts for only 9.7 per cent of total public expenditure in Ireland compared with an OECD average of 13 per cent. Finland spends 6 per cent of GDP on education, but has better outcomes in terms of literacy, numeracy and digital literacy. Education accounts for 12 per cent of total public expenditure in Finland (OECD, 2014). Over much of the last decade, as national income has increased, the share allocated to education has slowly increased; a development we strongly welcome. Table 9.1 (CSO 2014) details a real expenditure increase per student of 16.4 per cent at first level and 11.6 per cent at second level over the period 2003-2012. During the same period real expenditure per student at third level declined by one fifth (20.1 per cent). Real expenditure per student in 2012 at primary level was three quarters that at third level. Between 2003 and 2012 the numbers of students in Ireland grew by 17 per cent at first level and by 6.5 per cent at second level. Over the same period, the number of full-time third level students increased by 24.1 per cent (CSO 2014). The number of part-time third-level students increased by just 0.3 per cent in the same period. It should also be noted, however, that Ireland's young population as a proportion of total population is large by EU standards and, consequently, a higher than average spend on education would be expected.

Investment and planning for future education needs

Education is now regarded as a central plank in the economic, social and cultural development of Irish society (Department of Education and Skills, 2004). Education and training are also crucial to achieving the objective of an inclusive society where all citizens have the opportunity to participate fully and meaningfully in social and economic life. The development of the education and skills of people is as important a source of wealth as the accumulation of more traditional forms of capital.

The fundamental aim of education is to serve individual, social and economic well-being and to enhance quality of life. Policy formulation in education should value and promote all dimensions of human development and seek to prepare people for full participation in cultural, social and economic life. This requires investment in education at all levels, from early childhood right up to lifelong learning.

Social Justice Ireland welcomes the fact that the Department of Education has begun to use the population projections by the CSO based on the census results to plan for future education needs, timing and spatial distribution. Using these figures, the Department of Education now projects the following possible increases in enrolment across the system:

- an additional 44,000 places will be needed at primary level between now and 2017[59] with enrolments to peak at 573,777 by 2018[60];

- an additional 25,000 places will be needed at second level between now and 2017 with significant increases projected in the years 2021-2026, to peak at an enrolment of 404,915 in 2025[61];

- at third level, the number of full-time students is expected to continue to rise every year between 2015 and 2028; reaching 211,709 by 2028[62].

The Department of Education has published a capital works programme amounting to €2.2 billion between now and 2016 to address this issue and increase the number of places available through a School Building Programme. *Social Justice Ireland* believes it is critically important that Government, and in particular the Department of Education and Skills, pays attention to the population projection by the CSO for the years to come in order to adequately plan and provide for the increased places needed within the education system in the coming decades. Budget 2012 introduced an increase in the number of pupils required to gain and retain a classroom teaching post in small primary schools. The reasoning given for this change was that small schools benefitted disproportionately from the staffing schedule and that it acted as a disincentive to consider amalgamation. A Value for Money Review of small primary schools was submitted to the Minister for Education and Skills in April 2013 but has yet to be published. The Minister has announced that the recommendations of the report have not been accepted and that Government will implement two new policies to better support small rural schools[63]. These policies include changes to the staffing schedule for small rural schools and a voluntary protocol for one teacher schools. To date 79 schools have lost a classroom post and 42 schools have not gained a classroom post as a result of this decision. A further 75 posts were removed from rural schools in 2014 with the last phase of budget measures relating to small primary schools being implemented in the 2014/2015 academic year. This policy, which has had a significant impact on rural schools and education in rural areas seems to be based on a philosophy that rural schools should be forced to amalgamate. Such a philosophy ignores the economic and social impact of the closure of a school on rural communities.

---

[59] http://www.education.ie/en/Press-Events/Press-Releases/2014-Press-Releases/PR14-12-18.html
[60] http://www.education.ie/en/Publications/Statistics/Statistical-Reports/Projections-of-full-time-enrolment-Primary-and-Second-Level-2014-2032.pdf
[61] ibid
[62] http://www.education.ie/en/Publications/Statistics/Statistical-Reports/Projections-of-demand-for-Full-Time-Third-Level-Education-2014-2028.pdf
[63] http://education.ie/en/Press-Events/Press-Releases/2015-Press-Releases/PR15-02-17A.html

Education is widely recognised as crucial to the achievement of our national objectives of economic competitiveness, social inclusion and active citizenship. However, the overall levels of public funding for education in Ireland are out of step with these aspirations. This under-funding is most severe in early childhood education and in the areas of lifelong learning and second chance education – the very areas that are most vital in terms of the promotion of greater equity and fairness. The projected increased demand outlined above in all areas of our education system must be matched by a policy of investment at all levels that is focussed on protecting and promoting quality services for those in the education system.

Early Childhood Education

It is widely acknowledged that early childhood (pre-primary) education helps to build a strong foundation for lifelong learning and ensure equity in education. It also improves children's cognitive abilities, reduces poverty and can mitigate social inequalities (OECD 2012: 338). It is seen as the essential foundation for successful lifelong learning, social integration, personal development and later employability (European Commission, 2011). It is important that adequate resources are invested in this area because early childhood education plays a crucial role in providing young people with the opportunity to develop to their fullest potential.

The most striking feature of investment in education in Ireland relative to other OECD countries is our under-investment in early childhood education relative to international norms. Ireland spends 0.1 per cent of GDP on pre-primary education compared with the OECD average of 0.5 per cent (OECD 2012: 339). The introduction of the Early Childhood Care and Education Scheme (ECCE) has been a positive move in addressing this under investment. The ECCE Scheme entitles every child between the ages of 3 years and 3 months and 4 years and 6 months to three hours of pre-school care for thirty-eight weeks in one year free of charge. The ECCE scheme is availed of by over 68,000 children and is administered by the Department of Children and Youth Affairs at a cost of approximately €175 million[64]. In 2011, 95 per cent of 4 year olds in Ireland were enrolled in early childhood education as a result of this initiative. However only 47 per cent of 3 years olds were enrolled in early childhood education compared with an OECD average of 67 per cent. Clearly Ireland still has quite a way to go to catch up with the OECD average. The establishment of the Early Years Education Advisory Group by the Minister for Education and Skills is a welcome development. The Minister has made improving the quality of early years education in Ireland a policy priority in 2015. The commitment to ensuring equal educational opportunities to all children from the start of their lives is welcome. A coherent Early Childhood Education and Care

---

[64] Budget 2015 estimate http://www.dcya.gov.ie/docs/01.07.2014_Speech_by_Charlie_Flanagan_TD_Minister_for_Childr/3221.htm

strategy requires adequate resources and policy coordination between the Department of Education and Skills and the Department of Children and Youth Affairs. A commitment to ensuring equal opportunities to all children at the start of their lives should be at the core of all Government policy and not just confined to a number of key departments.

Early childhood is also the stage where education can most effectively influence the development of children and help reverse disadvantage (European Commission, 2011). It has the potential to both reduce the incidence of early school leaving and to increase the equity of educational outcomes. Early childhood education is also associated with better performance later on in school. A recent OECD study found that 15-year-old pupils who attended pre-primary education perform better on PISA testing (Programme for International Student Assessment) than those who did not, even allowing for differences in their socio-economic backgrounds (OECD, 2012:338). This is mirrored in the PISA 2012 results for Ireland which show that Irish students who attended pre-school scored significantly better than those who did not (Department of Education and Skills, 2013).

Chart 9.1 below illustrates that the highest return from investment in education is between the ages of 0 to 5. This is the point in the developmental curve where differences in early health, cognitive and non-cognitive skills, which are particular sources of inequality, can be addressed most effectively. The evidence shows that early childhood education has the greatest potential to provide more equal educational opportunity to those students from lower socio-economic backgrounds. The importance of investment in education is widely acknowledged and the rewards for both individuals and the state are clear. The Oireachtas Spotlight on Early Childhood Education and Care details that the return on investment can be as much as €7 for every €1 invested in a child. Longitudinal studies internationally also show returns of between three and ten times the original investment in children[65]. It is critically important that Ireland invest in this area and provide universal early childhood education services for children. This will provide an economic and social return for many years to come.

The European Commission believes that Europe's future will be based on smart, sustainable and inclusive growth and that improving the quality and effectiveness of education systems is essential to this (European Commission, 2011). Achieving such growth, and honouring the educational commitments outlined in the Programme for Government and National Recovery in the process, will require significant strategic investment in early childhood education and lifelong learning through a policy making process that has long-term planning at its core. Our success in educating future generations of pre-school children will be a major determinant of our future sustainability.

---

[65] http://www.dcya.gov.ie/viewdoc.asp?DocID=1751

Chart 9.1: The Heckman Curve

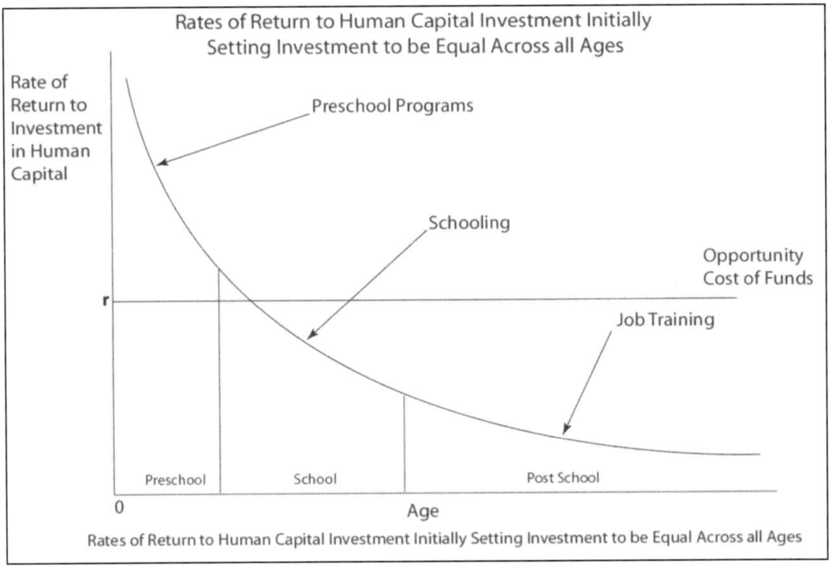

```
Rates of Return to Human Capital Investment Initially
Setting Investment to be Equal Across all Ages
```

[Curve showing Rate of Return to Investment in Human Capital declining with Age, with arrows pointing to Preschool Programs, Schooling, and Job Training. A horizontal line labeled "Opportunity Cost of Funds" at level r. X-axis divided into Preschool, School, Post School.]

Rates of Return to Human Capital Investment Initially Setting Investment to be Equal Across all Ages

Source: Carneiro and Heckman, 2003

Primary and Second Level Education

Ireland has a pupil teacher ratio (PTR) of 15.7 at primary level and 14.4 at second level (CSO, 2014), the eleventh highest in the EU. The average class size in Ireland at primary level is 24.4, the second highest in the EU. Government should address this issue and take action to reduce class sizes at primary level. In 2011 Ireland took part in the Progress in International Reading Literacy Study (PIRLS) and the Trends in International Mathematics and Science Study (TIMSS). These test primary school pupils in the equivalent of fourth class in reading, mathematics and science in over 60 countries. Ireland preformed relatively well, ranking 10th out of 45 participating countries in reading, 17th out of 50 participating countries in mathematics and 22nd out of 50 participating countries in science. A detailed analysis has been published by the Educational Research Centre (Eivers and Clerkin eds., 2013).

Some of the most interesting findings are in the differences in results for children in Northern Ireland and the Republic. Northern Irish primary school pupils performed better in reading and numeracy than any other English speaking country, coming 5th out of 45 participating countries in reading and 6th out of 50 participating countries in mathematics. A revised primary school curriculum and targeted literacy and numeracy programmes were introduced in Northern Ireland in 2007. The new curriculum is based on the skills that children should attain rather than on content to be covered, with a focus on preparation for learning and child-led learning. The revised curriculum has been a considerable success and provides an excellent example of how to redesign a school curriculum, putting quality programmes and services at the heart of the system. This is particularly relevant at a time when the Minister for Education and Skills has set tackling educational disadvantage in schools as one of three priorities for 2015. Recent research from the Educational Research Centre (ERC) (2015) examined English Reading and Mathematics at 2nd and 6th class in primary schools. Students' performance has improved significantly, for this first at primary level since the early 1980s. These very welcome improvements were evident in both DEIS and non DEIS schools. These results show that the targets set out in the National Literacy and Numeracy Strategy 2011-2021 for children and primary level have already been achieved. This strong performance gives the Minister for Education scope to set an ambitious new target following the interim review f the strategy in 2015. There is ample evidence to support more ambitious targets following the interim review. The ERC study also shows that there is still significant scope for improvement. The large proportion of very low achievers in reading in DEIS band 1 schools is worrying (44 per cent of pupils in 2nd class in DEIS band 1 schools performed at or below the lowest proficiency level on overall reading) and there is room for improvement on mathematics and problem solving across all schools.

At second level, Irish students performed relatively well in the 2012 PISA tests in reading, literacy, mathematics and science. The performance of Ireland's fifteen-year-olds shows a significant improvement on the 2009 performance. However, when compared with 2003 PISA results, the overall performance showed very little progress. Students from fee paying schools significantly out-performed those from non-fee paying schools, and students who never attended pre-school performed less well than those who attended pre-school (Perkins et al, 2013). The PISA findings suggest that while reading levels among the school-going population are better than the population generally, this difference is much smaller than might be expected. The fact that the proportion of male students unable to read at the most basic level (Level 2 PISA) is almost unchanged since 2000 (Perkins et al., 2013:143) must be a cause of considerable concern for policymakers. It is clear that fundamental reforms are needed to Ireland's education system[66] to address this problem.

Social Justice Ireland welcomes the reforms to the Junior Cycle and the implementation of the national literacy and numeracy strategy *'Literacy and Numeracy for Learning and Life'*. The strategy sets out national targets and a range of

---

[66] A discussion paper by Áine Hyland for the HEA Summer School 2011 suggested that the emphasis on rote learning at second level might have affected our results as the PISA test is based on the application of prior knowledge.

significant measures to improve literacy and numeracy in early childhood education and in primary and post-primary schools. These measures include improving the performance of children and young people in PISA literacy and numeracy tests at all levels. The impact of these measures and of Project maths should be seen in the next round of PISA 2015. The strategy also proposes fundamental changes to teacher education and the curriculum in schools and radical improvements in the assessment and reporting of student progress at student, school and national level. Progress on this issue is overdue and budgetary and economic constraints must not be allowed to impede the implementation of the strategy.

The 'reform agenda' currently pursued by the Minister for Education and Skills is being implemented at second level with the phased replacement of the Junior Certificate examination with the new Junior Cycle Student Award incorporating a school-based approach to assessment. This award was developed in response to weaknesses in the current model highlighted by the National Council for Curriculum and Assessment[67] and to address the issue of second level students not achieving their potential and the wake-up call in Irish education of students failing PISA tests[68]. *Social Justice Ireland* welcomes the new student centred approach to the Junior Cycle and the new emphasis on helping students who are not performing well in Irish schools. It is important that such reforms be followed through to the Leaving Certificate to ensure policy coherence and a truly student centred approach in the second level education system. It is equally important that policymakers, whilst implementing a reform agenda, remember that the primary focus of education is to prepare students for life, not just for work.

Literacy and Adult Literacy

The OECD PIAAC study 2013 provides the most up to date data on adult literacy in Ireland. On literacy, Ireland is placed 17th out of 24 countries with 18 per cent of Irish adults having a literacy level at or below level 1. People at this level of literacy can understand and follow only basic written instructions and read only very short texts (OECD, 2013). On numeracy, Ireland is placed 19th out of 24 countries with 26 per cent of Irish adults scoring at or below level 1. In the final category, problem solving in technology rich environments, 42 per cent of Irish adults scored at or below level 1. In other words, a very significant proportion of Ireland's adult population does not possess the most basic literacy, numeracy and information-processing skills

---

[67] For more detail see Junior Cycle Briefing Note http://www.education.ie/en/Schools-Colleges/Information/Curriculum-and-Syllabus/A-Framework-for-Junior-Cycle-Briefing-Note.pdf

[68] See Speech by Minister Quinn http://www.education.ie/en/Press-Events/Speeches/2012-Speeches/04-October-2012-Speech-by-Ruair%C3%AD-Quinn-TD-Minister-for-Education-and-Skills-On-the-launch-of-his-Junior-Cycle-Framework.html

considered necessary to success in the world today. The report also found that there is no statistical difference between average literacy scores of adults in Ireland from IALS in 1994 and PIAAC in 2012. In other words, the adult literacy strategy implemented by successive governments in the intervening years was grossly inadequate in terms of dealing with Ireland's adult literacy problem. People with literacy and numeracy difficulties are more likely to be long-term unemployed (O'Connell *et al*, 2009), to have lower earnings and career aspirations (Dorgan, 2009) and are less likely to take part in education and training (Expert Group on Future Skills Needs, 2007). A significant proportion of Ireland's labour force is not equipped with the skills required for the modern labour market. Those with low literacy skills are almost twice as likely to be unemployed (OECD, 2013) and are more likely to report poor health outcomes and are less likely to participate in social and civic life.

The Programme for Government and National Recovery states that the government will address the widespread and persistent problem of restricted adult literacy through the integration of literacy in vocational training and through community education. The previous target for adult literacy policy set out in NAPInclusion was that 'the proportion of the population aged 16-64 with restricted literacy will be reduced to between 10 per cent to 15 per cent by 2016 from the level of 25 per cent found in 1997'. It seems that the targets in the NAP Inclusion were destined for attainment without any policy action on adult literacy (because of the trend for younger people to have overall better literacy levels) (Dorgan, 2009). The European Commission recently noted the slow rate of progress in reform of further education and training (2014). This target was completely unacceptable and unambitious at the time and showed a lack of interest in seriously addressing the problem. The recent PIAAC results confirm this analysis. The lack of focus on this issue has been further underscored by successive budget cuts to funding for adult literacy programmes. Successive Government budgets cut funding for adult literacy since 2010[69] and only a relatively modest additional allocation was made in Budget 2015 (€6million).

No new target or strategy for adult literacy has yet been outlined, despite the Department of Education and Skills commencing a review of adult literacy provision in late 2012, and publishing the report of the review group in September 2013. The Department accepted the findings of the Report and as an initial step the Adult Literacy Operational Guidelines were revised to incorporate many of the recommendations. These guidelines were published in December 2013. A new *Further Education Strategy ('FET strategy') 2014-2019* published by SOLAS in 2014 includes reference to the issue of literacy and numeracy and includes 12 actions described as a 'literacy and numeracy strategy'. Key amongst these is a promotional

---

[69] Budget 2011 reduced capitation grants for adult and further education courses by 5%; there was a 2% reduction in Budget 2012, 2% in 2013 and 1% in 2014.

campaign to elicit higher levels of engagement (SOLAS, 2014, p.100). However, it is disappointing that the FET strategy fails to set specific literacy targets[70] or to commit additional funding. The serious issue of adult literacy deserves a detailed high-level strategy, one that that is more comprehensive than the commitments incorporated in the FET strategy and such a strategy should now be developed. *Social Justice Ireland* believes that public policy aimed at tackling literacy problems among adults has to date simply been inadequate and unacceptable and has left too many people with serious literacy problems unable to function effectively or to obtain meaningful jobs. *Social Justice Ireland* recommends that the new ambitious adult literacy targets o be set in the context of the future social and economic development of Ireland, and that the necessary funding is provided to ensure that this target is met.

Lifelong learning

Equality of status is one of the basic democratic principles that should underpin lifelong learning. Access in adult life to desirable employment and choices is closely linked to level of educational attainment. Equal political rights cannot exist if some people are socially excluded and educationally disadvantaged. The lifelong opportunities of those who are educationally disadvantaged are in sharp contrast to the opportunities for meaningful participation of those who have completed a second or third level education. Unlike the rising earnings premium and earnings rewards enjoyed by those who have completed higher education, the earnings disadvantage for those who have not completed upper secondary education increases with age. Therefore, lifelong education should be seen as a basic need. In this context, second chance education and continuing education are vitally important and require on-going support.

The OECD recommends that lifelong learning opportunities should be accessible to all through systems that combine high-quality initial education with opportunities and incentives for the entire population to continue to develop proficiency in reading and numeracy skills, whether outside work or in the workplace, after initial education and training are completed. It notes that the joint impact of investing in the skills of many individuals may exceed the sum of the individual parts.

There is a strong link between educational attainment and employment. Those aged 25 to 64 with only primary level qualification are three times more likely to be unemployed than those with a third level qualification (24 per cent versus 7 per cent) (CSO 2011:1). This gap has increased 10 percentage points since 2009, demonstrating the difficulties faced by Government in helping those with low levels

---

[70] It instead commits to setting appropriate targets between 2015 and 2019

of educational attainment up-skill and improve their prospects of getting a job. The Programme for Government makes reference to lifelong learning as a high priority for jobseekers. However, labour market activation cannot be the sole factor defining the lifelong learning agenda and education and training curricula. Various reports identify generic skills and competences as a core element of the lifelong learning framework. The Forfás Report *'Sharing our future: Ireland 2025'* (Forfas 2009) highlights the increasing range of generic skills that individuals require to operate within society and the economy. These include basic skills such as literacy, numeracy, use of technology, language skills, people related and conceptual skills. The report of the Expert Group on Future Skills Needs *'Tomorrow's Skills – Towards a National Skills Strategy'* (2007) indicates that there is substantial evidence to show that employers regard generic skills as equal to, if not more important than, technical or job specific skills.

Eight key competences for lifelong learning have been identified by the Council of Europe and the European Parliament (Council of Europe, 2006):

- Communication in the mother tongue (reading, writing, etc.);
- Communication in foreign languages;
- Mathematical and basic competences in science and technology;
- Digital competence;
- Learning to learn;
- Social and civic competences;
- Sense of initiative and entrepreneurship;
- Cultural awareness and expression.

These key competences are all interdependent, with an emphasis in each on critical thinking, creativity, initiative, problem solving, risk assessment and decision making. They also provide the framework for community education and training programmes within the European Education and Training 2010 work programme and the Strategic Framework for European Cooperation in Education and Training (ET 2020) (European Commission 2011). These key competences should be included as part of the reform of apprenticeship programmes. Many of these key competences are already included in one of the recommendations of the report of the review group of apprenticeship training which recommends that apprenticeship programmes should provide for the appropriate integration of transversal skills, particularly literacy, numeracy, maths, science and ICT. These competences could also form the basis of a system to recognise the enhanced skills of the flow of returning migrants. These migrants have gained significant and diverse skills whilst in employment abroad and a system to formally recognise this non-formal skill development will be needed. SOLAS, the Further Education and Training (FET) authority published the new FET strategy in 2014. The publication has brought some strategic planning to the delivery of further education and training that had been lacking previously. The implementation of the strategy will be challenging and more needs to be done at government level to ensure that the further adult and community education sector achieves parity of esteem with other sectors within the formal system. This is particularly important when one considers that is it expected to respond to the needs of large sections of the population who have either been failed by the formal system of for whom it is unsuitable as a way of learning.

A recent Forfas (2014) report urged Government to invest in developing FET and Apprenticeship systems in order to ensure the delivery of more high quality, flexible and responsive education and training programmes that explicitly meet the needs of the learner and the employer and are flexible to local needs.

The same report notes that skills development across all levels of the education and training system must remain priority and that managers be suitably upskilled to that they can recognise the value of education and training in terms of upskilling those who are in employment as well as those seeking employment.

The reform of apprenticeship training in Ireland will be important in terms of providing training and lifelong learning opportunities to those who are low skilled or those who are early school leavers. A reformed system has the opportunity to provide relevant skills and meaningful and clear progression paths to those involved. It can contribute to a strategy to help long-term unemployed people whose skills are now redundant to retrain for employment opportunities that have been identified in particular regions. It could also provide an opportunity to provide people with opportunities to upskill throughout their working life and contribute to a strategy to combat labour market polarisation. A reformed and flexible apprenticeship system could help ensure that low skilled workers at risk of losing their jobs in the future due to automation and the polarisation of the labour market have the skills required to remain in the labour market and take up other employment opportunities. The Apprenticeship Council, established in late 2014 is currently calling for proposals for the expansion of the new Irish Apprenticeship system into new sectors of the economy, across a range of qualification levels. The National Competitiveness Council (2015) has called on Government to ensure that an apprenticeship is seen as an attractive education option offering real career opportunities. It also proposes that apprenticeships be developed in key sectors such as modern manufacturing and engineering. In a welcome move the Minister has set the development of 21st century apprenticeships as one of three key policy priority areas for 2015.

Access to educational opportunity and meaningful participation in the system and access to successful outcomes, are central to the democratic delivery of education. Resources should be made available to support people who wish to engage in lifelong learning, in particular those people who completed second level education but who chose not to progress to third level education at that point. *Social Justice Ireland* welcomes the provision in the Technological Universities Act 2014 that a combined minimum of 30 per cent of all enrolments are to be in flexible learning programmes; professional or industry based programmes or mature learners. It is important that enrolment policies for higher education are revised and amended in conjunction with the reforms to further education and training.

Early school leaving

The proportion of persons aged 18-24 who left school with, at most, lower secondary education in Ireland was 9.7% in 2012 (CSO, 2014). The rate has been decreasing steadily since 2002 and positive progress has been made in this area. However it still remains a serious issue. Early school leaving not only presents problems for the young people involved but it also has economic and social consequences for society. Education is the most efficient means by which to safeguard against unemployment. The risk of unemployment increases considerably the lower the level of education. Early school leavers are:

- at higher risk of poverty and social exclusion;
- confronted with limited opportunities to develop culturally, personally and socially;
- likely to have poor health status; and
- face a cyclical effect associated with early school leaving, resulting in the children of early school leavers experiencing reduced success in education (European Commission, 2011).

The unemployment rate for early school leavers is 37 per cent, almost twice that for other persons in the same 18 to 24 age cohort. They also had an employment rate that was half that of their peers (21 per cent compared to 42 per cent) (CSO 2011:7). Government has invested heavily in trying to secure a school-based solution to this problem through, for example, the work of the National Educational Welfare Board (NEWB). Seventy nine per cent of early school leavers are either unemployed or classified as economically inactive, a situation that is simply unacceptable and cannot be allowed to continue. Combined with Ireland's very high NEET (young people aged 15-24 not in education, employment or training) rate of 18.4 per cent, early school leaving is a major issue for government that requires a long-term policy response. It may well be time to try alternative approaches aimed at ensuring that people in this cohort attain the skills required to progress in the future and participate in society. With this in mind the review of apprenticeship training should include this cohort of young people as one of its target groups.

Funding higher education

The purpose of higher education and how it is to be funded has become a topic of much discussion in Ireland. The CSO population projections indicate that considerable investment is required to ensure that the higher education sector in Ireland can continue to cope with the projected increased demand. However public funding for higher education in Ireland has been decreasing since 2009 despite steadily increasing enrolments both full and part time.

A recent report by the Oireachtas Library and Research Service outlines the changing purpose and nature of higher education and how the higher education sector has developed over time in Ireland. This report also outlines some of the challenges Ireland faces in terms of future funding for the sector. The *National Strategy for Higher Education to 2030* made 26 recommendations regarding the future of higher education in Ireland. One of the recommendations is to establish some form of student loan system to make the financing of higher education sustainable. There are arguments both for and against this recommendation.

There are strong arguments from an equity perspective that those who benefit from higher education and who can afford to contribute to the costs of their higher education should do so. This principle is well established internationally and is an important component of funding strategies for many of the better higher education systems across the world. People with higher education qualifications reap a substantial earnings premium in the labour market which increases with age (OECD, 2012:140). The earnings premium in Ireland for those with higher education has increased by 22 percentage points since 2010. Third-level graduates in employment in Ireland earn on average 64 per cent more that those with a leaving certificate only (OECD, 2011), and 81 per cent of people aged 25 to 64 with a third-level qualification are in employment compared with 35 per cent of those with a primary level qualification only. Ireland is one of the few countries where the relative earnings of 25-64 year olds with qualifications from tertiary type A (largely theory based) and advanced research programmes are more than 100 per cent higher than the earning of people with upper secondary or post-secondary education (OECD, 2013).

Ireland is the highest ranking country in the EU in terms of higher education attainment, with 48 per cent of all 25-34 year olds having a third-level qualification. At present third-level students do not pay fees but do incur a student contribution charge at the beginning of each academic year. Undergraduate students are supported through the provision of maintenance grants under the Student Grant Scheme 2013. As a result of decisions taken in Budget 2012 postgraduate students are no longer eligible for maintenance grant support. Without the introduction of some form of income-contingent loan facility this decision is likely to have a significant impact on entry into postgraduate courses in Ireland over the coming years.

There has been much discussion regarding the future funding for Higher Education Institutions (HEIs) and how they might be configured in the future. In the *'National Strategy for Higher Education to 2030'* the Higher Education Authority (HEA) discusses broadening the base of funding for HEIs and sets out in detail how a student contribution framework might be developed and managed. Various policy options for student contributions are discussed in a report to the Minister (Department of Education, 2009) and the fiscal impact of these options are outlined in detail. Further research concludes that an income contingent student loan rather than a graduate tax system would be the most equitable funding option for Ireland (Flannery & O'Donoghue, 2011).

There are also arguments against the introduction of fees for third level education, particularly in light of the absence of any complimentary strategy to ensure the long term future funding for the sector. These arguments relate to the possible costs of administering such a scheme, the risk of escalation in tuition fees and the prospect of there being no immediate saving to public expenditure as Government's loan guarantee would be recorder as General Government Expenditure (Healy and Delaney, 2014). The policy challenge posed by these arguments is made more difficult by the lack of any alternative funding strategy for higher education. The IMF in its most recent country mission emphasises the need for higher education funding reforms to control growth in public spending while protecting low income students[71]. Given the projected increases in student intake it is difficult to see how public spending on higher education can be curtailed and it would be extremely difficult to fund the sector on student loans alone. The sector will require long-term, sustainable Government funding to ensure that it can deliver what is expected of it in terms of human capital and engaging with society. These are the challenges that the Expert Group[72] established to examine the funding policy for higher education must consider when presenting their recommendations at the end of 2015. The recently published discussion paper by the expert group notes that the existing funding system for higher education in Ireland is unsustainable given demographic projections and insufficient to maintain quality. The paper considers the value that higher education in Ireland contributes in terms of economic growth, social development and civic and cultural engagement. Clarity on the nature and

---

[71] http://www.imf.org/external/np/ms/2015/012715.htm
[72] http://www.education.ie/en/Press-Events/Press-Releases/2014-Press-Releases/PR14-07-01A.html

purpose of higher education, its contribution to society and how to enhance this contribution is key in order to guide future funding mechanisms argues the expert group.

Key Priorities on Education and Educational Disadvantage

- Invest in universal, quality early childhood education.
- Set an ambitious adult literacy target and ensure adequate funding is provided for adult literacy programmes.
- Increase resources available to lifelong learning and alternative pathways to education.
- Develop a long-term, sustainable funding strategy for all levels of education (primary, post-primary and higher education).

10.
PEOPLE AND PARTICIPATION

> **CORE POLICY OBJECTIVE: PEOPLE AND PARTICIPATION**
> To ensure that all people from different cultures are welcomed in a way that is consistent with our history, our obligations as world citizens and with our economic status. To ensure that every person has a genuine voice in shaping the decisions that affect them and that every person can contribute to the development of society.

People have a right to participate in shaping the decisions that affect them and to participate in developing and shaping the society in which they live. These rights are part of *Social Justice Ireland*'s Governance policy pillar as set out in Chapter 2. In this chapter we set out some of the implications of these rights and how they might be met in Ireland today.

People

Migration issues of various kinds, both inwards and outwards, present important challenges for Government and Irish society. The circumstances that generate involuntary emigration must be addressed in an open, honest and transparent manner. For many migrants immigration is not temporary. They will remain in Ireland and make it their home. Irish society needs to adapt to this reality. Ireland is now a multi-racial and multi-cultural society and Government policies should promote and encourage the creation of an inclusive and integrated society in which respect for and recognition of all cultures is an important right for all people.

The key challenge of integration

The rapid internationalisation of the Irish population in recent years presents Ireland with the key challenge of avoiding mistakes made by many other countries. The focus should be on integration rather than on isolating new migrant communities. Census 2011 showed that there were a total of 544,357 non-Irish nationals – representing 199 different nations - living in Ireland in 2011 (CSO, 2012: 8). It also showed that that 268,180, or 15.1%, of the workforce are non-Irish nationals (CSO, 2012: 19). These figures are unlikely to change significantly over the next few years, even when allowance is made for emigration. Spending cuts have had significant impact on strategies on integration. The fourth report (2012) of the European Commission against Racism and Intolerance (ECRI) highlighted:

- the closing of the National Consultative Committee on Racism and Interculturalism (NCCRI) in December 2008, and the subsequent loss of the reporting of racist incidents carried out by the NCCRI;

- the lack of adequate language support in the classroom for the 10% of primary school and 12% of post-primary school children from an immigrant background;

- the withdrawal of funding of the Integrate Ireland Language and Training centres; and

- the non-renewal of the Action Plan Against Racism (2005-2008).

Discrimination against Travellers

In Irish society, Travellers have often faced discrimination and the state has been slow to recognise Traveller's culture to be respected as a right. In the Programme for Government and National Recovery 2011-2016 the Government commits to promoting 'greater coordination and integration of delivery of services to the Traveller communities across Government, using available resources more effectively to deliver on principles of social inclusion particularly in the area of Traveller education' (Government of Ireland 2011: 53). While the structures recommended by the Task Force on the Travelling People have been established, it is very important to ensure that the recommendations of the report are fully implemented. The fourth report of the ECRI highlighted the fact that Travellers still face problems related to adequate accommodation and recommended that Government introduce measures binding on local authorities to support the National Traveller/Roma Integration Strategy and fully implement the 1998 Traveller Accommodation Act. It also called on the Government to reduce health inequalities, particularly in relation to the Travelling Community. This is particularly important as Travellers have a lower life expectancy rate and a higher rate of chronic diseases than the rest of the population (Pavee Point, 2012).

Migrant Workers

The latest figures from the Central Statistics Office for nationality and employment are presented in Table 10.1. They show that after a significant fall between 2008 and

2011 the numbers of non-Irish nationals in employment has begun to increase, though the numbers in employment have yet to recover to the peak level in the fourth quarter of 2007.

Table 10.1: Estimated number of persons aged 15 years and over in employment and classified by nationality Q4 2007- Q3 2014, by '000

	2007	2008	2009	2010	2011	2012	2013	2014
Irish	1,804.20	1,736.00	1,632.50	1,603.20	1,584.30	1,579.70	1,626.20	1,642.3
Non-Irish	334.7	316	255.2	220	223.5	269.2	283.6	284.6
Including								
UK	51.4	51.8	44.9	34.1	29.4	46.5	49.8	49.3
EU15*	34.5	33.7	28.5	22.9	21.1	29.1	27.7	22.0
EU15/28	167.7	150.9	114	107.8	114.3	125.9	130.2	129.9
Other	81	79.6	67.9	55.3	58.7	67.7	75.9	83.4
Total	2,138.9	2,052.0	1,887.7	1,823.2	1,807.8	1,848.9	1,909.8	1,926.9

Source: CSO QNHS Series (2008-2014). 2007-2013 Q4/ 2014 Q3. *excluding Ireland and UK

There has been criticism of Irish immigration policy and legislation specifically due to the lack of support for the integration of immigrants and a lack of adequate recognition of the permanency of immigration. Three significant areas of concern are:

- Work permits are issued to employers, not to employees, which ties the employee to a specific employer, increasing their vulnerability to exploitation and reducing their labour market mobility.

- The Irish asylum process can take many years to reach a conclusion and most refugees coming onto the Irish labour market are *de facto* long-term unemployed. A process for training and education of asylum seekers is needed so that they can retain and gain skills (ECRI, 2006 & Employers Diversity Network, 2009).

- The existence of up to 26,000 undocumented migrants working in Ireland, one in five of whom has been here for over ten years[73]. Without credentials they are denied access to basic services and vulnerable to exploitation by employers. The Irish Migrant Rights Centre has proposed an Earned Regularisation Scheme to provide a pathway to permanent residency (Migrant Rights Centre Ireland, 2014).

---

[73] http://www.mrci.ie/wp-content/uploads/2014/11/MRCI_policy-paper_FINAL.pdf

Refugees and Asylum Seekers

Until recently, the number of refugees forced to flee from their own countries in order to escape war, persecution and abuses of human rights had been declining worldwide over a number of years. Recent reports by the United Nations High Commission for Refugees (UNHCR) and the Internal Displacement Monitoring Centre signal a sizeable reversal of this trend. In 2013 there were at least 33.3 million people internally displaced by armed conflict, generalised violence and human rights violations across the world, a 16 per cent increase on 2012 (IDMC, 2014). Of the 8.2 million people newly displaced in 2013, the majority (78 per cent) come from five countries affected by conflict: Syria, Democratic Republic of Congo, Central African Republic, Nigeria and Sudan.

Irish people have had a long tradition of solidarity with people facing oppression within their own countries, but that tradition is not reflected in our policies towards refugees and asylum-seekers. *Social Justice Ireland* believes that Ireland should use its position in international forums to highlight the causes of displacement of peoples. In particular, Ireland should use these forums to challenge the production, sale and free access to arms and the implements of torture.

Despite this tradition of solidarity with peoples facing oppression, racism is an everyday reality for many migrants in Ireland. Preliminary figures from the Immigrant Council of Ireland show an 114 per cent increase in the number of racist incidences reported in the first six months of 2014 with the majority of cases occurring in a person's local workplace or in the home[74]. This increase in reported racism is very worrying and *Social Justice* Ireland urges Government to provide leadership in dealing with the issue. An integrated policy response is needed to address the root causes of racism within communities; political and institutional responses are required to address this problem in order to prevent it deteriorating. The establishment of Citizenship Ceremonies by the Minister for Justice, Equality and Defence and the reforms to the procedure of assessing and processing citizenship applications are welcome and have the potential to promote inclusiveness and integration.

Table 10.2 shows the number of applications for asylum in Ireland between 2000 and 2014. In 2014 Ireland experienced a 53 per cent increase in asylum applications. 2,360 people were deported from Ireland in 2014, of whom 2,147 were refused entry into the country at ports of entry (Department of Justice and Equality, 2014).

In the third quarter of 2014, there were 177,000 applicants for asylum in the European Union; the top three largest nation of origin for applicants were

---

[74] http://www.immigrantcouncil.ie/index.php/media/press-releases/847-racism-reports-increase-by-114-in-first-six-months-of-2014

Afghanistan, Eritrea and Syria, reflecting the terrible situations in those countries (Eurostat, 2014). The UNHCR estimates that at least 3,419 migrants died at sea in 2014 trying to cross the Mediterranean to get into Europe. It has warned that the policies of some governments were increasingly seeing keeping foreigners out as being a higher priority than upholding asylum[75].

Table 10.2 Applications for Asylum in Ireland, 2000-2014

Year	Number	Year	Number	Year	Number
2000	10,938	2005	4,323	2010	1,939
2001	10,325	2006	4,314	2011	1,290
2002	11,634	2007	3,985	2012	956
2003	7,900	2008	3,866	2013	946
2004	4,766	2009	2,689	2014	1,456

Source: Office of the Refugee Applications Commissioner (2014), *Statistical Report December 2014*

The third report of the ECRI identified difficulties in gaining recognition for professional qualifications as a major challenge facing refugees and asylum-seekers when they have been granted leave to stay in Ireland. It means refugees are often unable to find employment commensurate with their qualifications and experience, impeding their full integration into society. It also means their valuable skills, which could contribute to the Irish economy, are unused or underused (ECRI, 2006). *Social Justice Ireland* proposes that asylum-seekers who currently are not entitled to take up employment should be allowed to do so with immediate effect and that structures are established to recognise professional qualifications. The fourth ECRI report has already been highlighted; its recommendations should be implemented in full.

While asylum-seekers are assigned initial accommodation in Dublin, most are subsequently allocated accommodation at locations outside Dublin, pending the completion of the asylum-seeking process. The Reception and Integration Agency (RIA) was established to perform this task. The latest statistics from the RIA show that there are 34 accommodation centres throughout the country accommodating 4,360 people, of whom one third are children (RIA, 2014). Over 3,000 people have been in direct provision centres for two or more years and 1,600 have been in direct provision for five or more years. The system of direct provision relies heavily on private operators. €54.22 million was spent on direct provision in 2014 of which €43.7 million went to 25 commercially owned centres.

---
[75] http://www.unhcr.org/5486e6b56.html

The policy of "direct provision" employed in these centres results in these asylum-seekers receiving accommodation and board, together with €19.10 direct provision per week per adult and €9.60 per child. Over time this sum has remained unchanged and its value has therefore been eroded by inflation. Between 2001 and 2014 the purchasing power of these payments has been decreased by almost 20 per cent. Furthermore, many asylum-seekers have been placed for long periods of time in these centres, with 9 per cent residing in the centres for over seven years (Joyce, C. & Quinn, E., 2014). This situation, combined with the fact that asylum-seekers are denied access to employment, means that asylum-seekers are among the most excluded and marginalised groups in Ireland.

Social Justice Ireland proposes that asylum-seekers who currently are not entitled to take up employment should be allowed to do so with immediate effect and that the direct provision payments should be increased immediately to at least €65 per week for an adult and €38 per week for a child. Removing employment restrictions and increasing the direct provision allocation would cost €12.5m per annum[76] and provide noticeable improvements in the subsistence life being led by these asylum-seekers. The accommodation centres must also be examined; some of the centres, which include a former leisure centre, are not appropriate places for people to live, and serve to isolate asylum seekers. A recent report by the European Migration Network and the ESRI highlights some of the problems with Ireland's reception system. These are a lack of privacy, overcrowding, limited autonomy, and insufficient homework and play areas for children (Joyce, C. & Quinn, E. 2014). Despite Government acknowledging that the reception system is unsuitable for long-term residence of asylum seekers, progress on developing an alternative procedure has been extremely slow. The Minister for Justice, Equality and Defence established a Working Group to report to Government on improvements to the 'protection process' including direct provision and asylum seekers supports in late 2014. The Working Group is tasked with identifying a practical range of recommendations to Government on improvements to the direct provision system, improved supports for asylum applicants and improvements in the processing of applications. The establishment of the Working Group is a long overdue and welcome development, however it is unfortunate that the recommendations must ensure that the overall cost of the protection system to the taxpayer is reduced or remains close to current levels[77].

---

[76] *Social Justice Ireland* calculation based on 2010 data.
[77] http://www.inis.gov.ie/en/INIS/Pages/Ministers%20Fitzgerald%20and%20O%20R%C3%ADord%C3%A1in%20announce%20composition%20of%20Working%20Group%20to%20examine%20improvements%20to%20the%20Protection%20process%20and%20the%20Direct%20Provision%20system

Emigration

Emigration has increased dramatically since 2009. It should be noted that in all migration statistics the year end is April of the year in question. Net migration was negative in 2010; the first time since 1995 more people had left Ireland than returned or arrived from elsewhere. Net outmigration was 27,400 in 2011, rose to 34,400 in 2012, and fell slightly to 33,100 in 2013 and fell again to 21,400 in 2014. During 2008 and 2009 the majority of those emigrating were from the new accession countries. However, from 2010 the largest group emigrating were Irish nationals; 42,000 left in 2011, 50,900 left in 2013, while 40,700 left in 2014. Overall, emigration of all nationalities is estimated to have reached 81,900 in 2014. Table 10.3 below outlines the numbers of people leaving the country between 2006 and 2014, both Irish and non-Irish nationals.

Table 10.3: Estimated Emigration by Nationality, 2006 – 2014, by'000

Year	Irish	UK	EU 13*	EU 10/12**	Rest of World	Total
2014	40.7	2.7	10.1	14.0	14.4	81.9
2013[78]	50.9	3.9	14.0	9.9	10.3	89.1
2012[79]	46.5	3.5	11.2	14.8	11.1	87.1
2011	42	4.6	10.2	13.9	9.9	80.6
2010	28.9	3	9	19	9.3	69.2
2009	19.2	3.9	7.4	30.5	11	72
2008	13.1	3.7	6	17.2	9	49.2
2007	12.9	3.7	8.9	12.6	8.2	46.3
2006	15.3	2.2	5.1	7.2	6.2	36

Source: CSO (2013), *Population and Migration Estimates*.
*EU 15 excluding UK and Ireland. **EU MS that joined in 2004 and 2007

The rate of emigration of Irish nationals has more than tripled since 2008. This demonstrates the lack of opportunities available for people in Ireland, especially for those seeking employment in the 15-44 age group. Of those who emigrated in 2014, more than 33,500 were aged 15-24 and 37,600 were aged 25-44. The austerity programme is contributing to Ireland's loss of young people, the implications of which are stark as this loss will pose significant problems for economic recovery.

---

[78] Preliminary.
[79] Preliminary.

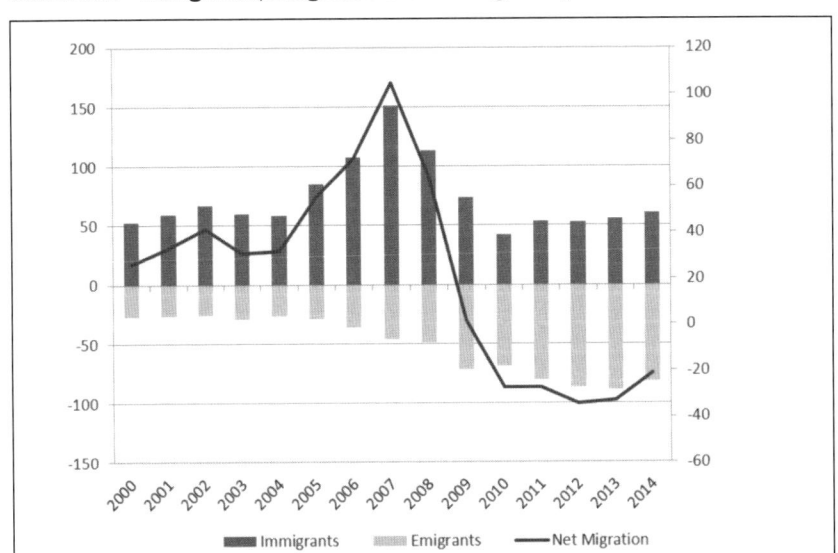

Chart 10.1 – Immigration, Emigration and Net Migration, 2000-2014

Source: CSO, *Population and Migration Estimates (2014)*.

This emigration 'brain drain', which in some quarters is perversely being heralded as a 'safety valve', is in fact a serious problem for Ireland. It may well result in a significant skills deficit in the long-term and hamper Ireland's recovery. *Social Justice Ireland* has highlighted the need for a skills transfer programme for returning migrants in order to ensure the skills that they have acquired whilst working abroad are recognised in Ireland (see chapter 9 for further details). Sadly, emigration has been one of the factors keeping the unemployment rate down. In December 2012, the IMF estimated that had all the employees who lost their job at the outset of the crisis remained in the labour force, the unemployment rate would have been 20 per cent (IMF, 2012: 5). In their latest staff working document on Ireland the IMF highlight the problem of high youth unemployment (22 per cent) and the challenge it poses. Given the continuing weakness of domestic demand and investment in the economy induced by austerity budgets it is likely that emigration will continue for the foreseeable future. Unless there are measures in place to increase employment at a faster pace by boosting domestic demand and investment, outmigration will continue.

Participation

The changing nature of democracy has raised many questions for policy-makers and others concerned about the issue of participation. Decisions often appear to be made without any real involvement of the many affected by the decisions' outcomes. The most recent in-depth analysis of voter participation was undertaken in 2011 by the CSO. In a quarterly national household survey module on voter participation and abstention, issued in November 2011, the CSO provided an insight into how people regarded the electoral process. It found that just over 62 per cent of those aged 18 to 24 voted in the 2011 general election. This contrasts with participation figures of 92 per cent for older voters aged 55 to 64 years (CSO 2011: 3). The survey also found that over one-third of those who did not vote were not registered to vote, 11 per cent of non-voters said they had 'no interest', 10 per cent were 'disillusioned' with politics and 11 per cent had difficulty getting to the polling station (this was particularly common among non-voters aged 55 and over). (CSO, 2011:4) Those educated to primary level only were most likely to say they did not vote because they were disillusioned with politics.

These findings suggest that many people, especially young people and those who have lower educational attainment levels, have little confidence in the political process. They have become disillusioned because the political process fails to involve them in any real way, while also failing to address many of their core concerns. Transparency and accountability are demanded but rarely delivered. Many of the developments of recent years will simply have added to the disillusionment of many people. A new approach is clearly needed to address this issue. Although Government is engaging with members of civil society on eight specific issues as part of the Constitutional Convention[80], it can ill afford to ignore the lack of trust and engagement of civil society in the democratic processes of the state.

Some of the decision-making structures of our society and of our world, allow people to be represented in the process. However, almost all of these structures fail to provide genuine participation for most people affected by their decisions, resulting in apathy towards participating in political processes. The decline in participation is exacerbated by the primacy given to the market by many analysts, commentators, policy-makers and politicians. Most people are not involved in the processes that produce plans and decisions which affect their lives. They know that they are being presented with a *fait accompli*. More critically, they realise that they and their families will be forced to live with the consequences of the decisions taken. This is particularly relevant in Ireland in 2015, where people are living with the consequences of the bailout programme and repaying the debts of European banks through a programme of austerity and upward redistribution of resources. Many feel disenfranchised by a process that produced this outcome without any meaningful consultation with citizens. It is crucially important as politicians and policy makers begin to talk of recovery that people feel engaged in this process. In order to ensure that the recovery reaches all sections of society then we must ensure that all voices are heard.

---

[80] For more information see https://www.constitution.ie/Convention.aspx

Many people feel that their views or comments are ignored or patronised, while the views of those who see the market as solving most, if not all, of society's problems are treated with the greatest respect. This situation seems to persist despite the total failure of market mechanisms in recent years and despite the role these very mechanisms played in producing Ireland's range of current crises and the associated EU-level crises that are not currently being recognised by most decision-makers. Markets have a major role to play. But it needs to be honestly acknowledged that they produce very mixed results when left to their own devices. Recent experience has shown clearly that markets are extremely limited in terms of many policy goals. Consequently other mechanisms are required to ensure that some re-balancing, at least, is achieved. The mechanisms proposed here simply aim to be positive in improving participation in a 21st century society. Modern means of communication and information make it relatively easy to involve people in dialogue and decision-making. The big question is whether the groups with power will share it with others?

A forum for dialogue on civil society issues

A new forum and structure for discussion of issues on which people disagree is becoming more obvious as political and mass communication systems develop. A civil society forum and the formulation of a new social contract against exclusion has the potential to reengage people with the democratic process. Democracy means 'rule by the people', which implies that people participate in shaping the decisions that affect them most closely. What we have, in practice, is a highly centralised government in which we are 'represented' by professional politicians. The more powerful a political party becomes, the more distant it seems to become from the electorate. Party policies on a range of major issues are often difficult to discern. Backbenchers have little control over, or influence on, Government ministers, opposition spokespersons or shadow cabinets. Even within the cabinet some ministers seem to be able to ignore their cabinet colleagues. The democratic process has certainly benefited from the participation of various sectors in different arenas. It would also benefit from taking up the proposals to develop a new social contract against exclusion and a new forum for dialogue on civil society issues.

The failure to discuss openly a range of civil society issues that are of major concern to large numbers of people is contributing to disillusionment with the political process. When discussion or debate does take place, furthermore, many people feel that they are not allowed to participate in any real way. The development of a new forum within which a civil society debate could be conducted on an on-going basis would be a welcome addition to Ireland's political landscape. Such a forum could make a major contribution to improving participation by a wide range of groups in Irish society.

Social Justice Ireland proposes that Government authorises and resources an initiative to identify how a civil society debate could be developed and maintained and to examine how it might connect to the growing debate at European level around civil society issues. There are many issues such a forum could address. Given recent developments in Ireland, the issue of citizenship, its rights, responsibilities, possibilities and limitations in the twenty-first century is one that springs to mind. Another topical issue is the shape of the social model Ireland wishes to develop in the decades ahead. Do we follow a European model or an American one? Or do we want to create an alternative – and, if we do, what shape would it have and how could it be delivered? What future levels of services and taxation will be required and how are resources to be distributed? The issues a civil society forum could address are many and varied and Ireland would benefit immensely from having one.[81]

Deliberative Democracy

To facilitate real participation a process of 'deliberative democracy' is required. Deliberative democratic structures enable discussion and debate to take place without any imposition of power differentials. Issues and positions are argued and discussed on the basis of the available evidence rather than on the basis of assertions by those who are powerful and unwilling to consider the evidence. It produces evidence-based policy and ensures a high level of accountability among stakeholders. Deliberative participation by all is essential if society is to develop and, in practice, to maintain principles guaranteeing satisfaction of basic needs, respect for others as equals, economic equality, and religious, social, sexual and ethnic equality.

Social Justice Ireland believes a deliberative democracy process, in which all stakeholders would address the evidence, would go some way towards ensuring that local issues are addressed. This process could be implemented under the framework of the Council of Europe's *Charter on Shared Social Responsibilities*. The Charter states that shared social responsibility in terms of local government requires that local government 'frame local policies which acknowledge and take into account the contribution made by everyone to strengthening social protection and social cohesion, the fair allocation of common goods, the formation of the principles of social, environmental and intergenerational justice and which also ensure that all stakeholders have a negotiation and decision-making power' (Council of Europe, 2011). We believe these guidelines can be adapted to the Irish context and would be useful tools for devising a policy to promote greater alignment between local government and the community & voluntary sector in promoting participation at local level. This would involve:

---

[81] For a further discussion of this issue see Healy and Reynolds (2003:191-197).

- Local government, the community & voluntary sector and the local community working together to ensure the design and efficient delivery of services for local communities to cater for the specific needs of that particular local community.
- Highlighting the key role of social citizenship in creating vibrant, participative and inclusive communities.
- Direct involvement of local communities, local authorities, state bodies and local entrepreneurs in the policy making and decision making processes.
- Ensuring all voices are heard (especially those of people on the margins of society) in the decision making process.
- Reform of current local government structures to better involve local communities in the governance of and decision making in their local area.
- An increased sense of 'ownership' over local government by the local community, which will only come about with increased participation. The community & voluntary sector has a key role to play in this.

All communities are different and not every community has the capacity or the infrastructure to engage meaningfully with and participate in local government. This is where the community and voluntary sector has a key role to play in informing, engaging with and providing the local communities with the skills to participate in and contribute to local government.

Citizen Engagement

In October 2012 the Department of Environment, Community and Local Government published *'Putting People First: Action Programme for Effective Local Government'*. The document outlines a vision for local government as 'leading economic, social and community development, delivering efficient and good value services, and representing citizens and local communities effectively and accountably' (Department of Environment, Community and Local Government, 2012: iii). One of the stated aims of this process of local government reform is to create more meaningful and responsive local democracy (DECLG 2012:148) with options for citizen engagement and participative democracy outlined in the report. The new framework for public engagement and participation, introduced after the local and European elections in May 2014 is called "The Public Participation Network" (PPN). The PPN facilitates input by the public into local government through a structure that ensures public participation and representation and decision-making committees within local government. The role of the PPN[82] is:

---

[82] For a detailed outline of the structure of the PPN see section 3 of the Working Group Report.

1. To contribute to the local authority's development for the County/City a vision for the well-being of this and future generations.
2. to facilitate opportunities for networking, communication and the sharing of information between environmental, community and voluntary groups and between these groups and the local authority.
3. to identify issues of collective concern and work to influence policy locally in relation to these issues.
4. to actively support inclusion of socially excluded groups, communities experiencing high levels of poverty, communities experiencing discrimination, including Travellers, to enable them to participate at local and county level and to clearly demonstrate same.
5. to encourage and enable public participation in local decision-making and planning of services.
6. to facilitate the selection of participants from the environmental, social inclusion and voluntary sectors onto city/county decision making bodies.
7. to support a process that will feed the broad range of ideas, experience, suggestions and proposals of the Network into policies and plans being developed by agencies and decision makers in areas that are of interest and relevant to the Network
8. to work to develop the Environmental, Community and Voluntary sectors so that the work of the sectors is clearly recognised and acknowledged and the sectors have a strong collective voice within the County/City.
9. to support the individual members of the Public Participation Network so that:
    - They can develop their capacity and do their work more effectively.
    - They can participate effectively in the Public Participation Network activities.
    - They are included and their voices and concerns are heard.

The PPN structure embeds the need to develop sustainable communities and to consider the well-being of communities at the heart of the local decision making process. It is important that the necessary resources are made available to ensure that the PPNs function effectively and that members are given the training and support required to enable them to represent their communities. Most of the PPNs were established by the end of Q1 2015. However several have not followed the correct processes in choosing representatives for local authority structures and this is an issue that must be rectified or the key focus of the PPNs will be lost and they will not deliver on their potential impact on local development.

A deliberative democracy structure and framework embedded into the citizen engagement and local government structures can enhance community involvement in decision making and the policy making process at a local level. It can also ensure that governance, participation and policy evaluation are reformed in line with the Good Governance part of the Policy Framework for a Just Ireland detailed in chapter 2.

Supporting the Community & Voluntary Sector

The issue of governance is of major importance for Government and for society at large. Within this wider reality it is an especially crucial issue for the community & voluntary sector. The community & voluntary sector is playing a major role in responding to both the causes and the consequences of these crises. It should also play a major role in public discussion regarding what type of economic and social vision Ireland wants to pursue in the future. Support for the work of the community and voluntary sector is crucial and it should not be left to the welcome but very limited charity of philanthropists. Funding required by the sector has been provided over many years by Government. In recent years, however, the level of state funding has been reduced, with obvious consequences for those depending on the community & voluntary sector. It is crucial that Government appropriately resource this sector into the future and that it remains committed to the principle of providing multi-annual statutory funding.

Social dialogue is a critically important component of effective decision making in a modern democracy. Now that the economy is beginning to improve and some additional resources are likely to be available, Government is proposing to begin a process of social dialogue as it prepares a multi-annual plan for Ireland's development. A social dialogue process would be a very positive development for Ireland at this point in our recovery. Government needs to engage all sectors of society. Otherwise it is likely to produce lop-sided outcomes that will benefit those who are engaged in the social dialogue process while excluding others, most notably the vulnerable. If Government wishes the whole society to take responsibility for producing a more viable future then it must involve all of us. Responsibility for shaping the future should be shared among all stakeholders. There are many reasons for involving all sectors in this process: to ensure priority is given to well-being and the common good; to address the challenges of markets and their failures; to link rights and responsibilities.

A process of social dialogue involving all and not just some of the sectors in Irish society would be a key mechanism in maximising the resources for moving forward and in ensuring the best possible outcomes for Ireland. Ireland urgently needs to set a course for the future that will secure macroeconomic stability, a just tax system, strengthened social services and infrastructure, good governance and a real commitment to sustainability. A social dialogue process that includes all the stakeholders in Irish society would go a long way towards achieving such a future.

The Community & Voluntary Pillar provides a mechanism for social dialogue that should be engaged with by Government across the range of policy issues in which the Pillar's members are deeply engaged. All aspects of governance should be characterised by transparency and accountability. Social dialogue contributes to both transparency and accountability. We believe governance along these lines can and should be developed in Ireland.

Key Policy Priorities on People and Participation

- Immediately increase the weekly allowance allocated to asylum-seekers on 'direct provision' to at least €65 per week for an adult and €38 for a child and give priority to recognising the right of all refugees and asylum-seekers to work.

- Adequately resource the PPN structures for citizen engagement at local level and ensure capacity building is an integral part of the process.

- Ensure that there is real and effective monitoring and impact assessment of policy implementation using an evidence-based approach. Involve a wide range of perspectives in this process, thus ensuring inclusion of all sectors in a new deliberative process of social dialogue.

11.
SUSTAINABILITY

CORE POLICY OBJECTIVE: SUSTAINABILITY
To ensure that all development is socially, economically and environmentally sustainable

The search for a humane, sustainable model of development has gained momentum in recent times. After years of people believing that markets and market forces would produce a better life for everyone, major problems such as resource depletion and pollution have raised questions and doubts. There is a growing awareness that sustainability must be a constant factor in all development. Sustainability is about ensuring that all development is socially, economically and environmentally sustainable. This understanding underpins all the other chapters in this review. This chapter focuses in more detail on promoting sustainable development and on reviewing environmental issues. These are key policy areas that must be addressed urgently as part of sustainability in the Policy Framework set out in Chapter 2.

Promoting Sustainable Development

The World Economic Forum in its latest Global Competitiveness Report notes that those economies that have been balancing economic progress with social inclusion and good environmental stewardship will be better placed to maintain high prosperity for their citizens even accounting for external shocks (World Economic Forum 2014:73). It is clear at a global level that those countries who have been promoting sustainable development and who have been investing in medium to long-term policies whilst moving society to a more sustainable footing will be best placed to meet future challenges. It is clear that in order to live within the means of the planet whilst producing the kind of society in which we want to live a sustainable development framework should be at the centre of national and international policy making.

Sustainable development is defined as 'development which meets the needs of the present, without compromising the ability of future generations to meet their needs

(World Commission on Environment and Development, 1987). It encompasses three pillars; environment, society and economy. These three pillars of sustainability must be addressed in a balanced manner if development is to indeed be sustainable. Maintaining this balance is crucial to the long-term development of a sustainable resource-efficient future for Ireland. While growth and economic competitiveness are important, they are not the only issues to be considered and cannot be given precedence over others. They must be dealt with using a framework for sustainable development which gives equal consideration to the environmental, social and economic pillars. It is also important to note that, although economic growth is seen as the key to resolving many aspects of the current crisis across the EU, it is this very growth that may be damaging the possibility of securing sustainable development in the Global South (cf Chapter 13).

Sustainable development is our only means of creating a long term future for Ireland, with the environment, economic growth and social needs joined in a balanced manner with consideration for the needs of future generations. Sustainability and the adoption of a sustainable development model presents a significant policy challenge: how environmental policy decisions with varying distributional consequences are to be made in a timely manner while ensuring that a disproportionate burden is not imposed on certain groups e.g. low income families or rural dwellers. This policy challenge highlights the need for an evidence-based policy process involving all stakeholders. The costs and benefits of all policies must be assessed and considered on the basis of evidence only. This is essential in order to avoid the policy debate being influenced by hearsay or vested interests or the thoughtless exercise of power. Before the current recession began the global economy was five times the size it had been 50 years before and, had it continued on that growth path, it would be 80 times that size by 2100 (SDC, 2009). This raises the fundamental question of how such growth rates can be sustained in a world of finite resources and fragile ecosystems. Continuing along the same path is clearly not sustainable. A successful transition to sustainability requires a vision of a viable future societal model and also the ability to overcome obstacles such as vested economic interests, political power struggles and the lack of open social dialogue (Hämäläinen, 2013).

Promoting a sustainable economy requires that we place a value on our finite natural resources and that the interdependence of economy, wellbeing and natural capital are recognised[83] (EC 2011). A sustainable economy requires us to acknowledge the limitations of finite natural resources and the duty we have to preserve these for future generations. It requires that natural capital and ecosystems are assigned value

---

[83] The Sustainable Society Foundation has published a comprehensive global report 'Sustainable Society Index 2014' based on these three key areas. http://www.ssfindex.com/ssi2014/wp-content/uploads/pdf/SSI2014.pdf

in our national accounting systems and that resource productivity is increased. Policy frameworks and business models should give priority to renewable energy, resource efficiency and sustainable land use. One of the most cost effective measures to promote sustainable development is to increase building energy efficiency. Increasing building energy efficiency (through retrofitting for example), along with reducing food waste and increasing yields on large scale farms are the three most effective means to increase sustainability and meet international environmental targets (McKinsey, 2011). These three areas should be prioritised for investment by Government as they will yield significant long-term dividends in terms of increasing Ireland's sustainability and reducing emissions.

A sustainable economy would involve transformative change and policies being implemented similar to those being proposed by Stahel in the 'performance economy' and Wijkman in the 'circular economy'. The 'circular economy' theory is based on the understanding that it is the reuse of vast amounts of material reclaimed from end of life products, rather than the extraction of new resources, that is the foundation of economic growth (Wijkman, 2012:166). This theory involves a shift towards servicing consumer products rather than constantly producing new goods to be consumed. The policy instruments proposed to implement a circular economy are those which are also considered to be at the heart of the sustainable development debate. They are:

- Binding targets for resource efficiency;
- Sustainable innovation and sustainable design being given priority in terms of research; and
- Tax reform: lowering taxes on labour and raising taxes on the use of natural resources.

The business case to move towards a circular economy and decouple economic growth from resource consumption has been outlined by McKinsey[84] in 2014 which shows that such a move could add $1 trillion dollars to the global economy by 2025 and that the EU manufacturing sector could generate savings of up to $360 billion per annum by 2025. The European Commission announced a Circular Economy Package in July 2014 which aimed to create two million jobs, generate €600 billion net savings and deliver 1 per cent GDP growth. This was a very welcome development at the time. Unfortunately in December 2014 the package was withdrawn by the European Commission with a commitment to replace it with more ambitious plans by the end of 2015. This is extremely disappointing as it is clear that both Europe and Ireland should be moving towards a more sustainable model and the circular economy package would have provided an ambitious target.

---

[84] http://www.mckinsey.com/insights/manufacturing/remaking_the_industrial_economy

Alongside the theories of the 'performance economy' and the 'circular economy' is the concept of the 'Economy of the Common Good[85]'. This model, designed by Felber (2010) is based on the idea that economic success should be measured in terms of human needs, quality of life and the fulfilment of fundamental values. This model proposes a new form of social and economic development based on human dignity, solidarity, sustainability, social justice and democratic co-determination and transparency.

It is clear that the current economic path is not sustainable and consideration must be given to how we, as a society, can transform our present system and move to a more sustainable future pathway. Creating a sustainable Ireland is one of the five pillars of *Social Justice Ireland's* Policy Framework for a Just Ireland outlined in more detail in chapter 2

Beyond 2015 – Towards Sustainable Development Goals

Discussions and negotiations at the RIO+20 summit in June 2012 culminated in the *'Future We Want'* outcome document which outlines UN commitments for a sustainable future and the development of Sustainable Development Goals (SDGs[86]) to replace the Millennium Development Goals[87] (MDGs) after 2015. Work on developing SDGs began in earnest in January 2013 with the establishment of the Open Working Group (OWG) on Sustainable Development Goals[88]. When formulating SDG proposals and strategies, the OWG on Sustainable Development Goals must take into account the shortcomings of the MDGs, specifically their failure to address the structural causes of poverty, inequality and exclusion.

One of the failures of the MDG process was the inability to engage people who are impacted by poverty and experiencing marginalistion in a meaningful inclusive framework to develop the goals themselves. Lessons must be learned from the MDG process to ensure that those most impacted by these issues are involved in the development of the goals, not just the implementation. The common good must be at the core of sustainable development to ensure that natural resources are protected for future generations. It is also crucial that the SDG targets are equitable, that priority is given to meeting the challenge faced by the most disadvantaged and that fair allocation of resources is secured for both poor people and poor countries. The OWG state that in order to ensure that progress is measurable and measures quantified, targets will be required. Targets and measures are an integral part of the OWG proposal

---

[85] https://www.ecogood.org/en/information/ecg-idea/vision-economy-common-good
[86] SDGs are also discussed in chapter 14 – The Global South
[87] For a more detailed discussion on MDGs see Annex 14 of this socio-economic review
[88] For further information see http://sustainabledevelopment.un.org/index.php?menu=1549

for Sustainable Development Goals (UN, 2014). This OWG document contains seventeen SDGs for discussion and adoption at the UN Summit on post- 2015 development in September 2015. The proposed SDGs (listed in full in Annex 13) cover areas such as poverty, food security, health, water and sanitation, climate change, and gender equality. UNCTAD calculate that the annual investment gap for implementing the SDGs are in the region of $2.5 trillion per annum[89], the scale of the implementation challenge is immense. The on-going negotiations for the post-2015 development agenda already highlight the challenges the world faces, with delegates having different definitions of justice and different opinions on how to achieve a more equal society[90] and how to deliver a universal post-2015 development agenda. Ireland has been appointed as a co-facilitator of the post-2015 sustainable development negotiations. This represents an opportunity for Ireland to ensure that the common good and the fair allocation of resources are central to the post-2015 development agenda. Ireland should also work to ensure that all nations, especially those in the developed world take full responsibility for communicating and implementing the SDGs to ensure the world moves towards a sustainable path in order to guarantee a future for generations to come.

The strategy for SDGs being developed by the UN is in contrast with that adopted recently by the European Commission in the 2030 Framework on Climate and Energy. The European Commission commits to reducing emissions by 40% in Europe, but the document contains no national targets. The non-binding target of at least a 27 per cent improvement in energy efficiency is significantly weaker than that included in the Europe 2020 Strategy. Combined the European Commission's decision to withdraw the Circular Economy, Air Quality and Waste Packages the 2030 Framework appears to represent a significant weakening commitment among EU member states on climate and energy targets. This incoherence of policy at international level does not bode well for the successful adoption and implementation for SDGs and will pose challenges for the post-2015 development negotiations where targets are seen as critical to both implementation and monitoring by the OWG.

The need for shadow national accounts

According to Repetto, Magrath, Wells, Beer and Rossini (1989:3) the 'difference in the treatment of natural resources and other tangible assets [in the existing national accounts] reinforces the false dichotomy between the economy and "the environment" that leads policy makers to ignore or destroy the latter in the name

---

[89] http://unctad.org/en/pages/PressRelease.aspx?OriginalVersionID=194
[90] See note 'A Brief Analysis of the Meeting'
http://www.iisd.ca/vol32/enb3214e.html?&utm_source=www.iisd.ca&utm_mediu m=feed&utm_content=2015-02-06&utm_campaign=RSS2.0

of economic development.' By not assigning value to our natural capital and environmental resources, a major national asset, we are not measuring the cost to our society of the ongoing depletion of these resources.

Acceptance of the need to move away from money-measured growth as the principal economic target and measure of success towards sustainability in terms of real-life, social, environmental and economic variables must be central to any model of development with sustainability at its core. This is at the core of the 'circular economy' and 'Economy for the Common Good' theories and is a key part of our core policy framework. Our present national accounts are based on GNP/GDP as scorecards of wealth and progress and miss fundamentals such as environmental sustainability. These measures completely ignore unpaid work because only money transactions are tracked. Ironically, while environmental depletion is ignored, the environmental costs of dealing with the effects of economic growth, such as cleaning up pollution or coping with the felling of rainforests, are added to, rather than subtracted from, GNP/GDP.

It is widely acknowledged that GDP is 'an inadequate metric to gauge wellbeing over time, particularly in its economic, environmental, and social dimensions, some aspects of which are often referred to as sustainability (Stiglitz Commission 2009: 8). A new scorecard or metric model is needed which measures the effects of policy decisions on people's lives as well as the environmental, social and economic costs and benefits of those policies. The United Nations High Level Panel on Global Sustainability recommends that the international community measure development beyond GDP and that national accounts should measure and cost social exclusion, unemployment and social inequality and the environmental costs of growth and market failures.

Development of 'satellite' or 'shadow' national accounts should be a central initiative in this. Already a number of alternative scorecards exist, such as the United Nations' Human Development Index (HDI), former World Bank economist Herman Daly's Index of Sustainable Economic Welfare (ISEW) and Hazel Henderson's Country Futures Index (CFI). A 2002 study by Wackernagel et al presented the first systematic attempt to calculate how human demands on the environment are matched by its capacity to cope. It found that the world currently uses 120 per cent of what the earth can provide sustainably each year.

In the environmental context it is crucial that dominant economic models are challenged on, among other things, the assumptions that nature's capital (clean air, water and environment) are essentially free and inexhaustible, that scarce resources can always be substituted and that the planet can continue absorbing human and industrial wastes. These are issues that most economists tend to downplay as externalities. Shadow national accounts would help to make sustainability and 'green' procurement mandatory considerations in the decision and policy making process. They would also go some way towards driving a civil society awareness campaign to help decouple economic growth from consumption.

Social Justice Ireland welcomed the establishment of the Green Tenders Implementation group to implement the Action Plan for Green Public Procurement. This is a significant step on the road towards making green procurement mandatory in public sector procurement decisions. Green Public Procurement is referred to as an area for consideration in the forthcoming Rural Development Programme (RDP) 2014-2020[91]. Employment and growth possibilities in the green economy have been considered in the Government policy statement 'Delivering our Green Potential' which will guide any future initiatives in this area in the RDP. The document notes how up to 10,000 jobs could be created in six key sub-sectors of the green economy between 2012 and 2015. It would be extremely useful in term of policy making for Government to review progress on job creation in the green economy post 2015, whether or not the recommendations of the Expert Group on Future Skills Needs were implemented and the impact that these had on job creation in the green economy.

What should be measured?

Some governments and international agencies have picked up on these issues, especially in the environmental area and have begun to develop 'satellite' or 'shadow' national accounts that include items not traditionally measured. *Social Justice Ireland's* 2009 publication *Beyond GDP: What is prosperity and how should it be measured?* explored many of these new developments. It included contributions from the OECD, the New Economics Foundation, and other informed bodies and proposed a series of policy developments which would assist in achieving similar progress in Ireland.

There has, in fact, been some progress in this area, including commitments to better data collection and broader assessment of well-being and progress by the CSO, ESRI and EPA. The CSO published Sustainable Development Indicators Ireland in 2013 and this is a welcome development. However, much remains to be achieved in terms of communicating these sustainable development indicators to the public and the inclusion of well-being in the monitoring process. *Social Justice Ireland* strongly urges Government to adopt this broader perspective and commit to producing these accounts alongside more comprehensive indicators of progress. Measures of economic performance must reflect their environmental cost and a price must be put on the use of our natural capital.

---

[91] per.gov.ie/wp-content/uploads/Partnership-Agreement-Ireland-2014-2020.pdf

The OECD Global Project on measuring the progress of society recommends that sets of key environmental, social and economic indicators be developed and that these should be used to inform evidence-based decision making across all sectors (Morrone, 2009: 23).

Social Justice Ireland recommends that government commit to producing shadow national accounts and that these accounts include indicators that measure the following:

- the use of energy and materials to produce goods;
- the generation of pollution and waste;
- the amount of money spent by industry, government and households to protect the environment or manage natural resources;
- natural resource asset accounts measuring the quantity and quality of a country's natural resources;
- sustainability of the growth being generated *vis-a-vis* our social and natural capital;
- natural resource depletion and degradation as a cost to society;
- the output of waste and pollution as a result of commercial activity as a cost within the satellite national accounts; and
- the measures of the GPI (Genuine Progress Indicator) which measure and deduct for income inequality, environmental degradation and cost of crime, amongst other items. By measuring and differentiating between economic activities that diminish natural and social capital and those activities that enhance them, we can ensure that our economic welfare is sustainable (Daly & Cobb, 1987).

Stakeholder involvement

One of the key indicators of sustainability is how a country runs stakeholder involvement. Sustainable Development Councils (SDCs) are a model for multi-stakeholder bodies comprising members of all major groups – public, private, community, civil society and academic – engaged in evidence-based discussion.[92] The EU-wide experience has been that SDCs are crucial to maintaining a medium and long-term vision for a sustainable future whilst concurrently working to ensure that sustainable development policies are embedded into socio-economic strategies and budgetary processes.

---

[92] For more information see http://www.eeac.eu/images/doucments/eeac-statement-backgr2011_rio_final_144dpi.pdf

Ireland established its sustainable development council (Comhar) in 1999 and disbanded it in 2011, transferring its functions to NESC (National Economic and Social Council). This is unfortunate in the light of the United Nations recommendation that the link between informed scientific evidence and policy making on sustainable development issues be strengthened (United Nations, 2012). While it is admirable that Government wishes to place sustainable development at the core of policy making and has asked NESC to ensure it gives sustainable development major consideration in all it does, it is also important to note that NESC is not in a position to do the detailed work done previously by Comhar.

All areas of governance, from international to national to local, along with civil society and the private sector, must fully embrace the requirements of a sustainable development future (United Nations, 2012). In order to facilitate a move towards a sustainable future for all, stakeholders from all arenas must be involved in the process. Sustainable local development should be a key policy issue on the new local government agenda and the Public Participation Networks could be a forum where sustainable development issues at a local level become part of local policy making.[93] There is need for a deliberative democracy arena within which all stakeholders can discuss evidence without power differentials impeding outcomes.

Principles to underpin sustainable development

Principles to underpin sustainable development were proposed in a report for the European Commission prepared by James Robertson in May 1997. The report, *The New Economics of Sustainable Development*, argued that these principles should include the following:

- systematic empowerment of people (as opposed to making and keeping them dependent) as the basis for people-centred development;
- systematic conservation of resources and environment as the basis for environmentally sustainable development;
- evolution from a 'wealth of nations' model of economic life to a 'one-world' economic system;
- evolution from today's international economy to an ecologically sustainable, decentralising, multi-level one-world economic system;
- restoration of political and ethical factors to a central place in economic life and thought;
- respect for qualitative values, not just quantitative values; and
- respect for feminine values, not just masculine ones.

---

[93] For more detail on Public Participation Networks see chapter 10

At first glance these might not appear to be the type of concrete guidelines that policymakers so often seek. Yet they are principles that are relevant to every area of economic life. They also apply to every level of life, ranging from personal and household to global issues. They influence lifestyle choices and organisational goals. If these principles were applied to every area, level and feature of economic life they would provide a comprehensive checklist for a systematic policy review. Many of these principles underpin the 'Economy for the Common Good' Balance Sheets which rates companies based on areas including ecological sustainability, social justice and transparency[94].

A key challenge for Ireland is to ensure that the economy and key sectors develop in a sustainable way and that economic growth is decoupled from environmental pressures. This would require environmental considerations being placed at the centre of policy and decision making at national, regional and local levels (EPA, 2012). Protecting our natural resources and ensuring they are not missused or exhausted is crucial to the economic and social wellbeing of future generations in Ireland.

It is also important that any programme for sustainable development should take a realistic view of human nature, recognising that people can be both altruistic and selfish, both co-operative and competitive. It is important, therefore, to develop the economic system to reward activities that are socially and environmentally benign (and not the reverse, as at present). This, in turn, would make it easier for people and organisations to make choices that are socially and environmentally responsible. Incorporating social and environmental costs in regulating and pricing both goods and services, combined with promoting those goods and services which are sustainable, should also become part of sustainable development policy. In order to transition to an economy based on sustainable development and a 'green growth strategy' a policy framework is needed that is adaptive and supports shifts away from traditional economic models. This would include user charges for environmental resources to reflect environmental costs and environmental taxes to shift the tax base towards environmental pollutants and consumption and away from labour and production (EPA, 2012).

Any programme for sustainable development has implications for public spending. In addressing this issue it needs to be understood that public expenditure programmes and taxes provide a framework which helps to shape market prices, rewards some kinds of activities and penalises others. Within this framework there are other areas which are not supported by public expenditure or taxed. This framework should be developed to encourage economic efficiency and enterprise, social equity and environmental sustainability. Systematic reviews should be carried out and published on the sustainability effects of all public subsidies and other

---

[94] https://www.ecogood.org/en/common-good-balance-sheet

relevant public expenditure and tax differentials. Governments should identify and remove those subsidies which cause the greatest detriment to natural, environmental and social resources (United Nations, 2012:14). Systematic reviews should also be carried out and published on the possibilities for re-orientating public spending programmes, with the aim of preventing and reducing social and environmental problems.

Social Justice Ireland welcomed the publication entitled *'Our Sustainable Future – A Framework for a Sustainable Development for Ireland'* (Department of the Environment, Community and Local Government, 2012) which is a late but positive step on the road towards a sustainable development model. One area of concern, however, is the failure by governments to implement earlier sustainability strategies (2000 & 2007) and another is the lack of quantitative and qualitative targets and indicators to accompany the Framework itself. *Social Justice Ireland* welcomes the Framework's emphasis on the need for a whole of government approach to sustainability and the need for all areas of government policy to have regard for sustainable development. Clear leadership from Government and public bodies are needed to ensure that existing and future activities maintain and improve the quality of the environment (EPA, 2012). At a time when leadership on sustainable development and climate change is needed it is disappointing that the recently published Climate Action and Low Carbon Development Bill 2015 fails to include any specific targets on emissions reductions. Without clear targets the work of the Cabinet Committee on Climate Change and the Green Economy and the High-Level Inter-Departmental Group on Sustainable Development in order to ensure that the framework and its recommendations is at the heart of policy making in all Government departments will be much more challenging.

Monitoring sustainable development

Many studies have highlighted the lack of socio-economic and environmental data in Ireland required to assess trends in sustainable development. The empirical and methodological gaps which continue to impede the incorporation of sustainable development issues into public policy making and assessment are known (ESRI, 2005). It is only through a sustained commitment to data collection in all of these areas that these deficiencies will be addressed. We welcome recent developments in this area, particularly at the CSO, and look forward to all of these data impediments being removed in the years to come.

Comhar undertook a lot of work developing indicators in order to set targets and quantitative means of measuring the progress of sustainable development. *Social Justice Ireland* does not believe that the full range of the work of Comhar[95] has been

---

[95] http://www.comharsustainableindicators.ie/explore-the-indicators/comhar-indicators.aspx

satisfactorily adopted by NESC to date and a great deal of work needs to be done in the area of indicators. There should be real consultation between NESC, the CSO, and the Community & Voluntary Pillar (which has done extensive work in this area[96]) to ensure that these issues are addressed, appropriate indicators are immediately put in place and the necessary data collected. These could be used in conjunction with indicators developed by the CSO and data being collected by the EPA and ESRI to measure Ireland's progress towards sustainable development.

In a study of national strategies towards sustainable development in 2005 (Niestroy, 2005: 185) Ireland's sustainability strategy was criticised for:

- having no systematic monitoring system;
- having no general timetable;
- its lack of quantitative national targets.

The lack of quantitative and qualitative targets and indicators to accompany the new sustainability framework means that Ireland remains open to similar criticism for its current strategy. Implementation, targets and monitoring will be crucial to the success of any policy approach that genuinely promotes sustainable development. It is important that these targets and indicators and the mechanisms for monitoring, tracking and reviewing them are developed and clearly explained to ensure that responsibility is taken across all departments and all stakeholders for its implementation.

The publication by the Central Statistics Office of *Sustainable Development Indicators Ireland 2013*, aims to achieve continuous improvement in the quality of life and well-being for present and future generations through linking economic development with protection of the environment and social justice (CSO, 2013). These sustainable development indicators should be discussed and debated in the Dáil along with satellite or shadow national accounts and indicators of well-being as a step towards integrating sustainable development across the entire policy agenda in Ireland.

Environmental Issues

Maintaining a healthy environment remains one of the greatest global challenges. Without concerted and rapid collective action to curb and decouple resource depletion and the generation of pollution from economic growth, human activities may destroy the very environment that supports economies and sustains life (UNEP 2011: II).

---

[96] This work involved extensive engagement with a range of government departments on agreeing appropriate indicators to measure progress on the high-level goals contained in the national agreement *'Towards 2016'*. Much of this work remains valid despite the changing context.

Our environment is a priceless asset. It is also finite – a fact that is often ignored in current debates. Protection and conservation of our environment is of major importance as it is not just for our use alone; it is also the natural capital of future generations.

For environmental facts and details for Ireland see Annex 11.

The economic growth of recent decades has been accomplished mainly by drawing down natural resources without allowing stocks to regenerate and causing widespread degradation and loss to our eco-system. Careful stewardship of Ireland's natural resources is required to ensure the long term health and sustainability of our environment. Unsustainable use of natural resources is one of the greatest long-term threats to humankind (European Commission, 2012:3). It is crucial therefore, that Ireland meets the challenges of responding to climate change and protecting our natural resources and biodiversity with policies that are based on scientific evidence and protecting the common good.

Climate change

Climate change is one of the most significant and challenging issues currently facing humanity. Ireland produces an estimated 160,359 tonnes of greenhouse gas emissions every day (EPA, 2014). Increased levels of greenhouse gases, such as CO_2, increase the amount of energy trapped in the atmosphere which leads to global effects such as increased temperatures, melting of snow and ice and raised global average sea-level. If these issues are not addressed with urgency the projected effects of climate change present a serious risk of dangerous and irreversible climate impacts at national and global levels. Food production and ecosystems are particularly vulnerable. The latest research from the World Meteorological Organisation has ranked 2014 as the hottest year on record, and finds that fourteen of the fifteen hottest years have been in this century. In Ireland, six of the ten warmest years on record have occurred since 1990 (EPA, 2014). Among the predicted adverse impacts of climate change are sea level rise, more intense storms, increased likelihood and magnitude or river and coastal flooding, adverse impacts on water quality, and changes in distribution of plant and animal species (EPA, 2014).

The 2013 report by the Intergovernmental Panel on Climate Change (IPCC) outlines the global challenge of climate change. The report sets out the effect climate change and greenhouse gas emissions have had on the planet and the impact of human influence on the climate system. Some of the main findings are:

- More than 60% of the net energy increase in the climate system is stored in the upper ocean;

- The global ocean will continue to warm during the 21st century and global mean sea level will continue to rise;
- Sea level rise is projected in more than 95% of the ocean area with 70% of coastlines worldwide expected to experience sea level change;
- It is virtually certain that global mean sea level rise will continue beyond 2100, with sea level rise due to thermal expansion to continue for many centuries;
- Carbon dioxide concentrations have increased by 40% since pre-industrial times. The ocean has absorbed 30% of the emitted carbon dioxide, causing ocean acidification;
- Global surface temperature change for the end of the 21st century is likely in the range 1.5C to 4.5C;
- It is very likely that heat waves will occur with a higher frequency and duration;
- The contrast in precipitation between wet and dry regions and between wet and dry seasons will increase, although there may be regional exceptions;
- Cumulative emissions of CO2 largely determine global mean surface warming by the late 21st century and beyond. Most aspects of climate change will persist for many centuries even if CO_2 emissions are stopped.

The IPCC report serves to highlight the challenges ahead for all countries in dealing with climate change. It is very disappointing therefore that the European Commission Policy Framework for Climate and Energy 2020-2030 published in January 2014 does not contain any binding national targets for member states for reducing energy use or for increasing renewable energies. This is despite the fact that the plan commits the European Commission to reducing gas emissions by 40 per cent. By not setting binding or measurable targets the European Commission is taking the opposite approach to that recommended by the SDG Open Working Group. The European Commission claims that the 2030 climate plan sets in stone a commitment to cap the temperature increase at 2°C. The IPCC data shows that a 40 per cent emissions target for 2030 means in effect there is a 50/50 chance of exceeding the 2°C threshold. This is consistent with the 450 Scenario of the IEA's *World Energy Outlook 2011* which shows that an energy pathway consistent with a 50 per cent chance of limiting global temperature increase to 2°C requires CO_2 emissions to peak at just 1.0 Gt above 2011 levels in 2017. This will be very difficult to achieve.

A new report from the United Nations Environment Programme (UNEP) published to coincide with the Lima climate talks[97] shows how the cost of adapting to climate change in developing countries is likely to reach two to three times the previous estimates of $70billion -$100billion per year by 2050. The report assesses the global

---

[97] http://unfccc.int/meetings/lima_dec_2014/meeting/8141.php

adaptation gaps in finance, technology and knowledge. Adaptation plans are not a required outcome of the Lima climate talks despite their obvious importance in helping developing countries adapt to climate change and the heavy cost of inaction as outlined by the UNEP report. It is disappointing that the UN Climate talks in Lima failed to reach substantial progress or commitment towards adopting ambitious and binding climate targets in Paris, 2015.

Climate change and implementation of climate policy have been challenges for Ireland. Despite two National Climate Change Strategies (one in 2000 and one in 2007), there have been significant delays in implementing these policies. In some cases policies have still not been implemented. The mobilisation of vested interests has been a decisive factor in many of these delays and cases of non-implementation (Coughlin (2007). This is very disappointing because if these policies had been implemented on time, and as specified, Ireland's climate policy commitments could have been met from domestic measures. Now Ireland is faced with the prospect of overshooting its EU 2020 emissions targets as early as 2016 (EPA 2012).

Social Justice Ireland welcomes the publication of the *Climate Action and Low Carbon Development Bill 2015* by the Department of Environment, Community and Local Government. The provision for five yearly National Climate Change Adaptation Frameworks and the establishment of a National Expert Advisory Council on Climate Change is welcome. However there are a number of areas of concern:

Social Justice Ireland is concerned the failure to include any specific targets on emissions reductions other than those committed to under European Union law to reach by 2020 and those under the Kyoto Protocol. The absence of sectoral targets and quantitative measures and outputs has already impeded climate change policy progress internationally (UNEP 2011: vii). Without sectoral targets and a system whereby they are regularly reviewed, the monitoring of progress on climate change policy will be very difficult. It will also make enforcing responsibility and accountability for implementation of climate policy across all Government departments and stakeholders in all sectors extremely challenging.

The failure to include the recommendations of the Oireachtas Committee on Environment, Culture and the Gaeltacht Climate Bill Report 2013[98] . Of particular concern are the omission of the committee's interpretation of 'Low Carbon Development' as near zero emissions for 2050, the omission of the committee's proposal on the incorporation of principles of climate justice and the establishment of a national Green Climate fund to support climate mitigation and adaptation in developing countries.

---

[98] http://www.oireachtas.ie/parliament/mediazone/pressreleases/name-19163-en.html

A National Low Carbon Transition and Mitigation Plan and a National Climate Change Adaptation Framework are to be submitted within 24 months of the passing of the Bill. This means that Government does not have to adopt a national policy position on climate legislation and the transition to a low carbon future until mid-2017 at the earliest. This will give the Government less than three years to reach the targets set in the EU 2020 strategy (European Commission, 2010). Given that we are on course to overshoot emissions targets by 2016, there is a real danger that short-term planning to limit our liabilities in respect of missed targets will overshadow the requirement for long-term planning and policy goals for a sustainable and low carbon future. The long-term goal of a low carbon economy beyond 2020 must be at the core of climate policy.

Social Justice Ireland is concerned that the Bill refers to the objective of achieving the national low carbon roadmap at the least cost to the national economy by adopting cost-effective measures that do not impose an unreasonable burden on the Exchequer. By failing to take appropriate actions and measures on climate change and carbon emissions now Ireland's economy and society will bear a far greater cost in the future. It is important that the National Expert Advisory Body on Climate Change is not constrained by economic and cost issues and that its recommendations should be based solely on scientific evidence and best practice.

A recent study examining climate change and governance in Ireland points out that local authorities have made little progress on climate change due to barriers related to resources, prioritisation and integration and a lack of public consensus for proactive measures (EPA, 2013). The report concludes that the national government has side-lined the climate change issue by not establishing a separate ministry for climate change; this signals a lack of priority on this issue at national level, resulting in a limited response at regional and local level. An integrated, cross-departmental approach is recommended and the potential of local authorities for innovative solutions is highlighted. Government must support local authorities to coordinate climate change policy and adopt legislation that clearly signals climate change as a priority. Without a shift in attitudes and strong leadership nationally Ireland will remain unprepared for upcoming challenges related to climate change. A Climate Action and Low Carbon Development Bill without targets, without refereeing to climate justice and with a focus on cost-effectiveness means a significant opportunity to provide long-term leadership in this area has been lost.

Emissions challenge[99]

Ireland has two sets of emissions targets to meet: the Kyoto Protocol and the EU 2020 Targets. Ireland is on track to meet its Kyoto commitments when the effects of the EU Emissions Trading Scheme and forest sinks are taken into account. However, it is already facing significant challenges in meeting its future EU emissions targets for greenhouse gases under the EU Climate and Energy package for 2020 and further anticipated longer term targets up to 2050. This is despite substantial declines in greenhouse gas emissions between 2009 and 2011 which the EPA attributes primarily to the economic recession.

Under the *Climate and Energy Package,* as part of the EU 2020 targets Ireland is required to deliver a 20 per cent reduction in non-Emissions Trading Scheme (ETS) greenhouse gas emissions by 2020 (relative to 2005 levels). Ireland also has signed up to binding annual emissions limits over the period 2013 to 2020 to ensure movement towards the EU 2020 target. The latest EPA projections indicate that Ireland will meet the 2013 target but will exceed its annual binding limit over the 2013 to 2020 period with emissions exceeding the binding limits from 2015 onwards.

Ireland's emissions profile is dominated by emissions from the energy supply, transport and agriculture sectors (EPA, 2014). The domestic sector comprises transport, agriculture and residential waste activities and is also responsible for 72 per cent of Ireland's total emissions. The immediate challenge for Irish climate policy is to meet the EU 2020 targets for the domestic sector, which is a reduction of at least 20 per cent on the 2005 emission levels by 2020. If achieved, the projected strong growth in the agriculture sector set out in the Department of Agriculture, Fisheries and Food vision *Food Harvest 2020* will likely result in agricultural emissions increasing by 7 per cent by 2020. There is a significant challenge for Government in achieving the binding EU 2020 targets whilst also pursuing its *Food Harvest* agenda.

Support for sustainable agricultural practice is important to ensure the long-term viability of the sector and consideration must also be given to how the projected increase in agriculture emissions can be offset. It is important that the agriculture sector be at the fore of developing and implementing sustainable farming practices and be innovative in terms of reducing emissions. Consideration should also be given to the European Commission proposals to establish a framework for land use, land use change and forestry (LULUCF) to be included in the emission reduction targets. This is important for Ireland because it is estimated that forest sinks could provide significant relief in reaching emissions targets (see Annex 11). The European Council Conclusions on Climate recognised the 'limited' mitigation potential of the agriculture sector and commits to considering emissions from forestry and land use and agriculture together. Agriculture accounts for the largest proportion of

---

[99] More detail on emissions and targets is available in Annex 11

Ireland's greenhouse gas emissions, account for 32.3 per cent of the total. Pursuing Food Harvest 2020 and increasing milk production in 2015[100] means that emissions from agriculture are likely to continue to increase over the coming years. Agricultural emissions increased between 2012 and 2013 and is driven by higher animal numbers reflecting plans to expand milk production (EPA, 2014). A recognition of the 'limited' mitigation potential of the sector must not reduce efforts to reduce agricultural emissions and meet international targets and obligations.

Transport and agriculture represent the most intractable sectors in terms of carbon offsets and emissions mitigations, with the transport sector recording a 115.5 per cent increase in emissions between 1990 and 2013[101]. A national sustainable transport network would represent a major step towards a low carbon, resource efficient economy. Capital investment will be required in sustainable transport infrastructure projects to ensure the reduction of transport emissions. Agriculture, which accounted for 32 per cent of total emissions in 2011, faces major difficulties in limiting emissions and meeting future targets. In the agriculture sector progress towards changing farm practices has been limited and incentives to reduce on-farm greenhouse emissions have not been delivered on a wide scale (Curtin & Hanrahan 2012: 9). The agriculture and food sector must build on its scientific and technical knowledge base to meet the emissions challenge.

The European Network for Rural Development has highlighted a number of opportunities for Ireland to use the development of renewable energy to mitigate the effects of climate change by delivering additional reductions to Ireland's CHG emissions. The opportunity and capability exist to significantly mitigate climate change through growth in afforestation and renewable energy sources. Forestry can play a significant role in combating climate change and the development of the forestry sector and renewable energy should be supported in the Irish CAP Rural Development Programme 2014-2020. It is important, therefore, that Government departments work together to tackle climate change and recognise that action on climate change is not just a challenge but a great opportunity to create jobs and develop a genuine, indigenous, low carbon economy.

Biodiversity

Nature and biodiversity are the basis for almost all ecosystem services and biodiversity loss is the greatest challenge facing humanity (EPA 2011: vii). Biodiversity loss and ecosystem degradation directly affect climate change and undermine the way we use natural resources (EEAC 2011: 114). Pollution, over-

---

[100] Milk Quotas are due to be abolished by the European Union in 2015.
[101] Transport emissions have decreased for four consecutive years and are now 22% below peak levels in 2007.

exploitation of natural resources and the spread of non-native species are causing a decline in biodiversity in Ireland. The Environmental Protection Agency (EPA) has identified the four main drivers (EPA 2011: 11) of biodiversity loss in Ireland all caused by human activity:

- habitat destruction and fragmentation;
- pollution;
- over-exploitation of natural resources; and
- the spread of non-native species.

Our eco-system is worth €2.6 billion to Ireland annually (EPA 2011) yet our biodiversity capital is decreasing rapidly. Ireland missed the 2010 target to halt biodiversity loss and lacks fundamental information on such issues as the distribution of species and habitats that inform planning and policy in other countries. *Social Justice Ireland* is concerned that responsibility for biodiversity now lies with the Department of Arts, Heritage and the Gaeltacht, whereas responsibility for all environmental issues lies with the Department of Environment, Community and Local Government. Both departments must work together to ensure that the policies they implement are designed to complement each other and will not have any negative consequences on other areas of environmental concern.

Biodiversity underpins our eco-system, which supports our natural capital and in particular the agriculture industry. It is critically important that our biodiversity is preserved and maintained and that the effects of policies and developments on biodiversity are monitored in order to inform environmental policy in the short and long-term. Ireland has less land designated as a Special Protected Area under the EU Habitats Directive than the EU average The majority of Ireland's habitats listed under the Habitats Directive are reported to be in poor or bad conservation status (EPA 2012:76).

The economic value of biodiversity and how it contributes to our well-being needs to be better promoted and understood. The data collected by the National Biodiversity Data Centre on the environment and the eco-system goods and services provided by biodiversity should be included in any proposed shadow national accounting system. This is our greatest national asset yet we do not factor it into our present national accounting system. Without biodiversity and our eco-system the development of a sustainable, low-carbon future for Ireland will not be possible and the value of our natural capital will be lost. Climate change will not go away and initial costs will have to be incurred in order to preserve and conserve our natural resources. Environmental and socio-economic decision making should be integrated with biodiversity and resource management to maximise the benefit to society of our natural resources.

11. Sustainability

The long-term benefits of these investments, both for the present and future generations, will far outweigh the initial cost. It is important that the economic value of biodiversity be factored into decision making and reflected in national accounting and reporting systems. The EPA notes that the continuing loss of biodiversity is one of the greatest challenges facing us (EPA 2012:82). *Social Justice Ireland* believes that Government should implement the EPA's recommendations regarding evidence-based decision making on biodiversity issues and the integration of the economic value of ecosystems into the national accounting and reporting systems.

Environmental taxation

The extent of Ireland's challenge in terms of climate change and maintaining and preserving our national resources is clear from the information outlined above. One way of tackling this challenge whilst also broadening the tax base is through environmental taxation. Eco-taxes, which put a price on the full costs of resource extraction and pollution, will help move towards a resource efficient, low carbon green economy. Environmental taxation enforcing the polluter pays principle and encouraging waste prevention can help to decouple growth from the use of resources and support the shift towards a low carbon economy. Carbon taxation was introduced in Ireland in Budget 2010 and was increased from €15 to €20 per tonne in Budget 2012. *Social Justice Ireland* welcomed the introduction of a carbon tax but is disappointed that Government has not used some of the money raised by this tax to target low income families and rural dwellers who were most affected by it. When considering environmental taxation measures to support sustainable development and the environment and to broaden the tax base, the Government should ensure that such taxes are structured in ways that are equitable and effective and do not place a disproportionate burden on rural communities or lower socio-economic groups. Environmentally damaging subsidies should be abolished with the resulting savings invested in renewable energies.

Key Policy Priorities on Sustainability

- A common understanding of sustainable development must be communicated across all Government departments, policy makers, stakeholders and civil society. This should underpin all public policy decisions.
- The economic value of biodiversity must be accounted for in all environmental policy decisions.
- Shadow national accounts should be developed to move towards a more sustainable, resource efficient model of growth.
- A progressive and equitable environmental taxation system should be developed in a structured way that does not impose a disproportionate burden on certain groups.
- Investment should be made in sustainable infrastructure projects which will have substantial long-term dividends.

12.
RURAL DEVELOPMENT

CORE POLICY OBJECTIVE: RURAL DEVELOPMENT
To secure the existence of substantial numbers of viable communities in all parts of rural Ireland where every person would have access to meaningful work, adequate income and to social services, and where infrastructures needed for sustainable development would be in place.

Rural Ireland continues to change dramatically. The composition and population patterns of rural Ireland are changing and there is a need to revise and update how we measure rurality in Ireland. No county has shown an increase in the share of rural population since 2006, however the numbers living in small towns (<3,000 population) has doubled since 2002. The Central Statistics Office definition of rural (places with a population of less than 1,500) shows that the population living in rural areas has declined to 28 per cent. However, examining the next category above rural (towns of 1,500 to 2,999 people) the population living in this category increased by 33 per cent (Walsh & Harvey, 2013). Areas of the countryside close to the main cities and rural towns have experience substantial growth in their populations, in contrast with remote or less accessible rural areas. In these more remote areas a high proportion of the population is older with lower education levels (O'Donoghue et al, 2014). This changing composition shows the need to redefine rural areas and how we measure them. In European discourse the concept of 'rural' is often linked to regional development and includes 'non-urban' and 'non-metropolitan' areas[102]. The need for an integrated transition from an agricultural to a rural and regional development agenda to improve the quality of life for all rural dwellers has never been more pressing. This will require policy coherence in terms of investment, social services, governance and sustainability as part of the policy framework discussed in details in chapter 2.

---

[102] See O'Hara, P in Healy & Reynolds (Eds) (2013) for a more detailed discussion on rurality and the regions.

Rural and Regional Development

The Commission for the Economic Development of Rural Areas (CEDRA) adopts a holistic definition of rural areas as those areas being outside the main metropolitan areas and recognises the relational nature of economic and social development and the interconnections between urban and rural areas[103]. Among the objectives of the commission is to ensure that rural areas can benefit from and contribute to economic recovery and to provide research to inform the medium term economic development of rural areas to 2025. The CEDRA report 'Energising Ireland's Rural Economy' provides a list of recommendations to Government on how to safeguard the future of rural Ireland, a valuable national resource. It establishes that many of the key issues facing rural communities are part of a long term economic and social transformation. The report calls for new integrated approaches to rural economic development aligning national goals with regional, county and local strategies. It calls on Government to prepare a clear and detailed Rural Economic Development policy and to outline in details how Government proposes to support rural economic development to 2025. *Social Justice* Ireland endorses this call and urges Government to implement the recommendations of the CEDRA report. The first White Paper on Rural Development (1999) defined rural development policy in Ireland as *"all Government policies and interventions which are directed towards improving the physical, economic and social conditions of people living in the open countryside, in coastal areas, in towns and villages and in smaller urban centres outside of the five major urban areas"*. Given the changing population patterns and composition of rural Ireland it is now an appropriate time to revisit this definition of rural development policy in Ireland. The present model of rural development policy in Ireland has a dominant agricultural focus. There is a need to broaden this model of rural development to encompass coastal areas, towns and small urban centres and to support the diversification of the rural economy.

Rural development is often confused with agricultural development. This approach fails to grasp the fact that many people living in rural Ireland are not engaged in agriculture. This, in turn, leads to misunderstanding when the income from agriculture increases because many people fail to realise that not everyone in rural Ireland benefits from such an increase. The challenge is the ensure that rural economic development fosters economic diversification and development in rural areas as well as continuing to support farming and other traditional rural-based economic activity (O'Donoghue et al, 2014:22). Long-term strategies to address the failures of current and previous policies on critical issues, such as infrastructure development, the national spatial imbalance, local access to public services, public transport and local involvement in core decision-making, are urgently required. The 1999 White Paper on rural development provided a vision to guide rural development policy (something *Social Justice Ireland* had advocated for over a decade previously). Rural economies are increasingly designed around towns of various sizes

---

[103] http://www.ruralireland.ie/index.php/objectives-of-the-commission

which provide a local labour market area. It is important that rural development is seen in the context of the relationship between a particular rural area and the nearest town or centre of economic activity. The interactions between more rural areas and the small towns and villages with which they connect should provide the framework and foundation for a rural development policy. In order to have successful rural communities, rural development policy must move beyond one dominated by agricultural development and towards policies designed to support the provision of public services, investment in micro businesses and small or medium enterprises, innovation and the sustainable use of natural resources and natural capital. In order to access employment rural workers will require the right skills. This will require coordinated strategies between the Local Enterprise Offices, Education and Training Boards, local businesses in order to ensure that rural workers have the skills required in order to take up employment in their local area.

Rural areas and small villages are connected and networked to the local regions and these local regional economies are dependent on the interaction with the rural areas they connect with for sustainability (Walsh & Harvey, 2013). Given this interconnection it is important that rural and regional development are integrated in order to support sustainable local economies and to ensure that local services are utilised most effectively to address the specific needs of a particular region and the rural communities within it.

The new Rural Development Programme 2014-2020 will be funded by the European Agricultural Fund for Rural Development and the national Exchequer. A plan for the Rural Development Programme (RDP) 2014-2020 was submitted to the European Commission but final approval for the plan has yet to be signed off on at European level. The Department of Agriculture, Food and the Marine propose a national co-financing rate of 46 per cent be applied to measures under the RDP via this Department in the period 2014-2020. The allocation for the delivery of LEADER is 7 per cent of Pillar 2 under the new programme. Irish Rural Link has called for this to be increased to 10 per cent in order to ensure real investment in rural areas to support job creation, biodiversity and environmental protection. The new RDP is based on six priority areas for rural development whilst contributing to the Europe 2020 Strategy objectives of smart growth, inclusive growth and sustainable growth.

The six priority areas are:
- Fostering knowledge transfer and innovation,
- Enhancing competitiveness,
- Promoting food chain organisation and risk management in agriculture,
- Restoring, preserving and enhancing ecosystems,,
- Promoting resource efficiency and supporting the shift towards a low carbon and climate resilient economy,
- Promoting social inclusion, poverty reduction and economic development in rural areas.

The European Commission have proposed community led local development (CLLD) as one of the cohesion policy tools to help rural communities build capacity, stimulate innovation, increase participation and assist communities to ensure that they can be full actors in the implementation of EU objectives in all areas. The reform of local government and work on citizens engagement could consider the CLLD process as a means of ensuring local communities have a voice in designing, shaping and delivery policy in their local area. The Department of Agriculture, Food and the Marine have published a draft RDP Consultation paper outlining some proposals under each of the six priority areas. The changes to the composition of rural areas and rural economies and the subsequent need to move rural development away from a focus dominated by agriculture has been well documented[104]. Therefore it is disappointing that the draft proposals for the RDP 2014-2020 are still predominantly focussed on agriculture and supporting the agri-sector and insufficient attention is given to diversifying and developing rural areas and the rural economy. The draft plan is predominantly focussed on complimenting and supporting the Food Harvest 2020 strategy. It points to LEADER measures to address areas of need in rural Ireland including support for enterprise development and job creation, supporting local development of rural areas and initiatives to improve broadband and communications infrastructure. Given the scope of the challenges facing rural Ireland and the recommendations of the CEDRA report the lack of a broader rural development and diversification focus in the draft plan is disappointing.

Diversification of rural economies

A study on rural areas across Europe (ECORYS, 2012:26) identified the key drivers of and key barriers to growth in rural economies. The key drivers of employment and growth were identified as (i) natural resources and environmental quality, (ii) the sectoral nature of the economy, (iii) quality of life and cultural capital and (iv) infrastructure and accessibility. The key barriers to growth in rural areas were identified as (i) demographic evolutions and migration (loss of young people and ageing), (ii) infrastructure and accessibility and (iii) the sectoral structure of the economy. Across Europe the secondary and tertiary sectors[105] are now the main drivers of economic growth and job creation in rural regions. These sectors support activities such as tourism, niche manufacturing and business services (ECORYS: 2010). For rural areas to become sustainable in the long-term these sectors must form an integral part of any future rural development strategy both in Ireland and in Europe. The *AGRI Vision 2015* report (Department of Agriculture, Food and the

---

[104] See O'Hara, P in Healy & Reynolds (Eds) 2013, Shucksmith, M (2012), ECORYS (2010) and Walsh, K. & Harvey, B. (2013)

[105] The EU traditionally splits economic activities into three sectors. Primary sector includes agriculture, forestry and fisheries; secondary sector includes industry and construction, tertiary sector includes all services.

Marine, 2004), highlighted the fact that many rural dwellers are not linked to agriculture and that in order to improve the standard of living and quality of life in rural communities opportunities must be created so that the rural economy can develop agriculture in conjunction with much needed alternative enterprises. The report also stated that the primary purpose of rural policy development is to underpin the economic and social wellbeing of rural communities. It is clear that in order to diversify the rural economy Ireland needs to move from agricultural development to rural development, from maritime development to supporting coastal communities and to support small, local, sustainable and indigenous enterprises, farming and fishing. Supporting rural households to ensure that they have sufficient incomes will be crucial to the future of rural Ireland. This requires both social and economic supports and broader skills and economic development strategies. About two-thirds of farm families requires off-farm income to remain sustainable, and while recent gains in agriculture based incomes have had an impact on the most commercial farms, solutions to the wider income problems requires a broader approach, both for farm and non-farm rural families (O'Donogue et al, 2014:30)The areas that are highlighted as possible drivers of rural job creation are social enterprise and social services (e.g. childcare and elder care), tourism, 'green' products and services and cultural and creative industries. In order to promote development of these drivers of employment and to support local entrepreneurs and local enterprises in rural and coastal areas the economic policies for these areas must take into account specific local needs such as accessible transport and access to childcare.

The economies of rural areas have become increasingly dependent on welfare transfers, with the 'at risk of poverty' rate in rural areas being 6.7 percentage points higher than that of urban areas. In 2013 the 'at risk of poverty' rate in rural areas was 19.3 per cent and 12.6 per cent in urban areas. The economic recession and restructuring of agriculture and subsequent decline in off farm employment has led to a narrowing of the economic base in rural areas. Low-paid, part-time and seasonal work and long-term underemployment are significant factors in rural poverty and exclusion (Walsh & Harvey (2013). The problem of underemployment is further highlighted by the recent assessment of the Rural Social Scheme (RSS) by the Department of Public Expenditure and Reform. It found that 60 per cent of participants have been on the scheme for more than six years, and 82 per cent for more than three years. The majority of participants are male and over 70 per cent of these are aged fifty and over. The RSS was designed as an income support scheme for people in rural occupations, not as an employment activation scheme. The assessment acknowledges that the RSS was established to support people who were underemployed in their primary activity. However in light of Government's new labour market activation policies whereby income supports must be integrated with activation measures the RSS is under increasing scrutiny. The assessment concludes that the RSS is not having a meaningful impact in terms of moving people into sustainable employment and that the social cohesion objective of the RSS needs to be set against broader high level policy objectives. What this assessment does not consider is the lack of sustainable and appropriate employment in rural areas, nor does it appropriately measure the social value of such a scheme in terms of combating social exclusion and isolation. In contrast, the value for money review of the Disadvantaged Area Scheme noted the multiplier effect of economic supports in rural economies and the contribution the payment makes to both farmers and rural families in terms of income support. The RSS is also a direct income support for rural families and its economic contribution should be considered carefully in light of the CEDRA report recommendation on the matrix of economic and social supports required to contribute to rural recovery. To ensure policy coherence no changes should be made to the RSS without a corresponding commitment from Government to develop and deliver a strategy to promote sustainable employment creation in rural areas.

Rural development and the challenges facing rural areas in terms of generating sustainable employment are either absent or barely referenced in key national policies such as the Medium Term Economic Strategy and the National Skills Strategy. As a result there is a mismatch between a Government policy aimed at attracting Foreign Direct Investment (FDI) and export-led industry and rural areas which are dominated by micro-businesses and small and medium sized enterprises. This mismatch has been acknowledged by the IDA in its review of 2014. Only 30 per cent of investments since 2009 have been made outside of the main cities. The IDA acknowledges the difficulty in persuading multinationals to move outside of Dublin and Cork and is committed to increasing investment outside of the main cities in the forthcoming 5 year strategy. This focus on relying on FDI to generate employment in rural areas will not create the sustainable employment required in these areas. A focus on rural niche investment and supporting rural start-ups in this area is also required. The Action Plan for Jobs (APJ) 2015 contains a welcome commitment to 'Delivering Regional Potential' with nineteen headline actions. However it is unlikely that sustainable employment will be generated on the scale required in rural areas without the roll-out of rural broadband. The CEDRA Report notes the strategic role of broadband and calls on Government to ensure the delivery of 30Mbps to all rural areas by the end of 2015. The headline action on broadband in the APJ 2015 is to issue the tender for the delivery of high speed broadband by Q4 2015. This means that rural areas and rural businesses will continue to be disadvantaged by poor broadband infrastructure in the coming year and that Government will not meet one of the key recommendations of the CEDRA Report.

Lack of quality broadband in rural areas is a considerable barrier to the diversification and growth of the rural economy in Ireland. Case studies show that several large firms have moved out of the South West of Ireland as a result of poor broadband speed and quality (ECORYS, 2010:237:241). The provision of quality broadband to rural areas must be a priority in the future if rural development is to be facilitated in a meaningful manner. The commitment to between 40Mbps and 30Mbps broadband speed in rural areas contained in the National Broadband Plan for Ireland is insufficient to encourage diversification and economic growth in rural areas. The commitment of Government to rollout the fibre infrastructure to provide broadband to areas which will not be served by commercial operators is welcome. However despite the commitment made in 2014, the tender is not due to be issued until Q4 2015. State intervention must be prioritised in order to prevent the two-tier digital divide developing between urban and rural areas growing any wider.

Employment and enterprise policy should have a rural specific element designed to support local enterprises, rural specific jobs and be cognisant of the need to create full-time, high quality jobs with career progression opportunities. Approximately 90 per cent of enterprises in the regions employ ten people or less and underemployment and flat career structures are particular features of rural areas that require attention (Walsh & Harvey, 2013).

With the on-going challenges facing traditional rural sectors, including agriculture, the future success of the rural economy is inextricably linked with the capacity of rural entrepreneurs to innovate and to develop new business opportunities that create jobs and income in rural areas. Some of the key needs of rural entrepreneurs have been highlighted as:

- Better, more locally-led access to finance;
- Harnessing local knowledge at all stages of policy formulation, delivery and evaluation;
- Developing better communication between national, regional and local actors to ensure the needs of entrepreneurs can be met;
- Acknowledgement that rising costs and Government revenue raising measures can hit rural businesses disproportionately compared to their urban counterparts e.g. fuel is often a bigger cost for rural businesses and entrepreneurs who need to transport produce or goods greater distances. (EU Rural Winter Review 2011)

Small rural firms and rural entrepreneurs need to be supported in developing their businesses and in overcoming the spatial disadvantage to benefit from the growth in the 'knowledge economy'. The €25 million to support regional enterprise strategies contained in the APJ 2015 is welcome but far below the €200 million called for by *Social Justice Ireland* in Budget 2015. Sustainable, integrated public transport serving rural Ireland and reliable high speed broadband must be given priority in order to support rural businesses and the development of the rural economy through diversification and innovation. The current strategy of relying on 'global demand' and foreign direct investment (FDI) has led to a widening of the development gap between urban and rural areas. One of the major problems faced by the government in trying to develop and promote sustainable rural communities is the restricted opportunities in secondary labour markets in rural areas. Data from the IDA and Forfás highlight the need for a rural and regional employment strategy. In 2014 only 37 per cent of IDA investments were located outside of Dublin and Cork (IDA, 2014). Significant regional disparities also show up in the Forfás annual employment survey. In the period 2003-2013 agency supported employment in Dublin increased by 14.6 per cent. In the same period agency supported employment in North West fell by 12.2 per cent, in the South East fell by 15.3 per cent and in the Mid West fell by 18.2 per cent (Forfás, 2014). This shows a trend of falling agency assisted employment in rural areas. The commitment to the development of Rural Economic Development Zones in the APJ 2015 is welcome, however without broadband it is difficult to see how this commitment can be delivered to its full potential.

Emigration

A recent Irish study on emigration showed that at least one household in four in rural areas has been directly affected by the emigration of at least one member since 2006 (Mac Éinrí et al, 2013). The same study found that 28 per cent of the households in this cluster expected that another member would emigrate within the next three years. This has profound implications for the future of rural areas. Rural areas in Ireland have already suffered a loss of young people due to out migration to urban areas and an ageing demographic prior to the recession. Such an enduring loss of educated young people will have a negative impact on social structures, service provision, cultural capital and levels of poverty and social exclusion.

The impact of sustained high levels of unemployment and subsequent high levels of emigration among young people in rural communities cannot be overestimated. It has led to a loss of young people in rural communities. This in turn means that the development of the rural economy has been hindered and it will continue to struggle in any future upturn due to the lack of skilled workers and the corresponding emergence of an ageing population. By failing to support young people to stay in their communities Government is potentially failing to address a key aspect of sustainability while supporting the emergence of an ageing demographic profile for rural areas which undermines both employment and growth targets (ECORYS, 2010:249).

Public services and rural transport

The provision of public services in rural areas in the context of a falling and ageing population is a cause for concern. With increased levels of emigration the population in rural areas has become dominated by those who are more reliant on public services (the elderly, children and people with disabilities). There is a need to develop a new rural strategy to take account of the changes in rural areas since the 1999 White Paper. Decisions need to be made regarding the provision and level of public services in rural areas, investment in childcare and transport and the integration of rural and regional development into a new Spatial Strategy[106]. Some European countries adopt the equivalence principle for the provision of services in rural areas, which decrees that public services in rural areas should be equivalent quality to those in urban areas. Walsh and Harvey (2013) propose that this would be a useful guidance for investment in an Irish context. The OECD has also noted the need for investment in rural areas in key sectors of transport, information technologies, quality public services, rural firms, conservation and development of local amenities and rural policy proofing (OECD, 2006). Investment in childcare, transport, progression and outreach are all required as part of a cohesive strategy in order to promote employment and innovation in rural areas.

The design and implementation of a new rural development strategy would provide Government and all stakeholders with the opportunity to consider how public services should be provided and delivered in the regions and rural areas. It would also provide an opportunity for the consideration of social, ecological and cultural benefits to and reasons for investing in rural areas. The benefits of such investment must be considered in terms which can encompass more than just economic measurements. The withdrawal of services or lack of provision of services in rural areas undermines rural development and compromises the needs of those most reliant on these services (Shucksmith, 2012). It is critical that the costs of not investing in rural areas, including social exclusion, continued under-employment, poverty and isolation, are taken into account in any new strategy.

The lack of an accessible, reliable and integrated rural transport system is one of the key challenges facing people living in rural areas. Rural dwellers at present shoulder a disproportionate share of the burden of insufficient public transport, according to a recent report (EPA 2011: 10), 45 per cent of the rural district electoral divisions in Ireland have a minimal level of scheduled public transport services with varying frequency and timing. Among the main identified issues contributing to rural deprivation and depopulation are:

- access to secure and meaningful employment;
- availability of public transport in order to access employment and public services;
- access to childcare; and
- access to transport.

(McDonagh, Varley & Shortall 2009: 16)

---

[106] Government stated in February 2013 that a new Spatial Strategy would be developed. It has yet to be published.

Government has acknowledged the importance of an integrated and accessible rural transport network and has pledged to maintain and extend the Rural Transport Programme with other local transport services as much as possible (Government of Ireland 2011: 63).

Car dependency and the reliance of rural dwellers on private car access in order to avail of public services, employment opportunities, healthcare and recreational activities is a key challenge for policy makers. Transport policy must be included in planning for services, equity and social inclusion. The social inclusion element of an integrated rural public transport system can no longer be ignored. The links between better participation, better health, access to public services, access to employment opportunities and a public integrated rural transport service have been documented (Fitzpatrick, 2006). Thus far there has been a failure to incorporate this knowledge fully into rural development policy. The Rural Transport Programme (RTP) (formerly the Rural Transport Initiative) has certainly improved access in some areas. However, the lack of a mainstream public transport system means that many rural areas are still not served. People with disabilities, women, older people, low income households and young people are target groups still at a significant disadvantage in rural areas in terms of access to public transport. Policy makers must ensure that local government and the local community are actively involved in developing, implementing and evaluating rural transport policies as national planning has not worked to date. In 2000 there was a call for a national rural transport policy and the prioritisation of government funding in this area (Farrell, Grant Sparks, 2000). Fourteen years later this policy has yet to be delivered. By 2021 it is estimated that the number of people with unmet transport needs could number 450,000 and of this group an estimated 240,000 will be from the target groups of vulnerable rural dwellers outlined above.

The National Transport Authority (NTA) has been given responsibility for the rural Transport Programme and progressing integrated local and rural transport. It published plans for restructuring the rural transport programme in 2013. The previous RTP Groups will be replaced by eighteen Transport Coordination Units with responsibility for delivering rural transport services. The restructuring plan also outlines the relationship between local authority, Socio-Economic Committees and Transport Coordination Units in terms of developing local transport policies and objectives. The National Integrated Rural Transport Committee was established to oversee six pilot programmes to integrate all state transport services in rural areas and provide access for the whole community to health services, education, employment and retail, recreational and community facilities and services. While the integration of rural transport with national transport policy is welcome, it is important that the models of best practice that emerge from the pilot programmes are put into a national rural transport strategy without delay. Ongoing monitoring will required to ensure that it continues to meet the needs of rural areas. A mainstreamed rural public transport service is required to service those in need of rural public transport and those who are potential users. Investment in a national sustainable rural transport network is required to support rural development. It is required to ensure access to employment, access to services and to ensure rural economies are supported in terms of economic diversification.

Improved rural public transport and improved accessibility to services also provide Ireland with an opportunity to deliver a key change which would in turn help deliver a significant reduction of climate harming gas (CHG) emissions (Browne 2011: 12). This is all the more pressing in terms of Ireland's EU 2020 emissions target and CHG emissions from private vehicles. By investing in a sustainable national public transport system covering all rural areas government could significantly reduce CHG emissions in the long run. The long term costs of not investing in rural areas and not providing adequate and quality public services to rural and regional communities should be factored into all Government expenditure decisions. A new rural strategy is required which should incorporate the social infrastructure, governance and sustainability elements of the core policy framework outlined in Chapter 2.

Farm incomes

The average family farm income was €25,437 in 2013 (Teagasc, 2014), a marginal decline on the 2012 figure. As ever, there was a wide variation in farm incomes with 23 per cent of farms producing a family farm income of less than €5,000 and 14 per cent of farms producing an income of between €30,000 and €50,000. In 2013 direct payments comprised on average 77 per cent of total farm income across all farms. Teagasc projections[107] for 2015 show that the forecast reduction in milk prices, as milk quotas are eliminated and production rises, could see a reduction of income in excess of 50 per cent on dairy farms with income across the entire farm sector falling by up to 25 per cent. Such a high and continued reliance on subsidies combined with the projected fall in milk prices in 2015 highlight the challenges still facing the sector.

Rural income data from the SILC reports was reviewed in chapter 3. This shows that rural Ireland has high dependency levels, increasing outmigration and many people living on very low incomes. The data from the most recent SILC study (CSO 2015) shows there is a very uneven national distribution of poverty. The risk of poverty in rural Ireland is 7 percentage points higher than in urban Ireland – 19.3 per cent and 12.6 per cent respectively.

---

[107] http://www.teagasc.ie/news/2014/201412-02.asp

Key farm statistics:

- Average family farm income was €25,437 in 2013, a 15.5 per cent decrease since 2011. The preliminary Teagasc estimates for 2014 indicate that average family farm income fell by 2 per cent in 2014.
- The number of farm households in which the farmer and/or spouse were engaged in off-farm employment was 51.1 per cent in 2013 (Teagasc, 2014).
- Just 35 per cent of farms were considered economically viable in 2013.
- Direct payments comprised 77 per cent of farm income in 2013 and averaged €19,474 per farm.

These statistics mask the huge variation in farm income in Ireland as a whole. Only a minority of farmers are at present generating an adequate income from farm activity and even on these farms income lags considerably behind the national average. An important insight into the income of Irish farmers is provided by Teagasc in its National Farm Survey 2011 and the IFA's Farm Income Review 2012. Table 13.1 below outlines the huge variations in farm income in Ireland in 2011, with 65 per cent of farms in Ireland having an income of less than €20,000.

Table 12.1: Distribution of Family Farm Income in Ireland 2013

€	< 5,000	5,000 – 10,000	10,000 – 20,000	20,000 – 30,000	30,000 – 50,000	> 50,000
%	23	16.5	22	20.5	14	4
Number	18,200	13,050	17,400	16,213	11,040	3,200

Source: Teagasc 2014/IFA 2015

The majority of farm families rely on income support and payments from the state to supplement their income. As outlined earlier in this chapter solutions to falling farm incomes require broader strategies, both for farm and non-farm rural families. This will require both economic and social supports and broader skills development strategies to find employment and require policy planning and coherence across all areas of the framework outlined in chapter 2. Table 13.2 shows that by the end of 2013 there were 10,303 families receiving the Farm Assist payment, an increase of 2,653 since 2006. This increase can be attributed to a combination of falling product prices and the loss of off-farm employment. Off farm employment and income is extremely important to farming households. From the mid-1990's off-farm employment by farmers increased by about 50 per cent. This gain was subsequently wiped out by the recession. This has increased the dependence of farms on direct subsidies to avoid rural poverty and social exclusion.

Table 12.2: Farm Assist Expenditure (€m) 2006-2013

Year	Expenditure (€m)	Number Benefiting	Average Payment (€/week)
2006	71	7,650	179
2007	79	7,400	205
2008	85	7,710	213
2009	96	8,845	209
2010	111	10,700	199
2011	112	11,300	190
2012	108	11,029	182
2013	99	10,303	180

Source: Teagasc, 2012 and Department of Social Protection, 2014

Agriculture and direct employment from agricultural activities have been declining in Ireland. The Department of Agriculture, Food and the Marine has outlined its vision of the future of Irish Agriculture in *Food Harvest 2020* (Department of Agriculture, Food and the Marine, 2011). It envisages that by 2020 the Irish agri-food industry will have developed and grown in a sustainable manner by delivering high quality, natural-based produce. This requires the industry to adopt a 'smart economy' approach by investing in skills, innovation and research. This signals a move away from traditional farming methods and to a method of collaboration across the agricultural, food and fisheries industries. In implementing this policy there needs to be significant investment in sustainable agriculture, rural anti-poverty and social inclusion programmes in order to protect vulnerable farm households in the transition to a rural development agenda.

Future of rural Ireland

Rural Ireland is a valuable natural resource with much to contribute to Ireland's future social, environmental and economy development. However it faces significant challenges in terms of job creation, service provision for an ageing population, ensuring the natural capital and biodiversity of rural areas is protected and encouraging young people who have left to return and settle in rural areas.

The cumulative impact of measures introduced in Budgets 2012-2015 are likely to have a negative effect on rural families[108] and on the weakest people in rural Ireland

---
[108] For further detail c.f. Social Justice Ireland (2014) *Budget 2015 Analysis and Critique* p.11

as inflation rises, unemployment persists, employment creation is disproportionately urban-based, and services are either reduced or have their charges increased. The removal of resources from rural areas will make it difficult to maintain viable communities. Concern has already been raised about the significant socio-economic impact of the possible closure of these schools on rural communities. Combined with the closure of 139 rural Garda stations in 2012 and 2013,[109] the quality of life for rural dwellers and the sustainability of our rural communities is facing a significant threat. The removal of resources from rural areas will make it difficult to maintain viable communities. Government is failing to deal with the new challenges an ageing population brings to rural areas in relation to health services, social services and accessibility for older and less mobile people. Employment, diversification of rural economies, adapting to demographic changes and supporting young people to stay in their communities are areas that need immediate attention from Government.

Social Justice Ireland believes that we are now reaching a crucial juncture that requires key decisions on social infrastructure, governance and sustainability to ensure the necessary structures are put in place so that rural communities can survive and flourish. The CEDRA Report contains research, analysis and recommendations on how we can face these challenges and ensure a future for rural Ireland. Government should ensure that these recommendations are implemented immediately.

Key Policy Priorities on Rural Development

- Prioritise rolling out high speed broadband to rural areas.
- A new national rural strategy should be developed. This strategy should make up a part of a new national spatial strategy.
- A rural and regional economic development policy statement should be published and incorporated into national economic and employment strategies.
- Ensure all policies are based on equity and social justice and take account of rural disadvantage.
- Decisions around services and provision of services must be made in the context of a national spatial strategy.
- Support young people to remain in their communities and implement policies to ensure rural areas can adapt to a changing demographic profile in the longer-term.

---

[109] 39 Garda Stations were closed in 2012 and 100 Garda Stations were closed in 2013.

13.
THE GLOBAL SOUTH

CORE POLICY OBJECTIVE: THE GLOBAL SOUTH
To ensure that Ireland plays an active and effective part in promoting genuine development in the Global South and to ensure that all of Ireland's policies are consistent with such development.

The theme of inequality dominated 2014, both in Ireland and abroad. Thomas Piketty's *Capital* proved a bestselling hit, provoking heated debates across political divides and publications across the globe as it detailed the problematic rise in inequality between the world's richest one per cent and the rest. In the months leading up the World Economic Forum (WEF) in January 2015 in Davos, Switzerland, inequality was also a key theme for NGO Oxfam as it released a report entitled *Even it Up: Time to end extreme inequality* in October 2014 (and followed this up with a subsequent briefing paper, *Wealth: Having it all and wanting more*). Oxfam highlighted the startling fact that "in 2014, the richest 1 per cent of people in the world owned 48 per cent of global wealth, leaving just 52per cent to be shared between the other 99 per cent of adults on the planet". By 2016, if present wealth share trends continue, "the top 1 per cent will have more wealth than the remaining 99 per cent of people in just two years". This theme was echoed at the organisation's Oxfam-Oxford Symposium in the week leading up to Davos, where Oxfam began its push for a global compact on taxation. In a seven-point plan, the NGO called for a new global approach to rein in inequality and tax avoidance:

- Clamp down on tax avoidance by corporations and rich individuals
- Invest in universal, free public services such as health and education
- Share the tax burden fairly, shifting taxation from labour and consumption towards capital and wealth
- Introduce minimum wages and move towards a living wage for all workers
- Introduce equal pay legislation and promote economic policies to give women a fair deal

- Ensure adequate safety-nets for the poorest, including a minimum income guarantee
- Agree a global goal to tackle inequality 2015

(*Wealth: Having It All And Wanting More*, Oxfam Issue Briefing, January 2015, p.9-10).

The UN Human Development Report 2014 (UNHDR) released in July of last year echoes, in many respects, the Oxfam report and gives us a current snapshot of human development across the Globe at this time. The UN Report entitled *Sustaining Human Progress: Reducing Vulnerabilities and Building Resilience* offered a somewhat more optimistic note in certain areas, yet also noted worrying trends. Whilst the 2013 UN HDR Report pointed to positive (unpredicted) outcomes with forty developing countries having "greater HDI (Human Development Index) gains than would have been predicted given their situation in 1990" (UN HDR 2014, p.33), the 2014 report warns that "there is evidence that the overall rate of progress is slowing—and this is worrying." (UN HDR 2014, p.33) Reflecting on welcome reductions in certain select inequality parameters, the report cautions that "Declines in inequality should be celebrated, but offsetting growing income disparities with progress in health is not enough. To tackle vulnerability, particularly among marginalized groups, and sustain recent achievements, reducing inequality in all dimensions of human development is crucial".(UN HDR 2014 Summary, p.2) The key emphasis within the 2014 report rests on vulnerability and individuals ability to respond to the shocks and uncertainties of a globalised world, in terms of climatic, economic and political upheavals. Whilst greater numbers around the world are emerging from poverty, "more than 2.2 billion people are either near or living in multidimensional poverty." (UN HDR 2014, p.3). As the recent outbreak of Ebola in West Africa attests, progress for some of the poorest nations can be easily eroded if safety nets and protective mechanisms- both at an institutional and social level- are weak or in some cases non-existent.

The reality of income inequality is graphically reported in both the Oxfam report and briefing paper. Promoting genuine development in the Global South is one of the key policy areas that must be addressed urgently as part of the Core Policy Framework we set out in Chapter 2.

The 2014 UN HDR notes that there are 1.2 billion people living on $1.25 a day or less and 2.7 billion living on less than $2.50 (HDR 2014, p.71). In a world with resources many times what is required to eliminate global poverty this situation is intolerable.

The 2014 United Nations Human Development Report gives an outline of the size of underdevelopment and inequality. Table 13.1 shows this outline.

Table13.1: United Nations development indicators by region and worldwide

Region	GNI per capita (US$ PPP)*	Life Expectancy at Birth (yrs)	Adult Literacy %**
Least Developed Countries	2,126	61.5	59.3
Arab States	15,817	70.2	77.0
East Asia + Pacific	10,499	74.0	94.4
Europe + Central Asia	12,415	71.3	97.7
L. America + Caribbean	13,767	74.9	91.5
South Asia	5,195	67.2	62.9
Sub-Saharan Africa	3,152	56.8	58.9
Very High HDI^	40,046	80.2	n/a
Worldwide total	13,723	70.8	81.3

Source: UNDP (2014: 34, 163, 195)
Notes: * Gross National Income (GNI) Data adjusted for differences in purchasing power.
** Adult defined as those aged 15yrs and above.
^49 Countries including the OECD with very high human development indicators.

The comparable rates for Ireland are: GNI per capita: $33,414; Life expectancy: 80.7; adult literacy: not available

Tables 13.1 and 13.2 show the sustained differences in the experiences of various regions in the world. These differences go beyond just income and are reflected in each of the indicators reported in both tables. Today, life expectancies are years higher in the richest countries than in Sub-Saharan Africa. Similarly, the UN reports that more than 1 in 3 Southern Asians and Sub-Saharan Africans are unable to read.

These phenomena are equally reflected in sizeable differences in income levels (GNI per person) and in the various mortality figures in table 13.2.. Table 13.2 shows that there are 389 deaths per 100,000 live births in Least Developed Countries as against 16 in OECD countries

Table 13.2: Maternal and Infant Mortality Rates

Region	Maternal Mortality Ratio#	Under-5yrs mortality rate*
Least Developed Countries	389	84
Arab States	164	37
East Asia + Pacific	72	21
Europe + Central Asia	31	23
L. America + Caribbean	74	19
South Asia	202	57
Sub-Saharan Africa	474	97
Very High HDI^	16	6
Worldwide total	**145**	**47**

Source: UNDP 2014 (175, 187)
Notes: Ratio of the number of maternal deaths to the number of live births expressed per 100,000 live births
^49 Countries including the OECD with very high human development indicators.
*number of deaths per 1,000 live births. Figures up to 2012.
The comparable rates for Ireland are: Maternal mortality: 2; Under 5 mortality: 6

The Human Development Report 2015 will be titled *Rethinking Work for Human Development*. The emphasis of the next Report will be to "zoom in on the fundamental question – how work can be rethought for human development" and will set about "rethinking the linkages between work and human development identifying the positive intrinsic relationship between work and human development...but also those situations where linkages are broken or eroded - child labour, human trafficking, etc." (Selim Jahan, Director of the Human Development Report Office, http://hdr.undp.org/en/rethinking-work-for-human-development). The report will be released in October.

UN millennium development goals

The UN Millennium Declaration was adopted in 2000 at the largest-ever gathering of heads of state. It committed countries - both rich and poor - to doing all they can to eradicate poverty, promote human dignity and equality and achieve peace, democracy and environmental sustainability. World leaders promised to work together to meet concrete targets for advancing development and reducing poverty by 2015 or earlier. Emanating from the Millennium Declaration, a set of Millennium Development

Goals (MDGs) was agreed. These bind countries to do more in the attack on inadequate incomes, widespread hunger, gender inequality, environmental deterioration and lack of education, healthcare and clean water. They also include actions to reduce debt and increase aid, trade and technology transfers to poor countries. These goals and their related targets are listed in Annex 13.

Progress on the Millennium Development Goals has been mixed, with some countries outperforming others. As Liberian President Ellen Johnson Sirleaf noted in 2013, "Two years from the 2015 deadline, Africa's progress on the Millennium Development Goals remains uneven. Remarkable advances have been made in some areas, such as net primary school enrolment, gender parity in primary education, the representation of women in decision-making, some reduction in poverty, immunization coverage, and stemming the spread of HIV/AIDS. Notwithstanding this progress, there is ample room for more good news. Some areas have been neglected when they should have been put upfront, for example malaria, the number one killer of children in sub-Saharan Africa and many other places in the world. Additionally, the goal for school enrolment did not take into account the need for quality education." (UN HDR 2014, p.11). As noted in our previous annual Socio-Economic Review reports, many advances are at a national-level and not due to any particular regional co-operation or projects.

Critics of the MDGs argue that these goals were dictated by donors, written by donors, and made sense in the Aid Effectiveness agenda and process (Paris 2005 - Accra 2008 –(Busan 2011), rather than in the development agenda. As a consequence, there was very little ownership of the MDGs by development actors, very few countries attempted to localise them. In the years ahead a different approach is needed, one that engages the people who are meant to benefit from this process. It is also essential that the focus be on development that is sustainable (environmentally, economically and socially) and focused on all countries and not just the poorest.

As the MDGs timeline come to an end, a major focus of governments and NGOs is now on the nature of the post-2015 development agenda. This year will be crucial in assessing progress thus far and defining what next in the efforts to combat conflict, disease, inequality and poverty. The UN Rio+20 conference on Sustainable Development in 2012 began the process of determining the post-2015 developmental agenda. A series of high-level events are occurring in 2015 as governments and organisations come together to map the best way forward for the coming decades, including a Millennium Development Goals Report 2015 (July 2015) and a Special Summit on Sustainable Development (September 2015). Organisations such as 'Beyond 2015', representing 1,200 organisations in 140 countries, have come together to ensure the post-2015 Agenda is an inclusive and people-driven process, rather than externally dictated. They call upon the nations of the world to seize this unique opportunity to ensure "that a new paradigm based on democracy and good governance, empowerment of the poorest and most marginalised, and strong citizen voices on social, environmental and economic justice, solidarity, common but differentiated responsibilities, and accountability of all development actors" ('Inspiring and Aiming Higher Recommendations to the Post-2015 Political Declaration', Beyond 2015, p.5).

Wars, inter-community disputes and the easy availability of arms increase vulnerability and instability for many communities. Scarcity of resources especially water, energy and land have become more acute and highlight the need for urgent action. The Intergovernmental Panel on Climate Change (IPCC) estimates that such scarcity will lead to increased conflict and regional instability in many of the poorest parts of the world: "Climate change can indirectly increase risks of violent conflicts in the form of civil war and inter-group violence by amplifying well-documented drivers of these conflicts such as poverty and economic shocks. Multiple lines of evidence relate climate variability to these forms of conflict" (IPCC Climate Change 2014: Impacts, Adaptation, and Vulnerability, Summary for Policymakers, p.20). The overwhelming majority of violent conflicts are intra-state conflicts, their victims are mostly civilians. These conflicts are fought with small arms. The production and trade of these arms is the least transparent of all weapons systems. Stockholm International Peace Research Institute (SIPRI) report that world military expenditure in 2012 is estimated to have been $1,756 billion or $249 for each person. Nearly three-quarters of the companies in the Top 100 for 2012 are headquartered in North America or Western Europe, and they account for 87 per cent of the total arms sales. Ireland as a neutral country should have a role in researching, challenging and advocating for tight controls in the production and distribution of these weapons.

A number of Irish Aid's partner countries neighbour nations currently mired in conflict, such as Ethiopia (which shares a border with South Sudan and Somalia) and Uganda (which shares a border with Democratic Republic of Congo and South Sudan). Ireland should ensure its country offices and overseas programs engage in mediation efforts where possible and promote positive reconciliation efforts amongst civil society groups. Lessons learned from the Department of Foreign Affairs and Trade's (DFAT) Reconciliation Fund projects- fostering peace and community interaction within Northern Ireland, as well as between communities in Northern Ireland, Republic of Ireland and Britain, would allow the DFAT to offer positive insights on reconciliation and cross-border co-operation in other settings.

Climate change will affect all citizens of the world, yet as countless reports indicate those from poorer nations will suffer most. While Irish citizens have not been insulated from the effects of climate change, the consequences are much more acute for those living in developing countries. The effects of climate change have increased the vulnerability of many communities leading to enforced migration, internal displacement, poverty and hunger. Food production is a huge challenge for communities constantly forced to move. An increasingly important issue for developing nations is adaptation strategies to combat the severe effects of Climate Change. As a World Bank report in 2009 indicated, "the major challenge is to identify actions that will support and/or accelerate ongoing development efforts while making them more resilient to climatic risks" (*Making Development Climate Resilient: a World Bank Strategy for Sub-Saharan Africa*, 2009, p.xvi). The African *Union Common African Position (Cap) On The Post- 2015 Development Agenda* (2014) stressed that African nations "recognize that adaptation to the phenomenon represents an immediate and urgent global priority" (p.13), however research by the Overseas Development Institute (ODI) and Climate and Development Knowledge Network (CDKN) noted the worrying situation that many African countries are not preparing adequately for the effects of Climate Change. In a range of case studies- looking at Malawi, Rwanda and Zambia, and a combined urban case study in Accra, Ghana and Maputo, Mozambique, the study showed a lack of integrating thinking on Climate Change and "identified very few long-term decision-making processes that currently use climate information to inform the planning and delivery of investments" (*Promoting the use of climate information to achieve long-term development objectives in sub-Saharan Africa: Results from the Future Climate For Africa scoping phase*, 2015, p.15).

The most recent Inter-Governmental Panel on Climate Change (IPCC) report in 2014 noted that "African ecosystems are already being affected by climate change, and future impacts are expected to be substantial" (IPCC 5th Report, 2014, p.1022). The majority of Irish ODA is focused on African countries and the Irish Government must ensure Irish Aid engages and fosters the use of climate change planning in future planning. Ireland should be a world leader in combating climate change and it should lead the EU 2020 Strategy on climate change and sustainability. However the Government's own commitment to Climate Change has been called into question by the draft Climate Action and Low Carbon Development Bill 2015. The Bill's lack of firm commitments on CO2 emission reductions has seen it criticised by opposition parties and a host of NGOs It is imperative the richer nations of the world take the lead on Climate Change for the simple reality that "The richest seven percent of world's population (equal to half a billion people) are responsible for 50 percent of global CO2 emissions; whereas the poorest 50 percent emit only seven percent of worldwide emissions" (*Even it Up*, Oxfam, 2014, p.41). (A fuller treatment of this issue is to be found in chapter 11).

In February 2015, world leaders gathered in Geneva to prepare a draft text to set the basis for a global agreement in Paris in November 2015. Although 200 countries agreed to an 86-page draft agreement, the document (http://unfccc.int/files/bodies/awg/application/pdf/negotiating_text_12022015@2200.pdf, accessed 14 Feb. 2015) incorporated conflicting approaches to combat Climate Change and overall withheld any firm commitments on cutting emissions ('Geneva talks: countries agree draft text for deal to fight climate change', *The Guardian*, 13 February 2015).

The Irish Government should work within the EU and UN for a broad-based, inclusive agreement at Paris later this year, one that reflects the Global nature of Climate Change and the responsibility of richest nations to contribute most to combat the dangerous effects of increased emissions.

Human Rights and Governance.

Social Justice Ireland is a signatory of the *Galway Platform on Human Rights in Irish Foreign Policy*. This document reflects the views of many groups and academics and is a comprehensive contribution to development policy.

Social Justice Ireland welcomed the 'Review of Ireland's Foreign Policy and External Relations' and the release of *The Global Island* in January 2015 by the Department of Foreign Affairs and Trade. In our submission to the Review, we noted the importance of articulating a vision that is inspirational, attractive and achievable and how this vision can be promoted at home and abroad. We urged that a major focus of this review be on human rights and governance.

The Review is welcome in many respects, offering a revised outlook of Ireland's foreign policy in the years ahead. This is especially important given the decline in ODA contribution as a percentage of GDP and the cuts to Irish Aid's budget in recent years. The Review puts forward a vision of Ireland's Foreign Policy under five interrelated themes: 'Our People', 'Our Values', 'Our Prosperity', 'Our Place in Europe', 'Our Influence'. Whilst *The Global Island* places a great deal of importance on Human Rights obligations, it is vaguer on specific incorporation of Human Rights criteria throughout DFAT operations- this should be spelled out clearly in all future policy documents and country-specific projects.

In order to ensure good governance strong independent civil society organisations are necessary to articulate the views of the people, challenge injustices, and highlight social exclusion. The Irish Aid Report 2014 emphasises the Irish Government's commitment to foster civil society in host countries and Ireland should continue to ensure a space and support for a vibrant promotion of human rights and democratic participation across the globe. This is especially important given some of Ireland's key partner countries- including Ethiopia and Uganda- have a record of stifling democratic opposition and civil society activism.

Trade and debt

The fact that the current inequality between rich and poor regions of the world persists is largely attributable to unfair trade practices and to the backlog of unpayable debt owed by the countries of the South to other governments, to the World Bank, the International Monetary Fund (IMF) and to commercial banks.

The effect of trade barriers cannot be overstated; by limiting or eliminating access to potential markets the Western world is denying poor countries substantial income. In 2002 at the UN Conference on Financing and Development Michael Moore, the President of the World Trade Organisation (WTO), stated that the complete abolition of trade barriers could 'boost global income by $2.8 trillion and lift 320 million people out of poverty by 2015'.

Supporting developing countries to develop and implement just taxation systems would give a huge boost to local social and economic activity. *Social Justice Ireland* notes the initiatives outlined in the 2013 Irish Aid Report, to help developing countries to raise their own revenue and the reiteration of this in the *Global Island* (p.41). We urge Government to learn from and expand these programmes. We support Oxfam's call for a Global Compact on Taxation. Whilst some critics argue that such a deal may be difficult to achieve, as our previous Socio-Economic Review reports have noted the losses that developing countries incur due to tax evasion is sizeable and galling. The Human Development Report 2014 noted that "For the least developed countries illicit financial flows increased from $9.7 billion in 1990 to $26.3 billion in 2008, with 79 percent of this due to trade mispricing. To put this in context, for every dollar of official development assistance that the least developed countries received, an average of 60 cents left in illicit flows between 1990 and 2008" (HDR, 2014, p.119).

Social Justice Ireland also supports the introduction of a financial transaction tax (FTT) which it sees as progressive since it is designed to target only those profiting from speculation. It is clear that all countries would gain from trade reform.

The high levels of debt experienced by Third World countries have disastrous consequences for the populations of these indebted countries. Governments that are obliged to dedicate large percentages of their country's GDP to debt repayments cannot afford to pay for health and educational programmes for their people. Ellmers & Hulova (2013) estimate that the external debt of countries of the global South has doubled over the past decade to reach $4.5 trillion. Debt and Development Coalition estimate that revenue lost from global South countries through illicit capital flight is at €660 - €870 billion per year. It is not possible for these countries to develop the kind of healthy economies that would facilitate debt repayment when millions of their people are being denied basic healthcare and education and are either unemployed or earn wages so low that they can barely survive.

The debt relief initiatives of the past 10 years have been very welcome. These initiatives need to be further developed as there is growing concern that the debts of the poorest countries are beginning to rise again. It is now important that Ireland campaign on the international stage to reduce the debt burden on poor countries. Given Ireland's current economic circumstances, the Irish population now has a greater appreciation of the implications of these debts and the merit in having them reduced.

International Development post 2015

2015 is the European Year for Development (EYD). Within the EU, this means development issues are subject to increased awareness and publicity campaigns for 2015. In planning for the post-2015 development agenda, *Social Justice Ireland* believes that the international community needs to play an active role in developing the proposed UN Sustainable Development Goals and in assisting less developed countries achieve their potential. *Social Justice Ireland* welcomed the Government's publication of *One World, One Future: Ireland's Policy for International Development* (2013) with its overall vision to work for *"A sustainable and just world where people are empowered to overcome poverty and hunger and fully realise their rights and potential"*. The key areas highlighted in this document are a basis for an integrated framework for global development post-2015. These included the three goals of Reduced Hunger, Stronger Resilience; Better Governance, Human Rights and Accountability and Sustainable Inclusive Economic Growth; with the six priority areas for action of Global hunger; Fragile states; Climate change and development; Trade and economic growth; Essential services and; Human rights and accountability (ibid, p.2.).

In the development of this framework we recommend the following

- Priorities should be shaped by the views of those on the ground. People living in poverty should be supported in an appropriate manner so they can participate fully in processes that are influencing the post 2015 framework. This principle should also apply to goal setting, targets, monitoring and evaluation processes. Too often policies are detached from the communities they are meant to be serving.

- As spelled out in the *Galway Platform on Human Rights in Irish Foreign Policy*, the framework should affirm the full set of social, economic, cultural, civil and political rights of all people everywhere. Goals and targets (global and national) should be linked to human rights obligations.

- Equality should be mainstreamed across all goals and targets. Groups experiencing discrimination should be enabled to actively participate in identifying appropriate indicators to provide disaggregated data to assess progress.

- Establish effective accountability mechanisms for the implementation of the post-2015 framework. The mechanisms should operate at local, national and global levels. Involve people living in poverty and marginalisation in these evaluations.

- Sustainability should be the core concept around which international development post 2015 is organised. This should include environmental, economic and social sustainability.

One of the main outcomes of the UN Rio+20 Conference was the agreement by member States to establish a process to develop sustainable development goals. It is envisioned that all member states would contribute to and 'buy in' to these goals. In early 2013 the UN General Assembly established the Open Working Group to establish a process to draft these goals. The draft Sustainable Development Goals (SDGs) has been published. (A copy of these draft goals is included in Annex 13). It is expected that these goals will be adopted by the UN Summit when it meets in late September 2015. The draft SDGs are very general and aspirational. More work is needed on the draft. In particular, it will be important that budget lines, structures and measurements of progress are put in place to achieve these goals.

Ireland's commitment to ODA

As noted above, Ireland's Foreign Policy was subject to a significant review which resulted in the January 2015 publication of *The Global Island: Ireland's Foreign Policy for a Changing World*. The publication set out to offer the latest comprehensive outline of Irish Foreign policy since the 1996 White Paper *Challenges and Opportunities Abroad* (*The Global Island*, Foreword, p.1).

Social Justice Ireland welcomes the emphasis on Human Rights and Governance in this review, reflecting priorities as set out by the Galway Platform for Human Rights in Irish Foreign Policy in December 2013 (of which *Social Justice Ireland* is a signatory). The report emphasises "Good governance and accountability are vital for the realisation of human rights, and key to addressing inequality, discrimination and exclusion which lie at the core of poverty. We will continue to focus on building effective institutions and policies as well as encouraging popular participation in the democratic process" (The Global Island p.40). Governance is the institutional context within which rights are achieved or denied. It is about how power and authority are exercised in the management of the affairs and resources of a country. *Social Justice Ireland* welcomes this emphasizes on good governance, both at home and abroad, and urges the Irish Government to ensure such guiding principles are maintained in all its development projects.

Ireland's Policy for International Development, *One World, One Future,* published in 2013 reiterated the Programme for Government's commitment to achieve the target of 0.7 per cent of Gross National Income allocated to international development cooperation. It went on to state that: 'Recognising the present economic difficulties, the Government will endeavour to maintain aid expenditure at current levels, while moving towards the 0.7 per cent target' (p3). *Social Justice Ireland* welcomed this commitment but is disappointed that a date by which this target would be met has not been set.

As table 13.3 shows, over time Ireland had achieved sizeable increases in our ODA allocation. In 2006 a total of €814m (0.53 per cent of GNP) was allocated to ODA – reaching the interim target set by the Government. Budget 2008 further increased the ODA budget to reach €920.7m (0.6 per cent of GNP). However, since then the ODA budget has been a focus of government cuts and has fallen by €318m – more than 34 per cent.

Table 13.3: Ireland's net overseas development assistance, 2005-2014

Year	€m's	% of GNP
2005	578.5	0.42
2006	814.0	0.53
2007	870.9	0.53
2008	920.7	0.59
2009	722.2	0.55
2010	675.8	0.53
2011	657.0	0.50
2012	628.9	0.47
2013	637.1	0.46
2014	601.6	0.43
2015	602	0.38*

Source: Irish Aid (2012:73) and various Budget Documents.

Figures based on adjusted figure of GDP and GNI as introduced earlier this year by Eurostat.

The Government has been silent on this 0.7 per cent target in this new Foreign Policy review. The ODA budget was cut every year between 2006-2014 both in terms of allocation and as a percentage of GNP (Table 13.3). This is an allocation to the poorest people on the planet and should have been given first priority. Ahead of Budget 2015, *Social Justice Ireland* called for an increase of €60 million in the ODA budget to reach 0.45 per cent of GDP. However, Budget 2015 saw ODA remain at 2014 levels meaning the ODA allocation will fall below 0.4 per cent of GDP for the first time in 10 years ('Questions over Aid commitments', *Irish Examiner*, Oct. 15, 2014). We urge Government to halt this slide and begin the process of increasing the allocation to reach the 0.7 per cent of GNP target. An Ipsos MRBI poll in July 2014 found that over 77 per cent of respondents were in favour of Government meeting its commitment of providing over 0.7 per cent of GDP in ODA. Opinion polls have consistently shown public support for high levels of ODA and Government meeting its UN obligation in this regard.

Rebuilding our commitment to ODA and honouring the UN target should be important policy paths for Ireland to pursue in the years to come. Not only would its achievement be a major success for government, and an important element in the delivery of promises made but it would also be of significance internationally. Ireland's success would not only provide additional assistance to needy countries but would also provide leadership to those other European countries who do not meet the target. The DFAT and the Irish Government regularly cite the positive assessment international bodies give of Irish overseas aid. The OECD's Development Assistance Committee (DAC) Peer Review of Ireland noted how Ireland's "institutional structures enable it to deliver co-ordinated, quality development co-operation and to be a pragmatic and flexible partner" (*OECD Development Co-operation Peer Reviews: Ireland 2014*, p. 17). However, if ODA contributions continue to decline aid programs- and poor communities in host countries- will suffer. As the Dóchas 2015 budget submission stated: "The 0.7 per cent target is based on a percentage, meaning that the growth or shrinkage of a country's economy should not affect its progress towards the target. This in-built mechanism ensures fairness and demonstrates the 0.7 per cent target is not a matter of economic prosperity but a direct indicator of a county's commitment to development" (Dóchas Budget 2015 Submission to the Minister for Finance, "Demonstrating Ireland's Commitment to Development Cooperation", Summary). Despite the challenges in Ireland at present, we believe that we should care for those less well-off particularly the world's poorest people.

HIV/AIDS

Progress against the spread of HIV/AIDS has been one of the more notable successes of the MDGs. Target seven of the Goals committed the international community to have halted by 2015 and begun to reverse the spread of HIV/AIDS'. In July 2014, UN AIDS released its *Gap Report* indicating the progress thus far in combating HIV/AIDS and where further work needs to be done. As the Report notes, much progress has been made in the past decade:

- Nearly 12.9 million people were receiving antiretroviral therapy globally at the end of 2013. Of these 12.9 million people, 5.6 million were added since 2010 (p.14).
- At the end of 2013, US$ 19.1 billion was being invested annually in the AIDS response in low- and middle-income countries (p.16)
- There has been notable progress in Sub-Saharan Africa, the region most affected by HIV/AIDS, with significant declines in new infections. New HIV infections have dropped 33 per cent (amongst all age groups) between 2005 and 2013 and there has been a 19 per cent reduction in new infections since 2010 (p.30).

Despite these gains, deficiencies do remain, including:

- New infections are declining, but they still remain very high. 0.8 per cent of adults aged 15-49 years worldwide are living with HIV (p.17).
- New infections in eastern Europe and central Asia started increasing in the late 2000s and the region now has 0.6 per cent of adults living with HIV.
- Rising levels of new infections in the Middle East and North Africa are a worrying development. Numbers of those infected has increased 31 per cent since 2001, from 19,000 to 25,000 (p.19).
- Young women and adolescent girls are disproportionately vulnerable and at high risk of infection. 15 per cent of all women living with HIV aged 15 years or older are young women 15-24 years old (p.20)

In September 2014, UN AIDS released a report *Fast-Track - Ending the AIDS epidemic by 2030*. The ambitious goals including a commitment to 90-90-90 by 2020, meaning:

- 90 per cent of people living with HIV being aware of their HIV status, 90 per cent of people who know their status receiving treatment and 90 per cent of people on HIV treatment having a suppressed viral load so their immune system remains strong and they are no longer infectious. This would mean 500,000 new adult infections by 2020 (p.10).
- By 2030, the goal is to further increase coverage to 95-95-95 with a reduction to 200,000 new adult infections. (p.10-11).

Following on from this ambitious report, Mayors from cities across the world came together to reiterate these goals and sign the Paris Declaration on December 1, 2014, representing a new commitment on the part of world leaders to combat the disease. They committed themselves to "Support a greater involvement of people living with HIV/AIDS through an initiative to strengthen the capacity and coordination of networks of people living with HIV/AIDS and community-based organizations. By ensuring their full involvement in our common response to the pandemic at all national, regional and global levels, this initiative will, in particular, stimulate the creation of supportive political, legal and social environments".

The international community must take its commitment seriously and act with urgency. Despite our difficulties *Social Justice Ireland* urges Government to meet its commitments in this area and ensure Ireland plays a key role internationally in responding to this crisis.

Key Policy Priorities

- The Irish Government should renew its commitment to meet the United Nations target of contributing 0.7 per cent of GNP to Overseas Development Assistance. Recognising that the deadline of 2015 will be missed, *Social Justice Ireland* proposes that the new date should be 2020 and a clear pathway should be set out to achieve this.

- Take a far more proactive stance at government level on ensuring that Irish and EU policies towards countries in the South are just. Ensure that Irish businesses operating in developing countries - in particular Irish Aid country partners - are subject to proper scrutiny and engage in sustainable development practices.

- Continue to support the international campaign for the liberation of the poorest nations from the burden of the backlog of unpayable debt and take steps to ensure that further progress is made on this issue.

- Ireland should play a prominent role in the development of Sustainable Development Goals for the planet and, within these, maintain the focus on the issues raised earlier in this chapter.

- Work for changes in the existing international trading regimes, to encourage fairer and sustainable forms of trade. In particular, resource the development of Ireland's policies in the WTO to ensure that this goal is pursued.

- Ensure that the government takes a leadership position within the European and international arenas to encourage other states to fund programmes and research aimed at resolving the AIDS/HIV crisis.

14.
VALUES

"Few can doubt that we have been in a period of economic transition. The financial collapse has shown that many aspects of the 'new economy', so widely praised just a few years ago, are unstable and unsustainable. For years we were told that we had entered a brand new world of unlimited financial possibilities, brought about by sophisticated techniques and technologies, starting with the internet and the information technology revolution, spread through the world by "globalisation" and managed by 'financial engineers' who, armed with the tools of financial derivatives, could eliminate risk and uncertainty. Now we can see that the new financial structure was a house of cards built on sand, where speculation replaced enterprise, and the self-interest of many financial speculators came at the expense of the common good.

"While there were many factors that contributed to the financial meltdown of 2008, they start with the exclusion of ethics from economic and business decision making. The designers of the new financial order had complete faith that the 'invisible hand' of market competition would ensure that the self-interested decisions of market participants would promote the common good." (Clark and Alford, 2010).

While the initial shock of the meltdown has been absorbed, many questions remained. Why did we fail to see the crash coming? "Where did the wealth go?" People want to know who benefitted from the meltdown. The people who are bearing the cost of the economic crash are obvious, the unemployed, emigrants who were forced to leave Ireland, poor, sick and vulnerable people who have had their income and social services cut. We are conscious of much fear, anxiety and anger in our communities. There is a pervasive distrust of all institutions. The critical question now is how do we prevent a recurrence of this type of economic crash? While some people advocate good regulation as the solution, others are sceptical and search for more radical approaches.

Now seven years after the economic crash some commentators are urging us to look to the new 'shoots' and new signs of economic recovery. We are being encouraged to accept the current reality and 'move on'. We are discouraged from taking a critical look at what has happened to sections of our society especially people on middle and lower incomes and the socio-economic gap that has opened between them and the better off.

These observations, reflections and questions bring to the fore the issue of values. Our fears are easier to admit than our values. Do we as a people accept a two-tier society in fact, while deriding it in principle? The earlier chapters of this review document many aspects of this divided society. It is obvious that we are becoming an even more unequal world. Scarce resources have been taken from poorer people to offset the debts of bankers and speculators. This shift of resources is made possible by the support of our national value system. This dualism in our values allows us to continue with the status quo, which, in reality, means that it is okay to exclude almost one sixth of the population from the mainstream of life of the society, while substantial resources and opportunities are channelled towards other groups in society. This dualism operates at the levels of individual people, communities and sectors.

To change this reality requires a fundamental change of values. We need a rational debate on the kind of society in which we want to live. If it is to be realistic, this debate should challenge our values, support us in articulating our goals, and formulating the way forward. *Social Justice Ireland* wishes to contribute to this debate. We approach the task from the concerns and values of Christian thinking. While many people are not Christians they support the concerns and values identified here.

Christian Values

Christianity subscribes to the values of both human dignity and the centrality of the community. The person is seen as growing and developing in a context that includes other people and the environment. Justice is understood in terms of relationships. The Christian scriptures understand justice as a harmony that comes from fidelity to right relationships with God, people and the environment. A just society is one that is structured in such a way as to promote these right relationships so that human rights are respected, human dignity is protected, human development is facilitated and the environment is respected and protected (Healy and Reynolds, 2003:188).

Human rights are the rights of all persons so that each person is not only a right-holder but also has duties to all other persons to respect and promote their rights. Thus there is a sharing of the benefits of rights and the burden of duties. Alan Gewirth notes that human rights have important implications for social policy. On the one hand the State must protect equally the freedom and basic well-being of all persons and on the other hand it must give assistance to persons who cannot maintain their well-being by their own efforts.

Social Justice Ireland believes that every person should have the following basic socio-economic rights:

- Sufficient income to live life with dignity,
- Access to meaningful work,
- Access to appropriate accommodation.
- Opportunity to participate in the decisions that affect their lives.
- Access to appropriate education
- Access to essential healthcare
- An environment which respects their culture

As our societies have grown in sophistication, the need for appropriate structures has become more urgent. The aspiration that everyone should enjoy the good life, and the goodwill to make it available to all, are essential ingredients in a just society. But this good life will not happen without the deliberate establishment of structures to facilitate its development. In the past charity, in the sense of alms-giving by some individuals, organisations and Churches on an arbitrary and ad hoc basis, were seen as sufficient to ensure that everyone could cross the threshold of human dignity. Calling on the work of social historians it could be argued that charity in this sense was never an appropriate method for dealing with poverty. Certainly it is not a suitable methodology for dealing with the problems of today. As recent world disasters have graphically shown, charity and the heroic efforts of voluntary agencies cannot solve these problems on a long-term basis. Appropriate structures should be established to ensure that every person has access to the resources needed to live life with dignity.

Few people would disagree that the resources of the planet are for the use of the people - not just the present generation, but also the generations still to come. In Old Testament times these resources were closely tied to land and water. A complex system of laws about the Sabbatical and Jubilee years (Lev 25: 1-22, Deut 15: 1-18) was devised to ensure, on the one hand, that no person could be disinherited, and, on the other, that land and debts could not be accumulated. This system also ensured that the land was protected and allowed to renew itself

These reflections raise questions about ownership. Obviously there was an acceptance of private property, but it was not an exclusive ownership. It carried social responsibilities. We find similar thinking among the leaders of the early Christian community. St John Chrysostom, (4th century) speaking to those who could manipulate the law so as to accumulate wealth to the detriment of others, taught that *"the rich are in the possession of the goods of the poor even if they have acquired them honestly or inherited them legally*" (Homily on Lazarus). These early leaders also established that a person in extreme necessity has the right to take from the riches of others what s/he needs, since private property has a social quality deriving from the law of the communal purpose of earthly goods (*Gaudium et Spes* 69-71).

In more recent times, Pope Paul VI (1967) said "*private property does not constitute for anyone an absolute and unconditional right. No one is justified in keeping for his/her exclusive use what is not needed when others lack necessities.... The right to property must never be exercised to the detriment of the common good*" (*Populorum Progressio* No. 23). Pope John Paul II has further developed the understanding of ownership, especially in regard to the ownership of the means of production.

One of the major contributors to the generation of wealth is technology. The technology we have today is the product of the work of many people through many generations. Through the laws of patenting and exploration a very small group of people has claimed legal rights to a large portion of the world's wealth. Pope John Paul II questioned the morality of these structures. He said "*if it is true that capital as the whole of the means of production is at the same time the product of the work of generations, it is equally true that capital is being unceasingly created through the work done with the help of all these means of production*". Therefore, no one can claim exclusive rights over the means of production. Rather, that right "*is subordinated to the right to common use, to the fact that goods are meant for everyone*". (*Laborem Exercens* No.14). Since everyone has a right to a proportion of the goods of the country, society is faced with two responsibilities regarding economic resources: firstly, each person should have sufficient to access the good life; and secondly, since the earth's resources are finite, and since "more" is not necessarily "better", it is time that society faced the question of putting a limit on the wealth that any person or corporation can accumulate. Espousing the value of environmental sustainability requires a commitment to establish systems that ensure the protection of our planet.

In his recent exhortation, *The Joy of the Gospel,* (Evangelii Gaudium) Pope Francis named the trends that are detrimental to the common good, equality and the future of the planet. He says:

> "While the earnings of the minority are growing exponentially, so too is the gap separating the majority from the prosperity enjoyed by those happy few. This imbalance is the result of ideologies which defend the absolute autonomy of the marketplace and financial speculation. Consequently, they reject the right of states, charged with vigilance for the common good, to exercise any form of control. A new tyranny is thus born, invisible and often virtual, which unilaterally and relentlessly imposes its own laws and rules. Debt and the accumulation of interest also make it difficult for countries to realise the potential of their economies and keep citizens from enjoying their real

purchasing power. To all this we can add widespread corruption and self-serving tax evasion, which have taken on worldwide dimensions. The thirst for power and possessions knows no limits. In this system, which tends to devour everything which stands in the way of increased profits, whatever is fragile, like the environment, is defenceless before the interests of a deified market, which become the only rule." (par 56)

The concern of Pope Francis to build right relationships extends from the interpersonal to the inter-state to the global.

Interdependence, mutuality, solidarity and connectedness are words that are used loosely today to express a consciousness which resonates with Christian values. All of creation is seen as a unit that is dynamic - each part is related to every other part, depends on it in some way, and can also affect it. When we focus on the human family, this means that each person depends on others initially for life itself, and subsequently for the resources and relationships needed to grow and develop. To ensure that the connectedness of the web of life is maintained, each person depending on their age and ability is expected to reach out to support others in ways that are appropriate for their growth and in harmony with the rest of creation. This thinking respects the integrity of the person, while recognising that the person can achieve his or her potential only in right relationships with others and with the environment.

As a democratic society we elect our leaders regularly. This gives an opportunity to scrutinise the vision politicians have for our society. Because this vision is based on values it is worth evaluating the values being articulated. Check if the plans proposed are compatible with the values articulated and likely to deliver the society we desire.

Most people in Irish society would subscribe to the values articulated here. However these values will only be operative in our society when appropriate structures and infrastructures are put in place. These are the values that *Social Justice Ireland* wishes to promote. We wish to work with others to develop and support appropriate systems, structures and infrastructures which will give practical expression to these values in Irish society.

SOCIO-ECONOMIC REVIEW 2015

Annex 3
INCOME DISTRIBUTION

To accompany chapter 3, this annex outlines details of the composition of poverty in Ireland over recent years alongside offering an overview of Ireland's income distribution over the past two decades. It also reviews the process by which the basic social welfare payment became benchmarked to 30 per cent of Gross Average Industrial Earnings. The material underpins the development of many of the policy positions we have outlined in chapter 3.

Poverty - Who are the poor?

Two interchangeable phrases have been used to describe those living on incomes below the poverty line: *'living in poverty'* and *'at risk of poverty'*. The latter term is the most recent, introduced following a European Council meeting in Laeken in 2001 where it was agreed that those with incomes below the poverty line should be termed as being 'at risk of poverty'.

The results of the *SILC* survey provided a breakdown of those below the poverty line. This section reviews those findings and provides a detailed assessment of the different groups in poverty.

Table A3.1 presents figures for the risk of poverty facing people when they are classified by their principal economic status (the main thing that they do). These risk figures represent the proportion of each group that are found to be in receipt of a disposable income below the 60 per cent median income poverty line. In 2013 the groups within the Irish population that were at highest risk of poverty included the unemployed and those not at work due to illness or a disability. Over one in five classified as being "on home duties", mainly women, have an income below the poverty line. The "student and school attendees" category represents a combination of individuals living in poor families while completing their secondary education and those attending post-secondary education but with low incomes. The latter element of this group are not a major policy concern, given that they are likely to only experience poverty while they gain education and skills which should ensure they live with sufficient income subsequently. Those still in school and experiencing poverty are more aligned to the issue of child poverty, which is examined later in this annex.

Despite the increase in poverty between 2009 and 2013 (see chapter 3), the table also reveals the groups which have driven the overall reduction in poverty over the period (falling from 19.7 per cent to 15.2 per cent). Comparing 2003 and 2013, the poverty rate has fallen for all groups other than students while there have been pronounced falls among the welfare-dependent groups, i.e. the unemployed, retired and those not at work due to illness or a disability.

Table A3.1: Risk of poverty among all persons aged 16yrs + by principal economic status, 2003-2013

	2003	2006	2013
At work	7.6	6.5	5.0
Unemployed	41.5	44.0	36.7
Students and school attendees	23.1	29.5	28.2
On home duties	31.8	23.8	21.1
Retired	27.7	14.8	10.0
Unable to work as ill/disabled	51.7	40.8	18.1
Total	19.7	17.0	15.2

Source: CSO SILC reports (2005:11, 2007:15, 2014: table 2), using national equivalence scale

One obvious conclusion from table A3.1 is that further progress in reducing poverty is closely associated with continued enhancements to the adequacy of welfare payments.

The working poor

Having a job is not, of itself, a guarantee that one lives in a poverty-free household. As table A3.1 indicates 5 per cent of those who are employed are living at risk of poverty. Despite decreases in poverty among most other groups, poverty figures for the working poor have remained static, reflecting a persistent problem with low earnings. In 2013, almost 82,000 people in employment were still at risk of poverty.[110] This is a remarkable statistic and it is important that policy makers begin to recognise and address this problem.

---

[110] See table 3.6.

Many working families on low earnings struggle to achieve a basic standard of living. Policies which protect the value of the minimum wage and attempt to keep those on that wage out of the tax net are relevant policy initiatives in this area. Similarly, attempts to highlight the concept of a 'living wage' (see section 3.3) and to increase awareness among low income working families of their entitlement to the Family Income Supplement (FIS) are also welcome; although evidence suggests that FIS is experiencing dramatically low take-up and as such has questionable long-term potential. However, one of the most effective mechanisms available within the present system to address the problem of the working poor would be to make tax credits refundable. We have addressed this proposal in chapter 3 of this review.

Recent data from Eurostat estimates the proportion of the Irish workforce who are low paid, defined as those below 66 per cent of the median hourly wage. Using data for 2010, they found that threshold to be €12.20 for Ireland and that an estimated one in five Irish workers earn below that threshold.

Child poverty

Children are one of the most vulnerable groups in any society. Consequently the issue of child poverty deserves particular attention. Child poverty is measured as the proportion of all children aged 17 years or younger that live in households with an income below the 60 per cent of median income poverty line. The 2013 *SILC* survey indicates that 17.9 per cent were at risk of poverty.

Table A3.2: Child Poverty – % Risk of Poverty Among Children in Ireland.

	2006*	2007*	2009	2013
Children, 0-17 yrs	19.0	17.4	18.6	17.9

Source: CSO (various editions of SILC)
Note: * 2006 and 2007 data exclude SSIA effect.

Translating the data in table A3.2 into numbers of children implies that in 2013 almost 218,000 children lived in households that were experiencing poverty.[iii] The scale of this statistic is alarming. Given that our children are our future, this situation is not acceptable. Furthermore, the fact that such a large proportion of our children are living below the poverty line has obvious implications for the education system, for the success of these children within it, for their job prospects in the future and for Ireland's economic potential in the long-term.

[iii] See table 3.6.

Child benefit remains a key route to tackling child poverty and is of particular value to those families on the lowest incomes. Similarly, it is a very effective component in any strategy to improve equality and childcare. We welcomed the Budget 2015 initiative to restore some of the recent cuts to this payment; cuts which were regressive and hit low incomes families hardest.

Older people

According to the CSO's 2011 *Census Results* there were 535,393 people aged over 65 years in Ireland in 2011. Of these, more than a quarter live alone comprising over 87,000 women and 49,000 men (CSO, 2012:26, 27). When poverty is analysed by age group the 2013 figures show that 9.2 per cent of those aged above 65 years live in relative income poverty.

Among all those in poverty, the retired have experienced the greatest volatility in their poverty risk rates. As table A3.3 shows, in 1994 some 5.9 per cent of this group were classified as poor; by 1998 the figure had risen to 32.9 per cent and in 2001 it peaked at 44.1 per cent. The most recent data record a decrease in poverty rates, mainly driven by increases in old age pension payments. While recent decreases are welcome, it remains a concern that so many of this county's senior citizens are living on so little.

Table A3.3: Percentage of older people (65yrs+) below the 60 per cent median income poverty line.

	1994	1998	2001	2003	2004	2005	2009	2013
Aged 65 +	5.9	32.9	44.1	29.8	27.1	20.1	9.6	9.2

Source: Whelan et al (2003: 28) and CSO (various editions of SILC)

The Ill /People with a Disability

As table A3.1 showed, those not employed due to illness or a disability are one of the groups at highest risk of poverty with 18.1 per cent of this group classified in this category. Much like the experience of Ireland's older people, the situation of this group has varied significantly over the last decade and a half. The group's risk of poverty climbed from approximately three out of every ten persons in 1994 (29.5 per cent) to over six out of every ten in 2001 (66.5 per cent) before decreasing to approximately two out of every ten in the period 2008-2013. As with other welfare dependent groups, these fluctuations parallel a period where policy first let the value of payments fall behind wage growth before ultimately increasing them to catch-up.

Overall, although those not at work due to illness or a disability only account for a small proportion of those in poverty, their experience of poverty is high. Furthermore, given the nature of this group *Social Justice Ireland* believes there is an on-going need for targeted policies to assist them. These include job creation, retraining (see chapter 5 on work) and further increases in social welfare supports. There is also a very strong case to be made for introducing a non-means tested cost of disability allowance. This proposal, which has been researched and costed in detail by the National Disability Authority (NDA, 2006) and advocated by Disability Federation of Ireland (DFI), would provide an extra weekly payment of between €10 and €40 to somebody living with a disability (calculated on the basis of the severity of their disability). It seems only logical that if people with a disability are to be equal participants in society, the extra costs generated by their disability should not be borne by them alone. Society at large should act to level the playing field by covering those extra but ordinary costs.

Poverty and education

The *SILC* results provide an interesting insight into the relationship between poverty and completed education levels. Table A3.4 reports the risk of poverty by completed education level and shows, as might be expected, that the risk of living on a low income is strongly related to low education levels. These figures underscore the relevance of continuing to address the issues of education disadvantage and early-school leaving (see chapter 9). Government education policy should ensure that these high risk groups are reduced. The table also suggests that when targeting anti-poverty initiatives, a large proportion should be aimed at those with low education levels, including those with low levels of literacy.[112]

Table A3.4: Risk of poverty among all persons aged 16yrs + by completed education level, 2007-2013

	2007	2009	2013
Primary or below	24.0	18.6	16.7
Lower secondary	20.7	19.7	23.0
Higher secondary	13.8	12.8	16.2
Post leaving certificate	10.9	9.1	17.5
Third level non-degree	8.4	4.9	8.8
Third level degree or above	4.2	4.8	5.0
Total	15.8	14.1	15.2

Source: CSO (various editions of SILC).

---

[112] We address the issues of unemployment and completed education levels in chapter 5 and adult literacy in chapter 9.

Annex 3 – Income Distribution

Poverty by region and area

Recent SILC reports have provided a regional breakdown of poverty levels. The data, presented in table A3.5 suggests an uneven national distribution of poverty. Using 2013 data, poverty levels are recorded as higher for the BMW region compared to the South and East. Within these regions, the data highlights that in Dublin less than one in ten people are living in poverty (9.1 per cent) while figures were twice this in the Boarder, Midlands, West and South-East. The table also reports that poverty is more likely to occur in rural areas than urban areas. In 2013 the risk of poverty in rural Ireland was 6.7 per cent higher than in urban Ireland with at risk rates of 19.3 per cent and 12.6 per cent respectively.

Table A3.5: Risk of poverty by region and area, 2005-2013

	2005	2009	2010	2013
Border, Midland and West	-	16.2	13.8	21.4
South and East	-	13.3	15.0	14.7
Urban Areas	16.0	11.8	12.5	12.6
Rural Areas	22.5	17.8	18.1	19.3
Overall Population	18.5	14.1	14.7	15.2

Source: CSO (various editions of SILC).

Deprivation: food and fuel poverty

Chapter 3 outlines recent data from the SILC survey on deprivation. To accompany this, we examine here two further areas of deprivation associated with food poverty and fuel poverty.

Food poverty

While there is no national definition or measure of food poverty, a number of reports over the past decade have examined it and its impact. A 2004 report entitled *Food Poverty and Policy* considered food poverty as "the inability to access a nutritionally adequate diet and the related impacts on health, culture and social participation" (Society of St. Vincent de Paul et al, 2004). That report, and a later study entitled *Food on a Low Income* (Safefood 2011), reached similar conclusions and found that the experience of food poverty among poor people was that they: eat less well compared to better off groups; have difficulties accessing a variety of nutritionally balanced good quality and affordable foodstuffs; spend a greater proportion of their weekly income on food; and may know what is healthy but are restricted by a lack of financial resources to purchase and consume it.

Recently, Carney and Maitre (2012) returned to this issue and used the 2010 SILC data to construct a measure of food poverty based on the collected deprivation data. They measured food poverty and profiled those at risk of food poverty using three deprivation measures: (i) inability to afford a meal or vegetarian equivalent every second day; (ii) inability to afford a roast or vegetarian equivalent once a week; (iii) whether during the last fortnight there was at least one day when the respondent did not have a substantial meal due to lack of money. An individual who experienced one of these deprivation measures was counted as being in food poverty (2012: 11-12, 19).

The study found that one in ten of the population experienced at least one of the food poverty/deprivation indicators; approximately 450,000 people and an increase of 3 per cent since 2009. Those most at risk of food poverty are households in the bottom 20 per cent of the income distribution, households where the head of household is unemployed or ill/disabled, household who rent at less than the market rent (often social housing), lone parents and households with three adults and children (2012: 29, 38-39).

The results of these studies point towards the reality that many household face making ends meet, given their limited income and challenging living conditions in Ireland today. They also underscore the need for added attention to the issue of food poverty.

Fuel poverty

Deprivation of heat in the home, often also referred to as fuel poverty, is another area of deprivation that has received attention in recent times. A 2007 policy paper from the Institute for Public Health (IPH) entitled *"Fuel Poverty and Health"* highlighted the sizeable direct and indirect effects on health of fuel poverty. Overall the IPH found that the levels of fuel poverty in Ireland remain "unacceptably high" and that they are responsible for "among the highest levels of excess winter mortality in Europe, with an estimated 2,800 excess deaths on the island over the winter months" (2007:7). They also highlighted the strong links between low income, unemployment and fuel poverty with single person households and households headed by lone parents and pensioners found to be at highest risk. Similarly, the policy paper shows that older people are more likely to experience fuel poverty due to lower standards of housing coupled with lower incomes.

Subsequently, the Society of St Vincent de Paul's (SVP) has defined energy poverty as the inability to attain an acceptable level of heating and other energy services in the home due to a combination of three factors: income; energy price and energy efficiency of the dwelling. The 2013 SILC study found that 15.7 per cent of individuals were without heating at some stage in that year; a figure which is 30.8

per cent for those in poverty (see table 3.10). The SVP points out that households in receipt of energy-related welfare supports account for less than half of the estimated energy poor households and over time these payments have been cut while fuel prices and carbon taxes have increased. Clearly, welfare payments need to address energy poverty. Other proposals made by the SVP include detailed initiatives on issues such as: the prevention of disconnections; investing in efficiency measures in housing; education and public awareness to promote energy saving; and the compensation of Ireland's poorest households for the existing carbon tax. [113]

Social Justice Ireland supports the IPH's call for the creation of a full national fuel poverty strategy similar to the model currently in place in Northern Ireland. While Government have made some inroads in addressing low-income household energy issues through funding a local authority retrofitting campaign, progress to date has been limited given the scale of the problem and its implication for the health and wellbeing of many low-income families. Clearly, addressing this issue, like all issues associated with poverty and deprivation, requires a multi-faceted approach. The proposals presented by the SVP should form the core of such a fuel poverty strategy.

The experience of poverty: Minimum Income Standards

A 2012 research report from the Vincentian Partnership for Social Justice (VPSJ) and Trinity College Dublin casts new light on the challenges faced by people living on low incomes in Ireland (Collins et al, 2012). Entitled '*A Minimum Income Standard for Ireland*', the research established the cost of a minimum essential standard of living for individuals and households across the entire lifecycle; from children to pensioners. Subsequently the study calculated the minimum income households required to be able to afford this standard of living. The data in this report has been updated annually by the VPSJ and published on their website.[114]

A minimum essential standard of living is defined as one which meets a person's physical, psychological and social needs. To establish this figure, the research adopted a consensual budget standards approach whereby representative focus groups established budgets on the basis of a household's minimum needs, rather than wants. These budgets, spanning over 2,000 goods, were developed for sixteen areas of expenditure including: food, clothing, personal care, health related costs, household goods, household services, communication, social inclusion and participation, education, transport, household fuel, personal costs, childcare, insurance, housing, savings and contingencies. These budgets were then benchmarked, for their nutritional and energy content, to ensure they were sufficient to provide appropriate nutrition and heat for families, and priced. The

---

[113] We address these issues further in the context of a carbon tax in chapter 4.
[114] See www.budgeting.ie

study establishes the weekly cost of a minimum essential standard of living for five household types. These included: a single person of working age living alone; a two parent household with two children; a single parent household with two children; a pensioner couple; and a female pensioner living alone. Within these household categories, the analysis distinguishes between the expenditure for urban and rural households and between those whose members are unemployed or working, either part-time or full-time. The study also established the expenditure needs of a child and how these change across childhood.

Table A3.6 summarises the most recent update of these numbers following Budget 2015 (October 2014). Looking at a set of welfare dependent households, the study found that when the weekly income of these households is compared to the weekly expenditure required to experience a basic standard of living, they all received an inadequate income. As a result of this shortfall these households have to cut back on the basics to make ends meet (Collins et al, 2012:105-107). The comparison between 2014 and 2015 highlights the impact of price increases and budgetary policy over that period. In each case the challenges facing households is increasing as the gap between income and expenditure widens.

Table A3.6: Comparisons of minimum expenditure levels with income levels for selected welfare dependent households (€ per week)

	2A 2C 3 & 10 yrs	2A 2C 10 & 15 yrs	1A 1C Baby	1A 2C 3 & 10 yrs	Single Adult	Single Pensioner
2014						
Expenditure	479.37	560.96	314.47	361.12	342.99	254.57
Income	434.32	438.17	257.80	319.52	276.00	236.70
Shortfall	*-45.05*	*-122.79*	*-56.67*	*-41.60*	*-66.99*	*-17.87*
2015						
Expenditure	489.50	571.99	321.01	368.14	348.82	258.82
Income	436.63	440.48	260.88	323.75	276.00	238.00
Shortfall	*-52.87*	*-131.51*	*-60.13*	*-44.39*	*-72.82*	*-20.82*

Source: VPSJ, 2014:2

These results, which complement earlier research by the VPSJ (2006, 2010), contain major implications for government policy if poverty is to be eliminated. These include the need to address child poverty, the income levels of adults on social welfare, the 'working poor' issue and access to services ranging from social housing to fuel for older people and the distribution of resources between urban and rural Ireland.[115]

Ireland's income distribution: trends from 1987-2011

The results of studies by Collins and Kavanagh (1998, 2006), Collins (2013) and CSO income figures provide a useful insight into the pattern of Ireland's income distribution over 24 years. Table A3.7 combines the results from these studies and reflects the distribution of income in Ireland as tracked by five surveys.[116] Overall, across the period 1987-2011 income distribution is very static. However, within the period there were some notable changes, with shifts in distribution towards higher deciles in the period 1994/95 to 2005.

Table A3.7: The distribution of household disposable income, 1987-2011 (%)

Decile	1987	1994/95	1999/00	2005	2011
Bottom	2.28	2.23	1.93	2.21	2.05
2nd	3.74	3.49	3.16	3.24	3.64
3rd	5.11	4.75	4.52	4.46	5.14
4th	6.41	6.16	6.02	5.70	6.39
5th	7.71	7.63	7.67	7.31	7.82
6th	9.24	9.37	9.35	9.12	9.18
7th	11.16	11.41	11.20	10.97	11.10
8th	13.39	13.64	13.48	13.23	13.32
9th	16.48	16.67	16.78	16.35	16.50
Top	24.48	24.67	25.90	27.42	24.85
Total	100.00	100.00	100.00	100.00	100.00

Source: Collins and Kavanagh (2006:156), CSO (2006:18-19) and Collins (2013:2)
Note: Data for 1987, 1994/95 and 1999/00 are from various Household Budget Surveys. 2005 and 2011 data from SILC.

Using data from the two ends of this period, 1987 and 2011, chart A3.1 examines the change in the income distribution over the intervening years. While a lot changed

---
[115] Data from these studies are available at www.budgeting.ie
[116] Comparable data for 2013 is not yet available.

in Ireland over that period, income distribution did not change significantly; the decile variations are all small. Compared with 1987, only two deciles saw their share of the total income distribution increase - the fifth decile and the top decile. However, the change for the former is small (+0.11 per cent) while the change for the latter is larger (+0.37 per cent). All other deciles witnessed a small decrease in their share of the national income distribution with the bottom two deciles recording the largest falls.

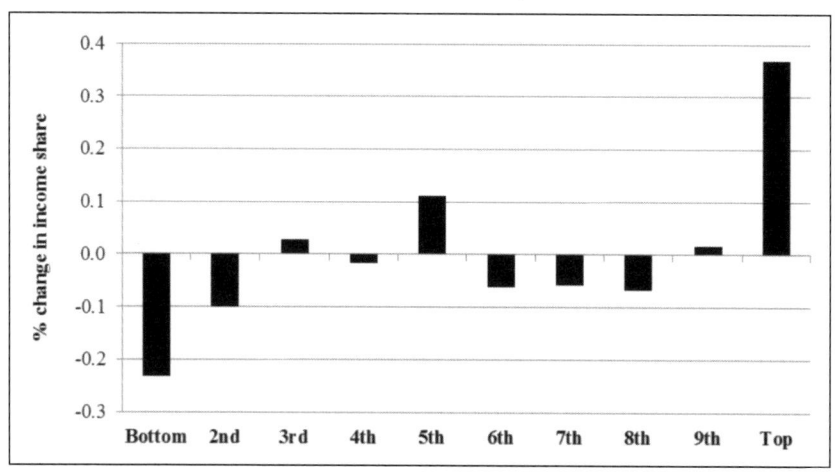

Chart A3.1: Change in Ireland's Income Distribution, 1987-2011

Source: Calculated using data from Collins and Kavanagh (2006:156), CSO (2006:18-19) and Collins (2013:2)

Benchmarking Social Welfare Payments, 2001-2011

While Chapter 3 considers the current challenges associated with maintaining an adequate level of social welfare, here we examine the transition to benchmarked social welfare payments.

The process of benchmarking social welfare payments centred on three elements: the 2001 *Social Welfare Benchmarking and Indexation Working Group* (SWBIG), the 2002 *National Anti-Poverty Strategy (NAPS) Review* and the *Budgets 2005-2007*.

Social welfare benchmarking and indexation working group
In its final report the SWBIG agreed that the lowest social welfare rates should be benchmarked. A majority of the working group, which included a director of *Social Justice Ireland*, also agreed that this benchmark should be index-linked to society's

standard of living as it grows and that the benchmark should be reached by a definite date. The working group chose Gross Average Industrial Earnings (GAIE) to be the index to which payments should be linked.[117] The group further urged that provision be made for regular and formal review and monitoring of the range of issues covered in its report. The group expressed the opinion that this could best be accommodated within the structures in place under the NAPS and the *National Action Plan for Social Inclusion* (now combined as *NAPinclusion*). The SWBIG report envisaged that such a mechanism could involve:

- the review of any benchmarks/targets and indexation methodologies adopted by government to ensure that the underlying objectives remain valid and were being met;
- the assessment of such benchmarks/targets and indexation methodologies against the various criteria set out in the group's terms of reference to ensure their continued relevance;
- the assessment of emerging trends in the key areas of concern, e.g. poverty levels, labour market performance, demographic changes, economic performance and competitiveness, and
- identification of gaps in the area of research and assessment of any additional research undertaken in the interim.

National Anti-Poverty Strategy (NAPS) review 2002
In 2002, the NAPS review set the following as key targets:

To achieve a rate of €150 per week in 2002 terms for the lowest rates of social welfare to be met by 2007 and the appropriate equivalence level of basic child income support (i.e. Child Benefit and Child Dependent Allowances combined) to be set at 33 per cent to 35 per cent of the minimum adult social welfare payment rate.

Social Justice Ireland and others welcomed this target. It was a major breakthrough in social, economic and philosophical terms. We also welcomed the reaffirmation of this target in *Towards 2016*. That agreement contained a commitment to 'achieving the NAPS target of €150 per week in 2002 terms for lowest social welfare rates by 2007' (2006:52). The target of €150 a week was equivalent to 30 per cent of Gross Average Industrial Earnings (GAIE) in 2002.[118]

---

[117] The group recommended a benchmark of 27 per cent although *SJI* argued for 30 per cent.

[118] GAIE is calculated by the CSO on the earnings of all individuals (male and female) working in all industries. The GAIE figure in 2002 was €501.51 and 30 per cent of this figure equals €150.45 (CSO, 2006: 2).

Table A3.8 outlines the expected growth rates in the value of €150 based on this commitment and indicates that the lowest social welfare rates for single people should have reached €185.80 by 2007.

Table A3.8: Estimating growth in €150 a week (30% GAIE) for 2002-2007

	2002	2003	2004	2005	2006	2007
% Growth of GAIE	-	+6.00	+3.00	+4.50	+3.60	+4.80
30% GAIE	150.00	159.00	163.77	171.14	177.30	185.80

Source: GAIE growth rates from CSO Industrial Earnings and Hours Worked (September 2004:2) and ESRI Medium Term Review (Bergin et al, 2003:49).

Budgets 2005-2007
The NAPS commitment was very welcome and was one of the few areas of the anti-poverty strategy that was adequate to tackle the scale of the poverty, inequality and social exclusion being experienced by so many people in Ireland today.

In 2002 *Social Justice Ireland* set out a pathway to reaching this target by calculating the projected growth of €150 between 2002 and 2007 when it is indexed to the estimated growth in GAIE. Progress towards achieving this target had been slow until Budget 2005. At its first opportunity to live up to the NAPS commitment the government granted a mere €6 a week increase in social welfare rates in Budget 2003. This increase was below that which we proposed and also below that recommended by the government's own tax strategy group. In Budget 2004 the increase in the minimum social welfare payment was €10. This increase was again below the €12 a week we sought and at this point we set out a three-year pathway (see table A3.9).

Table A3.9: Proposed approach to addressing the gap, 2005-2007

	2005	2006	2007
Min. SW payment in €'s	148.80	165.80	185.80
€ amount increase each year	14.00	17.00	20.00
Delivered	→	→	→

Following Budget 2004 we argued for an increase of €14 in Budget 2005. The Government's decision to deliver an increase equal to that amount in that Budget marked a significant step towards honouring this commitment.. Budget 2006 followed suit, delivering an increase of €17 per week to those in receipt of the minimum social welfare rate. Finally, Budget 2007's decision to deliver an increase of €20 per week to the minimum social welfare rates brought the minimum social welfare payment up to the 30 per cent of the GAIE benchmark.

Annex 3 – Income Distribution

Social Justice Ireland believes that these increases, and the achievement of the benchmark in Budget 2007, marked a fundamental turning point in Irish public policy. Budget 2007 was the third budget in a row in which the government delivered on its NAPS commitment. In doing so, the government moved to meet the target so that in 2007 the minimum social welfare rate increased to €185.80 per week; a figure equivalent to the 30 per cent of GAIE.

Social Justice Ireland warmly welcomed this achievement. It marked major progress and underscored the delivery of a long overdue commitment to sharing the fruits of this country's economic growth since the mid-1990s. An important element of the NAPS commitment to increasing social welfare rates was the acknowledgement that the years from 2002-2007 marked a period of 'catch up' for those in receipt of welfare payments. Once this income gap had been bridged, the increases necessary to keep social welfare payments at a level equivalent to 30 per cent of GAIE became much smaller. In that context we welcomed the commitment by Government in *NAPinclusion* to 'maintain the relative value of the lowest social welfare rate at least at €185.80, in 2007 terms, over the course of this Plan (2007-2016), subject to available resources' (2007:42). Whether or not 30 per cent of GAIE is adequate to eliminate the risk of poverty will need to be monitored through the SILC studies and addressed when data on persistent poverty emerges.

Annex 4
TAXATION

In this annex, we outline the background data on taxation in Ireland. We first compare the overall level of taxation in Ireland to that of other European countries and then trace how this has changed over time. We then examine trends in income tax levels, outline and compare income tax levels across the income distribution and examine the distribution of indirect taxes on household.

Ireland's total tax-take up to 2012

The most recent comparative data on the size of Ireland's total tax-take has been produced by Eurostat (2014) and is detailed alongside that of 27 other EU states in table A4.1. The definition of taxation employed by Eurostat comprises all compulsory payments to central government (direct and indirect) alongside social security contributions (employee and employer) and the tax receipts of local authorities.[119] The tax-take of each country is established by calculating the ratio of total taxation revenue to national income as measured by gross domestic product (GDP). Table A4.1 also compares the tax-take of all EU member states against the average tax-take of 36.3 per cent.

Of the EU-28 states, the highest tax ratios can be found in Denmark, Belgium, France, Sweden, Finland and Italy while the lowest appear in Lithuania, Latvia, Bulgaria, Slovakia, Romania and Ireland. Overall, Ireland possesses the sixth lowest tax-take at 28.7 per cent, some 7.6 per cent below the EU average. Furthermore, Ireland's overall tax take has notably decreased over recent years with the 2012 value representing a marginal increase from a record low figure in 2010 (see chart A4.1). The increase in the overall level of taxation between 2002 and 2006 can be explained by short-term increases in construction related taxation sources (in particular stamp duty and construction related VAT) rather than any underlying structural increase in taxation levels.

---

[119] See Eurostat (2014:268-269) for a more comprehensive explanation of this classification.

Table A4.1: Total tax revenue as a % of GDP for EU-28 Countries in 2012

Country	% of GDP	+/- from average	Country	% of GDP	+/- from average
Denmark	48.1	11.8	Ireland GNP	35.1	-1.2
Belgium	45.4	9.1	Czech Republic	35.0	-1.3
France	45.0	8.7	Greece	33.7	-2.6
Sweden	44.2	7.9	Malta	33.6	-2.7
Finland	44.1	7.8	Estonia	32.5	-3.8
Italy	44.0	7.7	Spain	32.5	-3.8
Austria	43.1	6.8	Poland	32.5	-3.8
Luxembourg	39.3	3.0	Portugal	32.4	-3.9
Hungary	39.2	2.9	**Ireland GDP**	28.7	-7.6
Germany	39.1	2.8	Romania	28.3	-8.0
Netherlands	39.0	2.7	Slovakia	28.3	-8.0
Slovenia	37.6	1.3	Bulgaria	27.9	-8.4
Croatia	35.7	-0.6	Latvia	27.9	-8.4
UK	35.4	-0.9	Lithuania	27.2	-9.1
Cyprus	35.3	-1.0	**EU-28 average**	36.3	

Source: Eurostat (2014:174) and CSO National Income and Expenditure Accounts
Note: All data is for 2012.

Chart A4.1: Trends in Ireland and EU-28 overall taxation levels, 2000-2012

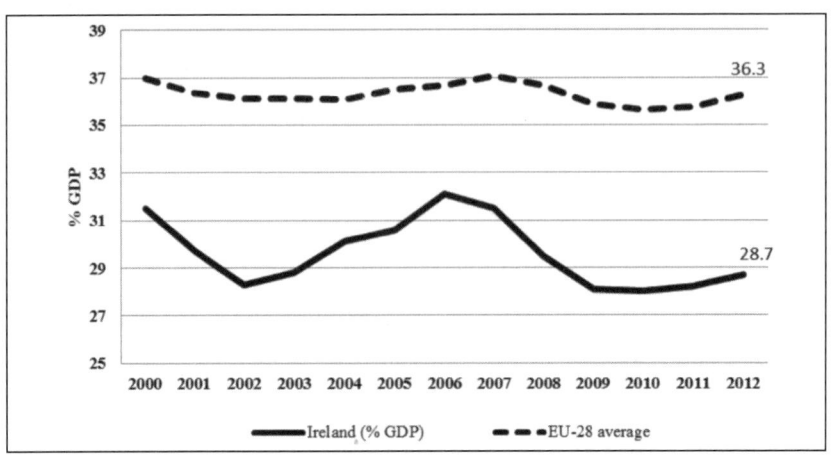

Source: Eurostat (2014:174) and CSO National Income and Expenditure Accounts

GDP is accepted as the benchmark against which tax levels are measured in international publications. However, it has been suggested that for Ireland gross national product (GNP) is a better measure. This is because Ireland's large multinational sector is responsible for significant profit outflows which, if included (as they are in GDP but not in GNP), exaggerate the scale of Irish economic activity.[120] Commenting on this, Collins stated that "while it is clear that multinational profit flows create a considerable gap between GNP and GDP, it remains questionable as to why a large chunk of economic activity occurring within the state should be overlooked when assessing its tax burden" and that "as GDP captures all of the economic activity happening domestically, it only seems logical, if not obvious, that a nations' taxation should be based on that activity" (2004:6).[121] He also noted that using GNP will understate the scale of the tax base and overstate the tax rate in Ireland because it excludes the value of multinational activities in the economy but does include the tax contribution of these companies. In this way, the size of the tax-take from Irish people and firms is exaggerated.

Social Justice Ireland believes that it would be more appropriate to calculate the tax-take by comparing either GNP or GNI (Gross National Income) and using an adjusted tax-take figure which excludes the tax paid by multi-national companies. As figures for their tax contribution are currently unavailable, we have simply used the unadjusted GNP figures and presented the results in table A4.1. In 2012 this stood at 35.1 per cent.[122] This also suggests to international observers and internal policy makers that the Irish economy is not as tax-competitive as it truly is.

In the context of the figures in table A4.1 and the trends in chart A4.1, the question needs to be asked: if we expect our economic and social infrastructure to catch up to that in the rest of Europe, how can we do this while simultaneously gathering less taxation income than it takes to run the infrastructure already in place in most of those other European countries? In reality, we will never bridge the social and economic infrastructure gaps unless we gather a larger share of our national income and invest it in building a fairer and more successful Ireland.

---

[120] Collins (2004:6) notes that this is a uniquely Irish debate and not one that features in other OECD states such as New Zealand where noticeable differences between GDP and GNP also occur.

[121] See also Collins (2014: 91) and Bristow (2004:2) who make a similar point.

[122] The 2012 tax take as a percentage of GNI is 33.3 per cent. The Irish Fiscal Advisory Council has made an attempt to adjust the tax level calculation to reflect these views and have produced a measure known as H. It is calculated as $H = GNP + 0.4(GDP-GNP)$ and, although there is limited detail on the derivation and appropriateness of the adjustment, the overall tax take figure for 2012 is 32.2% of H.

Effective income tax rates

To complement the trends and data outlined in chapter 4, it is possible to focus on the changes to the levels of income taxation in Ireland over the past decade and a half. Central to any understanding of these personal/income taxation trends are effective tax rates. These rates are calculated by comparing the total amount of income tax a person pays with their pre-tax income. For example, a person earning €50,000 who pays a total of €10,000 in tax, PRSI and USC will have an effective tax rate of 20 per cent. Calculating the scale of income taxation in this way provides a more accurate reflection of the scale of income taxation faced by earners.

Following Budget 2015 we have calculated effective tax rates for a single person, a single income couple and a couple where both are earners. Table A4.2 presents the results of this analysis. For comparative purposes, it also presents the effective tax rates which existed for people with the same income levels in 2000 and 2008.

In 2015, for a single person with an income of €15,000 the effective tax rate will be 1.9 per cent, rising to 14.4 per cent on an income of €25,000 and 42.3 per cent on an income of €120,000. A single income couple will have an effective tax rate of 1.9 per cent at an income of €15,000, rising to 7.6 per cent at an income of €25,000, 25.7 per cent at an income of €60,000 and 38.8 per cent at an income of €120,000. In the case of a couple, both earning and a combined income of €40,000, their effective tax rate is 9.1 per cent, rising to 32.9 per cent for combined earnings of €120,000.

Table A4.2: Effective Tax Rates following Budgets 2000 / 2008 / 2015

Income Levels	Single Person	Couple 1 earner	Couple 2 Earners
€15,000	13.9% / 0.0% / 1.9%	2.5% / 0.0% / 1.9%	0.8% / 0.0% / 0.0%
€20,000	13.9% / 0.0% / 10.2%	8.3% / 2.7% / 6.7%	6.1% / 0.0% / 1.1%
€25,000	24.0% / 8.3% / 14.4%	12.3% / 2.9% / 7.6%	11.0% / 0.0% / 1.3%
€30,000	28.4% / 12.9% / 17.1%	15.0% / 5.1% / 9.0%	14.6% / 1.7% / 4.3%
€40,000	33.3% / 18.6% / 23.7%	20.2% / 9.4% / 14.4%	17.5% / 3.6% / 9.1%
€60,000	37.7% / 27.5% / 32.8%	29.0% /19.8% / 25.7%	28.0% /12.2% / 17.1%
€100,000	41.1% / 33.8% / 40.4%	35.9% /29.2% / 36.1%	35.9% /23.8% / 29.2%
€120,000	41.9% / 35.4% / 42.3%	37.6% /31.6% / 38.8%	37.7% /27.2% / 32.9%

Source: Social Justice Ireland (2014:8).
Notes: Tax = income tax + PRSI + levies/USC
Couples assume 2 children and 65%/35% income division
All workers are assumed to be PAYE earners

While these rates have increased since 2008 for almost all earners they are still low compared to those that prevailed in 2000. Few people complained at that time about tax levels being excessive and the recent increases should be seen in this context. Taking a longer view, chart A4.2 illustrates the downward trend in effective tax rates for three selected household types since 1997. These are a single earner on €25,000; a couple with one earner on €40,000; and a couple with two earners on €60,000. Their experiences are similar to those on other income levels and are similar to the effective tax rates of the self-employed over that period.

Chart A4.2: Effective tax rates in Ireland, 1997-2015

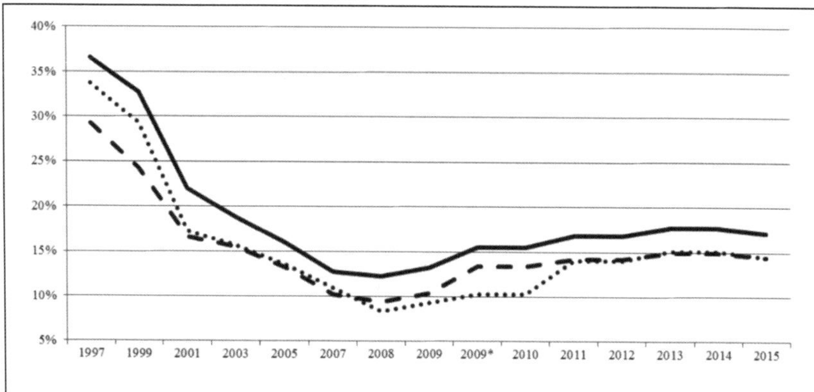

Source: Department of Finance, Budget 2015 and Social Justice Ireland (2014:8).
Notes: Tax = income tax + PRSI + levies/USC
Couples assume 2 children and 65%/35% income division
2009*= Supplementary Budget 2009 (April 2009)
All workers are assumed to be PAYE earners

The two 2009 Budgets produced notable increases in these effective taxation rates. Both Budgets required government to raise additional revenue and with some urgency - increases in income taxes providing the easiest option. Similarly, the introduction of the USC in Budget 2011 increased these rates, most notably for lower income earners, The subsequent Budget 2012 provided a welcome reduction for the lowest earners through raising the income level at which the USC applies. Despite that change, the employee PRSI increase in Budget 2013 targeted lowest income earners hardest and increased effective taxation rate for almost all workers. Budget 2015 further raised the USC entry point and decreased the effective income tax rates faced by all taxpayers.

However, income taxation is not the only form of taxation and, as we highlight in chapter 4, there are many in Ireland with potential to contribute further taxation revenues.

Income taxation and the income distribution

An insight into the distribution of income taxpayers across the income distribution is provided each year by the Revenue Commissioners. The Revenue's ability to profile taxpayers is limited by the fact that it only examines 'tax cases', or taxpayer units, which may represent either individual taxpayers or couples who are jointly assessed for tax. The latest data is the post-Budget 2015 projection by Revenue of the structure on income and income taxes in Ireland during 2015 (see table A4.3).

Table A4.3: Income taxation and Ireland's income distribution, 2015

From €	To €	No. of cases	Av. income	Av. Tax & USC	% Total Tax & USC
-	10,000	402,649	€4,436	€1.42	0.0%
10,000	12,000	73,234	€11,006	€27	0.0%
12,000	15,000	116,836	€13,540	€260	0.2%
15,000	17,000	82,408	€16,018	€354	0.2%
7,000	20,000	130,705	€18,507	€677	0.5%
20,000	25,000	216,626	€22,477	€1,329	1.6%
25,000	27,000	83,130	€25,995	€1,901	0.9%
27,000	30,000	117,955	€28,460	€2,416	1.6%
30,000	35,000	173,843	€32,466	€3,273	3.2%
35,000	40,000	150,662	€37,448	€4,567	3.9%
40,000	50,000	229,709	€44,678	€6,917	9.0%
50,000	60,000	157,805	€54,637	€10,240	9.2%
60,000	75,000	149,372	€66,920	€13,985	11.9%
75,000	100,000	126,352	€85,689	€20,791	14.9%
100,000	150,000	82,764	€119,025	€34,133	16.0%
150,000	200,000	22,512	€170,753	€55,259	7.1%
200,000	275,000	12,188	€231,129	€79,094	5.5%
Over	275,000	12,455	€540,666	€202,409	14.3%
Totals		2,341,205	€39,527	€7,523	100%

Source: Calculated from Revenue Commissioners (2014:4) projections for the 2015 income tax structure.

The progressivity of the Irish income taxation system is well demonstrated in table A4.3 – as incomes increase the average income tax paid also increases. The table also underscores the issues highlighted earlier in chapter 3; that a large proportion of the Irish population survive on low incomes. Summarising the data in the table, almost 18 per cent of cases have an income below €10,000; 52 per cent have an income below €30,000 and 89 per cent of cases are below €75,000. At the top of the income distribution, 5 per cent of households (almost 130,000) receive an income in excess of €100,000. The table also highlights the dependence of the income taxation system on higher income earners, with 27 per cent of income tax coming from cases with incomes of between €60,000 and €100,000 and 43 per cent of income tax coming from cases with incomes above €100,000. While such a structure is not unexpected, a symptom of progressivity rather than a structural problem, it does underscore the need to broaden the tax base beyond income taxes – a point we have made for some time and develop further in chapter 4.

Indirect taxation and the income distribution

As chapter 4 shows, the second largest source of taxation revenue is VAT and the third largest is excise duties. These indirect taxes tend to be regressive – meaning they fall harder on lower income individuals and households (Barrett and Wall, 2006:17-23; Collins, 2014: 13-19).

An assessment of how these indirect taxes impact on households across the income distribution is possible using data from the CSO's Household Budget Survey (HBS), which collects details on household expenditure and income every five years. Chart A4.3 and table A4.4 presents the results of an examination by Collins of the 2009/10 HBS data. It show that indirect taxation consumes more than 29 per cent of the lowest decile's income and more than 13 per cent of the income of the bottom six deciles. These findings reflect the fact that lower income households tend to spend almost all of their income while higher income households both spend and save. Consequently in our *Analysis and Critique of Budget 2012*, Social Justice Ireland highlighted the way that that Budget's increase in VAT was regressive and unnecessarily undermined the living standards of low income households. Other, fairer approaches to increasing taxation were available and should have been taken.

Table A4.4 brings together data for both the indirect and direct (income taxes) payments by households across the income distribution. Although income taxes are progressive, indirect taxes are regressive and the combine picture of overall household contributions offers a more nuanced understanding of the taxes people pay. Although the indirect taxes for the bottom decile are somewhat skewed by households recoding zero incomes (yet still spending, such as self-employed households), the picture from the 2nd decile upwards is one of a flat taxation system for most households, with increases only noticeable for the top three deciles.

Chart A4.3: Indirect Taxes as a % of household gross income, by decile

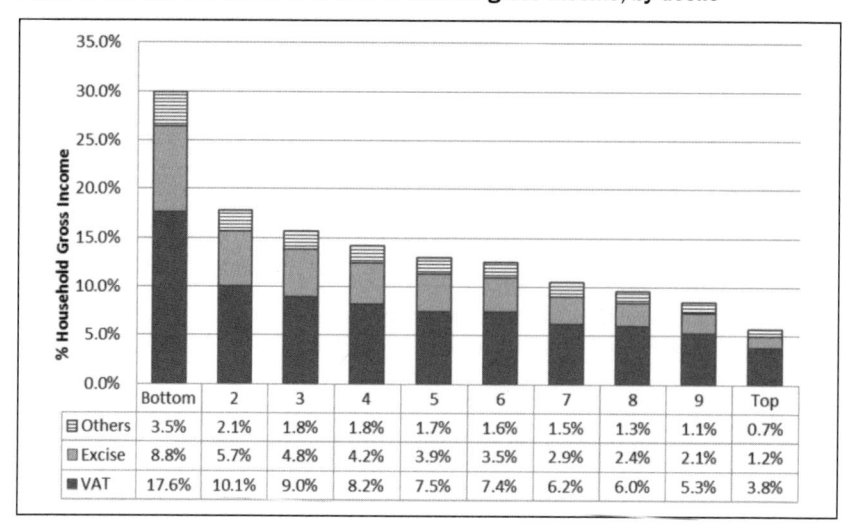

	Bottom	2	3	4	5	6	7	8	9	Top
Others	3.5%	2.1%	1.8%	1.8%	1.7%	1.6%	1.5%	1.3%	1.1%	0.7%
Excise	8.8%	5.7%	4.8%	4.2%	3.9%	3.5%	2.9%	2.4%	2.1%	1.2%
VAT	17.6%	10.1%	9.0%	8.2%	7.5%	7.4%	6.2%	6.0%	5.3%	3.8%

Source: Collins (2014: 18)
Note: Others include levies, vehicle taxes and TV licences.

Table A4.4: Direct, Indirect and Total Household Taxation as a % of Gross Income

Decile	Direct	Indirect	Total
Bottom	0.72%	29.93%	30.64%
2	0.49%	17.85%	18.34%
3	1.00%	15.66%	16.66%
4	2.62%	14.20%	16.82%
5	3.97%	13.05%	17.03%
6	7.38%	12.57%	19.95%
7	10.67%	10.53%	21.20%
8	14.12%	9.62%	23.74%
9	17.27%	8.50%	25.77%
Top	23.99%	5.70%	29.69%
State	13.60%	10.36%	23.95%

Source: Collins (2014: 19), equivalised data using national scale.

Annex 5
WORK, UNEMPLOYMENT AND JOB CREATION

Measuring the labour market

When considering terms such as "employment" and "unemployment" it is important to be as clear as possible about what we actually mean. Two measurement sources are often quoted as the basis for labour market data, the *Quarterly National Household Survey* (QNHS) and the *Live Register*. The former is considered the official and most accurate measure of employment and unemployment although, unlike the monthly live register unemployment data, it appears only four times a year.

The CSO's QNHS unemployment data use the definition of 'unemployment' supplied by the International Labour Office (ILO). It lists as unemployed only those people who, in the week before the survey, were unemployed *and* available to take up a job *and* had taken specific steps in the preceding four weeks to find employment. Any person who was employed for at least *one hour* is classed as employed. By contrast, the live register counts everybody 'signing-on' and includes part-time employees (those who are employed up to three days a week), those employed on short weeks, seasonal and casual employees entitled to Jobseekers Assistance or Benefit.[123]

Labour force trends

The dramatic turnaround in the labour market after 2007 (see chapter 5) contrasts with the fact that one of the major achievements of the preceding 20 years had been the increase in employment and the reduction in unemployment, especially long-term unemployment. In 1992 there were 1,165,200 people employed in Ireland. That

---

[123] See Healy and Collins (2006) for a further explanation of measurement in the labour market.

figure increased by almost one million to peak at 2,169,600 in mid-2007. During early 2006 the employment figure exceeded two million for the first time in the history of the state. Overall, the size of the Irish labour force has expanded significantly and today equals over 2.17 million people, eight hundred thousand more than in 1992 (see chart A5.1).

However, in the period since 2007 emigration has returned, resulting in a decline in the labour force. Initially this involved recently arrived migrants returning home but was then followed by the departure of native Irish. CSO figures indicate that during the first quarter of 2009 the numbers employed fell below two million and that the level continued to fall until achieving some growth in 2013. By the end of 2014 there were just over 1.9 million people employed (see chart A5.1).

Chart A5.1: The Numbers of People in the Labour Force and Employed in Ireland, 1991-2014

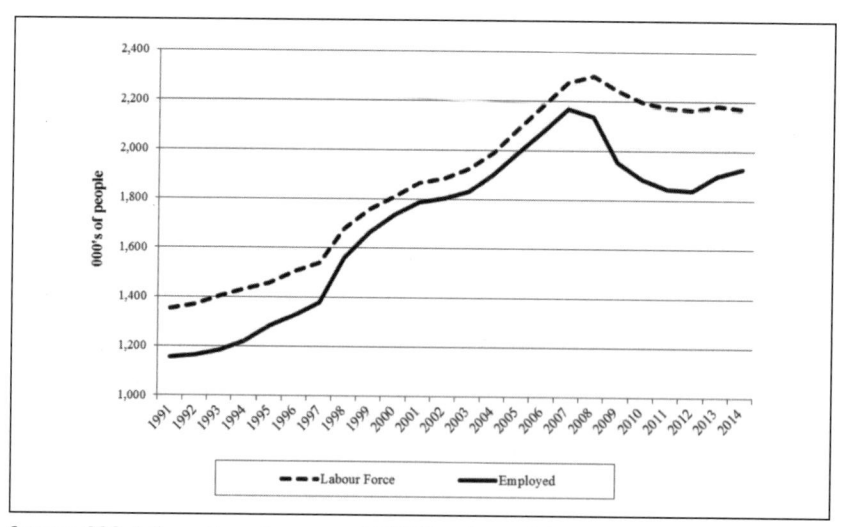

Source: CSO, Labour Force Survey and QNHS various editions

As chart A5.2 shows, the period from 1993 was one of decline in unemployment. By mid-2001 Irish unemployment reached its lowest level at 3.6 per cent of the labour force. Subsequently the international recession and domestic economic crisis brought about increases in the rate. During 2006 unemployment exceeded 100,000 for the first time since 1999 with a total of 105,100 people recorded as unemployed in mid-2006. As chart A5.2 shows, it exceeded 200,000 in early-2009, 300,000 in 2010 and peaked at 328,000 in 2011. Unemployment has since declined, reaching a figure of 245,000 in 2014. The chart also highlights the rapid growth in the number of long-term unemployed (those unemployed for more than 12 months). The CSO reports that there are now almost 140,000 people in long-term unemployment and that this figure has increased more than four-fold since 2007. Quite simply, given the nature and duration of the recent economic crisis, many of those who entered unemployment in 2007-2010 have remained unemployed for more than 12 months and therefore became long-term unemployed.

Chart A5.2: The Numbers of Unemployed and Long-Term Unemployed in Ireland, 1991-2014

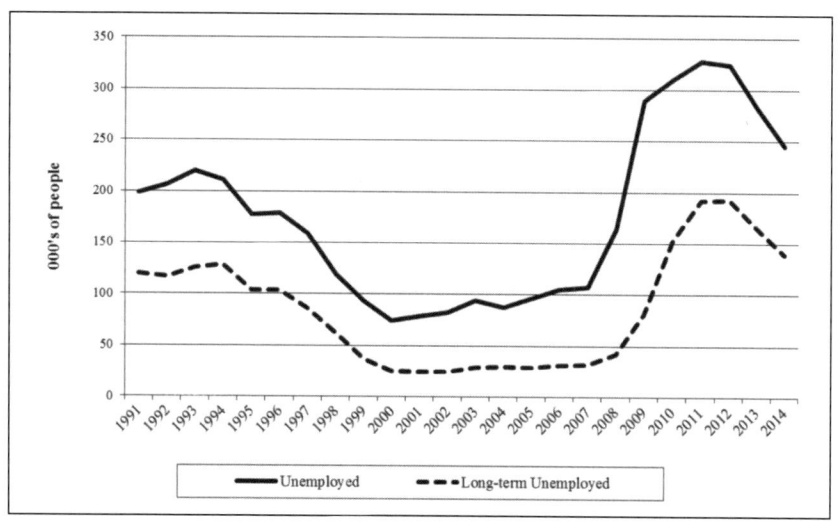

Source: CSO, Labour Force Survey and QNHS various editions

Annex 11
SUSTAINABILITY AND ENVIRONMENT

Ireland: some key environmental facts (CSO 2014, EPA 2014, SEAI 2014)

Greenhouse Gases and Climate Change

- For 2013, total national greenhouse gas emissions are estimated to be 57.81 million tonnes carbon dioxide equivalent (Mt CO2eq). This is 0.7% lower (0.41 Mt CO2eq) than emissions in 2012.

- Emissions from Energy (principally electricity generation) decreased by 11.1% (1.42 Mt CO2 eq) in 2013.

- Transport and Agriculture account for 51.4% of total emissions in 2013 and 70.5% of non EU ETS emissions. Emissions from both of these sectors increased in 2013.

- Agriculture remains the single largest contributor to the overall emissions at 32.3% of the total. Energy and Transport are the second and third largest contributors at 19.6% and 19.1% respectively.

- The transport sector has been the fastest growing source of GHG emissions, showing a 115.5 per cent increase between 1990 and 2013, although emissions from this sector have shown a 23.7% decrease from peak levels in 2007.

- Forest sinks in Ireland could provide a removal of 4.6Mtonnes of CO2 in 2020 and 32 Mtonnes of CO2 over the 2014-2020 period.

Transport

- There were 71,348 new private cars licensed in the year to the end of December 2013, a fall of 6.4% compared to the same period in 2012.

- Ireland's car density in 2013 was 533 cars per 1,000 adults.
- Road transport accounted for 68% of transport final energy consumption in 2013.
- Diesel consumption in transport grew by 251% between 1990 and 2013.
- There has been a substantial increase in the number of low emission vehicles licensed since the introduction in 2008 of motor taxation rates based upon emissions. In 2011, 90% of new private vehicles licensed were in emission bands A and B.

Energy

- Ireland's renewable energy targets for 2020 are to have 40% of electricity, 10% of transport and 12% of heat to be generated from renewable energy.
- In 2013 Ireland generated 20.9% of electricity, from renewable energy.
- In 2013 there was a fall in all fossil fuel used for electricity generation falling by 10.5% in total. Electricity generated from wind increased by 13.2% in 2013.
- Transport accounted for 39.5% of Ireland's final energy consumption in 2013.
- Oil accounted for 56.8% of Ireland's total final energy consumption in 2013.
- Renewable energy accounted for 7.8% of Ireland's gross final energy use in 2013. The target set for 2020 is 16%.
- Wind energy accounted for 42.9% of Ireland's renewable energy in 2013.
- Over the period 1990 to 2013 there was a 73% increase of total net imports with a 31% increase in net imports of oil and as a result Ireland's overall import dependency was 89% in 2013.

Water

- Food Harvest 2020 proposes a 50% increase in milk production. This will present a significant challenge if Ireland is to meet its Water Framework Directive goals as agriculture is one of the main sources of nitrates in groundwaters and of nutrient enrichment in surface waters.
- The Food Harvest target for milk production will potentially increase total nitrogen generation by as much as 14% by 2020.
- The proportion of Irish rivers classified as being unpolluted has declined from 77.3% in 1987-1990 to 68.9% in 1997-2009.
- The percentage of slightly polluted river water has increased steadily from 12% in 1987-1990 to 20.7% in the period 2007-2009.

Waste

- The amount of municipal waste generated in 2012 was 2,692,537 tonnes, a 4.6% decrease since 2011.
- Average household waste generation per capita was 344kg in 2012.
- Ireland is on course to meet the 2013 and 2016 Landfill Directive targets. However, economic recovery may lead to an increase in the disposal of biodegradable municipal waste to landfill which would put achievement of the 2016 target at risk.
- The recovery rate for packaging waste was 87% in 2012
- In 2012, Ireland achieved all its EU obligations across a broad range of waste legislation.
- 92% of Ireland's hazardous waste is exported to three European countries (Belgium, Germany and UK).

Land Use

- Forestry accounts for 11% of land cover, which is low compared with a European average of 35%.
- The area of forest owned privately in Ireland increased from 23% in 1980 to 46% in 2010.
- Although the area farmed organically increased by over 150% between 1997 and 2009, Ireland had the third lowest percentage of agricultural land designated as organic in the EU in 2009.

Biodiversity and Heritage

- Only 7% of Ireland's habitats listed under the Habitat's Directive are considered to be in a favourable state.
- The social and economic benefits of Ireland's biodiversity are worth at least €2.6 billion per annum.
- Ireland had the smallest percentage of land in the EU designated as a Special Protected Area, under the EU Birds Directive, at only 3% of total land area in 2010.
- Ireland at 11% had less land designated as a Special Protected Area under the EU Habitats Directive than the EU average of 14% in 2010.
- 30% of Irish bee species are threatened.

Environmental Taxation

- Environmental taxes accounted for 8.4% of Ireland's total tax revenues in 2012.

Table A11.3: Environmental tax revenue 2008-2012   *€million*

Tax	2008	2009	2010	2011	2012
Energy taxes	2,250	2,265	2,469	2,553	2,518
Transport taxes	2,003	1,523	1,522	1,449	1,471
Pollution and Resource taxes	61	57	62	62	67
Total	4,313	3,845	4,054	4,064	4,056
% of total receipts from Taxes and Social Contributions	8.0%	8.3%	9.0%	8.7%	8.4%

Source: CSO

Annex 13
UN MILLENNIUM DEVELOPMENT GOALS

The following are the UN Millennium Development Goals and the specific targets attached to each of these goals:

Goal 1: Eradicate extreme poverty and hunger
Target 1: Halve, between 1990 and 2015, the proportion of people whose income is less than $1.25 a day.
Target 2: Halve, between 1990 and 2015, the proportion of people who suffer from hunger.

Goal 2: Achieve universal primary education
Target 3: Ensure that, by 2015, children everywhere, boys and girls alike, will be able to complete a full course of primary schooling.

Goal 3: Promote gender equality and empower women
Target 4: Eliminate gender disparity in primary and secondary education, preferably by 2005 and in all levels of education no later than 2015.

Goal 4: Reduce child mortality
Target 5: Reduce by two-thirds, between 1990 and 2015, the under-five mortality rate.

Goal 5: Improve maternal health
Target 6: Reduce by three-quarters, between 1990 and 2015, the maternal mortality ratio.

Goal 6: Combat HIV/AIDS, malaria and other diseases
Target 7: Have halted by 2015 and begun to reverse the spread of HIV/AIDS.
Target 8: Have halted by 2015 and begun to reverse the incidence of malaria and other major diseases.

Goal 7: Ensure environmental sustainability
Target 9: Integrate the principles of sustainable development into country policies and programmes and reverse the loss of environmental resources.
Target 10: Halve by 2015 the proportion of people without sustainable access to safe drinking water.
Target 11: Have achieved by 2020 a significant improvement in the lives of at least 100 million slum dwellers.

Goal 8: Develop a global partnership for development
Target 12: Develop further an open, rule based, predictable, nondiscriminatory trading and financial system (includes a commitment to good governance, development, and poverty reduction - both nationally and internationally).
Target 13: Address the special needs of the least developed countries (includes tariff and quota free access for exports, enhanced programme of debt relief for and cancellation of official bilateral debt, and more generous official development assistance for countries committed to poverty reduction).
Target 14: Address the special needs of landlocked countries and small island developing states (through the Programme of Action for the Sustainable Development of Small Island Developing States and 22nd General Assembly provisions).
Target 15: Deal comprehensively with the debt problems of developing countries through national and international measures in order to make debt sustainable in the long term
Target 16: In cooperation with developing countries, develop and implement strategies for decent and productive work for youth.
Target 17: In cooperation with pharmaceutical companies, provide access to affordable essential drugs in developing countries.
Target 18: In cooperation with the private sector, make available the benefits of new technologies, especially information and communications technologies.

(UNDP, 2003: 1-3)

Open Working Group Proposals for Sustainable Development Goals – Headline Targets

Goal 1: End poverty in all its forms everywhere.

Goal 2: End hunger, achieve food security and improved nutrition and promote sustainable agriculture.

Goal 3: Ensure healthy lives and promote well-being for all at all ages.

Goal 4: Ensure inclusive and equitable quality education and promote lifelong learning opportunities for all.

Goal 5:   Achieve gender equality and empower all women and girls.

Goal 6:   Ensure availability and sustainable management of water and sanitation for all.

Goal 7:   Ensure access to affordable, reliable, sustainable and modern energy for all.

Goal 8:   Promote sustained, inclusive and sustainable economic growth, full and productive employment and decent work for all.

Goal 9:   Build resilient infrastructure, promote inclusive and sustainable industrialization and foster innovation.

Goal 10: Reduce inequality within and among countries.

Goal 11: Make cities and human settlements inclusive, safe, resilient and sustainable.

Goal 12: Ensure sustainable consumption and production patterns.

Goal 13: Take urgent action to combat climate change and its impacts.

Goal 14: Conserve and sustainably use the oceans, seas and marine resources for sustainable Development.

Goal 15: Protect, restore and promote sustainable use of terrestrial ecosystems, sustainably manage forests, combat desertification, and halt and reverse land degradation and halt biodiversity loss.

Goal 16: Promote peaceful and inclusive societies for sustainable development, provide access to justice for all and build effective, accountable and inclusive institutions at all levels.

Goal 17: Strengthen the means of implementation.

REFERENCES

Bank for International Settlements (2013) *Triennial Central Bank Survey of Foreign Exchange and Derivatives Market Activity*. Basel: BIS.

Barrett, A. and Wall C. (2005) *The Distributional Impact of Ireland's Indirect Tax System*. Dublin: Combat Poverty Agency.

Behan, J., J. McNaboe, C. Shally & N. Burke (2014) *National Skills Bulletin 2014*. Dublin: Exper Group on Future Skills Needs

Bennett, C. (2013) *MABS Clients and Mortgage Arrears, a profile of MABS clients in mortgage difficulty and factors associated therewith*. Dublin: MABS National Development Limited.

Bennett M., D. Fadden,. D. Harney, P. O'Malley, C. Regan and Sloyan L. (2003) *Population Ageing in Ireland and its Impact on Pension and Healthcare Costs - Report of Society of Actuaries Working Party on Population Studies*. Dublin: Society of Actuaries in Ireland.

Bergin, A., J. Cullen, D. Duffy, J. Fitzgerald, I. Kearney and McCoy D. (2003) *Medium-Term Review: 2003-2010*. Dublin: ESRI.

Bristow, J. (2004) *Taxation in Ireland: an economist's perspective*. Dublin: Institute of Public Administration.

Brown, C. and Scott, C. (2010) 'Regulation in Ireland: History, Structure, Style and Reform' *UCD Geary Institute Discussion Paper Series, September 2010*. Dublin: UCD.

Browne, D, Caulfield, B and O'Mahony, M (2011) Barriers to Sustainable Transport in Ireland. *Climate Change Research Programme (CCRP) 2007-2013 Report Series No. 7*: Dublin: EPA

Burke, S., Thomas, S., Barry, S., Keegan, C., (2014). *Measuring, Mapping and Making Sense of Irish Health System Performance in the Recession. A Working Paper from the Resilience project in the Centre for Health Policy and Management, School of Medicine, Trinity College Dublin*. March 2014.

Byrne, D., Duffy, D. and Fitzgerald, J. (2014) *Household Formation and Tenure Choice: Did the great Irish housing bust alter consumer behaviour?*, ESRI Working Paper No.487, July 2014. Dublin: ESRI.

Cacioppo J.T. and Hawkley, L.C. (2003) 'Social Isolation and Health' *Perspectives in Biology and Medicine, Summer 2003, Vol.46, number 3 supplement*.

Cahill, S., O'Nolan, C., O'Caheny, D., Bobersky, A., (2015) *An Irish National Survey of Dementia in Long-term Residential Care*. Dementia Services Information and Development Centre Carneiro, P and Heckman, J (2003) Human Capital Policy. *NBER Working Paper Series*. Cambridge MA: National Bureau of Economic Research

Carney, C and Maître, B. (2012) 'Constructing a Food Poverty Indicator for Ireland using the Survey on Income and Living Conditions', *Social Inclusion Technical Paper No. 3*. Dublin: Department of Social Protection.

Carrie, A (2005) "Lack of long-run data prevents us tracking Ireland's social health" in *Feasta Review No2 Growth: the Celtic Cancer* Dublin: Feasta

Central Bank of Ireland (2014) *Macro-prudential policy for residential mortgage lending, Consultation Paper CP87*. Dublin: Central Bank.

Central Bank of Ireland (2014) *Residential Mortgage Arrears and Repossession Statistics: Q.3 2014*. Dublin: Central Bank.

Central Bank of Ireland (2014) *Financial Statistics Summary Chart Pack*. Dublin: Central Bank.

Central Bank of Ireland (2013) *Research highlights positive experience of borrowers engaged in the Mortgage Arrears Resolution Process*. Dublin: Central Bank. Central Statistics Office (2004) *Industrial Earnings and Hours Worked*. Dublin: Stationery Office.

Central Bank of Ireland (2012) *Residential Mortgage Arrears and Repossessions Statistics: Q3 2012*. Available online at http://www.centralbank.ie/polstats/stats/mortgagearrears/documents/2012q3_ie_mortgage_arrears_statistics.pdf. (Accessed on 04/03/2013)

Central Statistics Office (2015) *Household Finance and Consumption Survey, 2013*. Dublin: Stationery Office.

Central Statistics Office (2015) *Quarterly National Household Survey Quarter 4 2014*. Dublin: Stationery Office.

Central Statistics Office (2015) *Statistical Yearbook of Ireland 2014*. Dublin: Stationery Office.

Central Statistics Office (2015) *Survey on Income and Living Conditions 2013*. Dublin: Stationery Office.

Central Statistics Office (2015) *Measuring Ireland's Progress 2013*. Dublin: Stationery Office.

Central Statistics Office (2014) *Measuring Ireland's Progress 2012* Dublin: Stationery Office.

Central Statistics Office (2014) *Population and Migration Statistics*. Dublin: Stationery Office.

Central Statistics Office (2014) *Statistical Yearbook of Ireland 2014*. Dublin: Stationery Office.

Central Statistics Office (2014) *Survey on Income and Living Conditions 2012*. Dublin: Stationery Office.

Central Statistics Office (2014) *Population and Migration Statistics*. Dublin: Stationery Office.

Central Statistics Office (2014) *Quarterly National Household Survey Parental Involvement in Children's Education Q2 2012*. Dublin: Stationery Office.

Central Statistics Office (2013) *Statistical Yearbook of Ireland 2013*. Dublin: Stationery Office.

Central Statistics Office (2013) *Sustainable Development Indicators Ireland 2013*. Dublin: Stationery Office.

Central Statistics Office (2013). *Quarterly National Household Survey, Effects on Households of the Economic Downturn Quarter 3 2012*. Dublin, Stationery Office.

Central Statistics Office (2013) *Population and Labour Force Projections 2016-2046*. Dublin: Stationery Office.

Central Statistics Office (various) *Survey on Income and Living Conditions Results*. Dublin: Stationery Office.

Central Statistics Office (2012) *Census 2011 Profile 2: Older and Younger.* Dublin: Stationery Office.

Central Statistics Office (2012) *Census 2011 Profile 6: Migration and Diversity.* Dublin: Stationery Office

Central Statistics Office (2012) *Environmental Indicators Ireland 2012.* Dublin: Stationery Office.

Central Statistics Office (2012) *Homeless persons in Ireland, A Special Census Report.* Dublin: Stationery Office.

Central Statistics Office (2012) *Measuring Ireland's Progress 2011.* Dublin: Stationery Office.

Central Statistics Office (2012) *Population and Migration Statistics.* Dublin: Stationery Office.

Central Statistics Office (2012) *Census 2011 Profile 4: The Roof over our Heads.* Dublin: Stationery Office.

Central Statistics Office (2012) *Census 2011 Profile 8: Our Bill of Health – Health, Disability and Carers in Ireland.* Dublin: Stationery Office.

Central Statistics Office (2012) *Statistical Yearbook of Ireland 2012.* Dublin: Stationery Office

Central Statistics Office (2012) *Census 2011 Profile 10: Door to Door.* Dublin: Stationery Office.

Central Statistics Office (2011) *Quarterly National Household Survey Voter Participation Quarter 2 2011.* Dublin: Stationery Office

Central Statistics Office (2011) *Quarterly National Household Survey, Educational Attainment Thematic Report 2011.* Dublin: Stationery Office.

Central Statistics Office (2010) *Mortality Differentials in Ireland.* Dublin: Stationery Office.

Central Statistics Office (2010) *National Disability Survey 2006 – Volume two.* Dublin: Stationery Office.

Central Statistics Office (2010) *Quarterly National Household Survey: Special Module on Carers Quarter 3 2009.* Dublin: Stationery Office.

Central Statistics Office (2010) *Statistical Yearbook of Ireland 2010.* Dublin: Stationery Office.

Central Statistics Office (2010) *Survey on Income and Living Conditions 2009 Results.* Dublin: Stationery Office.

Central Statistics Office (2009) *Survey on Income and Living Conditions Housing Module 2007.* Dublin: Stationery Office.

Central Statistics Office (2008) *National Disability Survey 2006 – First Results.* Dublin: Stationery Office.

Central Statistics Office (2004) *Quarterly National Household Survey: Special Module on Disability Quarter 1 2004.* Dublin: Stationery Office.

Chambers of Commerce of Ireland (2004) *Local Authority Funding – Government in Denial,* Dublin: Chambers of Commerce Ireland.

Children's Rights Alliance (2014) *Report Card 2014.* Dublin: Children's Rights Alliance.

Clark C.M.A. (2002) *The Basic Income Guarantee: ensuring progress and prosperity in the 21st century.* Dublin: Liffey Press and CORI Justice Commission.

Collins, M.L. (2015) 'Wealth in Ireland – at last some robust data'. *NERI Blog* 18/2/2015.

Collins M.L. (2014) "Taxation". In O'Hagan, J. and C. Newman (eds.) *The Economy of Ireland* (12th edition). Dublin: Gill and Macmillan.

Collins, M.L. (2014) 'Total Tax Contributions of Households in Ireland' *NERI Working Paper*, 2014/18. Dublin: NERI.

Collins, M.L. (2013) 'Income Distribution, Pre-Distribution and Re-Distribution: latest data for the Republic of Ireland' *NERI Research inBrief no5*, August 2013. Dublin: NERI.

Collins, M.L. (2013) 'Income Taxes and Income Tax Options – a context for Budget 2014' *NERI Working Paper*, 2013/05. Dublin: NERI.

Collins, M.L. (2011) *Establishing a Benchmark for Ireland's Social Welfare Payments*. Paper for Social Justice Ireland. Dublin: Social Justice Ireland.

Collins, M.L. (2006) "Poverty: Measurement, Trends and Future Directions", in Healy, S., B. Reynolds and M.L. Collins, *Social Policy in Ireland: Principles, Practice and Problems*. Dublin: Liffey Press.

Collins, M.L. (2004) "Taxation in Ireland: an overview" in B. Reynolds, and S. Healy (eds.) *A Fairer Tax System for a Fairer Ireland*. Dublin: CORI Justice Commission.

Collins, M.L. and Kavanagh, C. (2006) "The Changing Patterns of Income Distribution and Inequality in Ireland, 1973-2004", in Healy, S., B. Reynolds and M.L. Collins, *Social Policy in Ireland: Principles, Practice and Problems*. Dublin: Liffey Press.

Collins, M.L. and Kavanagh, C. (1998) "For Richer, For Poorer: The Changing Distribution of Household Income in Ireland, 1973-94", in Healy, S. and B. Reynolds, *Social Policy in Ireland: Principles, Practice and Problems*. Dublin: Oak Tree Press.

Collins, M.L. and Larragy, A. (2011) 'A Site Value Tax for Ireland: approach, design and implementation' *Trinity Economics Papers Working Paper 1911*. Dublin: Trinity College Dublin.

Collins, M.L. and Walsh, M. (2011) Tax Expenditures: Information and Revenue Forgone – the experience of Ireland. *Trinity Economic Papers Series*, 2011/12.

Collins, M.L. and Walsh, M. (2010) *Ireland's Tax Expenditure System: International Comparisons and a Reform Agenda – Studies in Public Policy No. 24*. Dublin: Policy Institute, Trinity College Dublin.

Collins, M.L., B. Mac Mahon, G. Weld and Thornton, R. (2012) 'A Minimum Income Standard for Ireland – a consensual budget standards study examining household types across the lifecycle – Studies'. *Public Policy No. 27*, Dublin: Policy Institute, Trinity College Dublin.

Comhar (2002) *Principles for Sustainable Development*. Dublin: Stationery Office.

Commission for the Economic Development of Rural Areas (2014) *Energising Ireland's Rural Economy*. Dublin: CEDRA.

Commission on Taxation (2009) *Commission on Taxation Report 2009*. Dublin: Stationery Office.

Commission on Taxation (1982) *Commission on Taxation First Report*. Dublin: Stationery Office.

Convention on the Constitution (2014) *Eight Report of the Convention on the Constitution: Economic, Social and Cultural (ESC) Rights*. available online at https://www.constitution.ie/AttachmentDownload.ashx?mid=5333bbe7-a9b8-e311-a7ce-005056a32ee4 (Accessed 12 March 2015)

Corr, C. (2006) *Financial Exclusion in Ireland: An exploratory study and policy review*. Dublin: Combat Poverty Agency.

Costanza, R., Hart, M., Posner S. and Talberth, J. (2009) *Beyond GDP: The Need for New Measures of Progress*. Boston University: The Pardee Papers.

Coughlan, O (2007) Irish Climate Change Policy from Kyoto to the Carbon Tax: a Two-level Game Analysis of the Interplay of Knowledge and Power. *Irish Studies in International Affairs*, Vol. 18 (2007), 131-153

Council of Europe (2011) *Council of Europe's charter of shared social responsibilities*. Brussels: Council of Europe.

Council of the European Union (2011) *Council Resolution on a renewed European Agenda for adult learning*. 20 December 2011. (2011/C 372/01)

Cullen, P. (2015) *'Hospital trolleys: Behind record figures lies much unnecessary suffering'*. The Irish Times. 6th January.

Cullen, P. (2015). 'Big gap in health between rich and poor young'. *The Irish Times* 14 February

Curtin, J and Hanrahan, G (2012) *Why Legislate? Designing a Climate Law for Ireland*. Dublin: The Institute of International and European Affairs.

Curtin, J. (2014) *Understanding the European Council Conclusions on Climate: A 10 Step Guide*. Dublin: The Institute of International and European Affairs.

Daft (2014) *The Daft.ie House Price Report, An analysis of recent trends in the Irish residential sales market, 2014 in Review*, available online at http://c0.dmstatic.com/620/report/Daft-Sale-Report-Q4-2014.pdf (Accessed 12 March 2015)

Daft (2014) *The Daft.ie Rental Report, An analysis of recent trends in the Irish rental market, 2014 Q3*, available online at https://c0.dmstatic.com/620/report/Daft-Rental-Report-Q3-2014.pdf (Accessed 12 March 2015)

Dáil Debates (2014) *Written Questions, 17 June 2014, available online at http://oireachtasdebates.oireachtas.ie/debates%20authoring/debateswebpack.nsf/takes/dail 2014061700078#WRR00600* (Accessed 12 March 2015)

Dalal-Clayton, B. & Bass, S. (2002) *Sustainable development strategies: a resource book*. OECD: Paris.

Daly, H.E and Cobb, J.B. (1987) *For the Common Good: Redirecting the Economy toward Community, the Environment and a Sustainable Future*. Boston: Beacon Press.

Debt and Development Coalition Ireland (2014) *Submission to the Review of Ireland's Foreign Policy and External Relations*, available online at http://www.dochas.ie/sites/default/files/ddci_submission_foreign_affairs_review040214.pdf (accessed 12 March 2015).

Delaney, A. (2011) *Árainn Mhór: A Case for Combining Social and Environmental Sustainability in an Irish Island Community*. Denmark: Aalborg University.

Delaney, A. (2012) *Donegal Islands Survival Plan 2012-2015*. Denmark: Aalborg University.

Department of Agriculture and Food (1999) *Ensuring the Future - A Strategy for Rural Development in Ireland*. Dublin: Stationery Office.

Department of Agriculture, Food and the Marine (2014) *The Rural Development Programme (RDP) 2014-2020 Consultation Paper*. Dublin: Department of Agriculture, Food and the Marine.

Department of Agriculture, Food and the Marine (2014) *Value for Money Review Disadvantaged Areas Scheme*. Dublin: Department of Agriculture, Food and the Marine

Department of Agriculture, Food and the Marine (2012) *Harnessing Our Ocean Wealth – An Integrated Marine Plan for Ireland*. Dublin: Stationery Office.

Department of Agriculture, Food and the Marine (2015) *A discussion document on the potential for Greenhouse Gas (CHG) mitigation within the Agriculture and Forestry Sector*. Dublin: Department of Agriculture, Food and the Marine.

Department of An Taoiseach (2012) *National Reform Programme for Ireland 2012 Update*. Dublin: Stationery Office.

Department of An Taoiseach (2006) *Towards 2016 - Ten-Year Framework Social Partnership Agreement 2006-2015*, Dublin, Stationery Office.

Department of An Taoiseach (2002) *Basic Income, A Green Paper*. Dublin: Stationery Office.

Department of An Taoiseach (2001) *Final Report of the Social Welfare Benchmarking and Indexation Group*. Dublin: Stationery Office.

Department of Education and Skills (2014) *An Action Plan for Solas*. Dublin: Stationery Office.

Department of Education and Skills (2014) *Apprenticeship Implementation Plan*. Dublin: Stationery Office.

Department of Education and Skills (2014) *Focussed Policy Assessment Early Start Programme*. Dublin: Early Years Education Policy.

Department of Education and Skills (2014) *General Scheme Technological Universities Bill*. Dublin: Department of Education and Skills.

Department of Education and Skills (2014) *Review of Apprenticeship Training in Ireland*. Dublin: Department of Education and Skills.

Department of Education and Sills (2012) Address by Minister for Education and Skills, Ruairí Quinn TD, at Nordic Education Seminar. Dublin: Department of Education and Skills.

Department of Education and Sills (2012) Speech by Minister for Education and Skills Ruairi Quinn, TD at the launch of his Junior Cycle Framework. Dublin: Department of Education and Skills.

Department of Education and Skills (2012) *A Framework for Junior Cycle*. Dublin: Stationery Office

Department of Education and Skills (2012) Press Release *Minister Quinn protects frontline services in Budget 2013*. Dublin: Department of Education and Skills.

Department of Education and Skills (2012) *Report to the Minister for Education and Skills on the impact in terms of posts in Budget measures in relation to The Withdrawal form DEIS Band 1 and Band 2 Urban Primary Schools of Posts from Disadvantage Schemes pre-dating DEIS*. Dublin: Department of Education.

Department of Education and Sills (2011) *2011-2031, Twenty Years of Radical Reform* Speech by Minister for Education and Skills Ruairi Quinn, TD at the MacGill Summer School, Glenties, Co. Donegal.

Department of Education and Skills (2011) *An Evaluation of Planning Processes in DEIS Post-Primary Schools*. Dublin: Stationery Office.

Department of Education and Skills (2011) *An Evaluation of Planning Processes in DEIS Primary Schools*. Dublin: Stationery Office

Department of Education and Skills (2011) *Comprehensive Review of Current Expenditure*. Dublin: Department of Education and Skills

Department of Education and Skills (2011) *Information Note regarding main features of 2012 Estimates for Education and Skills Vote*. Dublin: Department of Education and Skills.

Department of Education and Skills (2011) *Literacy and Numeracy for Learning and Life, The National Strategy to Improve Literacy and Numeracy among Children and Young People 2011 – 2020*. Dublin: Stationery Office.

Department of Education and Skills (2011) *National Strategy for Higher Education to 2030*. Dublin: Stationery Office.

Department of Education and Skills (2009) *Policy Options for New Student Contributions in Higher Education: Report to Minister for Education and Science*. Dublin: Stationery Office.

Department of Environment and Local Government (2000) *Part V of the Planning and Development Act, 2000 Housing Supply Guidelines for Planning Authorities*, December 2000 available online at http://www.environ.ie/en/Publications/DevelopmentandHousing/Housing/FileDownLoad,2114,en.pdf (Accessed 12 March 2015)

Department of Environment, Community and Local Government (2015) *Climate Action and Low Carbon Development Bill 2015*. Dublin: Stationery Office.

Department of Environment, Community and Local Government (2014) *Monthly Household Completions 1975 to date* available online at http://www.environ.ie/en/Publications/StatisticsandRegularPublications/HousingStatistics/

Department of Environment, Community and Local Government (2014) *Housing Statistics: House Prices, Loans and Profile of Borrowers*, available online at http://www.environ.ie/en/Publications/StatisticsandRegularPublications/HousingStatistics/

Department of Environment, Community and Local Government (2014) *Breakdown of Homeless Persons in Emergency Accommodation, April to November 2014*, available online at http://www.environ.ie/en/DevelopmentHousing/Housing/SpecialNeeds/HomelessPeople/

Department of Environment, Community and Local Government (2014) *Implementation Plan on the State's Response to Homelessness May 2014 to December 2016*, available online at http://www.environ.ie/en/Publications/DevelopmentandHousing/Housing/FileDownLoad,38053,en.pdf (Accessed 12 March 2015)

Department of Environment, Community and Local Government (2014) *Implementation Plan on the State's Response to Homelessness, Progress Reports for Q.2 and Q.3 2014*, available online at http://www.environ.ie/en/Publications/DevelopmentandHousing/Housing/#d.en.1796 (Accessed 12 March 2015)

Department of Environment, Community and Local Government (2014) *Report of the Working Group on Citizen Engagement with Local Government*. Dublin: Stationery Office.

Department of Environment, Community and Local Government (2013) *Building for the Future – A Voluntary Regulation Code For Approved Housing Bodies in Ireland*, July 2013 available online at https://www.housing.ie/Regulation/The-Code.pdf (Accessed 12 March 2015)

Department of Environment, Community and Local Government (2012) *Putting People First: Action Programme for Effective Local Government*. Dublin: Stationery Office.

Department of Environment, Community and Local Government (2012) *Final Report of the Local Government/Local Development Alignment Steering Group*. Dublin: Stationery Office.

Department of Environment, Community and Local Government (2012) *Our Sustainable Future. A Framework for Sustainable Development for Ireland*. Dublin: Stationery Office.

Department of Environment, Community and Local Government (2012) *Green Tenders – An Action Plan for Green Public Procurement* Dublin: Stationery Office.

Department of Environment, Community and Local Government (2011) *A Roadmap for Climate Policy and Legislation*. Dublin: Stationery Office.

Department of Environment, Community and Local Government (2011) *Review of National Climate Policy*. Dublin: Stationery Office.

Department of Environment, Community and Local Government (2011) *Housing Policy Statement, June 2011,* available online at http://www.environ.ie/en/Publications/DevelopmentandHousing/Housing/FileDown Load,26867,en.pdf (Accessed 12 March 2015)

Department of Environment, Community and Local Government (2009) *Interim Value for Money and* Policy Review of the Rental Accommodation Scheme, October 2009 available online at http://www.environ.ie/en/Publications/DevelopmentandHousing/Housing/FileDownLoad,22160,en.pdf (Accessed 12 March 2015)

Department of Environment, Heritage and Local Government (2008) *Statement of Strategy*. Dublin: Stationery Office.

Department of Finance (2014) *Budget 2015*. Dublin: Stationery Office.

Department of Finance (2014) *Effective Rates of Corporation Tax in Ireland*. Dublin: Stationery Office.

Department of Finance (2014) *Fiscal and Economic Outlook 2015*. Dublin: Stationery Office.

Department of Finance (2013) *Fiscal and Economic Outlook 2014*. Dublin: Stationery Office.

Department of Health (2015) *Second Annual Progress Report - National Carers Strategy*. Dublin: Department of Health.

Department of Health (2014) *First Annual Progress Report - National Carers Strategy*. Dublin: Department of Health.

Department of Health (2014) *Annual Report 2013*. Dublin: Department of Health.

Department of Health (2014) *Health in Ireland: Key Trends, 2014*. Dublin: Department of Health

Department of Health (2014) Publications and Statistics. Online website: http://health.gov.ie/publications-research/statistics/ (Accessed 26 January 2015)

Department of Health (2013) *Health in Ireland: Key Trends, 2013*. Dublin: Department of Health.

Department of Finance (2012) *Medium-Term Fiscal Statement November 2012*. Dublin: Stationery Office.

Department of Finance (various) *Budget Documentation – various years*. Dublin: Stationery Office.

Department of Health (2012) *Annual Output Statement, 2013 for Health Group of Votes 38-39*. Dublin: Department of Health.

Department of Health (2012) *National Carers Strategy*. Dublin: Department of Health.

Department of Jobs, Enterprise and Innovation (2015) *Action Plan for Jobs 2015*. Dublin: Department of Jobs, Enterprise and Innovation.

Department of Justice and Equality (2014) *Immigration in Ireland – 2013 in Review*. Dublin: Department of Justice and Equality.

Department of Justice and Equality (2013) *Immigration in Ireland – 2012 in Review*. Dublin: Stationery Office.

Department of Public Expenditure and Reform (2014) *Focused Policy Assessment of the Rural Social Scheme*. Dublin: Department of Public Expenditure and Reform.

Department of Public Expenditure & Reform (2014) *Comprehensive Expenditure Report, 2015-17*. Dublin: Stationery Office.

Department of Public Expenditure & Reform (2011) *Comprehensive Expenditure Report, 2012-14*. Dublin: Stationery Office.

Department of Social Protection (2014) *Statistical Information on Social Welfare Services 2013*. Dublin: Department of Social Protection.

Department of Social, Community and Family Affairs (2000) *Supporting Voluntary Activity*. Dublin: Stationery Office.

Department of Transport, Tourism and Sport (2015) *Sports Capital Programme Allocations, 2012 to 2014.* . Dublin: Stationery Office.

Department of Transport, Tourism and Sport (2013) *Strengthening the Connections in Rural Ireland – Plans for Restructuring the Rural Transport Programme*. Dublin: Stationery Office.

DKM Economic Consultants and Brady Shipman Martin (2012) *Review of Part V of the Planning and Development Act, 2000*, 27th November 2012 available online at http://www.environ.ie/en/Publications/DevelopmentandHousing/Housing/FileDown Load,33908,en.pdf (Accessed 12 March 2015)

DKM Economic Consultants, Ronan Daly Jermyn, ESRI and RedC (2014) *Future of the Private Rented Sector, Final Report, prepared for the Housing Agency on behalf of the Private Residential Tenancies Board* available online at http://www.housing.ie/Housing/media/Media/Our%20Publications/future-of-the-private-rented-sector-PRTB.pdf (Accessed 12 March 2015)

Dóchas (2014) *Demonstrating Ireland's Commitment to Development Cooperation*. Dublin: Dochas.

Donnellan, T., Hanrahan, K., Hennessey, T., Kinsella, A., McKeon, M., Moran, B. and Thorne, F. (2013) *Outlook 2014: Economic Prospects for Agriculture*. Galway: Teagasc.

Dorgan, J., (2009) *Adult Literacy Policy: A Review for the National Adult Literacy Agency*. Dublin: National Adult Literacy Agency.

Dorgan, J., (2009) *A Cost Benefit Analysis of Adult Literacy Training: Research Report, March 2009*. Dublin: National Adult Literacy Agency.

Downey, J. (2014) *Issues and Context – government reform of planning legislation, Oireachtas Library & Research Services, Spotlight, No.6*. Dublin: Stationery Office.

Dublin City Council (2014) *Official Street Count figures on rough sleeping for Winter 2014 across the Dublin Region*. Dublin: Dublin City Council.

Duffy, D. (2004) *A Note on Measuring the Affordability of Homeownership, ESRI Quarterly Economic Commentary, Summer 2004*. Dublin: ESRI.

Duffy, D., (2012) Irish Housing: A Role for Loan to Value Limits?, *ESRI Renewal Series, Paper 7*. Dublin: ESRI.

Duffy, D., Byrne, D., and Fitzgerald, J. (2014) *ESRI Special Article, Alternative Scenarios for New Household Formation in Ireland*. Dublin: ESRI.

Duffy, D., J. FitzGerald, K. McQuinn, D. Byrne and C. Morley (2014) *Quarterly Economic Commentary Autumn 2014*. Dublin: ESRI.

Dunne, T. (2004) "Land Values as a Source of Local Government Finance" in B. Reynolds, and S. Healy (eds.) *A Fairer Tax System for a Fairer Ireland*. Dublin: CORI Justice Commission.

Economy for the Common Good (2013) *The Economic for the Common Good – An Economic Model for the Future*. Gemeinwohl Oekonomie, available at https://www.ecogood.org/en (Accessed 13 February, 2015)

ECORYS (2010) *Study on Employment, Growth and Innovation in Rural Areas*. Rotterdam: ECORYS.

EEAC (2011) *The "Green Economy" Agenda in the context of SD Institutional framework for SD at National Level*. Brussels: EEAC.

Eivers, E. amd Clerkin, A. (2012) *PIRLS and TIMSS 2011: Reading, Mathematics and Science Outcomes for Ireland*. Dublin: Education Research Centre.

Ellmers, Bodo & Diane Hulova, (2013) *The New Debt Vulnerabilities, Why the Debt Crisis is Not Over*, Eurodad, Brussels.

Enterprise Ireland (2013) *Annual Report and Accounts 2012*. Dublin: Enterprise Ireland.

Environmental Protection Agency (2014) *Ireland's Provisional Greenhouse Gas Emissions in 2013*. Dublin: EPA.

Environmental Protection Agency (2014) *Greenhouse Gas Inventory 2012*. Dublin: EPA.

Environmental Protection Agency (2013) *EPA Releases figures for key air pollutants. Press release*. Dublin: EPA.

Environmental Protection Agency (2013) *Governance and Climate Change: Making the Transition to an Adapted Ireland*. Wexford: EPA.

Environmental Protection Agency (2013) *Ireland's Greenhouse Gas Emission Projections 2012-2030*. Dublin: EPA.

Environmental Protection Agency (2013) *SIMBIOSYS: Sectoral Impacts on Biodiversity and Ecosystems Services*. Dublin: EPA.

Environmental Protection Agency (2013) *Winners and Losers: Climate Change Impacts on biodiversity in Ireland*. Wexford: EPA.

Environmental Protection Agency (2012) *A Year in Review – Highlights from 2011*. Dublin: EPA.

Environmental Protection Agency (2012) *A Focus on Urban Waste Water Discharges in Ireland*. Dublin: EPA.

Environmental Protection Agency (2012) *Ireland's Climate Strategy to 2020 and beyond - A contribution to the Programme for Development of National Climate Policy and Legislation 2012*. Dublin: EPA.

Environmental Protection Agency (2012) *Ireland's Environment 2012 – An Assessment*. Dublin: EPA.

Environmental Protection Agency (2012) *Ireland's Greenhouse Gas Emissions in 2011 – Key Highlights*. Dublin: EPA.

Environmental Protection Agency (2012) *Ireland's Greenhouse Gas Emissions Projections 2011-2020*. Dublin: EPA.

Environmental Protection Agency (2012) *National Waste Report 2010*. Dublin: EPA.

Environmental Protection Agency (2012) *The EU Emissions Trading Scheme. A review of the first six years of operation*. Dublin: EPA.

Environmental Protection Agency (2011) *Biochange: Biodiversity and Environmental Change: An Integrated Study Encompassing a Range of Scales, Taxa and Habitats*. Wexford: EPA.

Environmental Protection Agency (2011) *Biodiversity Action Plan 2011-2013*. Dublin: EPA.

Environmental Protection Agency (2010) *Environmental Protection Agency Biodiversity Action Plan*. Dublin: EPA.

Environmental Protection Agency (2010) *Water Quality in Ireland 2007-200*. Dublin: EPA.

ESRI (various) *Quarterly Economic Commentary (QEC)*. Dublin: ESRI.

Eurofound (2012) *Third European Quality of Life Survey – Quality of Life in Europe: Impacts of the crisis*. Luxembourg: Publications Office of the European Union.

Eurofound (2014). *Access to Healthcare in times of crisis*. European Foundation for the Improvement of Living and Working Conditions. Luxembourg: Publications Office of the European Union.

European Centre for the Development of Vocational Training (2009) *Future skill supply in Europe: Medium-term forecast up to 2020 – synthesis report*. Luxembourg: European Centre for the Development of Vocational Training.

European Commission (2015) *Digital Economy and Society Index 2015 – Country Profile Ireland*. Brussels: European Commission.

European Commission (2014) *A Policy Framework for Climate and Energy in the period 2020-2030*. Brussels: European Commission.

European Commission (2014) *Post-Programme Surveillance for Ireland Spring 2014 Report*, European Economy Operational Papers 195. Brussels: European Commission.

European Commission (2013) *A Decent Life for All: Ending Poverty and Giving the World a Sustainable Future*. Brussels: European Commission.

European Commission (2012) *A View of Employment, Growth and Innovation in Rural Areas*. SWD 2012/44. Brussels: European Commission.

European Commission (2012) *The 2012 Ageing Report: Economic and budgetary projections for the EU27 Member States (2010-2060)*. Brussels: European Commission.

European Commission (2012) *The CAP towards 2020: Meeting the food, natural resources and territorial challenges of the future*. COM(2010) 672. Brussels: European Commission.

European Commission (2011) A *resource-efficient Europe – Flagship initiative under the Europe 2020 Strategy*. Brussels: European Commission.

European Commission (2011) *Early Childhood Education and Care: Providing all our children with the best start for the world of tomorrow*. Brussels: European Commission

European Commission (2011) *Our life insurance, our natural capital: an EU biodiversity strategy to 2020*. Brussels: European Commission.

European Commission (2011) *Roadmap to a Resource Efficient Europe. COM(2011) 571*. Brussels: European Commission.

European Commission (2011) *Strategic framework for European cooperation in education and training (ET 2020)*. Brussels: Brussels: European Commission.

European Commission (2011) *The Social Dimension of the Europe 2020 Strategy A report of the Social Protection Committee*. Luxembourg: Publications Office of the European Union.

European Commission (2010) *Eurobarometer 74 Autumn 2010 Report*. Brussels: European Commission.

European Commission (2010) *Europe 2020: A strategy for smart, sustainable and inclusive growth*. Brussels: European Commission.

European Commission/EACEA/Eurydice (2014) *Modernisation of Higher Education in Europe: Access, Retention and Employability 2014*. Luxembourg: Publications Office of the European Union

European Network for Rural Development (2010) *Climate Change and Renewable Energy measures in EU RDPs 2007-2013 Ireland*. Brussels: European Network for Rural Development.

Eurostat (2014) *Taxation Trends in the European Union*. Luxembourg: Eurostat.

Eurostat (2014). *Taxation trends in the European Union; Data for EU Member States, Iceland and Norway*. 2014 Edition. Luxembourg: Eurostat.

Eurostat (2012) *Population and Social Conditions, Asylum applicants and first instance decisions on asylum applications: third quarter 2012*. Luxembourg: Eurostat.

Eurostat (2008) Satellite accounts sharpen the focus. *Sigma – The bulletin of European Statistics, 2008.03*. Luxembourg: Eurostat.

Eurostat (2008) *Taxation Trends in the European Union*. Luxembourg: Eurostat.

Eurydice Network (2012) *Key Data on Education in Europe 2012*. Brussels: European Commission.

Expert Group on Future Funding for Higher Education, (2015) *The Role, Value and Scale of Higher Education in Ireland*. Dublin: Department of Education and Skills.

Expert Group on Future Skills Needs, (2007) *Tomorrow's Skills: Towards a National Skills Strategy. 5th Report*. Dublin: Expert Group on Future Skills Needs.

Expert Group on Future Skills Needs, (2012) *Addressing High Level ICT Skills Recruitment Needs Research Findings*. Dublin: Expert Group on Future Skills Needs.

Financial Regulator (2006) *Financial Stability Report 2006*. Dublin: Financial Regulator.

Flannery, D. and O'Donoghue, C. (2011) The Life Cycle Impact of Alternative Higher Education Finance Systems in Ireland. *The Economic and Social Review, Vol. 42, No.3, (Autumn, 2011):pp.237-270* Dublin: UCD.

Focus Ireland (2014) *Focus Ireland Briefing Note: Family Homelessness*. Dublin: Focus Ireland.

Forfás (2014) *Annual Employment Survey 2013*. Dublin: Forfás.

Forfás (2014) *National Skills Bulletin2014*. Dublin: Forfás.

Forfas and National Competitiveness Council (2012) *Ireland's Competitiveness Scorecard 2012*. Dublin: Stationery Office.

Forfás and National Competitiveness Council (2011) *Ireland's Competitiveness Challenge 2011*. Dublin: Stationery Office.

Future Analytics (2014) *Housing Supply Requirements in Ireland's Urban Settlements 2014-2018*, April 2014 available online at http://www.housing.ie/getattachment/Our-Publications/Latest-Publications/Future-Housing-Supply-Requirements-Report.pdf (Accessed 12 March 2015).

Future Climate for Africa (2015) *Promoting the use of climate information to achieve long-term development objectives in sub-Saharan Africa*. Climate and Development Knowledge Network.

GAA, 2014: *GAA Strategic Plan, 2015-2017*, available online at http://www.gaa.ie/content/documents/Strategic%20Report%202015%20INTERACTIVE.pdf http://www.housing.ie/getattachment/Our-Publications/Latest-Publications/Future-Housing-Supply-Requirements-Report.pdf

Gloukoviezoff, G. (2011) *Understanding and Combating Financial Exclusion in Ireland: A European Perspective. What could Ireland learn from Belgium, France and the United Kingdom?*. Dublin: The Policy Institute, TCD.

Gloukoviezoff, G. (2006) 'From Financial Exclusion to Over-indebtedness: The paradox of difficulties for people on low income?' in Anderloni, L., Braga, MD., Carluccio, E (eds), *New Frontiers in Banking Services: emerging needs and tailored products for untapped markets*, Berlin: Springer Verlag.

Gloukoviezoff, G. (2006) 'From Financial Exclusion to Over-indebtedness: The paradox of difficulties for people on low income?' in Anderloni, L; Braga, MD; Carluccio, E (eds), *New Frontiers in Banking Services: emerging needs and tailored products for untapped markets*, Berlin: Springer Verlag.

Glynn, I., Kelly, T., and Mac Éinrí, P. (2013) *Irish Emigration in an Age of Austerity*. Cork: Emgire.

Government of Ireland (2012) *Delivering our Green Potential*. Dublin: Stationery Office

Government of Ireland (2012) *Ireland's National Reform Programme 2012 – Update*. Dublin: Stationery Office.

Government of Ireland (2012) *Programme for Government and National Recovery 2011-2016*. Dublin: Stationery Office

Government of Ireland (2011) *Towards Recovery: Programme for a National Government 2011-2016*. Dublin: Stationery Office

Government of Ireland (2007) *National Action Plan for Social Inclusion 2007-2016*. Dublin: Stationery Office.

Government of Ireland (2007) *National Climate Change Strategy*. Dublin: Stationery Office.

Growing Up in Ireland (2013) *Growing Up in Ireland - Key Findings: Infant Cohort (at 5 years) No. 3 Well-being, play and diet among five-year-olds*. Dublin: Department of Health and Children.

Gutmann, A. and Thompson, D. (2004) *Why deliberative Democracy?*. Princeton: Princeton University Press.

H.M. Treasury (2004) *Financial Statement and Budget Report, 2004*. London: H.M. Treasury.

Hämäläinen, T. (2013) *Towards a Sustainable Well-being Society version 1.0*. Sitra: Helsinki.

Health Consumer Powerhouse (2015). *Euro Health Consumer Index 2014*. Brussels: Health Consumer Powerhouse.

Health Insurance Authority (2014). *Newsletter, November 2014 Edition*. Dublin: Health Insurance Authority.

Health Service Executive (2015) *Mental Health Division: Operational Plan 2015*. Dublin: HSE.

Health Service Executive (2014) *Health Service Performance Assurance Report*. October 2014. Dublin: HSE.

Health Service Executive (2014) *Health Service Performance Assurance Report*. November 2014. Dublin: HSE.

Health Service Executive (2014) *National Service Plan 2015*. November 2014. Dublin: HSE.

Health Service Executive (2013) *National Service Plan, 2014*. Dublin: HSE.

Health Service Executive (2013) *Management Data Report*. December 2013. Dublin: HSE.

Health Service Executive (2013) *Health Service Performance Assurance Report*. December 2013 Dublin: HSE.

Health Service Executive (2012) *December 2012 Supplementary Report, National Service Plan, 2012*. Dublin: HSE.

Healy, S. and Reynolds, B. (2014) 'Vision and Values – Public Services and Infrastructure' in Healy, S. and Reynolds. B. eds *Planning and Delivering a Fairer Future*. Dublin: Social Justice Ireland.

Healy, S. and Reynolds, B. (2011) 'Sharing Responsibility and Shaping the Future: Why and How? In Healy. S. and Reynolds, B. eds *Sharing Responsibility and Shaping the Future*. Dublin: Social Justice Ireland.

Healy, S., M. Murphy, S. Ward and Reynolds, B. (2012) '*Basic Income – Why and How in Difficult Economic Times: Financing a BI in Ireland*' Paper to the BIEN Congress 2012, Munich.

Healy, S. and Collins, M.L. (2006) "Work, Employment and Unemployment", in Healy, S., B. Reynolds and M.L. Collins eds. *Social Policy in Ireland: Principles, Practice and Problems*. Dublin: Liffey Press.

Hennessy, T., Buckley, C., Dillon, E., Donnellan, T., Hanrahan, K., Moran, B., and Ryan, M. (2013) *Measuring Farm Level Sustainability with the Teagasc National Farm Survey*. Galway: Teagasc.

Higher Education Authority (2010) *A Study of Progression in Irish Higher Education*. Dublin: HEA.

Higher Education Authority (2010) *National Plan for Equity of Access to Higher Education 2008-2013 Mid-Term Review*. Dublin: HEA.

Higher Education Authority (2010) *Review of Student Charge*. Dublin: HEA.

Higher Education Authority (2011) *Report on the Social and Living Conditions of Higher Education Students in Ireland 2009/2010*. Dublin: HEA.

Higher Education Authority (2012) *10/11 Higher Education Key Facts and Figures*. Dublin: HEA.

Higher Education Authority (2012) *Springboard 2011 First Stage Evaluation*. Dublin: HEA.

Higher Education Authority (2012) *Towards a Future Higher Education Landscape*. Dublin: HEA.

Higher Education Authority (2013) *Completing the Landscape Process for Irish Higher Education*. Dublin: HEA.

Hoegen, M. (2009) *Statistics and the quality of life. Measuring progress – a world beyond GDP*. Bonn: InWent.

Honohan, P. (2014) *Household Indebtedness: Rhetoric and Action – Address by Governor Patrick Honohan at the MABS Annual Conference*, available online at http://www.centralbank.ie/press-area/speeches/Pages/HonohanMABSHouseholdIndebtedness.aspx (Accessed 12March 2015).

Honohan, P. (2013) *Introductory remarks by Governor Patrick Honohan at the Central Bank Conference "How to Fix Distressed Property Markets"?*, Available online at http://www.centralbank.ie/press-area/speeches/Pages/IntroductoryremarksbyGovernorPatrickHonohanattheCentralBankConferenceHowtoFixDistressedPropertyMarkets (accessed on 04/03/2013)

House, J.S. (2001) 'Social Isolation Kills, But How and Why?' *Psychosomatic Medicine*. 2001; 63:273-74

Housing Agency (2013) *Summary of Social Housing Assessments 2013*. Dublin: Housing Agency.

Housing Agency (2014) *A-Z Organisation Listing*. Dublin: Housing Agency.

Housing Agency (2014) *Resolving Unfinished Housing Developments, Annual Progress Report on Actions to Address Unfinished Housing Developments*. Dublin: Housing Agency.

Hutton, W. (2003) *The World We're In*. London: Abacus.

Hyland, A (2011) *Entry to Higher Education in Ireland in the 21st Century*. (Discussion Paper for the NCCA/HEA Seminar 2011) Dublin: HEA

IDA Ireland (2013) *IDA Ireland Annual Report and Accounts 2012*. Dublin: IDA Ireland

IFA (2015) *Farm Income Review 2014*. Dublin: IFA.

Institute for Public Health (2007) *Fuel Poverty and Health*. Dublin: IPH.

Institute of Public Health in Ireland (2011) *Facing the Challenge: The Impact of Recession and Unemployment on Men's Health in Ireland*. Dublin/Belfast: The Institute of Public Health in Ireland.

Intergovernmental Panel on Climate Change (2013) *Climate Change 2013: The Physical Science Basis*. Switzerland: IPCC.

Internal Displacement Monitoring Centre (2014) *Global Overview 2014: People Internally Displaced by Conflict and Violence*. Geneva: IDMC.

International Energy Agency (2011) *World Energy Outlook 2011*. Paris: International Energy Agency.

International Monetary Fund (2013) *Ninth Review under the Extended Arrangement*, available online at http://www.imf.org/external/pubs/ft/scr/2013/cr1393.pdf (Accessed 12March 2015).

International Monetary Fund (2014) *Ireland: First Post-Program Monitoring Discussion.* IMF Country Report No.14/165 Washington D.C.: International Monetary Fund.

International Monetary Fund (2013) *World Economic Outlook Update.* Washington D.C.: International Monetary Fund.

International Monetary Fund (2014) *Ireland: First Post-Program Monitoring Discussion.* IMF Country Report No.14/165 Washington D.C.: International Monetary Fund.

International Monetary Fund (2004) *World Economic Outlook.* Washington DC: IMF.

International Monetary Fund (2008) *World Economic Outlook.* Washington DC: IMF.

Ireland's Foreign Policy (2015) *The Global Island: Ireland's Foreign Policy for a Changing World.* Department of Foreign Affairs and Trade.

Ireland's Policy for International Development (2013) *One World, One Future*, Department of Foreign Affairs & Trade.

Irish Aid (2014) *Annual Report 2013.* Department of Foreign Affairs and Trade.

Irish Fiscal Advisory Council (2012) *Fiscal Assessment Report: September 2012*, Available online at http://www.fiscalcouncil.ie/wp-content/uploads/2012/09/FAR_Sept2012.pdf. (accessed on 20/02/2013)

Irish Nurses and Midwives Organisation (2014). *Trolley Watch/Ward Watch Figures.* [online] www.inmo.ie (Accessed 26 January 2015)

Jahan, Selim. (2014) *Rethinking Work for Human Development.* UN Human Development Report 2015 (to be published in later in 2015)

Jarret, R., Sullivan, P. and Watkins, N. (2005) 'Developing social capital through participation in organized youth programs: qualitative insights from three programs'. *Journal of Community Psychology, Vol.33, No.1: 41-55*

Joint Committee on the Environment, Culture and the Gaeltacht (2013) *Report on the Outline Heads of the Climate Action and Low Carbon Development Bill 2013.* Dublin: Stationery Office.

Joint Oireachtas Committee on Arts, Sport, Tourism, Community, Rural and Gaeltacht Affairs (2005) *Volunteers and Volunteering in Ireland.* Dublin: Stationery Office.

Joyce, C. and Quinn, E. (2014) *The Organisation of Facilities for Asylum Seekers in Ireland.* Dublin: European Migration Network/ESRI.

Kelly, E., S. McGuinness and P. O'Connell (2012) *Literacy and Numeracy Difficulties in the Irish Workplace: Impact on Earnings and Training Expenditure.* Research Series Number 27 September 2012. Dublin: ESRI.

Kelly, E., S. McGuinness and P. O'Connell (2012) *Literacy, Numeracy and Activation among the Unemployed.* Research Series Number 25 June 2012. Dublin: ESRI.

Kempson, E. (2002) *Over-indebtedness in Britain, A report to the Department of Trade and Industry.* London: Personal Finance Research Centre.

Kempson, E. and Collard, S. (2012) *Developing a vision for financial inclusion.* Bristol: University of Bristol.

Kempson, E., McKay, S. and Willitts, M. (2004) *Characteristics of families in debt and the nature of indebtedness.* London: Department for Work and Pensions.

Kinsella, S. (2012) 'Is Ireland really the role model for austerity?,' *Cambridge Journal of Economics*, 36(1), pp. 223-235.

Korczak, D. (2004) *MABS Ireland. A Service to Help People with Financial Problems and to Tackle Over-indebtedness, Synthesis Report, Peer Review and Assessment*. Dublin: MABS.

KW Research & Associates (2014) *Why Travellers leave Traveller-specific Accommodation? A Research Report*. Dublin: Housing Agency.

Law Society of Ireland (2012) *Access to Justice: A Report of the Legal Aid Taskforce*. Dublin: Law Society of Ireland.

Leahy, A., M. Murphy, S. Mallon and Healy, S. (2012) *Ireland and the Europe 2020 Strategy – Employment, Education and Poverty*. Dublin: Social Justice Ireland.

Leahy, E., S. Lyons and Tol, R. (2010) 'The Distributional Effects of Value Added Tax in Ireland' *ESRI Working Paper 366*. Dublin: ESRI.

Legal Aid Board (2014) *Annual Report 2013*. Dublin: Legal Aid Board.

Levy, J. D. (1999) *Tocqueville's Revenge: State, Society, and Economy in Contemporary France*. Cambridge MA: Harvard University Press.

Living Wage Technical Group (2014) *Living Wage 2014*. Dublin, Living Wage Technical Group.

Living Wage Technical Group (2014) *Technical Paper*. Dublin, Living Wage Technical Group.

Local Government Management Agency (2014) *Service Indicators in Local Authorities 2013*. Dublin: Stationery Office.

Lunn, P., Kelly, E. and Fitzpatrick, N. (2013) 'Keeping them in the Game, Taking up and dropping out of Sport and Exercise in Ireland'. *Research Series Number 33, September 2013, ESRI*.

Mahon Tribunal (2012) *The Final Report of the Tribunal of Enquiry into Certain Planning Matters and Payments*, available online at http://www.planningtribunal.ie/images/finalReport.pdf (Accessed 12 March 2015).

Mallon, S. and S. Healy (2012), *Ireland and the Europe 2020 Strategy – Unemployment, Education and Poverty*. Dublin, Social Justice Ireland.
Martin, M.O., Mullis, I.V.S., Foy, P., & Stanco, G.M. (2012) *TIMSS 2011 International Results in Science*. Chestnut Hill, MA: TIMSS & PIRLS International Study Center, Boston College
McCoy, S, Byrne, D, O'Connell, P, Kelly, E & Doherty C (2010) *Hidden Disadvantage? A Study on the Low Participation in Higher Education by the Non-Manual Group*. Dublin: HEA.

McDonagh, J, Varley,T and Shortall, S *(eds)* (2009) *A living countryside?: the politics of sustainable development in rural Ireland*. Ashgate: England;

McGee, H. (2012) 'IFSC lobby group powerful in shaping policy', *The Irish Times*, October 8.

McGinnity, F. and Russell, H. (2008) *Gender Inequalities in Time*. Dublin: ESRI.

McGuinness, S., A. Bergin, E. Kelly, S. McCoy, E. Smyth and K. Timoney (2012) *A Study of Future Demand for Higher Education in Ireland*. Research Series Number 30 December 2012. Dublin: ESRI.

McKinsey Global Institute (2011) *Resource revolution: Meeting the world's energy, materials, food, and water needs*. London: McKinsey Global Institute.

Meredith, D and Van Egeraat, D. (2013) 'Revisiting the National Spatial Strategy ten years on', *IPA Administration Journal*, 60 (3) pp.3-9. Dublin: IPA.

Migrant Rights Centre Ireland (2014) *Ireland is Home*. Dublin: MRCI.

Morrone, Adolfo (2009) "The OECD Global Project on Measuring Progress and the challenge of assessing and measuring trust" in Reynolds, B. and Healy S. (eds.), *Beyond GDP: what is progress and how should it be measured*. Dublin.

Mullis, I.V.S., Martin, M.O., Foy, P., & Arora, A. (2012) *TIMSS 2011 International Results in Mathematics*. Chestnut Hill, MA: TIMSS & PIRLS International Study Center, Boston College.

Mullis, I.V.S., Martin, M.O., Foy, P., & Drucker, K.T. (2012) *PIRLS 2011 International Results in Reading*. Chestnut Hill, MA: TIMSS & PIRLS International Study Center, Boston College.

National Anti-Poverty Strategy (1997) *Sharing in Progress*. Dublin: Stationery Office.

National Clinical Programme for Older People (2012). *Specialist Geriatric Services Model of Care. Part 1: Acute Service Provision*. July

National Competitiveness Council (2015) *NCC Submission to the Action Plan for Jobs 2015*. Dublin: National Competitiveness Council

National Disability Authority (2006) *Indecon Report on the Cost of a Disability*. Dublin: NDA.

National Economic and Social Council (2014) *Homeownership and Rental: What Road is Ireland on?*, No.140 December 2014. Dublin: NESC.

National Economic and Social Council (2014) *Review of Irish Social and Affordable Housing Provision*, Secretariat Paper No.10 July 2014. Dublin: NESC.

National Economic and Social Council (2014) *Social Housing at the Crossroads: Possibilities for Investment, Provision and Cost Rental*, No.138 June 2014. Dublin: NESC.

National Economic and Social Council (2012) *Ireland and the Climate Change Challenge: Connecting 'How Much' with 'How To'. Final Report of the NESC Secretariat to the Department of Environment, Community and Local Government*. Dublin: NESC.

National Economic and Social Council (2009) *Well-being Matters: A Social Report for Ireland*. Dublin: Stationery Office.

National Office for Suicide Prevention (2011) *Annual Report 2010*. Dublin: HSE.
National Office for Suicide Prevention (2014) *Annual Report, 2013*. Dublin: HSE.

National Roads Authority 92014) *National Road Indicators 2013*. Dublin: NRA.

National Suicide Research Foundation (2013). *Second Report of the Suicide Support and Information System*. Cork: National Suicide Research Foundation.

National Suicide Research Foundation (2015) *Statistics: Suicides in Republic of Ireland, 2001-2012*. [Online] www.nsrf.ie. (Accessed 17 February 2015)

National Transport Authority (2013) *Strengthening the Connections in Rural Ireland: Plans for Restructuring the Rural Transport Programme*. Dublin: National Transport Authority.

NERI (2014) *Quarterly Economic Facts – Winter 2014*. Dublin: NERI.

Niestroy, I (2005) *Sustaining Sustainability*, Brussels: EEAC.

Nolan, B. (2006) "The EU's Social Inclusion Indicators and Their Implications for Ireland", in Healy, S., B. Reynolds and M.L. Collins eds., *Social Policy in Ireland: Principles, Practice and Problems*. Dublin: Liffey Press.

Normand, C. (2015). *Funding Universal Health and Social Care in Ireland: Ageing, dying and affordability*. Presentation at NERI Research Seminar, 11 February.

Norris, Michelle (2013) *Varieties of home ownership: Ireland's transition from a socialised to a marketised policy regime,* UCD Geary Institute Discussion Paper Series.

O'Donoghue, C., Conneely, R., Frost, D., Heanue, K., Leonard, B., and Meredith, D. (2014) *Rural Economic Development in Ireland.* Carlow: Teagasc.

O'Hara, P. (2013) 'What Future for the Regions?'. In: Healy, S. and Reynolds, B. eds. *A Future worth Living For: Sustainable Foundations and Frameworks.* Dublin: Social Justice Ireland.

O'Neill (2015) 'Second Opinion: Step-down care for older patients is often a backwards step'. *Irish Times.* 12 January

O'Siochru, E. (2004) "Land Value Tax: unfinished business" in B. Reynolds, and S. Healy eds. *A Fairer Tax System for a Fairer Ireland.* Dublin: CORI Justice Commission.

O'Siochru, E. (Ed.). (2012) *The Fair Tax.* Dublin: Smart Taxes Network.

O'Toole, F. and N. Cahill (2006) "Taxation Policy and Reform", in Healy, S., B. Reynolds and M.L. Collins eds., *Social Policy in Ireland: Principles, Practice and Problems.* Dublin: Liffey Press.

OECD (2014) *Education at a Glance 2014: Country Note Ireland.* Paris: OECD Publishing.

OECD (2014) *OECD Economic Outlook* Volume 2014 Issue 2. Paris: OECD Publishing.
OECD (2014) *OECD Health Data, 2014. How Does Ireland Compare?* Paris: OECD Publishing.

OECD (2014) *PISA 2012 Results: Students and Money: Financial Literacy Skills for the 21st Century (Volume VI).* Paris: OECD PublishingOECD (2014) *Revenue Statistics.* Paris: OECD Publishing.

OECD (2014). *Health at a Glance: Europe 2014.* Paris: OECD Publishing.

OECD (2013) *Action Plan on Base Erosion and Profit Shifting (BEPS).* Paris: OECD.OECD (2012) *Education at a Glance 2012: OECD Indicators.* Paris:OECD Publishing

OECD (2012) *Equity and Quality in Education: Supporting Disadvantaged Students and Schools Spotlight on Ireland.* Paris: OECD Publishing.

OECD (2010) *Better Regulation in Europe: Ireland.* Paris: OECD Publishing.

OECD (2010) *PISA 2009 Results: Ireland.* OECD Publishing OECD (2008) *Economic Survey of Ireland.* Paris: OECD Publishing.

OECD (2006) *The new rural paradigm - policies and governance.* Paris: OECD Publishing.

OECD (2004) *OECD Factbook.* Paris: OECD Publishing.

OECD (2000) *Literacy in the Information Age: Final Report of the International Adult Literacy Survey.* Paris: OECD Publishing.

OECD's Development Assistance Committee (2014) *Peer Review of Ireland 2014.* Paris: OECD Publishing.

Office of the Refugee Applications Commissioner (2012) *Statistical Report December 2012.* Dublin: Stationery Office.

Office of the Refugee Applications Commissioner (2013) *Statistical Report December 2013.* Dublin: Office of the Refugee Applications Commissioner.

Office of the United Nations High Commissioner for Refugees (2012) *Global Trends 2011.* New York: United Nations.

Office of the United Nations High Commissioner for Refugees (2013) *Global Trends 2012.* New York: United Nations.

Office of the United Nations High Commissioner for Refugees (2013) *Statistical Yearbook 2012, 12th Edition*. New York: United Nations.

Oireachtas (2004) *Residential Tenancies Act, 2004*. Dublin: Stationery Office.

Oireachtas (2013) *Residential Tenancies (Amendment) (No.2) Bill, 2012*. Dublin: Stationery Office.

Oxfam (2015) *Wealth: Having It All And Wanting More*, Oxfam Issue Briefing, *available online at* https://www.oxfam.org/sites/www.oxfam.org/files/file_attachments/ib-wealth-having-all-wanting-more-190115-en.pdf (accessed 12March 2015).

Oxfam (2014) *Even it Up: Time to end extreme inequality, available online at* https://www.oxfam.org/sites/www.oxfam.org/files/file_attachments/cr-even-it-up-extreme-inequality-291014-en.pdf (accessed 12 March 2015).

Pfizer (2012) *The 2012 Pfizer Health Index*. Pfizer Healthcare Ireland.

Pierce, M., Cahill, S., & O' Shea, E. (2014). *Prevalence and Projections of dementia in Ireland, 2011*. Genio: Mullingar.

Power, J. (2007) *Irish Mortgage Market, A Special Report Commissioned by Genworth Financial*. Dublin: Genworth Financial.

Rapple, C. (2004) "Refundable Tax Credits" in B. Reynolds, and S. Healy eds. *A Fairer Tax System for a Fairer Ireland*. Dublin: CORI Justice Commission.

Reception and Integration Agency (2014) *Monthly Statistics Report December 2014*.Dublin: Reception and Integration Agency.

Reception and Integration Agency (2012) *Monthly Statistics Report November 2012*. Dublin: Reception and Integration Agency.

Reeves, E. (2013) *Public-Private Partnerships in Ireland: A Review of the Experience*. Dublin: NERI.

Repetto, R., W. Magrath, M. Wells, C. Beer and F. Rossini (1989) *Wasting Assets, Natural Resources in the National Income Accounts*. Washington: World Resources Institute.

Revenue Commissioners (various) *Analysis of High Income Individuals' Restriction*. Dublin: Stationery Office.

Revenue Commissioners (various) *Effective Tax Rates for High Earning Individuals*. Dublin: Stationery Office.

Rissel, C., Curac, N., Greenaway, M. and Bauman, A. (2012) 'Physical Activity Associated with Public Transport Use – A Review and Modelling of Potential Benefits'. *Int J Environ Res Public Health*. 2012 July; 9(7) 2454–2478.

Robertson, J (2007) *The New Economics of Sustainable Development report to the European Commission*. Brussels: European Commission.

Ruane, F. (2010). *Report of the Expert Group on Resource Allocation and Financing in the Health Sector*. Dublin: Department of Health and Children.

Russell, H., Maître, B. and Donnelly, N. (2011) *Financial Exclusion and Over-indebtedness in Irish Households*. Dublin: ESRI.

Safefood (2011) *Food on a Low Income*. Safefood.

Scott S. and Eakins, J. (2002) *Distributive effects of carbon taxes*, paper presented to ESRI conference entitled "The sky's the limit: efficient and fair policies on global warming" December: Dublin

Shucksmith, M. (2012) *Future Directions in Rural Development?* Dunfermline: Carnegie UK Trust

Social Justice Ireland (2015) *Ireland and the Europe 2020 Strategy: Employment, Education and Poverty.* Dublin: Social Justice Ireland.

Social Justice Ireland (2014) *Analysis and Critique of Budget 2015.* Dublin: Social Justice Ireland.

Social Justice Ireland (2013) *Investing for Growth, Jobs & Recovery.* Dublin: Social Justice Ireland.

Social Justice Ireland (2013) '*What Would Real Recovery Look Like*', *Socio-Economic Review, 2013.* Dublin: Social Justice Ireland.

Social Justice Ireland (2010) *Building a Fairer Taxation System: The Working Poor and the Cost of Refundable Tax Credits.* Dublin: Social Justice Ireland.

Society of St. Vincent de Paul, Combat Poverty Agency and Crosscare (2004) *Food Poverty and Policy.* Dublin: Combat Poverty Agency.

Stahel, W. (2010) *The Performance Economy.* London: Palgrave-Macmillan.

Stamp, S. (2009) *A Policy Framework for Addressing Over-indebtedness.* Dublin: Combat Poverty Agency.

Stiglitz, J. (2012) 'After Austerity', *Project Syndicate*, May 7.

Stiglitz, J. (2002) *Globalization and it's Discontents,* London: Penguin Books.

Stiglitz Commission (2008) *Report by the Commission on the Measurement of Economic Performance and Social Progress.* Paris

Stockholm International Peace Research Institute (SIPRI). 2013 Yearbook Fact Sheet. London: Oxford University Press.

Sustainable Energy Authority of Ireland (2014) *Energy in Ireland Key Statistics 2014.* Dublin: SEAI.

Teagasc (2014) *Outlook 2015 - Economic Prospects for Agriculture.* Teagasc.

The African Union, (2014) *Common African Position (Cap) On The Post- 2015 Development Agenda,* Addis Ababa, Ethopia.

The Intergovernmental Panel on Climate Change (IPCC) (2014) *Impacts, Adaptation, and Vulnerability.* Switzerland: IPCC.

Threshold (2014) *Pre Budget Advisory on Rent Supplement.* Dublin: Threshold.

United Nations Development Programme (2014) Sustaining Human Progress: Reducing Vulnerabilities and Building Resilience *UN Human Development Report 2014.* New York: UNDP.

UNAIDS (2014) Paris Declaration (2014) *Fast-Track Cities: Ending the AIDS Epidemic, available online* at http://www.unaids.org/sites/default/files/media_asset/20141201_Paris_Declaration_en .pdf (accessed 12 March 2015).

UNAIDS (2014) *The Gap Report, available online at* http://www.unaids.org/sites/default/files/media_asset/UNAIDS_Gap_report_en.pdf (Accessed 12March 2015).

UNEP (2011) *Decoupling natural resource use and environmental impacts from economic growth, A Report of the Working Group on Decoupling to the International Resource Panel.* Paris: UNEP.

UNEP (2011) *Keeping track of our changing environment from RIO to RIO +20 1992-2012.* Nairobi: UNEP.

UNEP (2011) *Towards a Green Economy: Pathways to Sustainable Development and Poverty Eradication.* Norway: UNEP.

United Nations Development Programme (2014) *Sustaining Human Progress: Reducing Vulnerabilities and Building Resilience - Human Development Report 2014.* New York: UNDP.

United Nations Environment Programme (2014) *The Adaptation Gap Report 2014.* Nairobi: UNEP.

United Nations General Assembly (2014) *Open Working Group proposal for Sustainable Development Goals A/68/970.* United Nations.

United Nations General Assembly (2014) *Progress Report of the Open Working Group of the General Assembly on Sustainable Development Goals A/67/941.* United Nations.

United Nations General Assembly (2012) *Future We Want Resolution 66/288.* New York: United Nations.

United Nations Secretary-General's High-Level Panel on Global Sustainability (2012) *Resilient people, Resilient planet: A Future Worth Choosing.* New York: United Nations.

Van de Ker, G. and Manuel, A. (2014) *Sustainable Society Index 2014.* The Hague: Sustainable Society Foundation.

Vatican Council II (1965) *Gaudium et Spes.* New York: Orbis.

Vincentian Partnership for Social Justice (2014) *Budget 2015: Minimum Essential Budget Standards: Income Briefing.* Dublin: VPSJ.

Vincentian Partnership for Social Justice (2010) *Minimum Essential Budgets for Households in Rural Areas.* Dublin: VPSJ.

Vincentian Partnership for Social Justice (2006) *Minimum Essential Budgets for Six Households.* Dublin: VPSJ.

Walsh, K. and Harvey, B. (2013) *Employment and Social Inclusion in Rural Areas: A Fresh Start.* Dublin: Pobal

Watson, D, and Maître, B. (2013) 'Social Transfers and Poverty Alleviation in Ireland: An Analysis of the CSO Survey on Income and Living Conditions 2004 – 2011', *Social Inclusion Report No. 4.* Dublin: Department of Social Protection/ESRI.

Watson, D., & Nolan, B. (2011) *A Social Portrait of People with Disabilities in Ireland.* Dublin: Department of Social Protection.

Weir, S & Archer P (2011) *A Report on the First Phase of the Evaluation of DEIS.* Dublin: Educational Research Centre.

Whelan, C.T., R. Layte, B. Maitre, B. Gannon, B. Nolan, W. Watson, and Williams, J. (2003) 'Monitoring Poverty Trends in Ireland: Results from the 2001 Living in Ireland Survey', *Policy Research Series No. 51.* Dublin: ESRI.

Wijkman, A. and Rockstrom, J. (2012) *Bankrupting Nature: Denying our Planetary Boundaries.* Stockholm: Routledge.

World Bank. 2009. *Africa - Making development climate resilient: a World Bank strategy for Sub-Saharan Africa*. Washington, DC: World Bank.

World Commission on Environment and Development (1987) *Our Common Future (the Bruntland Report)*. Oxford University Press.

World Economic Forum (2014) *The Global Competitiveness Report 2014-2015*. Geneva: World Economic Forum.

World Economic Forum (2011) *Global Competitiveness Report 2011-12*. Geneva: World Economic Forum.

World Economic Forum (2008) *Global Competitiveness Report 2008-09*. Geneva: World Economic Forum.

World Economic Forum (2003) *Global Competitiveness Report 2003-04*. Geneva: World Economic Forum.

World Health Organisation (2011) *Environmental burden of disease associated with inadequate housing. A method guide to the quantification of health effects of selected housing risks in the WHO European Region*. London: WHO.

World Health Organization Regional Office for Europe. (2013) *Review of social determinants and the health divide in the WHO European Region. Final report.* Denmark: World Health Organisation.

World Health Organisation and European Observatory on Health Systems and Policies (2012). *Health System responses to pressures in Ireland: Policy Options in an International Context*. London: World Health Organisation.

Online databases:

CSO CPI online database, web address: http://www.cso.ie/en/databases/

CSO Live Register online database, web address: http://www.cso.ie/en/databases/

CSO National Accounts online database, web address: http://www.cso.ie/en/databases/

CSO QNHS online database, web address: http://www.cso.ie/en/databases/

CSO SILC online database, web address: http://www.cso.ie/en/databases/

Eurostat online database, web address: http://epp.eurostat.ec.europa.eu
    OECD.StatExtracts *Health Statistics* http://dx.doi.org/10.1787/health-data-en